Conceptualizing Racism

Conceptualizing Racism

Breaking the Chains of Racially Accommodative Language

Noel A. Cazenave

ROWMAN & LITTLEFIELD
Lanham • Boulder • New York • London

Published by Rowman & Littlefield
A wholly owned subsidiary of
The Rowman & Littlefield Publishing Group, Inc.
4501 Forbes Boulevard, Suite 200, Lanham, Maryland 20706
www.rowman.com

Unit A, Whitacre Mews, 26-34 Stannary Street, London SE11 4AB, United Kingdom

Copyright © 2016 by Rowman & Littlefield

All rights reserved. No part of this book may be reproduced in any form or by any electronic or mechanical means, including information storage and retrieval systems, without written permission from the publisher, except by a reviewer who may quote passages in a review.

British Library Cataloguing in Publication Information Available

Library of Congress Cataloging-in-Publication Data
Cazenave, Noel A., 1948– author.
Conceptualizing racism : breaking the chains of racially accommodative language / Noel A. Cazenave.
pages cm
Includes bibliographical references and index.
ISBN 978-1-4422-5235-6 (cloth : alk. paper) — ISBN 978-1-4422-5236-3 (electronic)
1. Racism in language. 2. Critical discourse analysis—Social aspects. 3. Sociolinguistics. I. Title.
P120.R32C39 2016
305.8001'4—dc23
2015026486

∞ ™ The paper used in this publication meets the minimum requirements of American National Standard for Information Sciences Permanence of Paper for Printed Library Materials, ANSI/NISO Z39.48-1992.

Printed in the United States of America

To my awesome granddaughter, Graciela Celestina, and to my students.
May understanding and challenging racism make your futures brighter.

Contents

Preface and Acknowledgments ... ix

Prologue: Sociology as Autobiography ... xiii

Introduction: Racial Accommodation and the Misconceptualization of Racism ... 1

1 Understanding Linguistic Racial Accommodation and Confrontation ... 13

2 Linguistic Racial Accommodation from Slavery to the Civil Rights Movement ... 29

3 Linguistic Racial Accommodation and Confrontation from the Civil Rights Movement to *The Declining Significance of Race* ... 65

4 Theoretical Fragmentation: The White Backlash and Its Legacy of Failure ... 99

5 Defining Racism: Beyond Mini-Racism and the "Race" as Agency Concept ... 131

6 Confronting Racially Accommodative Language by Conceptualizing Racism as a System of Oppression ... 163

Conclusion: Lessons Learned and Challenges Remaining: Toward a More Honest Conceptualization of Racism ... 189

Epilogue: Unfinished Business in Confronting Racially Accommodative Language ... 197

Notes	213
Index	233
About the Author	249

Preface and Acknowledgments

Words Matter!

Racial incidents and other more enduring evidence of systemic racism in the United States and other highly racialized democracies expose a huge racial divide in public opinion. Unfortunately, only rarely do their political and social policy leaders acknowledge the presence of the eight-hundred-pound gorilla in the room: the one whose name is Racism. And when the problem is acknowledged, it is often euphemistically referred to as "race" or "the race issue." These acknowledgments are often such obviously empty rhetoric that any ensuing conversation cannot be expected to reach beyond our own kitchen tables. However, on those even rarer occasions when actual public discourse is called for, such efforts fail because the nomenclature of "race" is not capable of sustaining a serious dialogue. Indeed, there is little agreement on even the most basic of questions implicit in that word's use: what exactly is "race"? and why is it an issue? The word that best explains such conceptual confusion is power. Although racism exists, persists, and has horrific social consequences, most of the racially privileged members of highly racialized societies rarely acknowledge it; and even during those rare moments when the phenomenon becomes undeniably visible, they are unlikely to comprehend what they see. Such racism evasiveness and denial go beyond individuals being deaf and blind to racism. Punitive sanctions await anyone who attempts to broach the topic in an honest and straightforward way. It is this environment of what I call *linguistic racial accommodation* that allows racial oppression to flourish.

Part of my motivation for writing this book, which stresses the need to break the chains of racially accommodative language, is more personal than my desire to embolden more honest racism-focused discourse and action. It is to give myself a second chance to reach my students. Some of the most disappointing moments I experience as a professor are, after having taught my white racism course or my racism theory graduate seminar, to receive e-mails or to read articles in which my former students so uncritically use racially accommodative words like "race," "black," "white," and "minority," and racism-evasive and analytically obfuscating phrases like "the race issue" or "due to race" as to suggest that they had never taken a course from me. After this happened more than a few times, I came to realize that it is not enough to provide students with safe, in-class "free space" to examine systemic racism or actually do racism studies. As long as the career structure of the discipline remains so closely aligned with society's racial power structure, most scholars, teachers, and students will continue to use the language of racial accommodation. Rejecting such language is clearly an uphill battle, but I believe it is one well worth fighting. This book provides a second chance for me to reach my students and urge them to stay on course in their racism conceptualization work. That second chance comes through having *Conceptualizing Racism* serve as what one of my graduate students once referred to as "a little Noel." It is the job of this little me, if you will, to sit on the shoulders of my former students and to whisper into their ears reminders of what is needed and what is possible if they are able to muster the political courage to both imagine and to realize racism studies and its goal of examining systemic racism directly and explicitly.

The abilities to see and to comprehend systems of racial oppression are essential analytical skills for those who would dismantle them. One cannot undo what is both invisible and unintelligible. To that end, two of the three goals of *Conceptualizing Racism* are embodied in the words "critique" and "toolkit." This book's critique mission is to make the case for moving beyond racially accommodative language to study systemic racism directly and explicitly, an interdisciplinary scholarly approach I call racism studies. One of the book's action aims is to contribute to the conceptual toolkit with which to both analyze and challenge linguistic racial accommodation and to build racism studies as a specialty area through what I refer to as *linguistic racial confrontation*. With those goals, *Conceptualizing Racism* fits what to some readers may seem a rather strange genre of scholarship—falling somewhere between social criticism and applied social science. Because of its location at that nexus of critique and practice, *Conceptualizing Racism* might best be called applied criticism in that its goal is not just to clear the field of what I consider to be the racially accommodative conceptual weeds of the failed race and ethnic relations paradigm, but to make its modest contribution to the sowing of some new conceptual seeds that, with much more work that is beyond the scope of this study, may blossom as part of a bountiful racism studies garden that is fertile ground for the cultivation of its requisite racism theory. The third, and most important, goal of *Conceptualizing Racism* is to encourage not only scholars, but antiracist activists, policy makers, and other opinion leaders to embrace language that allows racial oppression to be discussed in a candid and forthright manner in the words of the racially oppressed. As you will see, the single most important word in their liberation-focused lexicon is racism.

I hope that *Conceptualizing Racism* will make its mark in achieving those goals in three ways: as a language-centered critique of the limitations of the dominant race and ethnic relations paradigm of American sociology; as a conceptual toolkit for both exposing racism evasiveness and the building of racism studies; and, most importantly, as a call for more honest, racism-specific, public discourse on systemic racism, which I see as one of the most serious problems facing the United States and other highly racialized societies today.

I am grateful to a presentation by Nya Stevens in my racism theory graduate seminar that helped me to appreciate the analytical power of focusing on racially accommodative language. For their helpful comments and suggestions on an early draft of this book's prospectus I thank Angie Beeman, Eduardo Bonilla-Silva, Ashley Doane, Philomena Essed, Aldon Morris, Stephen Steinberg, John H. Stanfield, and Johnny E. Williams. I also thank my department colleague Matthew Hughey for steering me to useful literature on the importance of language. Thanks also to Chandra Waring for sharing with me an article that proved useful in my analysis, to Peter Allison and Dawn Cadogan for their advice on the use of library data search systems, to Arlene Goodwin for making copies of the manuscript, and to Marilyn Moir and Laurie Pudlo for their assistance in seeking funding sources—a task that, unfortunately, as is typically true for racism studies projects, proved futile.

I appreciate the useful assistance I received from developmental editors Elsa Peterson, Shannon Hassan, and Brenda Hadenfeldt; and from my daughter, Anika Tene Cazenave. Thanks also to *Hartford Courant* editorial cartoonist Bob Englehart for generously granting his permission to use one of his cartoons that I think masterfully illustrates the pitfalls of not treating the conceptualization of racism seriously.

Special thanks to Sarah Stanton, the acquisitions editor at Rowman & Littlefield who believed in this book project and shepherded it through its publication. I am also grateful for the assistance I received from her editorial assistants, Kathryn Knigge and Karie Simpson, and from the book's production editor, Alden Perkins, and for the useful comments and suggestions provided by the manuscript's external reviewers.

Finally, thanks to my granddaughter, Graciela Celestina Cazenave, for bringing so much joy and wonderment into my life by reintroducing me to the fascinating world of a little girl I have not known since her mother was a child.

Prologue

Sociology as Autobiography

He that is without sin among you,
let him first cast a stone.[1]

From the sociology of knowledge perspective, one can argue that the scholarship a sociologist produces is ultimately more revealing of that person's social location and worldview than the social phenomenon they study. In brief, their work is autobiographical. That is certainly true for this book. So let me begin with a brief introduction to who I am and how I came to be so obsessed with the racism-evasive language of the social sciences.

I was born nearly seven decades ago and was raised in one of the world's most magical cities, a city whose special place was and is marred by intense levels of racism, poverty, and ignorance. That city is New Orleans and to understand who I am, how I think, and what I do, you must begin with the fact that from my early years in Jim Crow to the present I have had what seems like an infinite stream of Louisiana gumbo coursing through my veins. While my New Orleans roots help explain my concern about racism as a driving force in my becoming a sociologist, it does not account for why in my graduate studies and early career I stayed largely within the discipline's mainstream in my choice of words to express that concern, nor why later I rejected such racially accommodative language.

CONFESSIONS OF A LINGUISTIC RACIAL ACCOMMODATIONIST

To explain how I began what to many may seem a quixotic effort to defeat what I call linguistic racial accommodation (LRA), I must first confess my own sins as a career-focused sociologist who has all too often served as a wizard to the rulers of racism evasiveness. I do so to make clear that when I criticize my fellow scholars for engaging in linguistic racial accommodation, I am not pointing a finger at *them*. I am instead referring to *us, all of us*. It is important for me to acknowledge this fact not only because my critiques of the work of many of my colleagues within the discipline are, appropriately, hard hitting; but because those criticisms have been couched in a way that makes it difficult not to take them personally. Such pain-evoking stepping on toes is unavoidable for any analysis that stresses the role of careerism in stifling the use of honest language. Indeed, some may read this book's bottom line as, "social scientists routinely sell their souls to the devil of careerism." While I admit that I do think such a construal rings truer than we generally care to acknowledge, I don't believe we do so as a part of some Faustian bargain. When it comes to human motives things are, indeed, as the expression goes, "complicated," and even when we humans engage in the most inhumane acts we can generally find ways to feel good about ourselves. Sociologists and other social scientists tend to think of ourselves not as unprincipled hustlers who serve power to make a buck, but as caring social-problems-focused professionals who in order to retain the legitimacy necessary to bring about the social changes we advocate must work carefully within the normative boundaries—linguistic and otherwise—of our academic disciplines and their "scientific" methods.

We all—and I am no exception—face pressures to accommodate our work and ideals to career expediency. In an autobiographical essay published in *The American Sociologist* more than a quarter of a century ago I reflected on how I tried to negotiate that tension during my early years as a sociologist. For example, under the heading "The Tulane Years: 'Ain't Misbehavin'" and the 'Invisible Man'" I recalled my graduate school days and noted how at that conservative institution, in a department with no faculty of color, I chose the relatively non-controversial topic of African American fathers as a dissertation topic. And in another section titled "The 'Phantom' Goes to Philadelphia" I recounted how I entered a tenure track position at Temple University under the "false pretenses" of being a "reasonable" Negro fascinated by the supposed "'white radical' ideas" of some of my European American department colleagues. I recalled that even after I earned tenure I continued to hide my true identity as an African American leftist whose politics went far beyond white liberalism. Consequently, I still felt very much like "The Spook

Who Sat by the Door"; the African American revolutionary posing as the CIA agent protagonist of the 1969 novel, and later film, of that same name.[2]

Those were very stressful times for me; times when I struggled intensely to manage the tensions of being true to myself and successful in my career. To navigate those turbulent currents I devised a political advocacy/career advancement strategy that metaphorically resembled the growth of a sunflower plant. Within that image I viewed my graduate study and tenure track years as "strategic 'stem growth'"; a period during which I balanced "'a delicate dialectic' between achievement and commitment" as I rose "as high and as rapidly as possible" to "the high vantage point and sturdy base from which a social science activist can exercise influence." I justified this form of intellectual and political accommodation with the rationale that "those who are able to negotiate this delicate dialectic (i.e., maintain their idealism and desire for fundamental change as they become professionally successful) may develop the influence that will make their voices heard on important issues." They would therefore "be able to push harder and farther on controversial topics and proposals than those who are less successful and less secure in their status." I concluded that once such scholar/activists reached the ultimate "'flower growth' stage" of their careers as radical social scientists, they would witness the blossoming of both their career aspirations and the social change they advocated as they became free to speak out honestly and forcefully on the issues they care about most.[3]

I later became aware of reasons why such a strategy may prove unwise. Chief among these is the fact that no one is guaranteed to live long enough to secure the relative safety of job tenure and promotions. It would, indeed, be tragic if a young scholar got hit by a bus while being distracted by the grand contemplation and anxious apprehension of "when I get tenure." Another reason that such a strategy is perilous is what it does to the mind, body, heart, and soul of a scholar/activist who manages to live long enough to achieve some of its career-safety benefits. By the time I received tenure I experienced burnout, and since then have endured at least a couple of decades of dealing with what some might call the "angry black man" syndrome.[4]

Such struggles and the mental confusion they fuel can make it that much harder to think, speak, and write clearly. Prior to my coauthored book, *Welfare Racism*, which I believe—despite the compromises required of such a joint venture—offers a model of how racism studies should be done, my scholarship had been relatively accommodative in its language. Throughout much of my career as a sociologist I worked largely within the language structure of the discipline as I uncritically used terms like "black," "white," "race," and "underclass." Moreover, much of my focus was on the poverty-driven social problems African Americans disproportionately face, such as those related to family structures and roles. While my intention was to do a backdoor analysis of the larger social structure that ultimately produced those problems, my work too easily fit into the sociological mainstream of analyzing the "Negro problem." Only after I abandoned applied sociology—upon realizing how useless it was without the power to make its most progressive recommendations happen—and after no longer being able to ignore what I increasingly saw as its glorified victim analysis, did I finally move beyond African American families and male gender roles. After placing my "black studies" projects on the shelf, I began working on what I deemed my new emphasis on "white studies"; that is, an analysis of the white power structure and its key players. It was then, with an increasingly direct and explicit examination of racial oppression, that I began to focus intensely on what forms the ideological core of such systems: words.

My increasing fascination with the power of words came to an explosive head in the mid-1990s after I decided to teach a course the title of which would dare to call a thing by its rightful name, White Racism.

ALL HELL BREAKS LOOSE

Although I had been told that the approval of special topics courses was pro forma, the reaction of my college's curricula and courses committee—which twice tabled the course proposal after some of its members reacted emotionally to the course title—offers useful insights into how the white power structure controls racial discourse in usually subtle, but if need be ruthless ways. That experience left me with a profound and enduring impression of just how much words matter and how little academic freedom and freedom of speech there is in the United States and other highly racialized democratic states when it comes to honest discourse about racial oppression. As a result of the struggle I became radicalized in my commitment to as June Jordan so aptly put it, "make our language conform to the truth of our many selves."[5] An example of what I refer to as linguistic racial confrontation (LRC) is my struggle to shift the focus away from the "racial minorities" subject of many sociology courses to systemic white racism; the actual people and the system they construct and defend to benefit from racial privilege.

"White Racism" as Fighting Words

Why such an uproar over the title of a course? The short answer is that in the United States and other highly racialized democracies, "white racism" are deemed fighting words by the racially dominant "white" racialized group whose racial actions and the privileges that accrue from them are increasingly invisible. In an article about that course controversy Darlene Alvarez Maddern and I highlighted the role of sociology curricula in maintaining that system-sustaining invisibility. From an inventory of thirty-four course syllabi included in an American Sociological Association race and ethnic relations course teaching guide published a couple years after that widely publicized dispute, we found only one course in that guide that contained the word racism in it: my White Racism course. The largest grouping of those courses—more than a fourth—had titles (e.g., the sociology of minority groups, minority groups, and racial and ethnic minorities) that identified their focus as "minority groups."[6] Implicit in such titles is the racially accommodative—through what I refer to as the conceptual misdirection—assumption that it is largely the racial "minorities" themselves who constitute America's racial problem.

In that article we included a table that detailed in the order of their frequency the major categories of both published (e.g., newspaper articles and letters to the editor) and unpublished (e.g., letters, e-mails, and other correspondence sent to me personally) criticisms of the course. Two large and closely related categories of criticisms were "Racially Offensive Title" and "Title Is Inflammatory or Racially Divisive." Fitting the "Racially Offensive Title" category was a letter sent to me by the CEO of a manufacturing firm that began with the objection, "I'm personally insulted." Following that same line of reasoning that racism is individual-level bigotry, with its attendant assumptions that the course focus was on racially bigoted individuals and that it was therefore unfair to focus exclusively on white racial bigotry, was a comment by a humanities professor who as a member of the college curricula and courses committee opposed the course. As he put it, "the title made it seem like an attack on whites rather than racism." Similar to these perspectives on the meanings of racism and whiteness were comments that best fit under the "Title Is Inflammatory or Racially Divisive" category. They included a letter from a University of Connecticut natural science professor who was a longtime antiracism activist and who could best be described as a critic-supporter of the course. He complained that "its proposed title as it stands now is a provocation, because it contains the implication that being white automatically carries with it a racist outlook." An alumnus who threatened to withdraw financial support to the university condemned me as "a black racist" and, with righteous indignation backed by a petite definition of racism, proclaimed that "racism, black or white, should not be tolerated anywhere."[7]

A posting made on the Progressive Sociologists Network Listserv that fit the White People are Not the Only Racists category argued if there is a course on white racism there should also be "'courses entitled Black Racism, Asian Racism, Native American Racism, etc.'" This conclusion was further justified by the assertion that "'racism is not limited to the white race, it is a cultural universal and is found among all races and in all periods of history.'"[8]

Because the focus of this book is linguistic racial accommodation, it is fitting to note that another category of criticism of the course proposal was what I call the linguistically realistic advice that I should "Be Practical: If Title Is a Problem Change the Title." In expressing his sympathy to the feelings of the "'many white people [who] were offended,'" an African American columnist for the *Hartford Courant* acknowledged that "'I, too, was a little taken aback. WHITE RACISM. It does get right in your face.'" He then gave this linguistically pragmatic advice. "'If the word 'white' gets in the way of attracting a cross-section of students, then spike the word. 'Racism,' 'Racism 101,' 'Intro to Racism,' whatever, would suffice.'" Similarly, after interviewing me about the course a European American student reporter for UConn's *Daily Campus* also supported teaching what he believed would be the same course, but under another name. In making that case, he told his readers that "'a less inflammatory course title would have breezed through the approval process with no controversy.'"[9]

In a *Hartford Courant* commentary I took an LRC stance as I gave the following reason why the White Racism course title faced such intense opposition and why it is language well worth fighting for.

> In contemporary America there is a militant refusal to acknowledge the existence of white racism. The very words "white racism" are not to be spoken. "White racism" are fighting words because they acknowledge the existence of a color- and race-based system of group privilege. In a society that holds both equality and the superiority of the so-called "white" race as core but conflicting values, such recognition is extremely unpopular.[10]

WHERE DID I GO FROM THERE?

After that controversy, my thinking about language, social science, and systemic racism would never be the same as I became captivated by just how much words matter in establishing, maintaining, and challenging systems of social oppression. I got to the point that I became useless for reviewing book and article manuscripts because I could not accept their basic linguistic and conceptual premises. I knew that I had to do something about that obsession when I realized that in making comments and suggestions for a collection a colleague of mine was editing I had scribbled nearly as much red ink on the paper as there was black ink. Mercifully that journey to fully explore the depths of what I refer to as linguistic racial accommodation and confrontation culminated in this book.

These autobiographical insights are intended to help you understand, and hopefully appreciate, what *Conceptualizing Racism* is and what it is not; what it does and what it does not attempt to do. This book is a multi-purposed intellectual inquiry that includes an argument and conceptual framework useful for sociology of knowledge analyses, a critique of the existing race relations and racism literatures, and conceptual work toward the advancement of racism studies. The content, range, and organization of its chapters reflect the fact that its purpose, scope, and method go far beyond, for example, a more positivistic, hypothesis-centered, content analysis of the relevant social-science literature. While *Conceptualizing Racism* exposes a problem and takes some concrete steps toward fixing it, it does not attempt to test hypotheses or to develop substantive theory.

Some readers may find this book to be a bit different from the sociological studies they are accustomed to. They may be especially disturbed by what they perceive as its irreverent and harsh treatment of my fellow sociologists, not to mention of sociology itself. What this book is, is of course a product of what I intend it to do. For example, its essence, as among other things a sociology of sociology, reflects its goal of exposing the racial politics behind professional social science's abysmal failure to explain the pervasiveness and persistence of racism. In doing so I hope to convince you, the reader, that as long as sociologists and others continue to pursue such a racially accommodative path they should not be taken seriously. In this way, I hope that *Conceptualizing Racism* will inspire and help legitimize the efforts of at least a few young racism scholars to survive graduate school, tenure, and promotion with their integrity, their language, and their sense of humor largely intact.

Introduction

Racial Accommodation and the Misconceptualization of Racism

We wear the mask that grins and lies,
It hides our cheeks and shades our eyes.
Paul Laurence Dunbar[1]

In 1896, the year in which the U.S. Supreme Court upheld the constitutionality of racial segregation laws and practices with its infamous Plessy v. Ferguson decision, Paul Laurence Dunbar published a poem that powerfully expressed the anguish of African Americans forced to "wear the mask that grins and lies" in deference to a vigilant and vengeful white power structure. Today, more than a century later, after the successes of the modern civil rights movement and the election—twice—of a Kenyan American as president in what some pundits touted as a "post racial" America, it is widely assumed by many European Americans that racial "minorities" need no longer be careful about expressing their true thoughts and feelings. In this new America they do not, for example, need to wait to complain about their treatment by "white folks" until they return to the safety of their often racially homogeneous homes, neighborhoods, churches, social organizations, and bars. Unfortunately, however, that is not the real America we live in today. Dunbar's poem still aptly describes the lives of the racially oppressed in the United States and other highly racialized but assumed to be "color-blind" societies where what is actually racism blindness makes racism difficult to conceptualize and challenge.[2]

This wearing of the racially accommodative mask is still very much required for even those journalists, intellectuals, political pundits, scholars, and other highly educated elites of color who have been properly credentialed to speak with authority about race relations. And their European American colleagues, while perhaps under less intense scrutiny, also know the political wisdom of staying within the tightly delimited and well-known boundaries of acceptable racial discourse where words like white racism are not to be spoken. They are all aware that despite such loudly trumpeted ideals like freedom of speech, freedom of the press, and academic freedom, those who stray from existing racial discourse boundaries—by, for example, not conforming to the use of ambiguous and therefore racism-evasive terminology like "race," "minorities," and "the race issue"—place at risk not only their customary workplace comfort, but their careers.

While violation of the norms of the racial order can have devastating personal consequences, conformity has its own price. Those of us who engage in racial discourse often find ourselves caught between the proverbial rock and a hard place. My students and I examine what it means to be in such a place in my Social Construction of Happiness class when I ask them to consider the importance of individuals being authentic in their career pursuits. To that end we contemplate Plato's conceptualization of happiness as a soul in harmony with itself, as he makes his case for an individual living a life of justice.[3]

Systems of oppression flourish when the language that camouflages their ideological core is accepted as a given and therefore goes both unexamined and unchallenged. In this chapter I introduce the problem of racial accommodation—more specifically, what I refer to as *linguistic racial accommodation* (LRA)—and place it within its larger historical and social context. I then begin to make my case as to why the ability to understand and communicate honestly about systems of racial oppression—what I refer to as *linguistic racial confrontation* (LRC)—is an essential analytical skill for those who would dismantle them.

THE HISTORICAL CONTEXT OF RACIAL ACCOMMODATION

The contemporary workings of linguistic racial accommodation in the United States can best be understood when viewed within their historical context. The best known and most influential racial accommodationist in U.S. history is Booker T. Washington, a man who helped shape the race and ethnic relations conceptual paradigm of American sociology. That was done largely through Washington's influence on one of his aides, Robert E. Park, who would become a pioneer in the formation of American sociology as an academic discipline and as a profession. The nation's white power structure anointed Washington as the leader of African Americans after he gave his famous "Atlanta Compromise" speech in 1895, only months after the death of the militantly outspoken African American leader Frederick Douglass.[4]

Those two ex-slaves were indeed very different in their responses to racial oppression. Douglass, a journalist, was a master wordsmith who boldly crafted some of the most powerful writings and speeches for the cause of African American freedom. Perhaps his best-known words are from an address given in 1857 in Canandaigua, New York, in which he stressed the inextricable link between power and enacted social change. "If there is no struggle there is no progress. Those who profess to favor freedom and yet depreciate agitation, are men who want crops without plowing up the ground, they want rain without thunder and lightning. They want the ocean without the awful roar of its many waters." Douglass's words soon reached their climax in two brief sentences that eloquently state the need for breaking the chains of racially accommodative language: "Power concedes nothing without a demand. It never did and it never will."[5]

Booker T. Washington, the head of Tuskegee Institute, an industrial training school for African Americans located in Tuskegee, Alabama, took a very different tack to race relations than did Frederick Douglass. In his historic 1895 speech at the Cotton States and International Exposition in Atlanta, Georgia, which promoted what was touted as the emergence of a new industrialized South, Washington supported the interests of both northern industrial capitalists and similarly ambitious Southerners through his assurance that the region's racial situation would remain sufficiently stable so as to not threaten new investments there.[6]

By adroitly laying out the ideology and language of racial accommodation, Washington established himself as the white power structure's most influential spokesperson for African Americans for decades to come. Challenging African Americans to "cast down your bucket where you are," accept the fact of racial segregation, and focus instead on making economic gains by appreciating the dignity of manual labor, Washington advised that "the wisest among my race understand that the agitation of questions of social equality is the extremist folly."[7]

Washington's preference for slow, and what he deemed to be natural and inevitable change reflected his acceptance of the evolutionary theory popular at that time—and explained why he stated in his autobiography that he no longer harbored, as he did as a young man, "ill will toward anyone who spoke in bitter terms against the Negro, or who advocated measures that tended to oppress the black man or to take from him opportunities for growth in the most complete manner." Now Washington realized that such a man deserves "pity" more than anything else because, "one might as well try to stop the progress of a mighty railroad train by throwing his body across the track." Maintaining that "the according of the full exercise of political rights is going to be a matter of natural, slow growth, not an overnight, gourd vine affair," Washington cautioned that "it is the duty of the Negro—as the greater part of the race is already doing—to deport himself modestly in regard to political claims."[8]

Surely, though, in more than a century since Washington wrote these words, we have moved on, have we not? One could point to the protest-dominated modern civil rights movement era of the mid-1950s through the late 1960s, and to subsequent decades characterized by neither accommodation nor protest. My rejection of that racial-accommodation-as-merely-history argument is based on what I consider to be a more accurate, dialectical, and power-driven view of race relations that sees them as neither static nor ever improving. While the intensity and pervasiveness of racial accommodation may diminish with generally improved race relations, it still persists in new, often more subtle manifestations—especially through the use of racially accommodative language.

RACIAL ACCOMMODATION TODAY

A major reason why it is so difficult to have serious discussions about racism today is the intense denial of its existence or significance. The racially oppressed face an environment in which the usually largest and always most powerful segment of the population—the group that benefits from systemic racism while wanting to retain good feelings about itself—refuses to even acknowledge its existence as a social problem. Such denial of the persistence, pervasiveness, and devastating social consequences of racism persists despite overwhelming evidence that its occurrence is no mere aberration among a few remaining racial bigots who somehow failed to get the memo announcing that modern democracies like the United States are now officially "color-blind."[9]

It was just that type of racial make-believe thinking that was evident after the election of Barack Obama as president when numerous social commentators trumpeted what they saw as irrefutable evidence that the United States had entered into its post-racial era. That fantasy did not last long. After that 2008 election there was an unprecedented number of threats to President Obama's life. In addition, sizable segments of the European American population, despite all evidence to the contrary, denied both Obama's U.S. birthplace—which established his constitutional right to be president—and his Christianity as they reconstructed him into an un-American social other. That highly racialized otherization of Barack Obama was backed by sinister images of him as an Islamic terrorist, a surreptitious socialist, a Hitler-like fascist, a black racist, and even the Antichrist. At right-wing Tea Party rallies and elsewhere, opposition to President Obama seemed much too personal and emotionally intense to be driven solely by policy disagreements. For example, consistent with a popular racist stereotype that has deep historical roots in American culture, Barack Obama has been depicted as a chimpanzee. And when the focus was on public policy that, too, was highly racialized, such as in the matter of the illegal immigration of Latinos/as. Despite—or perhaps because of—the election of an African American president, the social fabric of the United States continued to tear apart along precisely the same color line W. E. B. Du Bois, the renowned African American social scientist and intellectual, predicted would be its major challenge for the previous century.[10]

It is within this racial environment that, in his apparent efforts not to alienate European American voters, President Obama accommodated himself to a racism-evasive political strategy in his handling of several highly racialized events. Consider the controversy over the arrest of the African American Harvard University professor Henry Louis Gates by a European American Cambridge, Massachusetts police officer after the professor complained too loudly about being racially profiled in his own home. President Obama's handling of that incident offers an example of the problems that accrue from the use of racially accommodative language. He could have taken the opportunity to acknowledge that, aside from the yet undetermined facts of that particular case, he was well aware of the large volume of evidence on the pervasiveness of racial profiling nationwide. He might have then announced that he had requested his Attorney General to appoint a commission to study the issue and to make recommendations for both congressional and executive action. Instead, he commented that Professor Gates was his friend, thus making it a personal instead of a systemic issue; he charged that the police had acted "stupidly"; and he invited the professor and the police officer to the White House for what the media quickly dubbed and dismissed as a "beer summit" photo opportunity.[11]

We can better understand President Obama's handling of that situation by examining his strategy for dealing with another highly racialized political mess the previous year, when he was campaigning for his first term as president. In a speech on "race" in Philadelphia he responded to remarks by his former minister that included what Obama characterized as "incendiary language." Obama complained that he found particularly offensive and racially divisive comments by Reverend Wright that "expressed a profoundly distorted view" of the United States, "a view that sees white racism as endemic."[12] In an open letter to then-candidate Obama, a group of nearly fifty sociology professors and PhD candidates—all Obama supporters—responded to his politically calculated remarks that were so carefully built upon a platform of racism-evasive language.

> We believe that Wright is exactly right, that racism is not only endemic but is at the core of American society as reflected in a large and well established

body of social scientific research.... The problem with your equating racism with prejudice and your characterization of "race" as the key issue rather than racism is that it does not account for the fact that racism is not merely a product of intentional (though perhaps sometimes unconscious) interactions between individuals, but rather the result of deeply seated social and institutional practices and habits. The use of language like "the race issue" or, as you put it, "race is an issue" is therefore confusing and evades a more real and serious discussion of racism.[13]

Once Obama rejected the notion that racism was endemic, or "systemic," as those and many other social scientists would put it, he had no framework for discourse about issues like racial profiling. That lack of an apt way to communicate about racism would plague President Obama again three years after his White House Beer Summit when, in response to widespread African American social protest over the shooting of unarmed African American teenager Trayvon Martin by a neighborhood watch volunteer, who for more than six weeks was not charged with a crime, Obama once again made the issue personal rather than systemic. His statement, "If I had a son, he'd look like Trayvon," came only after protests had brought such a level of national attention to the incident that he could no longer remain silent. By shifting the public's attention away from a serious discussion of systemic racism, once again a president of the United States bowed to the pressure of racial accommodation that enables racial oppression to flourish.[14]

RACISM DENIAL AND RACISM EVASIVENESS

Why is there so little honest discussion and conceptualization of racism today? First, people who enjoy the benefits of white racial privilege prefer to believe they have earned whatever status, opportunities, experiences, and possessions they have by their own talents and hard work. Second, consistent with the widespread misconceptualization of racism as an individual-level phenomenon, complaints about racism are taken as personal affronts rather than as systemic critiques. Therefore the mere word racism is received as a fighting word. Finally, and most relevant to this study, overtly racist attitudes and practices are incongruent with highly touted democratic and egalitarian ideals and thus pose a conundrum for the color-blind pretensions of highly racialized democracies.

Such dissonance between societal ideals and actual beliefs and behavior is typically resolved through the intense denial of the existence of systemic racism. Along the same lines as Ruth Frankenberg's work in categorizing different types of racial thinking, I have prepared a continuum (see figure 0.1) to show how people of European descent—those typically designated as

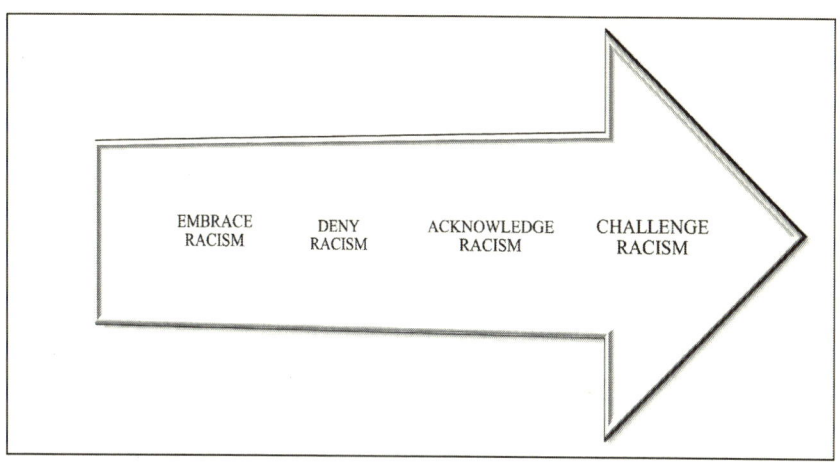

Figure 0.1. Continuum of Linguistic and Other Responses to Systemic Racism by Members of the Racially Dominant Group

"white" in race/color stratified societies—respond to systemic white racism.[15]

While racial bigots are most likely to openly *embrace* racism, most members of the racially dominant group are inclined to *deny* racism, those who are open to becoming educated about racism are inclined to *acknowledge* racism, and finally, it is the relatively small numbers of antiracist activists who are most motivated to *challenge* racism. When it comes to racism, even society's brightest intellectuals and best-trained social analysts tend to steer clear of controversy by remaining blind to racism.[16] This is not to suggest that all linguistic racial accommodation is conscious and rationally driven by careerist concerns. Social psychological experiments by Solomon Asch and Gregory Berns found that, because conformity to peer group pressure may be unconscious, those who are influenced to accept incorrect perceptions may be unaware of that influence. As one author succinctly concluded, the reason why such groups are "literally capable of changing our perceptions" is that "to stand alone is to activate primitive, powerful, and unconscious feelings of rejection."[17]

THE PROBLEM OF RACIALLY ACCOMMODATIVE LANGUAGE

It is through racially accommodative language that the existence, scope, and consequences of systemic racism are denied. According to sociologist Eduardo Bonilla-Silva, contemporary racial practices in the United States "(1) are increasingly covert, (2) are embedded in normal operations of institutions,

(3) avoid direct racial terminology, and (4) are invisible to most Whites." Bonilla-Silva's observation supports my position that in highly racialized democracies like the United States, where overt racism is inconsistent with democratic and egalitarian ideals, linguistic racial accommodation will persist even when there is an overall decline in overtly racist practices. As such societies forsake the use of whips, chains, and other implements of physical violence to maintain the racial order, white racial hegemony is increasingly maintained through words—especially those words that hide the very existence of systemic racism.[18]

This problem of racially accommodative language is evident today when there are efforts at honest racial discourse but the permissible lexicon proves not to be up to the task. Some time ago, I took part in an elaborate three-location televised forum on "race." Unfortunately, with each participant bringing his or her own agenda, we spent most of the night talking past one another. Some of those who participated argued that the forum was about the bad attitudes and behavior of individual bigots from any and all racial and ethnic groups. Others pushed a theme echoing the famous "can we all get along?" plea of Rodney King, the victim of a notorious videotaped beating in 1991 by officers of the Los Angeles Police Department. Still others came to complain about the stifling effects of various racial identity labels (e.g., "white" or "black") that they were forced to bear and that failed to capture the complexities of their racialized lives. And then there were the concerns of the people of color who were most likely to face racist stereotyping and systemic discrimination in their daily lives. As usual in such discussions, those who had the most at stake in racial dialogue and the least amount of collective power came away frustrated that their voices had been muddled amid the crowded discourse. Consequently many of us left feeling we had partaken in what amounted to a three-ring circus in which we were neither heard nor understood.[19]

Unlike that forum, in this book the voices of those who need it most are articulated in a strong and straightforward manner. *Conceptualizing Racism: Breaking the Chains of Racially Accommodative Language* confronts linguistic racial accommodation in such a way that concerned citizens, including social and public policy makers, can—if they are willing—finally have that honest conversation about racism that has for so long eluded this nation and many other highly racialized societies.

WHY WORDS MATTER

Conceptualizing Racism argues that words matter in both understanding and dismantling racism as a system of social oppression. That argument is based on three basic suppositions. First, racism is a highly organized *system* of "race"-justified oppression. Second, as is true for any oppressive system, *ideology* is the hegemonic glue that holds systemic racism together. And third, racist ideology is expressed largely through *language*. Therefore, as is true for all forms of human oppression, words matter mightily in any serious analysis of and challenge to systemic racism.

Because hegemonic ideologies are expressed in words—precise and carefully chosen words—it matters whether the words we choose are "race" or "racism," "black" or "African American," "minority" or "racially oppressed." It matters, for example, whether we select words that allow racism to be examined directly and explicitly or whether we opt to conform to what is comfortable and safe. In this book I do my best to free the voices of the racially oppressed from the fetters of racially accommodationist language. Understanding racism is not as complex as many people make it out to be. It does, however, necessitate our being precise in our analytical nomenclature (e.g., systemic racism) in the face of highly racialized group pressure and reward structures that encourage us to, instead, embrace society's racism-evasive program by being sufficiently vague (e.g., "race"). The only thing activist social scientists and other antiracists really need is the courage to see what is before us and to conceptualize it honestly without regard for what we are led to believe is the politically acceptable or career wise thing to do. Such courage entails something most liberals are uncomfortable with: confrontation, specifically linguistic racial confrontation.

Conceptualizing Racism can be viewed as a conceptual tool chest with two main compartments. One part contains the instruments used here to analyze how language is deployed to either support or challenge racism and other forms of oppression. The other stores various analytical devices I have assembled that should prove useful in building racism studies as a specialty area. It is around those key components that this book's chapters are organized.

FORTHCOMING CHAPTERS

Chapter 1, Understanding Linguistic Racial Accommodation and Confrontation

Here I review the existing theories of power, knowledge, language, and racism that help explain how linguistic racial accommodation, as a form of racism denial, works, and what that literature suggests is needed for successful linguistic racial confrontation. After presenting the study's key concepts I lay out my argument that in highly racialized democracies the use of racism-blind language is part of a historically normative pattern of racial accommodation to white power that requires people to work within the existing racial order rather than to examine it, much less challenge it. Finally, I name and define a dozen language-centered racism denial practices I use in later chapters in my critique of the existing race and ethnic relations literature.

Chapter 2, Linguistic Racial Accommodation from Slavery to the Civil Rights Movement

In this chapter I examine linguistic racial accommodation and the rise and fall of the dominant race and ethnic relations paradigm of American social science from the 1850s through the 1950s as both a reflection of and a source of racism evasiveness in the larger society.

Chapter 3, Linguistic Racial Accommodation and Confrontation from the Civil Rights Movement to *The Declining Significance of Race*

Here I examine efforts by progressive American sociologists, intellectuals, and policy makers to catch up with the dramatic racial events of the 1960s and by more conservative scholars the following decade to accommodate themselves to the white racial backlash.

Chapter 4, Theoretical Fragmentation: The White Backlash and Its Legacy of Failure

In chapter 4 I examine the legacy of the failure of race relations scholarship in American sociology from the 1980s to the present that is now evident in its theoretical fragmentation and petite conceptualizations of racism.

Chapter 5, Defining Racism: Beyond Mini-Racism and the "Race" as Agency Concept

This chapter's analytical center point is a discussion of influential definitions of racism organized around types of definitions, their basic theoretical assumptions, their advantages, and their limitations. After placing the relative size and robustness of those definitions within the context of changing race relations, I summarize the chapter's major findings and assess where defining racism is now and where it needs to go.

Chapter 6, Confronting Racially Accommodative Language by Conceptualizing Racism as a System of Oppression

Here I discuss the concept of linguistic racial confrontation as an alternative to linguistic racial accommodation and examine the dialectical, power-driven, relationship between the two. Next I share some of the lessons I have learned about racism from more than two decades of teaching undergraduate-

and graduate-level racism courses. I conclude this chapter with a list of criteria for an ample theory of systemic racism.

Conclusion, Lessons Learned and Challenges Remaining: Toward a More Honest Conceptualization of Racism

In this conclusion chapter I summarize this study's major findings and discuss its lessons that can be applied toward the construction of linguistically confrontational and intellectually radical racism studies. I then make my final plea that we take the conceptualization of racism more seriously.

Epilogue, Unfinished Business in Confronting Racially Accommodative Language

I end this book by discussing some additional LRA-related problems that must be overcome, as well as some emerging promises and challenges that should be embraced, if a more robust racism studies is to be developed.

Chapter One

Understanding Linguistic Racial Accommodation and Confrontation

> Anyone who challenges the status quo ... must expect intolerance.
> Oliver C. Cox[1]

In this chapter I conceptualize how linguistic racial accommodation (LRA) and linguistic racial confrontation (LRC) respectively strengthen and loosen systemic racism's hold on society by reviewing the scholarship that is most relevant to this study within four broad and overlapping categories of theories: power theories, knowledge theories, language theories, and racism theories (see figure 1.1).

WHAT WE KNOW

Power Theories

Pluralist Theory

The prevailing way of thinking about power in the United States and its impact on the nation's racial discourse is summed up nicely in pluralist theory. Best known through the work of political scientist Robert Dahl, pluralist theory assumes that when it comes to decision making the social system's power structure is open to the input of numerous countervailing groups, with no one group dominating that process.[2] Advocates of this view typically assume that the discourse is equally accessible to all parties, ideas, and language; and that in any disagreement it is the facts and logic of particular arguments that prevail. Therefore if terms like "race" or "the race issue" and "minority groups" are more likely to be used in racial discourse in the

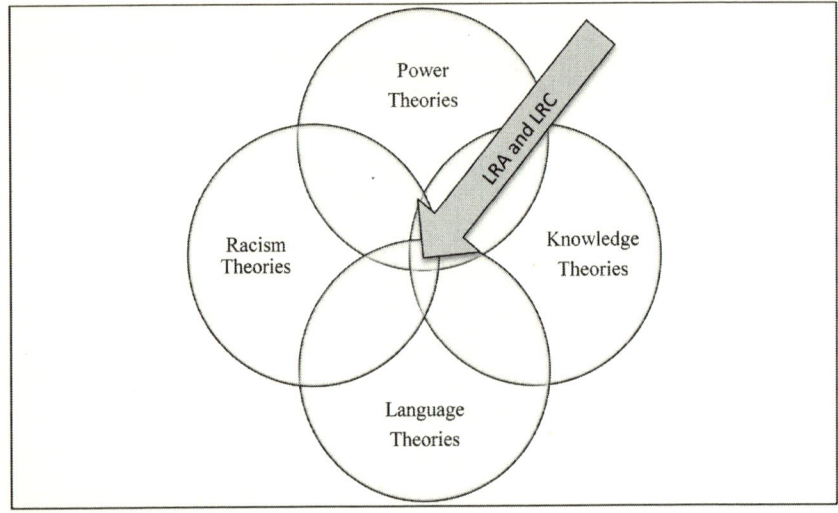

Figure 1.1. The Four Overlapping Categories of Theories Relevant to This Book's Linguistic Racial Accommodation and Confrontation Argument

United States than words like "racism," "racial oppression," and the "racially oppressed," it is simply because the former idiom is more factual and logical, not because a racially dominant group controls such discourse.

Power Elite Theory

The pluralist theory has been challenged by scholars who maintain that a society's decisions, including those about appropriate discourse, tend to be dominated by its most powerful individuals, groups, and institutions. The best known of these challengers is power elite theory, first articulated by sociologist C. Wright Mills. Power elite theory assumes that decision making and other manifestations of power are concentrated in the hands of a relatively small number of elites whose power is derived from the strategically important positions they hold within a society's key institutions and through their control of the production and dissemination of knowledge. For example, in regard to public policy, political elites determine whether racial matters are seen at all, and if so, how they are perceived and how they are conceptualized. Racism-evasive terms like "race" and "minority groups" tend to be used due to pressure from powerful elites who watch over the racial status quo: politicians, foundation officials, high-level government-agency bureaucrats, grant-funded academicians, and other policy experts.[3]

Other scholars have refined variants of power elite theory to better reflect the full complexity of power structures. E. E. Schattschneider made one of the first attempts to do so through his observation that "all forms of political organization have a bias in favor of the exploitation of some kinds of conflict and the suppression of others." It is this *"mobilization of bias"* that explains how "some issues are organized into politics while others are organized out." The power of such mobilization of bias can be seen in the largely successful efforts of politicians to keep the topic of systemic racism out of political discourse. Building on Schattschneider's idea, Peter Bachrach and Morton Baratz argued that power has not one, but two faces. Not only is there the face of decision making, recognized by both pluralist theory and power elite theory, but also the second face of agenda setting. This perspective accounts for the fact that elites within the white power structure can not only decide what, if anything, is known and done about systemic racism but, indeed, whether the issue is allowed onto the decision-making agenda.[4]

Class Theory

In his extension of Bachrach and Baratz's work, Steven Lukes added yet a third dimension of power to explain how power structures work. Lukes rejected Bachrach and Baratz's assumption that the absence of conflict over decision making, be it overt or covert, implied the existence of a consensus, and instead from a class-centered perspective examined how those who dominate power relationships prevent such conflict from surfacing in the first place. Influenced by Marxist theory, Lukes argued for the addition of a "third dimension" that "brings into view the fact that people may not be able to even perceive their own interests." Instead, what they perceive themselves as wanting "may themselves be a product of a system that works against their interests."[5] For example, there is no way that systemic white racism can be acknowledged to be a national problem if such words are not allowed within political discourse, and instead racial problems are assumed to be no larger than the bigotry of individuals from any racialized ethnic group.

Power and Powerlessness

John Gaventa, a graduate student of Lukes, was especially interested in the question of why the socially oppressed typically remain quiet about their social conditions. Were they just apathetic? Or was there something other than just brute force that kept them in a normal state of quiescence? And, finally, what accounts for rebellion when it does happen? Gaventa's thesis is that

> in situations of inequality, the political response of the deprived group or class may be seen as a function of power relationships, such that power serves for the development and maintenance of the quiescence of the non-elite. The emergence of rebellion, as a corollary, may be understood as the process by which the relationships of power are altered.[6]

With its dual focus on quiescence and rebellion, Gaventa's theory is useful in explaining why members of racially oppressed groups and their sympathizers, are usually—in public at least—quiet about racial oppression, but periodically become quite loud in their opposition to it. Central to this study is, of course, the role of racially accommodative and confrontational language in creating, maintaining, and breaking such quiescence.

Increasingly power manifests itself through the various mechanisms through which knowledge is produced and disseminated.

Knowledge Theories

The Sociology of Knowledge

The sociology of knowledge is "the branch of sociology which studies the relation between thought and society."[7] This theoretical perspective and analytical tool enhances our understanding of how the organization of a society, especially its racial organization, shapes its thinking about and conceptualization of racial oppression.

Karl Marx, in explaining that a society's class structure determines what an individual thinks and believes, articulated his famous précis of the sociology of knowledge: "it is not the consciousness of men that determines their existence, but on the contrary their social existence determines their consciousness."[8] Similarly, one could say that one's relative group position in a society's racial order determines if and how one views racism and how one is inclined to express such views linguistically.

Sociologist Karl Mannheim modified Marx's ideas by proposing a more general sociology of knowledge, one that applies not only to class dynamics but to other social groupings as well. According to Mannheim, the main thesis of the sociology of knowledge is "that there are modes of thought that cannot be adequately understood as long as their social origins are obscured." Mannheim's conceptualization is helpful in this study's analysis of racial discourse through the mobilization of both dominant and challenging ideological terminology.[9]

Whereas Marx and Mannheim examined the impact of objective social structures on knowledge production as mediated through ideologies, Peter L. Berger and Thomas Luckmann introduced an approach that stressed the more familiar subjective processes of knowledge building in ordinary life. In brief, to Berger and Luckmann the sociology of knowledge entailed nothing less than the process through which "a taken-for-granted 'reality' congeals for the man in the street." As they put it, "everyday life is, above all, life with and by means of the language I share with my fellowmen." With this emphasis on the language processes through which social reality is constructed, Berger and Luckmann's approach could prove to be useful in analyses of linguistic racial accommodation and confrontation, respectively, as processes through which certain language is censored out of racial discourse or forced into it.[10]

Social Epistemology Theory

The other variety of knowledge theory that informs my argument is social epistemology theory. Epistemology is the branch of philosophy concerned with "the study of knowledge," and social epistemology—with its rejection of the root epistemological assumption of "a universal rational knowledge that is not particular to one society or group"—entails the study of its "social dimensions." Steve Fuller saw the mission of the social epistemologist as being "to show how the *products* of our cognitive pursuits are affected by changing the social relations in which the knowledge *producers* stand to one another."[11] For the purpose of this study, this entails changes in acceptable racial knowledge congruent with shifts in race relations. This suggests that a society's intellectual and social-policy mainstream will only accept explicit discourse about racism during the disruption of usual racial power relations. A useful variant of social epistemology theory is the emerging sub-specialty of the epistemology of ignorance.

The Epistemology of Ignorance

In this book I argue that ignorance about systemic white racism can best be viewed linguistically as a verb rather than as a noun. That is to say, ignorance (as in *ignore*-ance) is not just a consequence of not knowing. It entails an active, highly organized, and persistent process I refer to as the *IPA Syndrome* that often afflicts members of socially dominant groups when it comes to acknowledging the oppression of others. That is the *ignorance* of not knowing, the *privilege* of not needing to know, and the *arrogance* of not wanting to know. IPA Syndrome fits nicely with what Charles Mills referred to as "the epistemology of ignorance," which works through an "epistemological contract" that frees members of racially dominant groups from the burdens of knowing about the racism they benefit from. In explaining this "agreement to *mis*interpret the world" and to therefore "see" it "wrongly," Mills states that "*on matters related to race, the Racial Contract prescribes for its signatories an inverted epistemology, an epistemology of ignorance, a particular pattern of localized and global cognitive dysfunctions (which are psychologically and socially functional), producing the ironic outcome that whites will in general be unable to understand the world they themselves have made.*"[12]

Mills's concept has given birth to a growing body of scholarship on the epistemologies of ignorance about gender and racial oppression, including a collection of articles entitled *Race and Epistemologies of Ignorance*. Editors Shannon Sullivan and Nancy Tuana state that "sometimes what we do not know is not a mere gap in knowledge, the accidental result of an epistemological oversight," but "especially in the case of racial oppression, a lack of knowledge or an unlearning of something previously known often is actively produced for purposes of domination and exploitation. . . . Sometimes these 'unknowledges' are consciously produced, while at other times they are unconsciously generated and supported."[13]

My study of linguistic racial accommodation and confrontation can be viewed as an investigation of the epistemology of ignorance and as a contribution to that literature—one that, of course, privileges the essential role of language.

Language Theories

The Dramatistic Approach

Literary critic Kenneth Burke stressed that by its nature language terminology includes some aspects of reality while excluding others. As he put it, "even if any given terminology is a *reflection* of reality, by its very nature as a terminology it must be a *selection* of reality; and to this extent it must function as a *deflection* of reality." Burke introduced the concept of "terministic screens" to explain this tendency for certain language terms to direct attention to or away from some phenomenon. For example, college courses that all focus on family life will employ very different terministic screens if they are taught in departments of sociology, economics, or history. And, of course, even within the same discipline radically different terminology may be deployed depending on the course taught or the theoretical paradigm chosen. This example illustrates Burke's point that "much that we take as observations about 'reality' may be but the spinning out of possibilities implicit in our particular choice of terms."[14] Such linguistic screens that steer people toward seeing some social phenomena while ignoring others can be especially powerful when they are further restricted by their donning ideological blinders.

Language, Ideology, and Power

More recent scholarship has engaged in more direct and extensive examination of the nexus of language, ideology, and power than did Burke or the post-modernist Michel Foucault. For example, in *Language and Symbolic Power*, Pierre Bourdieu criticized language studies that remove language from its sociohistorical and power contexts. Bourdieu stressed that "linguistic exchanges" are indeed "relations of power" and stated that language, as "symbolic power," is the ability to construct reality in one's own favor. Congruent with the linguistic racial accommodation focus of this study, Bourdieu defined symbolic power as "that invisible power which can be exercised only with the complicity of those who do not want to know what they are subject to or even that they themselves exercise it." By extension, I would argue that linguistic racial confrontation challenges the dominant symbolic power by making linguistic racial accommodation visible.[15]

In *Language and Power*, British social linguist Norman Fairclough crafted a useful set of conceptual and methodological tools with which scholars can study "how language functions in maintaining and changing power relations in contemporary society." Fairclough insisted that "sociolinguistic conventions," which "arise out of—and give rise to—particular relations of power," not be taken for granted, but instead, be explained as being "the outcome of power relations and power struggle." For example, for much of American history the problems facing African Americans have been framed linguistically as the "Negro problem." Only for a brief period—the late 1960s, after racial unrest in cities across the nation—was the terminology "white racism" endorsed by a commission of the federal government.[16]

In opposition to some post-modernists, who actually claim we are moving into a "'post-linguistic'" era, Fairclough argued that in this "linguistic epoch" in which "ideology is the prime means of manufacturing consent," "language has become perhaps the primary medium of social control and power." The gist of Fairclough's approach is that existing power relations are sustained through the uncritical acceptance of "common-sense assumptions" regarding appropriate language usage.[17]

Building on these ideas, Fairclough's conceptualization of "ideological common sense," and more specifically what might be referred to as *racialized linguistic common sense*, can be deployed to analyze the impact of social sanctions that follow the acceptance or rejection of racially accommodative language. Fairclough's work is also useful in explaining how insurgent groups challenge dominant language structures through linguistic racial confrontation. As Fairclough put it, "there is a constant endeavor on the part of those who have power to try to impose an ideological common sense which holds for everyone. . . . But there is always *some* degree of ideological diversity, and indeed conflict and struggle, so that ideological uniformity is never completely achieved." In the United States and other highly racialized societies, the dominant language term used in racial discourse is "race" and its insurgent "*anti-language*" challenger is *racism*.[18]

Finally, an adequate understanding of racially accommodative and confrontationist language requires that it be placed within its proper sociohistorical context of racial oppression and the challenges to it.

Racism Theories

By racism theories I mean intellectual work that examines racism directly and explicitly by explaining some or all of the following: its origins, nature, organization, dynamics, persistence, and consequences. Here I review only the racism theory most relevant to this book's focus and argument.

Systemic Racism Theory

Joe Feagin, the leading racism scholar in the United States, is also the most influential proponent of systemic racism theory. The evolution of his thinking on racism is based on the influence of African American intellectuals and activists going back to Oliver C. Cox, W. E. B. Du Bois, and Frederick Douglass. More recent influences on this theory include anticolonial movements and their impact on the development of the domestic colonialism perspectives among African American intellectuals and civil rights activists, as well as Stokely Carmichael and Charles Hamilton's related conceptualization of institutional racism.[19]

According to Feagin, such developments culminated in what is now a "revolution in the analysis of U.S. racism," an approach that has abandoned the long dominant individual-centered view that it is racial prejudice that results in racial discrimination for "one that views the U.S. social system as imbedding white racism at its very core."[20] This view of racial oppression as systemic is not limited to a small number of activists and elite social thinkers. While most European Americans are still likely to see racism as encompassing little more than the bad attitudes and behavior of a few isolated bigots, African Americans and other racially oppressed people tend to conceptualize racism as being systemic—as a highly organized *system* of oppression. For example, they see racism as a rigged game set up and maintained by "the man" for his benefit.

Feagin has used the concept of framing to explain the differences between how European Americans and African Americans typically view, speak about, and write about racism. According to Feagin, racism is built upon and sustained through what he referred to as "white-centered framing." Such framing, both within and outside of the social sciences, is based on language. As Feagin put it, "the language chosen to describe a society demographically or sociologically often reveals white perspective." For Feagin the prevailing ways of communicating about racial matters reflect the evasiveness and other interests of the dominant racialized group as the hegemonic white racial frame, whereas conceptualizations like institutional and systemic racism provide black "counter" or "resistance" frames.[21]

Building on the work of Joel Kovel and others, African-American political scientist Carter A. Wilson offered a historically grounded, comprehensive, and multi-faceted theory of systemic racism that incorporated not only its economic aspects, but also its political and psychocultural dimensions. Wilson's eclectic approach in *Racism: From Slavery to Advanced Capitalism* explained how racism has manifested itself during four historical periods, each of which has its own economic and psychocultural characteristics. They are: dominative racism during slavery through 1865; dominative aversive racism during sharecropping and debt peonage in the South from 1865 through 1965; aversive racism during industrial capitalism in the North, also from 1865 through 1965; and, finally, meta-racism in advanced capitalism from 1970 to the present.[22]

An obvious implication of Wilson's model of systemic racism is that the role of language in the construction of its core ideology changes from one historical period to the next. For example, as a racist system becomes more subtle and complex, its survival is increasingly based not on physical force or laws, but on hegemony imposed through the widespread distribution and enforced acceptance of its dominant racial ideology. Thus the workings of linguistic racial accommodation and confrontation would need to be much more sophisticated during the present meta-racism period of the most "advanced, rationalized, and bureaucratized form of racism,"[23] a period when racism is so covert, subtle, and institutionalized that it is widely assumed not to exist as much more than a residual of the past. This is in stark contrast to the overtly racist language that was commonplace during the earliest periods of racism, including during slavery when that oppressive system was maintained as much by the whip as it was by words. It should come as no surprise, then, that the dominant ideology for today's stealth meta-racism period of racism is color-blind ideology, constructed with language so evasive that it discourages even the mention of the word racism.

Wilson's theory of systemic racism is especially adept for analyses of battles over the linguistic framing of race relations. For example, its implicit model of the racial state—the political apparatus of white supremacy—assumes that although the racial state's ultimate aim is to maintain white racial hegemony, its actions are indeterminate and may even be paradoxical because it allows some minor, short-term changes in response to racial insurgency when racial state actors perceive such changes to be in their best interest. For example, after controversy over what has been statistically documented as widespread and sustained patterns of racial profiling, state government officials might accommodate some discourse that frames the problem as being indicative of systemic racism.[24]

Racial Contract Theory

As I show in figure 1.1, the various bodies of literature I reviewed to build my linguistic racial accommodation and confrontation argument are not distinct. There is considerable overlap that sometimes makes it impossible to confine a particular theory within a single circle. A case in point of such overlap is Charles Mills's racial contract theory, which can be categorized under both knowledge and racism theory. By combining elements of systemic racism with my previous discussion of Mills's racial contract theory, I can explain that at this meta-racism stage of racism history in the United States and other racialized democracies, during which color-blind ideology dominates, a key provision of what Mills referred to as the racial contract is the prohibition of words that acknowledge the existence and workings of systemic white racism.

GRAPHIC REPRESENTATION OF EXISTING THEORIES AND THE BOOK'S KEY ARGUMENT

Based on my review of the relevant literatures on theories of power, knowledge, language, and racism, in figure 1.2 I graphically represent the complexity of their relationships and their relevance to my linguistic accommodation and confrontation argument.

WHAT WE NEED TO KNOW

Power, knowledge, language, and racism are not only the key ingredients used in the making of linguistic racial accommodation and confrontation; they feed off the meals they have been used to prepare. As I show in figure

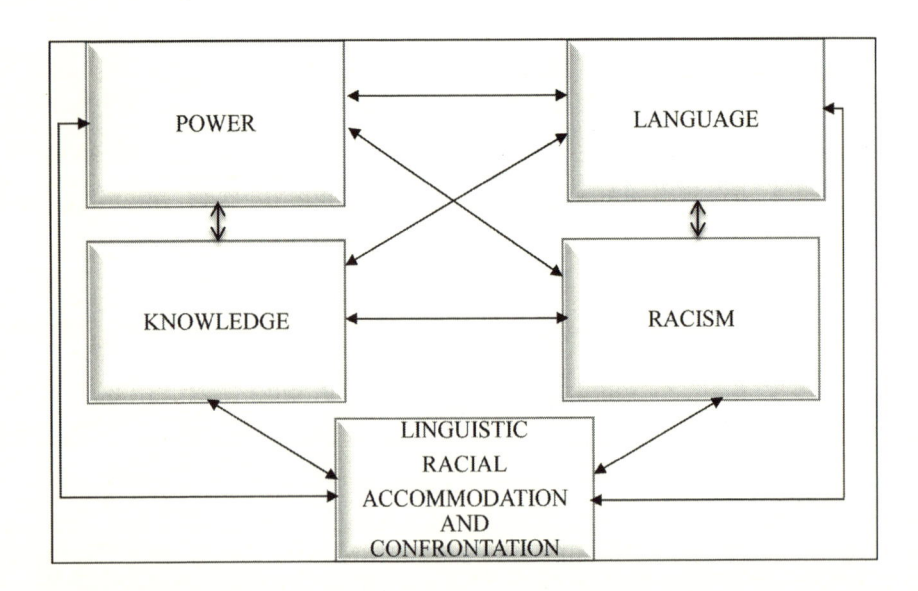

Figure 1.2. The Relationships among the Four Categories of Theoretical Literature Reviewed and the Book's Linguistic Racial Accommodation and Confrontation Argument

1.2, the relationships among these phenomena are complex and still only loosely specified. What remains to be known is *how* they impact and, in turn, are impacted by linguistic racial accommodation and confrontation. To this end I assemble the key concepts and the argument that are my analytical tools for exploring this largely uncharted maze of complex relationships.

KEY CONCEPTS AND ARGUMENT

Key Concepts

The ultimate function of linguistic racial accommodation is to evade racism as a serious social problem meriting societal attention. More specifically, *racism evasiveness* entails the deployment of various processes and practices that avoid treating systemic racism as a social problem by keeping society blind to the pervasive racism that would otherwise be obvious. By *racism blindness*, I mean the dominant ideology and practice of not seeing systemic racism in highly racialized societies in which strong sanctions are applied in the denial of its existence, pervasiveness, and consequences. I define *racism denial* as the refutation of the existence, pervasiveness, or seriousness of systemic racism despite overwhelming evidence to the contrary. While racism evasiveness and the racism blindness it produces are the dominant processes and practices through which racism remains invisible and unaddressed, racism denial is the means through which they are implemented. Building on these definitions, racism denial can be viewed as a racism-evasive process backed by numerous racism denial practices. Table 1.1 names, defines, and provides examples of some of the major racism denial practices that entail faulty linguistic conceptualizations.

For the purposes of this study, *racial accommodation* refers to the actions of individuals and organizations, including those of racially oppressed groups, that align their racial attitudes, behavior, and aspirations in keeping with the prevailing ideologies, practices, and sanctions of the dominant racialized group. More specific to my study, *linguistic racial accommodation* is the choice of words, concepts, phrases, and other language by individuals and organizations, including those of racially oppressed groups, that align their racial attitudes, behavior, and aspirations with the prevailing racial ideologies, practices, and sanctions of the dominant racialized group.

This book would, of course, have no purpose if there was no alternative to linguistic racial accommodation and its justification through *linguistic racial realism*, a system-sustaining form of extreme racial pragmatism. Its countervailing challenge—*linguistic racial confrontation*—is mobilized through a belief in a *linguistic racial idealism* rooted in the assumption that significant challenges to the racial order are possible only by speaking truth to power, despite the risks of doing so. It is through such language battles with the

Table 1.1. Language-Centered Racism Denial Practices Involving Faulty Conceptualizations

LANGUAGE-CENTERED RACISM DENIAL PRACTICES	DEFINITIONS	EXAMPLES
1. *Conceptual Colonization*	The treatment of racism as if it is merely derivative of and ancillary to some other, assumed larger and more important, form of oppression.	The privileging of terms like class or ethnic oppression over those like racism or racial oppression.
2. *Conceptual Conflation*	The confusion of racism with another form or with multiple forms of social oppression.	Terminology (e.g., ethnclass or ethnoracial) that conceptually fuses racism with class, ethnicity, gender, or a combination of various forms of oppression.
3. *Conceptual Extenuation*	The use of language that treats racism as simply one component of an assumed larger and more important set of social forces and trends.	Stressing language that refers to changes in macro-level phenomena (e.g., social forces, social transformation, social evolution, or social development) that are assumed to be larger and more consequential than racism.
4. *Conceptual Idealism*	The assumption that the demise of racism is inevitable because it is incompatible with other cherished national ideals.	Words or phrases (e.g., moral dilemma or color-blindness) that suggest that racism does not or will not exist because it should not exist.
5. *Conceptual Inflation*	Defining racism so broadly that it becomes conceptually meaningless by including nearly every form of social oppression.	Including within the definition of racism phenomena like ethnicism, anti-Semitism, and other types of oppression.
6. *Conceptual Minimization*	The refusal to use language that acknowledges that racism is systemic.	Terminology that reduces systemic racism to one of its components (e.g., ideology or individual-level racial bigotry).

7. *Conceptual Misdirection*	The use of terminology that shifts attention away from the racially oppressive system to its victims.	The selection of language (e.g., "minorities") that focuses on the various social problems of the racially oppressed.
8. *Conceptual Non-Definition*	The use of terms like race or racism without defining them.	The treatment of racism and other key terms as if they are so widely understood that they don't need defining.
9. *Conceptual Obfuscation*	The selection of language that is so vague and imprecise as to be virtually meaningless.	Abstruse words and phrases like "race," "the race issue," and "the issue of race."
10. *Conceptual Realism*	The use of language that uncritically accepts the racial status quo as a given.	The choice of terminology (e.g., caste) that treats the racial status quo as if it is natural and unchangeable.
11. *Conceptual Rejection*	The refusal to use racism-specific terminology.	The avoidance of using terms like racism or racial oppression.
12. *Conceptual Underdevelopment*	The need to further explicate concepts and theories.	Theoretical and conceptual frameworks that are so poorly conceptualized as to have limited analytical value.

dominant racial order that the racially oppressed are sometimes able to gain sufficient ground to have their voices heard, in their own words.

Argument

Linguistic Racial Accommodation, Its Consequence, and Its Alternative

Building upon the power, knowledge, language, and racism theories literatures I reviewed, the linguistic racial accommodation conceptual framework I developed, and including the language-centered racism denial practices presented above, I now introduce this book's key argument.

Linguistic racial accommodation is an instrument of racism evasiveness and denial in highly racialized—but otherwise democratic—societies that has resulted in the conceptual retardation and underdevelopment of the understanding of racism; and only by challenging such language censorship through linguistic racial confrontation is the development of an honest and full conceptualization and articulation of racism possible.

It is not, however, enough to know that linguistic racial accommodation exists and that it contributes significantly to the misconceptualization of racism. An equally important goal of this book is to explain *how* linguistic racial accommodation and confrontation work; for example, as I put it earlier, how *power* is used to effectively keep *knowledge* about *racism*—as articulated through *language*—out of societal discourse, and how a shift in power relations can force it into such places.

Figure 1.3 illustrates the cyclical organization, workings, and consequences of linguistic racial accommodation (LRA) in highly racialized democracies like the United States. The racial structure shapes career rewards and punishments in such a way that academic racial knowledge conforms to racially accommodative language. The resulting language-centered racism denial practices help sustain the racial structure, and the cycle strengthens as it repeats itself.

This proposition explains both how linguistic racial accommodation within sociology and the other social sciences is part of the same racism-evasive process within the larger society and the reciprocal relationship between LRA in society in general and more specifically its social sciences (see figure 1.4). Such linguistic racial accommodation within sociology and the other social sciences is not simply a reflection of LRA within the larger social structure but legitimizes it for that society. This suggests that one reason

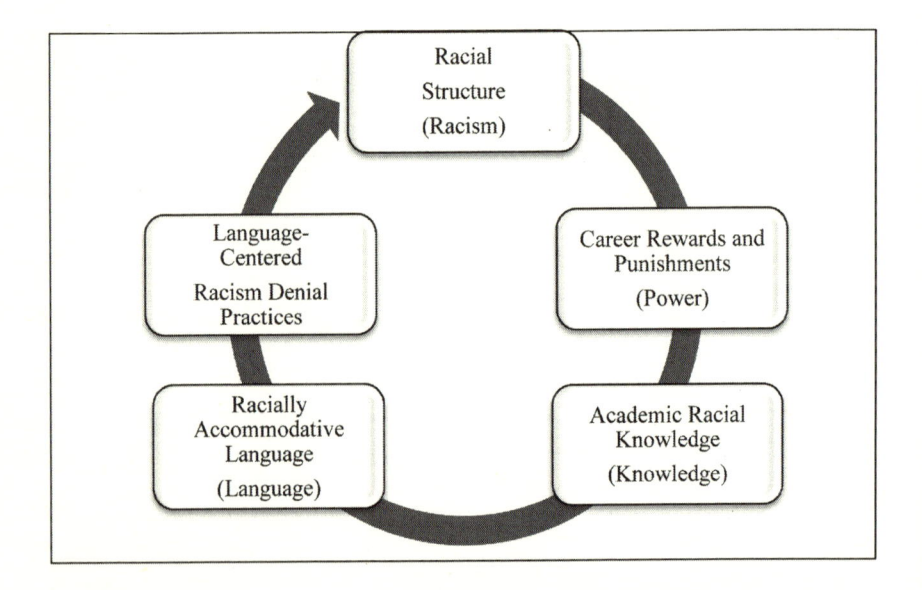

Figure 1.3. The Cyclical Relationship of a Society's Racial Structure, Its Career Rewards and Punishments, Its Academic Racial Knowledge, Its Racially Accommodative Language, and Its Language-Centered Racism Denial Practices

there is so little serious conceptualization of racism in the social sciences is that honest and straightforward discussion of the topic is not allowed by the white power structure of the larger society of which it is a part. Social scientists, like others who engage in the discourse about what is typically framed as "race," face punitive sanctions to stay within acceptable boundaries of racial discourse, those that pose no serious challenge to the racial status quo. But there's more. Such sanctions are not limited to punishment for wayward behavior; they also include rewards for appropriate behavior, including their disciplines' very status as professions. The social sciences gain and keep their legitimacy as professions by serving power, including of course a nation's white power structure. Of course, the same sets of factors shown in figures 1.3 and 1.4 also affect, and in turn are affected by, linguistic racial confrontation.

I now turn in the next three chapters to a closer look at the effects of linguistic racial accommodation in sociology and other social sciences, as well as to various efforts to challenge it through linguistic racial confrontation.

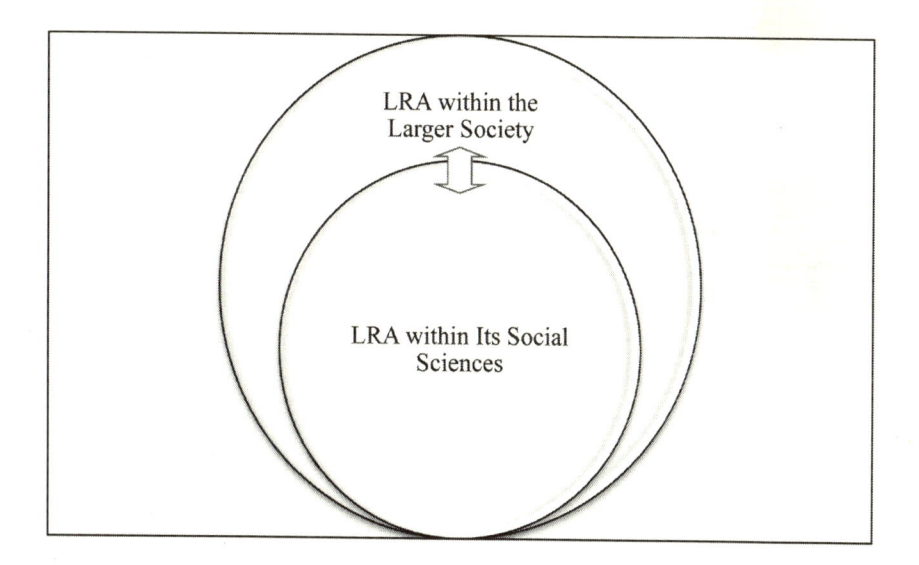

Figure 1.4. Linguistic Racial Accommodation within and between a Society and Its Social Sciences

Chapter Two

Linguistic Racial Accommodation from Slavery to the Civil Rights Movement

> It is difficult to get a man to understand something, when his salary depends upon his not understanding it.
> Upton Sinclair[1]

Sociology was established in the United States during a time of intense racial suppression. With roots that reach back into slavery, it came into its own within academia as the South ruthlessly reasserted its control over African Americans, control that had been threatened by their emancipation during the Civil War and the reconstruction period that followed. The other regions of the nation quickly followed suit. As Lerone Bennett Jr. so aptly put it, "by the 1890s the Southern view had become the American view" as America became "two nations—one white, one black, separate and unequal." This was the racially repressive environment I referred to in the Introduction chapter that caused the poet Paul Laurence Dunbar to lament how African Americans must "wear the mask" of acquiescence to racial oppression. Within the social sciences, it was not just the racially oppressed who wore that mask of racial accommodation. By the time sociology had been recognized as an academic discipline in the United States in the 1890s, it had already learned how to accommodate itself, linguistically and otherwise, to the racial status quo—a lesson that remains today as a highly institutionalized legacy of that era.[2]

LINGUISTIC RACIAL ACCOMMODATION WITHIN AMERICAN SOCIOLOGY DURING ITS FIRST CENTURY

I begin my analysis of LRA with an examination of its impact during the formative years of American sociology.

The Biological Justification of White Supremacy: 1850 through 1919

In the late nineteenth century numerous actions, ranging from the passage of segregation laws to lynchings, signaled in very concrete ways the resurgence of white racial power after the abolition of slavery. That racial crackdown on "free" African Americans, which included the 1896 Plessy v. Ferguson Supreme Court ruling, was advanced so quickly that it took "barely more than a decade" to construct "the system of legal segregation and racial domination that was to remain intact until after World War II." African American accommodation to that new system of racial coercion was also enforced through a rise of terroristic violence in the form of Ku Klux Klan activities, lynchings more generally, and white race riots in numerous American cities including New York, Chicago, and East St. Louis.[3]

Not surprisingly, during this period of intense racial oppression, a time when the emerging field of sociology sought legitimacy as a discipline, it largely abdicated what Thomas Pettigrew refers to as its "critic" role and remained mostly a compliant "supplicant" to the powers that be. Using language muddled by its own conceptual obfuscation, James McKee noted that, despite its twin focus on science and reform, "one issue was little discussed and not defined as reformable: the race problem." When sociologists did speak of it, all too often they went far beyond merely accommodating themselves to the racial status quo by aggressively justifying and otherwise supporting the white supremacy in which many of them firmly believed. For example, Yale professor and social Darwinist William Graham Sumner, who in 1875 taught the first sociology course in the United States, opposed the granting of voting rights to African Americans.[4] The chief linguistic racial accommodation denial practice deployed during that time was the conceptual misdirection from a social structural explanation of "white" racial dominance to a biological one of "black" racial inferiority.

That hardened approach to race relations remained unchallenged when the progressive era of reform took hold of the nation in the late nineteenth century with its emphasis on reducing rampant economic inequality, making government less corrupt and more efficient, and protecting the environment. And it wasn't simply that the leaders of that movement were blind to racism as an issue. Some of its most influential leaders, including presidents Theodore Roosevelt and Woodrow Wilson, were staunch promoters of white racial supremacy. Many progressive policies like highly racialized eugenics, immigration restrictions, and military-backed imperialism were fueled not just by ignorance and political calculus, but by strong racial animus. Progressive sociologists were certainly not immune to such sentiments. Edward Ross coined the phrase "'race suicide'" to express his support for legislation to restrict the immigration of southern and eastern Europeans, an inferior race of people, according to him, who might otherwise out-breed the superior race of Anglo-Saxons. Similarly, Ross favored measures to ensure that African Americans did not overwhelm Anglo-Saxons as a race. Although there were a few sociologists like Jane Addams, Lester Frank Ward, W. I. Thomas, and W. E. B. Du Bois who were troubled by the prevailing social theories that justified the racial disenfranchisement of African Americans through the scientific pretense of their biological and cultural inferiority, most were inclined to both accept and promote them.[5]

In a paper published in 1947, a year before his election as the first African American president of the American Sociological Society, E. Franklin Frazier introduced its readers to the racist underbelly of American sociology during its infancy by noting that the first two sociological studies published in the United States (both in 1854) not only focused on race relations but provided strong defenses of slavery. Other racist theories Frazier discussed in that article included William Graham Sumner's attribution of racial differences and relations to cultural mores, including racial norms that, he argued, must be respected and preserved (1906); Franklin Gidding's rooting of racial exclusiveness in a "'consciousness of kind'" (1908); Howard Odom's argument that African Americans constituted a social problem because they were unassimilable (1910); and Charles Ellwood's explanation of what was seen as the "Negro problem" as a matter of racial temperaments like "'shiftlessness and sensuality'"(1910). As Frazier explained it, with the North's acceptance of the South's solution to its racial problem through "the establishment of a quasi-caste system" that segregated and disenfranchised African Americans, "the famous formula of Booker T. Washington, involving the social separation of the races and industrial education, had become the accepted guide to future race relations." Consequently, "the sociological theories which were implicit in the writings on the Negro problem were merely rationalizations of the existing racial situation."[6]

One thing those early biological justifications of the racial status quo were not, was conflict evasive. In explaining why that was true James McKee stated that for those sociologists "conflict was the natural outcome of the antagonism of white people toward those they deemed to be racially inferior, who, in turn, were no longer willing to accept the continuance of an inferior status that had been legally removed a half century earlier." Implicit in this view was that one function sociology should serve is to provide an early warning system of threats to the racial status quo. This seemed to be the purpose of a paper entitled "Is Race Friction between Blacks and Whites in the United States Growing and Inevitable?" which was published in the *American Journal of Sociology* in 1908 by Alfred Holt Stone, a Southerner who, although not an academician, had written extensively on race relations. Stone attributed "racial antipathy" to biological rather than social causes and argued that such animus was natural and driven by "an instinctive feeling of dislike, distaste, or repugnance." Unlike later racially liberal theories that discount the existence of not only racial conflict but racial hierarchies, Stone's thesis was quite explicit in its advocacy of conceptual realism. When Stone stressed "the importance" of the "mutual recognition of a different racial status in minimizing racial friction," he did nothing less than express in academic-sounding language the popular racial warning familiar to all Southerners that to avoid trouble "the Negro must know his place."[7]

As the above examples suggest, the dominant trend during the early years of American sociology was toward the protection of the racial status quo. That was accomplished either through conceptual misdirection away from racism as a highly organized system of social oppression or through conceptual realism in which the existing racial order is taken as a given. Consequently there was no need to search for the social and economic causes of racial inequality. Moreover, any notion of changing the racial status quo was deemed to be not only foolish but dangerous. This is illustrated by the fate of African American sociologist W. E. B. Du Bois, who through his 1896 classic of survey research, *The Philadelphia Negro*, attempted to recast the "Negro problem" from one that had biological causes to one whose roots were clearly social. Du Bois was never able to find employment at a major American university and was unable to secure the funding he needed for the ambitious encyclopedia of African Americans he proposed.[8] He would eventually abandon science and academia to become one of the nation's most influential intellectuals and activists.

The race relations scholarship of the 1920s was more inclined to bypass biological explanations of presumed African American inferiority while offering a more sophisticated cultural justification of the racial status quo.[9]

Robert E. Park and the Chicago School of Race Relations: The 1920s

Historically, the participation of African Americans in the nation's various war efforts has increased both their expectations and raised their race consciousness. This was certainly true with the coming of World War I and continued with a dramatic postwar surge in migration of African Americans to Northern cities. It was there that they could not only find better job opportunities, including factory work in the growing defense industry, but be more outspoken about racial oppression and other political matters. Many found their racial voice through movements as diverse as the black nationalist Universal Negro Improvement Association founded by Marcus Garvey—the largest mass movement ever of African Americans—and the New Negro Movement, led by elite intellectuals, which later came to be known as the Harlem Renaissance. The tenor of those times of a new race consciousness and attitude was aptly captured by a poem published in 1919 by African American poet Claude McKay that, in stark contrast to Paul Laurence Dunbar's "we wear the mask," boldly broached the challenge "if we must die?"

and spoke of the glory of real men "pressed to the wall, dying, but fighting back!" It was within this racially confrontational environment that foundations offered fellowship money to train African American social scientists as an alternative to the growing numbers of radical socialist, nationalist, and pan-Africanist intellectuals and activists.[10]

During this racially transformative period a new generation of American sociologists came into prominence and articulated less overtly racist explanations of the African American condition that focused less on the purported biological inferiority of African Americans and more on what was seen as their deficient culture. However, with a few exceptions, the actual system of racial oppression still remained off limits to sociological discourse.

Park's Race Relations Cycle Theory and the Establishment of Race Relations as a Specialty Area of American Sociology

The most influential person in the formation of race relations as an area of study within American sociology was Robert Ezra Park, who was also a significant figure in the establishment of sociology as an academic discipline in the United States. As I mentioned earlier, Park developed many of his ideas about race relations as an aide to Booker T. Washington. He acknowledged his considerable intellectual debt to the nation's most celebrated racial accommodationist in a journal article in which he identified Washington as the person "from whom I learned more than from any of my other teachers." Washington's influence was so profound that one scholar has concluded that "Booker T. Washington, through his sponsorship of Robert E. Park, was a founder of the Chicago school of race relations," that specialty area's most influential paradigm. Indeed, at the core of Park's influential race relations cycle theory was Washington's racism-evasive notion that race relations will ease over time naturally as the social structure evolved, with no need for socially disruptive reforms. Park recalled that he learned from Washington "how deep-rooted in human history and human nature social institutions were, and how difficult, if not impossible it was, to make fundamental changes in them by mere legislation or by legal artifice of any sort."[11]

The assumption that it is naïve to try to address social problems through social policy is at the core of the LRA-centered racism denial practice of conceptual extenuation through which racial oppression, per se, is discounted as being just an unfortunate by-product of a set of much larger and more important global social and economic forces. Park began that long tradition within American sociology of ostensibly studying race relations but not really doing so at all, and instead focusing on what are assumed to be more encompassing phenomena of greater sociological scope and significance.

It is within this theoretical and careerism context that we can appreciate the lack of irony in the fact that, although Park is often considered to be the "father" of race relations, he is also remembered as "not" being "a specialist in race relations." Through the conceptual extenuation that allowed him to claim to explain race relations in the United States as but one example of larger and more general social processes—without actually examining its specific origins, history, functions, workings, and consequences—Park not only managed to discount obvious power relations but to make the racial status quo appear to be both biologically and socially natural—an inevitable and transitional process that was rooted in neither a highly organized system of exploitation nor group animus. Here is Park's summary of his race relations cycle theory from his 1939 article, "The Nature of Race Relations."

> It is obvious that race relations and all that they imply are generally, and on the whole, the products of migration and conquest. This was true of the ancient world and it is equally true of the modern. The interracial adjustments that follow such migration and conquest are more complex than is ordinarily understood. They involve racial competition, conflict, accommodation, and eventually assimilation, but all of these diverse processes are to be regarded as merely the efforts of a new social and cultural organism to achieve a new biotic and social equilibrium.[12]

In his review of Park's theoretical contributions, Lewis Coser concluded that social control is, as Park himself put it, "'the central fact and the central problem of society,'" and that it is only through such asymmetrical accommodation that a stable society is possible. Park's emphasis on social stability, cohesion, and consensus became the bedrock of the discipline's dominant structure functionalist perspective, which proved incapable of predicting or explaining the numerous issues involving power and conflict that emerged during the turbulent sixties.[13]

Finally, in explaining the neglect of the study of conflict in American sociology compared to the emphasis given to the topic by earlier American sociologists, Coser noted that as the discipline shifted away from the public as its audience to serving those with the power to make social and public policy, it became professionalized, more scientific, and more politically pragmatic and inclined to steer clear of controversy. Park, who was quite dogmatic in his anti-reformist sentiments, was a major figure in that conservative professionalization movement.[14]

Consistent with what I refer to as the conceptual minimization language-centered racism denial practice, when Park did focus on what might be called racial oppression, he limited his attention largely to prejudice. And even then, consistent with the conceptual realism view of race relations dominant in the South at that time, he stressed that such prejudice was natural, universal, and defensible. Park began his article "The Bases of Race Prejudice" by showing great compassion for racial bigots but none for their victims as he asserted that "prejudice, even race prejudice, no matter how reprehensible in itself, is a profoundly human phenomenon. As such, it deserves, perhaps, to be defended against those who inveigh against it, as if it were not a common human weakness in which we all, more or less share." And Park did not stop there. As a classic example of what came to be known in the 1960s as blaming the victim, when Park did allow group hierarchy into his analytical lens, his chief suspect in the rise of prejudice was not the ideology European Americans crafted to justify their privilege, but African American resistance to oppression. For when racial groups accepted their relative place "goodwill will exist," but when that "stable equilibrium" is disturbed prejudice arises. So, consistent with the admonition of his mentor, Booker T. Washington, Park concluded that the best solution to race relations is to simply leave it alone and let the larger social transformations play themselves out.[15]

Due to their marginal status within both the discipline and the larger society, African American scholars are especially vulnerable to pressures toward racial accommodation. However, because of their position as racially oppressed people, they are also more likely to experience racial oppression and to feel the need to speak out against it. So for African American sociologists, including Park's students, there existed during Park's times, as there does now, the need to respond skillfully to the delicate dialectical dance of caution and authenticity driven by pressures to both avoid and address the subject of racial oppression.

Although African American sociologists are trained to accept the dominant race relations paradigm and face great pressure not to overtly challenge the racial status quo, there are occasions when they manage to have their LRC voices heard within the discipline with a fairly high degree of authenticity. Or, to use the terminology of Thomas Pettigrew again, there are times when they embolden themselves to shift from being largely a "supplicant" to the larger society that makes their work and careers possible to its "critic."[16] Indeed, that was the case for Monroe Work, the first African American to publish in the *American Journal of Sociology*. In an article published years later in 1924 in *Social Forces*, a prestigious sociological journal that made its debut with a strong commitment to publish race relations articles, Work—who studied at the University of Chicago—sounded the alarm about the growing race consciousness, as W. E. B. Du Bois had done sixteen years earlier in *AJS*. If the discipline had paid serious attention to these and other African American scholars in its theory work, it might have avoided its failure to predict and explain the coming of the modern civil rights movement. This is what Work had to say in a section of that article entitled "Growing Race Consciousness" that explained that emerging "racial struggle" with words that were consistent with the racially bold idiom of that era's "New Negro" movement.

> The racial struggle of the years has gradually resulted in the negro thinking largely in terms of his race, and as a result of this there has evolved a racial consciousness. This group or group consciousness of the negro is growing. This growth is manifesting itself in various ways important among which are an increasing interest in race literature, more faith in race leadership, a demand for patronage of negro business, a tendency to boycott white firms which do not treat the negro with courtesy and a tendency to move away from communities in which lynchings have occurred.[17]

The African American sociologist most associated with Park's intellectual legacy was E. Franklin Frazier. As I noted earlier, Frazier was skillful enough in working within the acceptable parameters of mainstream sociology to be elected as the first African American president of the American Sociological Association. But Frazier, who was also heavily influenced by W. E. B. Du Bois, was no mere careerist who went along to get ahead. His career was full of the LRA and LRC contradictions and challenges of a man struggling to speak truth to power in a way that power would accept. For Frazier, as was true for Du Bois during his earlier years, that safe way was through assuming a posture of scientific objectivity. But sometimes he was not so careful.[18] There was also a much bolder side of Frazier as an intellectual who on occasion spoke his mind freely, regardless of the consequences. When that side of Frazier became visible in the late 1920s, it jeopardized not only his ambition to earn his doctorate in sociology, but—if the accounts of that incident are true—even his life.

The controversy erupted with the publication of Frazier's article "The Pathology of Race Prejudice," which began with an epigraph quote that characterized the attitudes of "white men" in America as "a form of insanity." With that bold opening, Frazier made it clear that he would not respect the acceptable social-science parameters of the "Negro problem" or even "the race problem."[19] For Frazier, the problem to be examined was European Americans and their racial prejudice. Moreover, by labeling such attitudes as pathological and insane, he implied that those European Americans who held such views were mentally ill—in a word, crazy. So in what is essentially his "White Racial Bigots are Crazy" theory of racial prejudice, Frazier not only focused directly on European Americans as the problem but managed to infuse into his "analysis" some rather bold name calling.

With his assertion that there is indeed hope for change if race prejudice is due to "psychopathology" rather than biology, Frazier began his essay with a decisive break from both the race essentialist assumptions championed by most of the early American sociologists and from the non-interventionism of his future mentor Robert Park. Frazier then revealed the rhetorical strategy he would deploy throughout his career: his claim to speak in the name of science. From his review of the latest scientific developments, Frazier concluded that "in each case . . . the behavior motivated by race prejudice shows precisely the same characteristics as that ascribed to insanity."[20]

It is important for me to note here that much of this article seems to have been intended tongue in cheek. It appears that what Frazier was writing here as "science" was meant as a science-tweaking farce, chock full of racially confrontational language. This is most evident when Frazier argued a point that makes for good satire but poor sociology by claiming that "certain manifestations of race prejudice" should be regarded "as abnormal behavior." While that assertion delivered potent pathological labeling, it reduced the sociological scope of the problem from a phenomenon that is systemic precisely because it is normative to one of "abnormal" behavior. For even though Frazier appeared to be referring to what he saw as the collective insanity of "the white man" as a group, the presumption was still that his actions can best be characterized as being irrational and socially deviant rather than as highly organized privilege seeking. I believe that Frazier knew better, but simply could not resist the temptation of venting his outrage over what he saw as the absurdity of racial oppression while having some fun at the expense of the dominant racialized group and its bigoted beliefs. In explaining the "dissociated systems of ideas" and intense emotions he referred to as "the Negro complex," Frazier argued that "just as the lunatic seizes upon every fact to support his delusional system, the white man seizes myths and unfounded rumors to support his delusion about the Negro." Basically Frazier was saying, with science as his backup, that "the white man" was a racial lunatic.[21]

But even that was not what would be found to be most offensive by the Southern European American segregationists in Atlanta where Frazier lived. Frazier crossed far beyond the line of southern racial etiquette when he suggested that a white woman's charge of rape by a black man might reflect her repressed sexual desires for him. As Frazier put it, using the jargon of psychological science, "Hallucinations often represent unacceptable sexual desires which are projected when they can no longer be repressed. . . . It is not unlikely, therefore, that imaginary attacks by Negroes are often projected wishes." Those words, which would certainly be controversial even today, placed much more at risk than Frazier's career aspirations. Frazier's wife recalled that after the outrage his article evoked, Frazier fled Atlanta with a 45-caliber pistol tucked under his belt.[22]

Stephen Steinberg notes that, fortunately for Frazier, his provocative article was published three months after he wrote to professors Park and Burgess of the University of Chicago to inquire about admittance into its sociology department as a doctoral student.[23] Under Park, Burgess, and others, and the mantle of science at the University of Chicago, Frazier became a model student as he was properly socialized as a sociologist who largely abandoned the controversy of topics like the pathology of prejudice for the much safer ground of the assumed pathology of African American families.

Race Relations as Caste Relations: The 1930s

The stock market crash of 1929 and the Great Depression that followed had a profound effect on every aspect of American life, race relations being no exception. While there continued to be initiatives for the advancement of the "New Negro," now economic survival was the most pressing goal for African Americans, who were hit especially hard by the Depression. To that end African Americans deployed every resource at their disposal, including self-help, electoral politics, social protest, and the creation of new organizations.[24] All four strategies were facilitated by what was perhaps the most significant movement involving African Americans at that time: their large-scale migration from the rural South to the relative freedom of Northern cities.

The numerous African American challenges to the racial and economic status quo in the 1930s included the NAACP's successful bid to block the confirmation to the Supreme Court of Robert Parker, who had opposed their political enfranchisement, and to achieve the electoral defeat of three senators who supported him; the formation of the Black Muslims; the beginning of efforts to free the Scottsboro Nine from trumped-up rape charges; Jesse Owens's winning four medals at the Olympics; Marian Anderson's triumphant concert for 75,000 in front of the Lincoln Memorial after being refused the use of Constitution Hall by the Daughters of the American Revolution; Joe Louis's winning of the heavyweight boxing title; and federal anti-lynching legislation that, lacking the support of President Roosevelt, ultimately failed. There were also numerous organizations, protests, and economic boycotts to pressure European Americans to hire African Americans and to prohibit discrimination in the dispersal of federal recovery funds and programs.[25]

In those desperate times, many European Americans saw any improvement of the conditions of African Americans as a threat to their own survival. Consequently the decade of the 1930s was one of considerable racial and class volatility. It was during that racial instability and backlash that what came to be known as caste theory was crafted; the period's dominant explanation of race relations, which through its potent ideology of conceptual realism supported the low racial and economic status of African Americans by making it appear both natural and unalterable. American race relations theorists accomplished that counterfactual feat by largely ignoring what was happening in Northern cities and focusing, instead, on what they depicted as the frozen-in-time race and economic relations of the rural South.[26]

Caste Theory

Although the notion of Southern race relations as caste relations was nothing new, the idea gained legitimacy as an academic theory in a brief paper W. Lloyd Warner published in 1936 in *The American Journal of Sociology*. In "American Caste and Class" Warner, a professor of anthropology and sociology at the University of Chicago best known for his studies of social class structures in the United States, introduced what became known as the Caste School of race relations. Warner's main thesis was that both a caste and a class system operated in the American South, with the difference between the two being that in a caste system there is no upward mobility through marriage or other means. As an example, Warner referred to the caste/class conflict experienced by an upper-class African American who saw himself as holding a superior social class position to a lower-class European American even though he could not break free of his racial caste ceiling. His quandary was rooted in the fact that the South's system of segregation functioned to ensure that no African American achieved a class level within the larger society high enough to threaten its caste system. Instability existed among upper-class African Americans to the extent to which they aspired and strived to be treated consistently with their intra-racial class as opposed to that of their racial caste.[27] As in Park's race relations cycle theory, Warner posited that racial tension occurred when African Americans did not accommodate themselves to the racial status quo; or, to put it in the less academic language of that time and region, when they did not stay in their place.

A year later, John Dollard—a Yale psychology professor trained at the University of Chicago—published a book in which he applied Warner's caste theory to the study of a small Southern town. In exchange for the cooperation he needed from local European Americans to conduct his study, Dollard was willing to totally submerge himself in the norms of its totalitarian "caste" structure. This meant being careful to avoid any behavior that might not conform to the caste norms of the Jim Crow South. In addressing the suspicions of local European Americans Dollard assured them that, from what he observed, "the situation seemed quite stable. If the Civil War could not change it, how could I hope to do so, even if I wanted to?"[28] As a psychologist, Dollard would have likely appreciated the influence that attitudes had on behavior, but it was only decades later that psychologists would understand the powerful influence of behavior on attitudes. So it is unlikely that Dollard fully grasped how his compliance with caste etiquette affected his thinking about that system.

Following Warner's lead, Dollard's main concern was the racial adjustment of African Americans. But Dollard went much further in his victim-centered analysis by focusing specifically on the impact of such racial accommodation on their personality development. Consistent with many popular racist images of the time that depicted happy-go-lucky slaves like the cheerful Mammy, shuffling minstrel figure, or a plantation darkie eating watermelon with a grin from ear to ear, Dollard's book lent psychological legitimacy to various racist stereotypes of African American docility and contentment.

> We shall discuss three gains of the lower-class Negro: first, greater ability to enjoy the sexual freedom possible in his own group; second, greater freedom of aggression and resentment within his own group; and third, the luxury of his dependence relationship to the white caste. All these types of freedom represent primitive biological values and none of them is constrained to the degree customary in white middle-class society.[29]

In these two sentences Dollard deployed science to advance not only those stereotypes portraying the caste system as being good for low-income African Americans, but also the popular racist and class-elitist stereotypes of them being sexually promiscuous, violent, and irresponsible. Through conceptual conflation he also managed to muddy the racial and class situations of low-income African Americans in ways that anticipated today's cultural pathology-focused sociological research on poverty among African Americans.

A chapter of *Caste and Class in a Southern Town* entitled "Accommodation Attitudes of Negroes" is of particular relevance to the racial accommodation focus of this study. As much as I disagree with Dollard's research assumptions, methods, and conclusions, as I read that chapter I found myself wondering whether, and if so to what degree, young untenured sociology professors of color could similarly be pressured to accommodate themselves to the power structures of overwhelmingly European American sociology departments. Referring the reader to Park and Burgess's *Introduction to the Science of Sociology*, Dollard defined "accommodation attitudes" as "those which enable the Negro to adjust and survive in the caste situation as it is presented to him."[30] Here we could substitute the words "require" for "enable," "faculty of color" for "the Negro" and "racial" for "caste" to explain the language professors of color often adopt to gain employment and obtain the grants and publications necessary for them to achieve their tenure, promotions, and other career ambitions.

The conservative implications of caste theory did not go unnoticed by African American scholars. Three decades later, E. Franklin Frazier criticized caste theory for being too static to explain the dynamics of race relations; being too simplistic to account for its complexities and contradictions, accepting the notion that African Americans acquiesced to their subjugation; and ignoring the festering tension and conflict beneath the surface of race relations.[31]

The conservative ideology of caste theory is similar to the more recent fatalistic conceptual realism that assumes that many if not most impoverished inner-city African American people are destined to remain a permanent underclass from one generation to the next with no chance for social mobility that might be facilitated by more progressive racial and economic policies. Terms like caste and underclass justify a worldview that accepts the racial and economic status quo as a given. Within this conceptual realism, no real change is needed because none is possible, and the best we can hope for is social stability based on an unjust peace in which those groups at the bottom accommodate themselves to things as they are. This essentially amoral view of race relations would soon be challenged by a conceptual idealism that placed morality at its core.

Race Relations as America's Moral Dilemma: The 1940s

The 1940s was a watershed decade both for American race relations and for its sociological study.[32] The war years and subsequent rising expectations of African Americans combined with their continued northward mass migration, the growth and strengthening of their organizations, various disappointments, and white repression to create a climate of social protest that set the stage for the civil rights movement of the 1950s and 1960s.

The expectations of African Americans were given a boost in 1940 when they played a significant role in electing Franklin Delano Roosevelt to an unprecedented third term as president. However, their reviews of Roosevelt's performance as president continued to be mixed at best. For example, while pleased with FDR's 1940 appointment of Benjamin Davis Sr. as the nation's first African American general, African American leaders were disappointed in Roosevelt failure's to integrate the troops. With the U.S. entry into World War II, the investment of African American lives in the war effort ushered in—as it had during previous wars—a period of high expectations combined with government repression of dissent, including in this case ruthless efforts to silence outspoken leaders like Paul Robeson and W. E. B. Du Bois.[33]

African Americans faced continued exclusion from most defense industry jobs and racial segregation within those branches of the armed forces that were open to them. Reflecting the growing impatience of many African American leaders with the slow pace of change under the Roosevelt administration, labor leader Asa Philip Randolph planned a huge march on Washington. Just a week after a meeting in which he failed to convince Randolph to call off the march, President Roosevelt signed an executive order that prohibited discrimination in defense jobs hiring and established the Fair Employment Practices Commission to enforce it.[34]

During the war, African Americans fought battles for racial justice both within the military abroad and in all arenas of life at home. Protests for racial equality in Northern cities intensified and there was mounting evidence of growing African American insurgency in the South. The Congress of Racial Equality was organized in Chicago in 1942, the same year racial unrest broke out in American cities, including Detroit and New York's Harlem, at a magnitude and intensity not seen since 1919. Foundations responded with funds to research the problem and various levels of government established race relations committees. It was in this racially volatile environment that *An American Dilemma*, the largest and best known study of American race relations, was initiated.[35]

Gunnar Myrdal's *An American Dilemma*

The driving force behind *An American Dilemma: The Negro Problem and Modern Democracy* was the increasingly rapid pace of African American challenges to the racial status quo and the perceived need of the nation's white power structure to keep tabs on what was happening before it got out of hand. Earlier sociological approaches to race relations were too accommodative of the racial status quo and too reliant on slow evolutionary change to account for the nation's quickly emerging new racial reality and to ideologically engage the racially oppressed and their rising aspirations.

Even the most progressive elements of the white power structure were not, however, open to a power-centered view of race relations that highlighted the problem as systemic oppression. Myrdal's racism-evasive approach instead reduced racial relations to a moral dilemma that, consistent with the old conceptual extenuation of Park's race relations cycle theory it challenged, was likely to resolve itself—in this case simply because racial prejudice and discrimination were incongruent with American democratic and egalitarian ideals. While providing a language-centered obfuscation of the true nature of American race relations, this conceptual idealism offered hope to those at the bottom that things were indeed changing at a quickening pace. It also allowed reform-oriented elites to rest assured that the remediation of the "Negro problem" remained firmly within their control as they tried to better balance it with the nation's highly touted humanitarian principles.[36]

One of the most interesting questions about Myrdal's study is how it came to be funded by a foundation known for its racial conservatism. As Myrdal suggested in the preface to the twentieth anniversary edition of that two-volume book, "I had happened to come to the study of the Negro problem in America at a time when big changes were pending and a new trend was at the point of asserting itself." In brief, the system worked and was in the process of reforming itself. That was, of course, an answer that pleased that study's major funder, the Carnegie Corporation.[37]

America's Negro Problem as Its Moral Dilemma

Using a thin conceptual thread, Myrdal stitched together the vast collection of research monographs that comprised *An American Dilemma*. It was this thesis, along with Myrdal's criticism of some influential race relations scholarship and his view about the need to make explicit the role of values in social scientific research, that made the study more than just a compilation of sociological facts about African Americans. In explaining how "the American Negro problem is a problem in the heart of the American," Myrdal asserted that

> the "American Dilemma," referred to in the title of this book, is the ever-raging conflict between, on the one hand, the valuations preserved on the general plane which we shall call the "American Creed," where the American thinks, talks, and acts under the influence of high national and Christian precepts, and, on the other hand, the valuations on specific planes of individual and group living, where personal and local interests; economic, social, and sexual jealousies; considerations of community prestige and conformity; group prejudice against particular persons or types of people; and all sorts of miscellaneous wants, impulses, and habits dominate his outlook."[38]

Here Myrdal replaced the materialist, political, and economic explanation of racial oppression—one we might expect from an economist—with his conceptually idealistic view of contemporary American race relations. That perspective conveniently looked away from the nation's highly organized system of racial oppression driven largely by economic interests as it instead aimed its analytical spotlight on a conflict of national ideals. And instead of the wary presumption that in the absence of a fundamental change in power relations such oppression is likely to persist, Myrdal brought the good news that due to the American exceptionalism of being an extraordinarily moral country, "the Negro problem in America represents" little more than "a moral lag" in its "development." Building upon that premise, Myrdal confidently predicted that *"not since Reconstruction has there been more reason to anticipate fundamental changes in American race relations, changes which will involve a development toward the American ideals."*[39] In Myrdal's view, this would happen not with successful African American challenges to the nation's racial order but simply because values-conflicted European Americans came to accept it as the right thing to do.

Myrdal's Criticism of American Race Relations Theory

In making his case that new thinking was needed on American race relations, Myrdal critiqued the then-dominant race relations theory of Robert Park. It was not only elements of Park's race relations cycle theory, but his philosophy regarding the proper use of social science, that were fundamentally at odds with Myrdal's interventionist model of applied social science. In building sociology as a profession, Park staked a claim that it was a value-neutral social science that stood outside the politically perilous world of social reform.[40] In stark contrast, Myrdal attempted to demonstrate the usefulness of social science to those, like the Carnegie Corporation, with a stake in managing the change they saw coming. Unfortunately, in rejecting Park's contributions to race relations theory, Myrdal threw the proverbial baby out with the bathwater by also discarding Park's idea regarding conflict being central to racial dynamics—an insight that might have allowed Myrdal to foresee the fast-approaching modern civil rights movement.

To make his case for the need for an applied social science to help guide what he saw as inevitable changes in race relations, Myrdal compared the "fatalism" of Robert Park to that of William Graham Sumner, whose earlier concepts of folkways and mores had been used to justify the racial status quo, especially in the South. Myrdal argued that Park, while not as deeply committed to preserving the status quo, like Sumner was fatalistic due to his "systematic tendency to ignore practically all possibilities of modifying—by conscious effort—the social effects of the natural forces."[41]

Myrdal's Challenge to the Social Science Ideology of Value Neutrality

Perhaps the most important potential contribution of Myrdal's study was its challenge to an emergent trend within the discipline, the ascendency of quantitative sociology and its ideology of value neutrality. This approach would soon come to dominate race relations research and contribute significantly to its scientific pretense, its conceptual sterility, and its inability to address society's big social issues. If Myrdal's challenge had been accepted, today's American race relations scholarship would be much harder to ignore.

With his assertion that "social science is essentially a 'political' science," Myrdal boldly sought to thrust a stake into the heart of the claim of Park and others that social science was a science-legitimized profession. Consistent with the relationship between social science and its larger society (illustrated in figure 1.4), Myrdal concluded that in their fatalistic anti-policy bias American "social scientists simply reflect the general distrust of politics and legislation that is widespread among the educated classes of Americans."[42] Their actions were not above and beyond politics, he argued, but were instead shaped by them.

Because the bulk of it was tucked away in an appendix entitled "A Methodological Note on Facts and Valuations in Social Science," Myrdal's critique of social-science methodology received scant attention. It was there that Myrdal made his case that rather than pretend to be value-free it would be better for social scientists to control for their value-based biases by acknowledging their existence. To this end, Myrdal identified six specific "Biases in the Research on the American Negro Problem" placed along scales of: "*'Friendliness' to the Negro*," "*'Friendliness' to the South*," "*Radicalism–Conservatism*," "*Optimism–Pessimism*," "*Isolation–Integration*," and "*Scientific Integrity*." While the conceptual misdirection of the existing race relations research is evident in his reference to "biases in the research on the American Negro Problem," the names Myrdal gave to his scales located those social-science biases clearly within the racial biases of its larger society.[43]

Consistent with this study's conceptualization of linguistic racial accommodation, Myrdal had the following to say about the biases of social science scholars rooted in their "*'Friendliness' to the Negro*": "white scholars until the last two or three decades worked more or less consistently in the interests of the dominant white group's need for rationalization or justification of the system of color caste." Myrdal then noted that even scholars considered to be "'friendly'" to African Americans and their cause were "'friendly' to the Negroes only when compared with the very unfriendly general public opinion, but not when compared with what disinterested scholarship should have demanded." Myrdal linked that anti–African American bias to the inclination of European American social scientists to take a non-interventionist stance. "These ideological tendencies are biased in a static and do-nothing (*laissez-faire*) conservative direction, which, in the main, works against a disfavored group like the American Negroes." Finally, Myrdal observed that their efforts to fit in with the "public and academic opinion in the dominant majority group" combined with their "desire to lean backwards and to be strictly scientific, and other reasons, may often cause even the Negro scientist to interpret the facts in a way which is actually biased against his own people." This is reminiscent of contemporary African American graduate students and job applicants who must prove themselves both knowledgeable about and accepting of William J. Wilson's thesis on "the declining significance of race."[44]

Not only did Myrdal assert that much of the bias of American race relations social science is political, but he also argued that the complexity of such bias extended beyond simple political labels like conservative, moderate, or radical. He noted, for example, that being moderate or even radical does not ensure that European American scholars will overcome the European American bias against African Americans. As Myrdal put it, "where public opinion in the dominant white group is traditionally as heavily prejudiced in the conservative direction as in the Negro problem, even a radical tendency might fail to reach an unprejudiced judgment. . . . The prevalent opinion that a 'middle-of-the road' attitude always gives the best assurance of objectivity is, thus, entirely unfounded."[45]

Responses to An American Dilemma by People of African Descent

An American Dilemma was largely protected from criticism from African American leaders, intellectuals, and scholars by the presence of prominent and influential African Americans who worked with the project in various capacities (e.g., Sterling Brown, Ralph J. Bunche, Horace Cayton, Kenneth B. Clark, Allison Davis, St. Clair Drake, W. E. B. Du Bois, E. Franklin Frazier, Charles S. Johnson, Alain Locke, Ira De A. Reid, and Walter White).[46] Not surprisingly, the harshest criticisms of the project came from those outside of its work-team orbit. One of the most scathing of those reviews was by the novelist Ralph Ellison.

Ellison located his critique of *An American Dilemma* within his larger appraisal of American social science. He observed that although from its beginning American social science was closely tied to the "destiny" of African Americans (e.g., in justifying slavery by asserting that African Americans were not human), "sociology did not become closely concerned with the Negro, however, until after Emancipation gave the slaves the status—on paper at least—of nominal citizens." That is, sociology was useful in helping the larger European American society, especially industrial capitalists, deal with its freed African American population and the various challenges they presented. Indeed, Ellison specifically mentioned the use of social science as one of four strategic actions Northern elites deployed to manage their post-slavery "Negro problem." In addition to its promotion of "Negro education in the South," the control of "his economic and political destiny" either directly or by allowing "the South to do so," and making "Booker T. Washington into a national spokesman of Negroes with Tuskegee Institute as his seat of power," the Northern power structure "organized social science as an instrumentality to sanction its methods." Following this class-based line of critique, Ellison drew a conclusion about "the real motivation" behind *An American Dilemma* that is remarkably similar to the historical context of Booker T. Washington's famous Atlanta Compromise speech. The study provided nothing less than "*the blueprint for a more effective exploitation of the South's natural, industrial and human resources.*" Next Ellison criticized what he saw as Myrdal's need "throughout the book . . . to carry on a running battle with Marxism." By doing so, Ellison continued, Myrdal "avoids the question of power *and* the question of who manipulates that power." Ellison also took that opportunity to critique "the sterile concept of 'race'" used by both Myrdal and African American scholars and called on African Americans to do two things Myrdal did not advocate: develop race consciousness and engage in struggle.[47]

Not surprisingly, the *American Journal of Sociology* review by project insider and by then well-socialized sociology professional E. Franklin Frazier was less critical. Frazier did, however, question how much European

Americans were really troubled by a moral dilemma over their treatment of African Americans and, like Ellison, took issue with what he saw as the power evasiveness of Myrdal's moral dilemma thesis. One of the most critical reviews of *An American Dilemma* from inside of the discipline came from Oliver C. Cox, a Trinidadian who, although an alumnus of the then-dominant Chicago School, was very much an outsider because of his radical class-centered perspective. Although Cox's largely ignored *Caste, Class, and Race* was written as a critique of caste theory, that book, published in 1948, also contained a cutting review of *An American Dilemma*.[48]

Like other reviewers of African descent, Cox began with praise for *An American Dilemma*, but he quickly made clear that the facts Myrdal presented did not always support his arguments. Cox was especially put off by Myrdal's ignoring of the study's own data through his use of caste theory and his "'value-premise'" focus on American ideals. For example, he accused Myrdal of failing to "recognize the determining role of class interest." This failure was disturbing to Cox not just because of the threat it posed to good social science, but because he saw it as a menace to effective labor movement ideology. At that time Cox and many other Marxism-inspired leftists anticipated the coming of a major class struggle that would unite working-class European and African Americans in that common progressive cause. And because they believed race relations were merely a reflection of the larger, determinant, class relations, they thought that such a movement would simultaneously solve the nation's class and racial problems. For such a class-centered movement to succeed in its organizational efforts, it must be recognized that European Americans were divided along class lines and were therefore not a racial monolith, and that it was the ruling class, not working-class or poor European Americans, that was the real and common enemy. Cox therefore scoffed at Myrdal's assumptions that the elimination of prejudice would end what Cox referred to as racial antagonism and that because such prejudice was based on misperceptions it could be eradicated. To Cox such naïve thinking was akin to believing in "werewolves or fairies." The historical evidence was clear: Myrdal got things backward; exploitation came first, then came prejudice. Consequently the solution required convincing the "white masses" that they were being exploited by the ruling classes and should join forces with similarly exploited African Americans.[49] Building on this logic, Cox concluded that a movement focused specifically on racial oppression would not only be ineffective but would imperil the interracial coalition necessary for that class struggle to be successful.

Congruent with Cox's contribution of placing race relations within a systemic perspective, one of his main criticisms of Myrdal's *An American Dilemma* is that it treated racial prejudice as it did the moral dilemma issue and other manifestations of racial relations: as if they were discrete social phenomena rather than part and parcel of a larger system of oppression. That problem—what I refer to as conceptual minimization—plagued much of the racial-prejudice-focused research that would dominate race relations research during the 1950s. And it didn't stop there. Indeed, as I will show in later chapters, in the wake of the civil rights movement, the language-centered racism denial practice of conceptual minimization made a major comeback in the late 1970s that persists today.

Cox had mixed results in his conceptualization of the key concepts of race and racism. While he, unlike anthropologist Ruth Benedict in her *Race and Racism,* published six years earlier, clearly understood that the race concept was merely a social construction, unfortunately, like Benedict's, his view of racism was much too narrow. For Benedict racism, as an ism, was merely a set of beliefs. Although Cox went further by acknowledging that that set of beliefs was indeed an ideology used to justify a system of class exploitation, because of his own class-centered ideological lens and its resultant conceptual colonization, plus his apparent misunderstanding of the concept of ideology, he was unable to see that racist ideology was the core of its own system of "race"-justified oppression. For, as he understood things,

> the term "racism" as it has been recently employed in the literature seems to refer to a philosophy of racial antipathy. Studies on the origin of racism involve the study of the development of an ideology, an approach which usually results in the substitution of the history of a system of rationalization for that of a material social fact. Indeed, it is likely to be an accumulation of an erratic pattern of verbalizations cut free from any on-going social system.[50]

With this incomplete, and therefore faulty, logic, Cox was unable to consider the possibility that although racism was begun as an *ideology* to justify colonization, slavery, and other forms of economic exploitation, it was ultimately developed into its own, at least semi-autonomous *system* of oppression. Consequently, Cox had no language to refer to racial oppression. That term does not appear in his book's index. Racism appears only three times and each time he was critical of its use as just beliefs unattached to a material base. Finally, in his index, Cox referred to racial antagonism fifteen times: a conceptually minimizing term that is devoid of any conceptualization of hierarchy or system. As Cox wrapped up his critique of *An American Dilemma*, he stressed that the purpose of a revolution is not to reform a social system but to overthrow it. After stressing his view that Myrdal was not naïve, Cox surmised that "we cannot help concluding that the work in many respects may have the effect of a powerful piece of propaganda in favor of the status quo." Like Ellison and Frazier, Cox concluded that Myrdal's "moralist" approach was power evasive due to its focus on getting individuals to live up to their ideals rather than changing the social system.[51]

If a history of racism studies is ever written, Oliver C. Cox should hold a paradoxical place as a scholar who simultaneously advanced systemic racism theory by locating race relations within the Marxist systemic framework and stifled its development through his dogmatic and still influential insistence that racial oppression not be seen except as an epiphenomenon of class relations.[52] It is indeed ironic that although Cox engaged in conceptual colonization and minimization by dismissing the notion that race relations, per se, should be a focus of radical analysis, he also established that it was possible to analyze racism as a highly organized system of oppression. Perhaps equally important, through the work he did during the early decades of his career Cox inspired subsequent generations of intellectuals by demonstrating great courage in writing about social issues as he saw them, in spite of paying one of the most dreaded penalties for any ambitious social scientist—having one's work ignored by one's peers.

Other Criticisms of *An American Dilemma*

Other valid criticisms can be made of *An American Dilemma*. As I noted earlier, it is not really a coherent study but a collection of research monographs held together by a very thin moral dilemma conceptual thread. In addition to being atheoretical, the study is also ahistorical in that it did not attempt to locate the origins of American race relations or to otherwise place them into historical context, astructural because it made no attempt to explain race relations as a highly organized system of oppression, and not nationally comparative because it limited its analysis to the United States and treated that nation as morally exceptional without evidence to support that claim. *An American Dilemma* also assumed that the solution to the nation's racial problem rested within the hands of members of the dominant racialized group and consequently largely ignored what African Americans and other racially oppressed peoples did on their own to challenge the racial status quo. Finally, Myrdal's study uncritically accepted and used popular racism-evasive language like "caste" and "race."

An American Dilemma on and as Linguistic Racial Accommodation

Despite his own linguistic racism evasiveness, Myrdal was fully aware that race relations entailed a battle over language in determining what gets said and how. For example, in a section entitled "Explaining the Problem Away," consistent with the standpoint theory of Marx and feminist scholars, Myrdal made the following distinction between African Americans, for whom the "Negro problem" is central to their lives, and the less-concerned attitudes of European Americans.

> The difference between the two groups, with respect to the recognition of the Negro problem, corresponds, of course, to the fundamental fact that the white group is above and the Negro group is below, that the one is intent upon

preserving the *status quo*, while the other . . . has a contrary interest to see clearly and even make visible to others the existence of a real problem. This latter group may be hushed by fear or opportunistic calculations.[53]

In another section of that chapter, "The Etiquette of Discussion," Myrdal introduced other concepts that could prove useful for linguistic analyses of racism evasiveness. These include the "theory of Southern indirectness," which operated as an "escape machinery" protecting European American Southerners from having a frank discussion of race relations through its insistence that Northerners and other outsiders respect the norm that whatever is said must, no matter how factual, be "said 'in the right way'"; so that it does not "'offend'" or cause "'embarrassment.'" For as Myrdal put it, "a whole system of moral escape has become polite form in the South. This form is applicable even to scientific writings and, definitely, to public discussion and teaching on all levels. It is sometimes developed into an exquisite and absorbing art." As he continued, Myrdal seemed to be describing the linguistic consequences of the etiquette and polite form of contemporary race relations teaching, research, and policy making: "it renders the spoken or written word less effective. It is contrary to the aims of raising issues and facing problems; it makes difficult an effective choice of words." Within such a linguistically repressive environment, "people become trained generally to sacrifice truth, realism, and accuracy for the sake of keeping superficial harmony in every social situation."[54] Unfortunately, Myrdal was too racially polite in his own choice of the language of his study. More often than not he went with the linguistic flow of popular and social science conventions rather than challenge them.

Myrdal's theoretical focus on race relations as a moral dilemma for European Americans also made the discipline and field deaf to what African American scholars were saying about growing African American insurgency. As Charles P. Henry put it, "by locating the fundamental problem in the attitude of whites, the development by racial subordinates of power bases among themselves was obscured." Drowned out from the discourse dominated by *An American Dilemma*, for example, was the voice of Tuskegee activist sociologist Charles Gomillion, who in 1942, in the respected sociological journal *Social Forces*, noted the "increasing militancy on the part of the Negro" in the South who was "refusing to accept willingly the *status quo*." Also apparently unheard and unheeded was the more mainstream voice of Charles S. Johnson, whose article in that same journal two years later, "The Present Status of Race Relations in the South," had as its thesis that "the emotional disturbances of the present period, involving racial issues, are symptoms of accelerated social changes, and that these changes are wholesome, even if their temporary racial effects are bad." As evidence of the growing racial tensions in the South, Johnson noted that over a ten-month period there were "111 racial incidents in the South of sufficient importance to be given attention in the national press." Overall Johnson saw a shift from racial accommodation to social protest that was indicative of the fact that "the great majority of southern Negroes: are becoming increasingly dissatisfied with the present pattern of race relations and want a change."[55]

The Social Psychology and Sociology of Prejudice: The 1950s

It was finally in the mid-1950s that the modern civil rights movement arrived full force. Although that decade has often been depicted as a period of cultural and political quiescence in the United States, for African Americans it was an exciting time not only for the civil rights struggle but in the arts, in literature, and in intellectual pursuits. Like the previous decade, the 1950s had its own war—the Korean War—and the usual subsequent rise of African American expectations combined with government suppression of the dissent of prominent radical African American leaders, which then included Paul Robeson and W. E. B. Du Bois.[56] And as was also true during the 1940s, the northward migration of African Americans continued, as did the growing number and strength of African American organizations. Finally, even more so than in the decade of the forties, African Americans faced intense white racial resistance and managed even greater legal and civil rights movement successes.

The decade began on a positive note with Ralph Bunche becoming the first African American to win a Nobel Peace Prize, for his mediation of the Palestine crisis. During those years African Americans also made significant gains in education and employment, with a rise in the number of African American professionals. The power of protest was amplified greatly as it was placed on a national stage though the growing availability of television. Through organizations like local NAACP and CORE chapters, in the North African Americans were successful in using protest to integrate restaurants, hotels, and other public accommodations. And in the South by 1953 nearly one million African Americans had registered to vote.[57]

In the 1950s the NAACP Legal Defense Fund, under the leadership of Thurgood Marshall, shifted its strategy of bringing local lawsuits against racial segregation to challenging the very constitutionality of legally mandated segregation. That effort culminated in the May 17, 1954 Brown decision by the U.S. Supreme Court overturning the Plessy v. Ferguson decision that had confirmed the legality of Jim Crow. With that ruling, not only were African Americans moved toward insurgency, but European American segregationists were driven to organize a powerful resistance movement to protect their Southern way of life. The following year African Americans experienced both the horrendous killing of Emmett Till and the initiation of the Montgomery Bus Boycott when Rosa Parks refused to give up her seat to a

European American man. That successful year-long boycott was followed in 1957 by the integration of Central High School in Little Rock, Arkansas with the backing of federal government troops.[58]

During the 1950s, foundations continued their crisis mode of relatively high levels of funding for race relations research. With the backing of the Carnegie Corporation, Myrdal had been successful in his effort to overcome the resistance of Park and others to joining such research with a liberal reform agenda. Now untenable and unworkable claims of value neutrality were out and applied social science was in. This shift was facilitated by the rapid growth of a new profession of race relations practice known by such names as human relations, community relations, and intergroup relations. Ironically it was also accompanied by another seemingly contradictory movement for greater scientific precision in race relations research that tended to keep its focus narrowly psychological just as the civil rights movement came clearly within view.[59]

Another ironic fact of the 1950s was the relative absence of African American sociologists during that racially volatile decade and into the 1960s. In explaining the dearth of African American sociologists, John Stanfield noted that most had died, retired, or moved out of the discipline and largely European American sociology departments were not committed at that time to the generation of African American PhDs.[60] This relative absence of African American scholars leads me to wonder whether, had that not been the case, the research of the 1950s would have been so inclined to conceptual minimization and so slow in developing the system- and power-centered approach to racism more capable of accounting for the profound racial changes happening in the United States as the modern civil rights movement took flight.

Adorno et al., The Authoritarian Personality

The first year of that decade the American Jewish Committee released a major study of anti-Semitism that focused attention on what it found to be the extremely rigid personalities of those who held bigoted beliefs. That book was part of a larger initiative that brought together a team of social scientists to explain prejudice like that which motivated Nazi Germany to carry out a program of genocide during World War II that included the murder of six million European Jews as well as other targeted groups like gay and lesbian people and the Roma. In their foreword to the nearly thousand-page tome, series editors Max Horkheimer and Samuel H. Flowerman stated that the goal of *The Authoritarian Personality* and two other previously published books was to answer the question, "what is there in the psychology of the individual that renders him 'prejudiced' or 'unprejudiced,' that makes him more or less likely to respond favorably to the agitation of a Goebbels or a

Gerald K. Smith?" The researchers chosen to carry out that study were philosopher Theodor W. Adorno and psychologists Else Frenkel-Brunswik, Daniel J. Levinson, and R. Nevitt Sanford.[61]

Although a major limitation of their scholarship from a racism studies perspective was its conceptual minimization due to their focus on the psychological, they certainly were not psychologists within the racially accommodative tradition of a John Dollard. Adorno was a major figure in the development of critical theory at the Marxism-inclined Institute of Social Research based in Frankfurt, Germany that came to be known simply as the Frankfurt School. He was forced to flee Germany to escape the persecution of Jews and radicals just as Frenkel-Brunswik had to flee Poland and later Austria. Levinson was Frenkel-Brunswik's student and Sanford was among the faculty fired from the University of California at Berkeley for refusing to sign a McCarthy-era loyalty oath.[62]

In addition to anti-Semitism and fascism, another major focus of *The Authoritarian Personality*, the one that James McKee maintained had the greatest influence on the sociology of race relations, was the development of a thirty-four-item scale for the measurement of ethnocentrism. Especially noteworthy was its Negro Subscale, which included items such as "The Negroes would solve many of their social problems by not being so irresponsible, lazy, and ignorant"; "An occasional lynching in the South is a good thing because there is a large percentage of Negroes in many communities and they need a scare once in a while to prevent them from starting riots and disturbances"; and "Most Negroes would become officious, overbearing, and disagreeable if not kept in their place." That scale provided both legitimacy and a model for the development of measurement scales that would characterize the individually focused and usually social-structure and power evasive research on prejudice that came to dominate the field during the next decade. It also promoted the conceptual colonialism practice of language-centered racism evasiveness as was evident when the authors stated their intention to use the term "'ethnocentrism'" to shift "the emphasis from 'race' to 'ethnic group.'" Even though they argued that the Negro Subscale is needed because African Americans "are a large and severely oppressed group" who face substantial stereotyping, their focus on ethnicity moved attention away from the distinct social and historical characteristics of race-based oppression. According to McKee, another significant contribution of *The Authoritarian Personality* to future applied race relations research was its assumption that prejudiced behavior could be successfully challenged through enacting and enforcing appropriate laws.[63]

In the end, through the boost it gave to prejudice-centered research, Adorno et al.'s personality-centered study fit best the linguistic racial accommodation racism-evasive practice of conceptual minimization. The growing appetite for such research was evident in the influence of another prejudice-focused book published a few years later.

Gordon W. Allport's *The Nature of Prejudice*

Just before the U.S. Supreme Court handed down the Brown decision against legalized segregation in 1954, Harvard psychology professor and former American Psychological Association president Gordon Allport published his influential study, *The Nature of Prejudice*.[64] As you will see, although that book at least acknowledged the role of historical and social structural forces on race relations, like Adorno et al.'s *The Authoritarian Personality*, it legitimized the conceptual minimization characteristic of the spate of narrowly focused, ahistorical, astructural, and power-evasive quantitative studies of prejudiced individuals that would soon follow.

The Nature of Prejudice seems to have followed the lead of *The Authoritarian Personality* in numerous ways. For example, the authors of both studies preferred the use of the term "ethnicity" over what they considered the problematic conceptualization of "race"; neither study was concerned primarily with race relations, much less racism; and both chose personality as their main variable. Moreover, like Myrdal's *An American Dilemma*, *The Nature of Prejudice* stressed the idea that prejudice had multiple causes, with no one dominant factor. Finally, all three studies emphasized the increasing relevance of scientific research in solving social problems.[65]

In staking out the turf of his study's own contribution to the prejudice literature, Allport critiqued the work of Park, Myrdal, and Adorno et al. To make his case that applied social science was useful in addressing problems involving race relations, Allport challenged Park's extremely fatalistic race relations cycle theory. Allport seemed to have Park in mind when he said, "we are not rejecting the structural argument, but rather pointing out that it cannot be used to justify total pessimism." Allport also found Myrdal's moral dilemma claim to be exaggerated because although the moral dilemma Myrdal stressed often occurs, it is not always present. Allport noted, for example, the criticism that "since social tradition is responsible for caste and its attendant discriminations, the individual living within a caste system may feel no grounds for guilt over his infinitesimal role." With respect to Adorno et al.'s *The Authoritarian Personality*, Allport's criticisms involved methodology. For example, he noted that the study's overemphasis of extreme scores resulted in much analysis of authoritarian and democratic personality types to the neglect of those who had "mixed or run-of-the-mill personalities in whom prejudice does not follow the ideal pattern here depicted."[66]

One of the most problematic features of Allport's study is its assertion that prejudice is natural, universal, and inevitable: "everywhere on earth we find a condition of separateness among groups. People mate with their own kind. They eat, play, reside in homogeneous clusters. They visit with their own kind, and prefer to worship together." I am not suggesting that there is no truth in Allport's assertion, only that he overstated his case with insufficient attention to the societal-level determinants of prejudice. Unfortunately, this same natural, universal, inevitable, non-systemic, and power-evasive view fits what I refer to as the conceptual realism linguistic racism evasion pattern of much of today's unconscious racism and implicit bias psychological explanations of racism I discuss in this book's epilogue.[67]

Allport also tended to obfuscate race relations through the *conceptual colonization* of treating it as but one form of prejudice. He did, however, acknowledge that his focus was largely on one level of analysis and, as I mentioned earlier, that other perspectives were important.

> A person acts with prejudice in the first instance because he perceives the object of prejudice in a certain way. But he perceives it in a certain way partly because his personality is what it is. And his personality is what it is chiefly because of the way he was socialized (training in family, school, neighborhood). The existing social situation is also a factor in his socialization and may also be a determinant of his perceptions. Behind these forces lie other valid but more remote causal influences. They involve the structure of society in which one lives, long-standing economic and cultural traditions, as well as national and historical influences of long duration.[68]

Unfortunately, in the end, by discounting situational, sociocultural, and historical factors as "other valid but more remote causal influences," Allport's work provided yet another example of the language-centered racism denial practice of conceptual minimization. By privileging more proximate psychological factors, or what critics of such a micro-level focus might themselves too harshly dismiss as its mere symptoms, Allport—who acknowledged that "discrimination and prejudice" are products of both "the social structure" and "the personality structure"—was able to discount the macro-level sociocultural and historical forces that scholars in other disciplines would claim as the phenomenon's ultimate causes. But, again, while not placing them at the center of his analysis Allport at least acknowledged their importance. And, unlike other scholars, Allport did not simply ignore or demonize Marxist theory. In the book's preface he provided the following one-sentence synopsis that is consistent with a Marxist interpretation of the origin of racism: "Negroes were enslaved primarily because they were economic assets, but the rationale took a racial form." And as an example of what he referred to as the exploitation theory variant of the historical approaches, Allport did what most sociologists at that time would not do; he engaged the ideas of Oliver C. Cox. After quoting a sentence by Cox as a summary of "the *exploitation theory* of prejudice held by Marxists and others" in which Cox defined race prejudice as a tool of exploitation deployed by the ruling classes to further its own interests, Allport surmised that "while there is obvious truth in the exploitation theory it is weak in many particulars." Allport then made two points with which most contemporary racism scholars would likely agree: the inability of vulgar Marxist theory to explain why some exploited groups are targeted by a great deal of prejudice while some are not, and to account for the fact that the exploitation of African Americans is not purely an economic matter. Allport then concluded that "the Marxist theory of prejudice is far too simple, even though it points a sure finger at *one* of the factors involved in prejudice, viz., rationalized self-interest of the upper classes."[69]

I consider Allport's willingness to acknowledge the essential contribution of Marxist theory to understanding racial prejudice to be a noteworthy step forward in our understanding of racism. What is particularly impressive was his willingness to do so in the wake of the congressional hearings by Senator Joe McCarthy, which intimidated many American scholars for decades to come. It is indeed ironic that when most prominent sociologists and other social scientists were content to treat the nation's racial problem as a mere moral dilemma, it took a psychologist to acknowledge the value of Marxist theory for our understanding of the exploitative structures. By at least providing a broad sketch of multiple levels of causation, Allport helped his readers better appreciate the relationship between social structure and human agency as they impact both the causes of racial oppression and its solutions. It is also ironic that it was a psychologist who so readily accepted the role of social protest in the rapidly changing U.S. race relations when he cautioned that "the role of the militant reformer must not be forgotten" for "it is the noisy demands of crusading liberals that have been a decisive factor in many of the gains thus far made."[70]

Which, if any, of these lessons did sociologists take from Allport's influential study? And would they react to the success of the *The Nature of Prejudice* and *The Authoritarian Personality* by retreating, through conceptual minimization, from their own expertise in understanding social structures to the politically safer world of social psychology, or by engaging psychology in a professional turf battle over the growing public policy and popular interest in topics like prejudice and race relations?

Sociological Studies of Racial Prejudice

After World War II, sociologists reasserted their professional-turf claim to the study of race relations by stressing the link between prejudice and the discrimination they thought should be its main focus.[71] While one effect of the influence of psychology was more sociological focus on the social psychology of racial prejudice, the need for sociologists to compete with psychologists resulted in increased interest in a more systemic approach to the analysis of race relations.

One of the most explicit professional-turf challenges was made by sociologist Arnold Rose, Gunnar Myrdal's top assistant from the United States. An article he published in 1956 in the journal *Social Problems*, "Intergroup Relations vs. Prejudice: Pertinent Theory for the Study of Social Change," argued sociology's case over psychology as the premier applied social science for the new profession of intergroup relations. For example, to challenge the simplistic conventional wisdom of social psychologists that prejudice caused discrimination, Rose cited the theory work of sociologist Robert K. Merton that showed how prejudice and discrimination could operate independently of each other. Rose made his social systems approach explicit in his conceptualization of race relations as entailing "behavior patterns that occur in social systems—such as the caste system—which have their own historical development in the culture of a given society," with prejudice being viewed as "a mere rationalization of these social systems." Rose advocated for a distinctly sociological study of race relations by pointing out "advantages to division of labor, to the cultivation of one's own specialized garden."[72]

That same year in that same journal, another sociologist, R. A. Schermerhorn, also attempted to recast race and ethnic relations theory and research with a more sociological focus. Schermerhorn, albeit conflating racial and ethnic relations and retaining the use of the problematic term "minorities," insisted that racial and ethnic relations be viewed as power-driven, asymmetrical, and systemic. Consistent with the concerns Myrdal expressed in *An American Dilemma*, Schermerhorn warned against the field's moving into an extremely positivistic direction that would largely remove it from such harder to measure macro-level concerns. And like Myrdal, he placed the work of Robert Park plainly within his critical sights. According to Schermerhorn, Park and his colleague, Ernest W. Burgess, imposed a false equilibrium on racial and ethnic relations that obscured their power differentials. Schermerhorn's focus on oppression is clear in his definition of power as "*the asymmetrical relationship between two interacting parties in which a perceptible probability of decision resides in one of the two parties, even over the resistance of the other party*." He made explicit his systemic approach when he stated that "when contacts between two groups with different cultural lifelines become regular rather than occasional or intermittent, the resulting interaction crystallizes into a social structure reflecting the power differentials and the value congruence of the two social systems in tensional equilibrium."[73]

A year later, E. Franklin Frazier expanded his ideas about "race" and culture to include power- and oppression-explicit terms like "domination," "ideologies," and "the race concept." In *Race and Culture Contacts in the Modern World*, Frazier concluded that

> during the period when European nations were establishing their dominance over non-European peoples, there arose the idea of the superiority of the white race. Although this idea could not be maintained on scientific or moral grounds, it nevertheless served as a means of separating the white and colored races and of justifying political and economic domination by the Europeans. The separation of the races was facilitated by differences in culture and standards of living which were employed in conjunction with the race concept to stamp non-European peoples as inferior races.[74]

Although other sociologists had not advanced as far as Rose, Schermerhorn, and Frazier toward the articulation of a systemic theory of racial oppression, they still felt the need to rescue the study of prejudice from the conceptual clutches of psychologists. That seemed to be the goal of Herbert Blumer's 1958 article "Race Prejudice as a Sense of Group Position," in which he panned the conceptualization of the authoritarian personality for its "grievous misunderstanding of the simple essentials of the collective process that leads to a sense of group position" that was essential to understanding prejudice. Blumer was also more specific in his focus on "race prejudice" than Adorno et al. in *The Authoritarian Personality* or Allport in *The Nature of Prejudice*. However, unlike Allport, in staking his sociological claim to the topic Blumer did not explicitly discuss the advantages and limitations of different levels of theoretical analysis and he did not acknowledge the contributions of Marxist and other exploitation-focused theories outside of the discipline's mainstream. Blumer's professional turf-battle-driven critique of the psychological approach to race prejudice moved the topic just far enough into the realm of the sociological for sociologists to claim ownership without expending any real sociological resources on understanding the origins, nature, and operations of the social system that generates such prejudice.[75]

Behind Blumer's sociological façade was more social psychology than anything else. Consistent with his symbolic interactionist theoretical approach, Blumer's social structure was more phenomenological than it was materially based, ultimately consisting of a subjective *sense* of group position. Despite this conceptual minimization, Blumer touted his approach as "different from that which dominates contemporary scholarly thought on this topic." The main contribution of Blumer's article was its campaign to place prejudice within the broader social context of the relations of racialized groups. By treating racial prejudice as "fundamentally a matter of relationship between racial groups," Blumer shifted the focus away from psychologists' concern with the prejudice of individual racial bigots and back to the traditional attention of sociologists to race relations.[76]

That same year, sociologist Pierre L. van den Berghe also made the case that it was sociology that was best equipped to explain racial prejudice. Van den Berghe's historically comparative approach was systemic and incorporated objective components of the social structure that went far beyond the subjective and psychological. Indeed, had he substituted the word "asymmetrical" for the term "reciprocal," van den Berghe's definition of racial prejudice as "a system of reciprocal relations of stereotypy, discrimination and segregation existing between human groupings which are considered as 'races'" could have worked as a definition of racism.[77]

Unfortunately, in their engagement with psychologists in their focus on prejudice rather than racial oppression, many sociologists also followed their lead toward conceptual minimization. Sometimes it was done to exploit that popular trend; at other times to challenge it. But in one way or another it was psychologists who set the prejudice-centered agenda for the race relations research of sociologists in the 1950s. While there were some notable efforts to map a path back to race relations as a group-level phenomenon, and even some hints as to how racism might be viewed as systemic, with a few scholars inclined to place the social structure and power relations at its core, these conceptualizations remained largely underdeveloped as sociology found itself lacking the experiential and theoretical tools to see the profound implications of the civil rights movement, which by that time was right in front of it.

THE FAILURE OF THE RACE RELATIONS PARADIGM OF AMERICAN SOCIOLOGY

As many curious toddlers have discovered, the best way to find out how a toy works is to break it apart; it is broken things that reveal their inner secrets. The same was true for the race relations paradigm of American sociology—the remains of which today we call "race and ethnic relations" or just "race." Its inner workings became most visible after it failed to predict, or even account for, one of the nation's most profound and consequential changes in race relations and the modern civil rights movement that made it happen. Subsequent intellectual autopsies revealed the cause of the demise of that then-dominant paradigm to be the fact that it was held together more by the politics of racial accommodation than by keen social analysis.

The official acknowledgment of the discipline's failure to foresee and explain the modern civil rights movement came from Everett Hughes in his 1963 presidential address to fellow members of the American Sociological Association (ASA). By the time of that conference it was clear that sociology was caught off guard by a massive upheaval in race relations that it could no longer ignore and retain its professional credibility. Indeed, Hughes gave his talk the very same day as the March on Washington for Jobs and Freedom, the massive rally that symbolized the success of the civil rights movement after its crucial victory in Birmingham, Alabama earlier that year.[78] Hughes's remarks are revealing not only in what he said, but in how he said it, and what remained unspoken. Resting not far beneath the surface was the irony that in his explanation of that embarrassing failure of American sociology—a topic to which his address actually devoted very little time—Hughes deployed the same racism-evasive theory, concepts, and language that had caused that fiasco in the first place.

Hughes broached the failure issue by asking "why did social scientists—and sociologists in particular—not foresee the explosion of collective action of Negro Americans toward immediate full integration into American society?" But in the very next sentence he discounted the issue, reducing its singular significance by conceptually extenuating it to what he saw as its larger context. For, as Hughes put it, "it is but a special instance of the more general question concerning sociological foresight of and involvement in drastic and massive social changes and extreme forms of social action."[79]

Hughes did not return to the failure question he posed until several pages later, when he insisted that what sociology got wrong was not the direction and content of the African American freedom struggle but merely its "vigor and urgency." He revisited the issue another half-dozen pages later where he argued that the problem was merely methodological. The discipline's methodologies were too narrow and hypotheses and facts-centered to encompass the larger sociological imagination needed to address the topic. Finally, Hughes suggested that the professionalization of the discipline—which relied on such narrowly focused, empirically based methods to claim its scientific rigor—was also partially to blame because it discouraged the use of the wider variety of methods required to examine such large and complex issues.[80] To Hughes, the discipline was fine; it just needed to retrieve some of the more diverse methodological tools of its early years. An acknowledgment that the discipline's real failure was conceptual would have brought to the surface the role of racial politics and questioned the value neutrality, and therefore the "science," claim of sociology and the other social sciences that give them professional legitimacy.

That Hughes saw no major conceptual problem with the discipline was also evident by the fact that his talk relied heavily on the ideas of Robert Park—ironically, the very approach some critics saw as being emblematic of its failure. Early on Hughes wrapped his comments around Park's conceptualization of race relations, a term that tends to camouflage hierarchical relationships as those involving exchanges between relatively equal groups. In Hughes's talk the word "racism" was not mentioned and the term "oppressor" was used only once—the latter in reference not to what was happening in the United States, but in South Africa.[81]

Additionally, Hughes engaged in conceptual conflation by forcing the U.S. racial insurgency to share equal billing with French-English ethnic conflict in Canada. Still guided by Parkian theory, Hughes asserted that, unlike the French Canadians who have chosen to remain ethnically distinct, "the Negro Americans want to disappear as a defined group." As the civil rights movement spread, became more militant, and increasingly emphasized black power and pride, the racial assimilation cornerstone of Park's race relations cycle theory was bitterly challenged by African Americans, who insisted that their goal was not to relinquish their own ethnic identity as they assimilated into the dominant white society and culture, but rather to gain the power they needed to exercise their own ethnic choices.[82] Because of the assimilation-focused conceptual blinders he chose to wear, Hughes—who found himself having to acknowledge the failure of sociology to predict the coming of the civil rights movement—now failed to see the early signs of its black power and black pride phase.

The most comprehensive sociology of knowledge investigation of the failure of race relations scholarship in the United States is James McKee's *Sociology and the Race Problem: The Failure of a Perspective*. While McKee is on target in noting the general failure of the discipline's race relations specialty area to predict the racial turbulence of the 1960s, and in rooting that failure in the race relations of the larger society, he missed the mark in his sweeping claim that no "sociological scholar" sounded the alarm that race relations were about to "burst their bonds." Socially transformative movements typically take decades to emerge and the development of the race consciousness of African Americans that fueled the modern civil rights movement did not escape the eyes of all American sociologists. Earlier in this chapter I mentioned an article Alfred Stone published in 1908 in the *American Journal of Sociology*. That article, which focused on the growing race consciousness among African Americans, was followed by replies from other scholars within the same journal issue, including one by W. E. B. Du Bois. Other articles followed suit in subsequent decades leading up to the civil rights movement including, as I have noted, those of Work in 1924, Gomillion in 1942, and Johnson in 1944. So while word of that bubbling racial tension may not have found its way into race relations theory, it had certainly been observed and written about by American sociologists for some time, especially those of African descent. Indeed, more recently, Stephen Steinberg noted that, to the extent they erred, radical African American scholars did so in predicting that the movement would come sooner than it did. But as is often the case with scholars who work outside of a society's acceptable boundaries of racial discourse, they were ignored.[83]

The conceptual limitations of McKee's own analytical language are evident in his conclusion that at the root of the failure of American sociology's race relations approach was "its basic perspective on race in American life, that is, of the beliefs, values, and assumptions sociologists brought to bear on the persistent and always difficult problem of race." Here McKee is, consistent with the language-centered racism evasion practices of conceptual rejection (refusal to use racism-specific terminology) and conceptual obfuscation (use of vague and imprecise wording), not clear about what "race" is and why it is a problem. Because McKee's focus is the race problem rather than racism as a highly organized system of social oppression, his study tended to be narrow in its analytical scope. A notable exception, which nicely details the relationship shown in figure 1.4 between linguistic racial accommodation within American sociology and its larger society, is his explanation of why the specialty was less able to change than the discipline as a whole:

> The sociology of race relations developed at its own pace, with its own vocabulary, and always with a deep concern for the attitudes of a racially intolerant white population. A milieu that for a long time could justifiably be called racist provided the social context from which sociologists developed a perspective on race relations, and it is not surprising that they, too, were not immune to that context.[84]

That is, even when their own racial attitudes were not overtly bigoted and were more racially progressive than those of most of their fellow Americans of European descent—or, in the case of sociologists from racially oppressed groups, they simply knew better from personal experience—they adopted a racially realist political, ethical, intellectual, and career stance that, by accepting the racial status quo as a given, in turn required that they accommodate their work to its linguistic racial realism demands. McKee's failure to hold this broader perspective consistently, however, is again evident from his rather ahistorical conclusion that since that time the society has fundamentally changed.[85] As I will show later, despite significant changes, its legacy of linguistic racial accommodation lives on both generally and within the social sciences.

The same year that McKee's book was released, Stanford Lyman published a paper in which he concluded that American sociology did not see the civil rights movement coming because that type of social movement activity was inconsistent with the tradition of the race relations perspective that viewed changes in race relations as resulting from natural and inevitable transformations in larger social processes as opposed to enacted change brought forth through social protest. I refer to this type of analytical failure as conceptual extenuation.[86]

CONCLUSION: LRA IN AMERICAN SOCIOLOGY'S FIRST CENTURY

As you have seen, American sociologists were not exactly forthcoming in their writings about race relations during the discipline's first century. Racism as a highly organized system of "race"-justified oppression was evaded in sociological discourse through a number of language-centered racism denial practices. First, in its earliest scholarship beginning in the mid-nineteenth century *conceptual misdirection* ruled race relations theory through its assumption that because racial inequality was biological rather than social there was nothing in the existing racial order that should or could be changed. Biological explanations of white racial supremacy also fed the *conceptual realism* ideology that racial inequality was natural and inevitable, and therefore not subject to change. Next, as evolutionary theory prevailed in the 1920s, race relations discourse was encumbered by *conceptual extenuation* and its supposition that there is no need to try to change anything because racialized social relations will automatically dissolve over time with other macro-level changes in the social structure. That period was followed in the 1930s by a *conceptual realism* driven acceptance of the racial status quo as a largely static caste-based system that would not change. Then in the 1940s there was both a dominant and a challenging view of race relations within American sociology. The dominant liberal view was the *conceptual idealism* that race relations would inevitably improve as the nation resolved the moral incongruity between its race relations and its democratic ideals. In contrast, the radical and marginalized outlook called for discourse about the assumed class-based materialist roots of race relations. Unfortunately, both the language-centered racism evasion practices of *conceptual conflation* and *conceptual colonization* flowed easily from its premise that the focus of effective change must be class relations, not race relations, per se. Finally, in the 1950s psychological theory dominated with its reduction of race group relations to the prejudice of racially bigoted individuals under its *conceptual minimization* assumption that there was no social system that needed to be changed. When sociologists tried to reclaim the study of racial prejudice as part of their own academic turf by placing it in a larger social context, their focus remained restricted through conceptual minimization to racial prejudice; and even when their work suggested that the phenomenon was indeed systemic it suffered from *conceptual underdevelopment*. For the most part racial oppression and the system that held it in place had been both linguistically and analytically off limits.

In chapter 3 I examine linguistic racial accommodation and confrontation in American social science during the 1960s and the 1970s. I include in that analysis more on the failure of race relations theory to predict or account for the civil rights movement. Then I shift that chapter's focus to what happened later when, after having expanded their conceptualization of racism in response to the social protests of African Americans, social scientists then contracted it again as they accommodated their work to the white racial backlash.

Chapter Three

Linguistic Racial Accommodation and Confrontation from the Civil Rights Movement to *The Declining Significance of Race*

The more things change, the more they remain the same.
Alphonse Karr, 1849[1]

As racism and other forms of oppression become more sophisticated—less overt and less reliant on physical force and violence—the importance of ideas and language in concealing their very existence increases. This is especially true in highly racialized democracies like the United States that balance conflicting values like the assumed superiority and inferiority of certain groups against that of equal opportunity for all.[2] Systems of racial oppression are adept at reprogramming their linguistic practices to adapt and continue to operate in societies that staunchly deny their very existence. It is through this nimbleness of micro-linguistic changes that white racial hegemony persists, such that "the more things change, the more they remain the same."

RACIAL LANGUAGE BATTLES FROM THE CIVIL RIGHTS MOVEMENT THROUGH THE INSTITUTIONALIZED LEGACY OF THE WHITE BACKLASH

In this chapter I explore both the continuity and change in the racially accommodative language practices of American society and its sociology, as well as the rise of linguistic racial confrontation, from the racially turbulent 1960s through the 1970s as the white racial backlash to the African American freedom movement became institutionalized within the social sciences. Before reviewing the race relations literature of the 1960s, I briefly establish that period's historic context.

Catching Up with the Civil Rights Movement: The 1960s

The civil rights victories of the 1950s were followed by a frustrating lull in the movement, but expectations rose again on February 1, 1960, with the sit-in demonstrations in Greensboro, North Carolina. Another rise in expectations followed near the end of that year when African Americans demonstrated their political clout by helping to elect John F. Kennedy president after he made a supportive phone call to Coretta Scott King whose husband, Martin, had been arrested during a sit-in in Atlanta.[3]

As the sit-ins spread throughout the South, the movement attracted more young people, who proved to be not only less patient but much bolder. Audacious freedom riders tested the enforcement of a federal court decision banning the segregation of interstate buses and terminals. Before that decade reached its mid-point there would also be the failed Albany, Georgia movement to desegregate that town; the deployment of the National Guard and other armed federal personnel to integrate the University of Mississippi; the movement's most impressive victory in Birmingham, Alabama; its symbolic peak with the spectacular March on Washington for jobs and freedom; the passage of the Civil Rights Act of 1964; and the initiation of a national War on Poverty.[4]

If the early 1960s were emblematic of Martin Luther King Jr.'s "dream" vision of America, then the mid and late 1960s increasingly reflected Malcolm X's "nightmare" as the civil rights movement shifted from its goal of integration and strategy of nonviolence to black power by any means necessary. That turning point was especially evident after the vicious "Bloody Sunday" attack on peaceful marchers in Selma, Alabama by state troopers. After Selma and the achievement of many of its civil rights goals—culminating in the passage of the Voting Rights Act of 1965—the movement spread both northward and westward from the South, and became increasingly urban and focused on economic justice issues. Those developments, plus police brutality, the rising frustration of urban poor people of color with the slow pace of change, the declining influence of civil rights leaders and organizations, and the scorching heat of urban ghettoes, ignited a sequence of "long hot summers" of rebellion in hundreds of American cities. This, in turn, helped spark an intense and enduring white racial backlash. With the assassination of Martin Luther King Jr., followed by still more urban unrest and the subsequent failure of his planned Poor People's Campaign in 1968, the movement was virtually dead.[5]

The civil rights victories of the 1960s challenged the previously dominant psychological theories of race relations by demonstrating clearly that institutional change was possible without healing the "hearts and minds" of individual racial bigots.[6] With the failure of both psychological and sociological theories to account for race relations during the modern civil rights movement era, concerned race relations scholars found themselves hurrying to catch up with racial reality.

Bringing Conflict Back In: Joseph Himes's "The Functions of Racial Conflict"

While this was a time when African American sociologists could more safely flex the muscle of the increasingly militant civil rights movement, such challenges from within the discipline were typically more incremental than revolutionary. For example, in his presidential address to the Southern Sociological Society on the social functions of racial conflict, Joseph Himes walked a tightrope between the more conservative and more progressive elements of sociological thinking. To this end, Himes built on Lewis Coser's argument that due to its structure-functional theoretical leanings that emphasized social order and consensus, by the late 1950s the discipline had become so averse to conflict that it failed to foresee the turbulent 1960s decade marked by campus protests, the antiwar movement, the most recent wave of the women's movement, and of course the modern civil rights movement.[7]

By touting the positive social functions of racial conflict, Himes argued that because it would ultimately strengthen American society, the civil rights movement should not only be tolerated but supported, despite the racial tensions it provoked by challenging the status quo. Himes enlarged the consensus-oriented model of sociological theory to include conflict that, despite Coser's insights, many sociologists still considered to be its opposite. In making it clear that the conflict aversion of American sociology was relatively new, Himes pointed out that earlier sociologists placed the concept at the center of their analyses, including Park and Burgess, who were more likely to view conflict as not only natural but an integrative force in societies.[8] In brief, Himes guided his European American colleagues back to an old and respected path within the discipline that could help it to reassert its relevance by catching up with the events of the civil rights movement.

As valuable as Himes's article was in helping American social science come to grips with the nation's new racial reality, from a racism studies perspective it remained conceptually underdeveloped. For one thing, Himes devoted inordinate attention to showing that conflict was, indeed, compatible with the more conservative and still dominant consensus-oriented structure functional theoretical perspective. Because he was primarily concerned with elucidating the positive social functions of African American insurgency, his article explained relatively little about the nature and workings of the system of oppression that insurgency challenged. So at best it offered a partial theory of racial conflict.

In explaining how racial conflict leads to changes in communication styles, patterns, and content, Himes made an observation that is especially relevant to this study's linguistic racial accommodation and confrontation focus. While acknowledging that "racial conflict tends to interrupt and reduce traditional communication between whites and Negroes," Himes maintained that the loss of customary racial communication is not as bad as it appears since "traditional interracial communication assumes that communicators occupy fixed positions of superiority and inferiority, precludes the consideration of certain significant issues, and confines permitted interchanges to a rigid and sterile etiquette." This fits nicely my LRA/LRC premise that in contemporary American society such disruption of normal racial communication is due to African Americans challenging racially accommodative language structures. It suggests that in democratic societies, when racial oppression is no longer as overt as it was in the United States during slavery and Jim Crow, racial discourse becomes more direct, explicit, and confrontational during periods of effective challenges to the racial status quo—and more racism evasive, and thus more racially accommodative, during times of racial backlash or obliviousness. That is, contrary to the insinuations of post-modernist theorists, such language changes are more indicative of shifts in racial power relations at a particular point in time than they are of an inevitable and progressive evolution of a society's racial relations. Himes also noted that by increasing the attention given to race relations, such conflict challenges what Gunnar Myrdal referred to as "'the convenience of ignorance'" and thus allows for a relationship that is more symmetrical in both its content and form.[9] Backed by pressure from the civil rights movement, throughout much of the 1960s there would be a push toward social science and more popular writings in which racism was discussed directly and explicitly.

Pierre van den Berghe's *Race and Racism*

An example of such scholarship is Pierre van den Berghe's *Race and Racism*, published in 1967—a year of widespread urban unrest. Consistent with my linguistic racial accommodation and confrontation argument, decades later van den Berghe attributed his book's popularity to the fact that "the ideological climate was ripe to accept my thesis that the United States was a deeply racist society." Because of the racial heat generated by the civil rights movement at that time, van den Berghe felt comfortable that his work was "clearly in the ideological mainstream" of "the academic liberal establishment."[10]

Van den Berghe was uniquely equipped because of his biography—although of European descent, he was born in the Congo and lived and worked in a number of different countries—to do what American sociologists had rarely done: place race relations in a macro-level historical and nationally comparative perspective. This method and its epistemological assumptions are anathema to the narrow and ahistorical positivism that had come to dominate much of the race relations research, with its heavy emphasis on the study of the social psychology of prejudice through quantitative methods. Critical of positivism and its myth of scientific objectivity, van den Berghe echoed Myrdal in surmising that "to pretend that we can operate in a value vacuum when assuming the role of the scientist is, I believe, a naïve delusion which may lead us to *hide* our biases but not to eliminate their effect on our thinking." He went as far as to conclude that "in the race relations field, more than in many others, social science theory is little more than a weathercock shifting with ideological winds."[11]

Unfortunately, despite his useful review of the state of race relations research, including its challenges to the race concept, van den Berghe settled for the conceptual minimization and underdevelopment of racism as a mere "set of beliefs" rather than a "race"-justified system of oppression. Although van den Berghe's nationally comparative perspective allowed him to distinguish racism from ethnocentrism, his undersized definition of racism prevented him from giving it its proper global reach or historical specificity. Consequently, while van den Berghe treated Western racism as the most socially significant "strain of the virus," he concluded that racism existed "independently" "in a number of societies." By ignoring the impact of European colonization, van den Berghe surmised that racism, which he again limited to racist beliefs, existed independently in Rwanda and Burundi in the Tutsi domination of the physically different Hutu and Twa. And by overlooking the impact of Arab racism in Nigeria, he saw racism there as simply facilitating the Muslim Fulani dominance of the local Hausa. In this way van den Berghe obscured, and thus diminished, the centrality of Western colonization, slavery, and capitalism to the development of contemporary systemic white racism.[12]

It was van den Berghe who, even more than Park, made explicit the declining significance of race thesis that would dominate the discipline and public policy from the late 1970s to the present. Racism, he wrote, having "achieved its golden age approximately between 1880 and 1920" "has since entered its period of decline, although, of course, its lingering remains are likely to be with us at least for the next three or four decades."[13] Without conceptualizing the systemic nature of racism, van den Berghe failed to comprehend its persistence.

Perhaps van den Berghe's greatest contribution to our understanding of race and racism in the West is his insight into their ideological roots. He identified three factors in the origin of Western racism as a belief system (or what I would refer to as an ideology): the economic exploitation of capitalism and colonialism, the new Darwinian thinking in the natural sciences, and the egalitarian ideals of the Enlightenment and their influence on the French and American revolutions. It is with the latter that van den Berghe explained the irony that such egalitarian ideals are at the root of racism.

> Faced with the blatant contradiction between the treatment of slaves and colonial peoples and the official rhetoric of freedom and equality, Europeans and white North Americans began to dichotomize humanity between men and submen (or the "civilized" and the "savages"). The scope of applicability of the egalitarian ideals was restricted to "the people," that is, the whites, and there resulted what I have called "*Herrenvolk* democracies,"—regimes such as those of the United States or South Africa that are democratic for the master race but tyrannical for the subordinate groups. The desire to preserve both the profitable forms of discrimination and exploitation and the democratic ideology made it necessary to deny humanity to the oppressed groups.[14]

Due to such conflicting ideals, democracies are especially inclined to engage in racism evasiveness through linguistic racial accommodation. As such societies develop and politically enfranchise the racially oppressed, the new denial is not of their humanity but of the persistence of systemic racism.

Had van den Berghe expanded his definition of racism to a highly organized system of "race"-justified oppression, he could have explained the origin of Western racism as an ideology used to justify economic exploitation and its persistence in terms of its steady evolution from just that ideology to an entire system of oppression with the race concept as its ideological core. Unfortunately, conceptual minimization is not van den Berghe's only weakness. He also goes to the other extreme of conceptual colonialization and conflation by treating racism—or "race" as he puts it—not as a specific and discrete phenomenon, but instead as just "a special instance of stratification" that "shares many characteristics with ethnicity and class." Similar to the common misuse of the concept of intersectionality today, he gave no real reason to study racism per se, aside from what it can tell us about social inequality in general.[15]

Despite his book's bold *Race and Racism* title, its insightful critique of the limitations of existing race relations research, its promising methodology, and its provocative discernment of the origin of racist ideology, van den Berghe did not focus on racism as a system of oppression. Swayed by conceptual minimization, extenuation, colonization, conflation, and underdevelopment, he either zoomed his analytical microscope in too narrowly on racism's ideological component, or focused out so broadly that its contours could not meaningfully be distinguished from other forms of social stratification.

As the civil rights movement became more militant, van den Berghe moved decisively to the right on controversial racial issues like black power, affirmative action, ethnic studies requirements, "'politically correct' thinking," and "'diversity'" initiatives.[16] Scholars and activists of color—especially those from outside of the discipline of sociology—were less accommodating to the weathervane trends of the dominant racial order. That proved to be the case at least for the racially turbulent 1960s and early 1970s.

Stokely Carmichael and Charles Hamilton's *Black Power*

An early example of the new insurgent scholarship—what Stephen Steinberg referred to as the "'scholarship of confrontation'"—is Stokely Carmichael and Charles Hamilton's *Black Power: The Politics of Liberation in America*. Unlike van den Berghe's book, published that same year, *Black Power* went far beyond academic liberalism by making it clear that racism entailed much more than the attitudes of racially bigoted individuals. There was no more frightening concept for European Americans in the 1960s than that expressed by the two words "black power," which Carmichael popularized through a speech that charismatic and fiery Student Nonviolent Coordinating Committee civil rights activist and leader gave a year earlier in Greenwood, Mississippi. Within a racial order that found subversive the mere juxtaposition of those two words, black power evoked racial confrontation, not accommodation.[17]

From its preface it is clear that *Black Power* was not intended as just another academic enterprise that carefully negotiated the demands of the truth of social science facts with the consequences of white racial power. "This book is about why, where and in what manner black people in America must get themselves together. It is about black people taking care of business—the business of and for black people." That opening verbal salvo made clear that above all else *Black Power* was a black nationalist manifesto. Carmichael and Hamilton spoke specifically about the need for African Americans to muster the courage to break free of the fetters of racial accommodation they wore as individuals for the sake of their collective betterment. "It is crystal clear that the society is capable of and willing to reward those individuals who do not forcefully condemn it—to reward them with prestige, status and material benefits. But these crumbs of co-optation should be rejected. The over-riding, all-important fact is that *as a people*, we have absolutely nothing to lose by refusing to play such games." And "such games" were often language games: "we have no intention of engaging in the rather meaningless language so common in discussions of race in America. . . . We reject this language and these views, whether expressed by black or white; we leave them to others to mouth, because we do not feel that this rhetoric is either relevant or useful." However, despite these bold challenges, linguistically (e.g., in their uncritical use of terms like "race," "black," and "white") Carmichael and Hamilton stayed largely within the boundaries of conventional racial discourse. As another example, note their use of the following conceptually obfuscating, racism-evasive language. "The whole question of race is one that America would much rather not face honestly and squarely. To some, it is embarrassing; to others, it is inconvenient; to still others, it is confusing." Of course nothing is more "confusing" than what is meant by the "question of race." Also puzzling is their assumption that all of America was opposed to honest discourse in the problem. Here they erroneously conflated being an American with being a European American with a stake in the maintenance of the racial status quo.[18]

Despite its language limitations, *Black Power* achieved a major breakthrough in the area of racism studies through its honest and straightforward conceptualization of what Carmichael and Hamilton deemed "institutional racism," a view congruent with the long-held belief among African Americans that racism is systemic and the belief among African American and African intellectuals and activists in the 1960s that racism in the United States could best be viewed through the metaphor of domestic colonialism. But the road there was often a rocky one. For example, in choosing the term racism over race relations and defining racism as "the predication of decisions and policies on considerations of race for the purpose of *subordinating* a racial group and maintaining control over that group," Carmichael and Hamilton made it clear that they were referring to a phenomenon that is both hierarchical and oppressive. But there is a major problem with this definition: It conceptually minimizes racism as requiring only conscious "race"-based decision making. On the very next page, however, the authors provided their now famous description of racism and its multiple dimensions that, without acknowledging the fact, proves the inadequacy of their previous intent-centered definition.

> Racism is both overt and covert. It takes two, closely related forms: individual whites acting against individual blacks, and acts by the total white community against the black community. We call these individual racism and institutional racism. The first consists of overt acts by individuals. . . . The second type is less overt, far more subtle, less identifiable in terms of *specific* individuals committing the acts. But it is no less destructive of human life. The second type originates in the operation of established and respected forces in the society.[19]

Carmichael and Hamilton then gave the following cogent example to distinguish those two forms of racism.

> When white terrorists bomb a black church and kill five black children, that is an act of individual racism, widely deplored by most segments of the society.

But when in the same city—Birmingham, Alabama—five hundred black babies die each year because of the lack of proper food, shelter and medical facilities, and thousands more are destroyed and maimed physically, emotionally and intellectually because of conditions of poverty and discrimination in the black community, that is a function of institutional racism.[20]

The inconsistencies found in *Black Power* suggest that it best be viewed as a work in progress, one that is conceptually underdeveloped. Although I argue that all racism is systemic and that the notion of individual racism is therefore oxymoronic, the idea that racism could be covert and institutional was a major breakthrough in conceptualizing racism at that time—one that would enable progressive academics to, perhaps for the first time, fall in line with the systemic racism perspective widely held by African Americans. If we conceptualize a social system as comprising all of a society's interrelated institutions, the leap from an institutional to a systemic racism perspective is a short one.

Black Power was published in 1967, the year of a "long hot summer" that included shocking conflagrations of urban unrest in Newark, Detroit, and numerous other American cities. Such events not only gave African Americans license to speak and write in such LRC terms as domestic colonialism, black power, and institutional racism, but set the stage for the 1968 publication of a federal government report under the leadership of European American moderates who mustered the temerity to identify white racism as the nation's top social problem.[21]

The Kerner Commission Report

During that especially intense long hot summer of 1967, marked by racial rebellions in nearly a hundred and fifty American cities, President Johnson established his National Advisory Commission on Civil Disorders to explain what happened, why, and how it could be prevented from recurring. In the spring of 1968 the commission, chaired by Illinois Governor Otto Kerner, released its report, which found that "white society is deeply implicated in the ghetto. White institutions created it, white institutions maintain it, and white society condones it," and boldly blamed "white racism" for the fact that the United States was splitting into "two societies, one black, one white—separate and unequal." Thus it took nothing short of a national racial crisis of scores of burning cities for the influential moderate and liberal elements of the white power structure in the United States to drop the pretense of racially accommodative language and to place the LRC words white racism at the center of its racial discourse. However, while naming white racism as a problem, the Kerner report remained conceptually underdeveloped in that it did little to advance our understanding of what white racism is and how it works. Unfortunately, like a flare shot high into the darkness of night, that report at once signaled the peak of European American concern about race relations and a white racial backlash that culminated in the election of Richard Nixon as president on a highly racialized platform of restoring "law and order."[22]

The 1970s reflected a continuation of the same two contradictory movements of African American insurgency and the more general societal accommodation to the white racial backlash. Consequently there remained a huge gap between the linguistic tools available to conceptualize the race relations of that time and those that were needed.

Back to the Future: The Bipolar Race Relations Scholarship of the 1970s

While the 1960s can be described as a decade of racial insurgency, the 1970s are more difficult to characterize. Just as the black power phase of the civil rights movement reached its peak, it began to dissolve under an intense white racial backlash. The same was true for race relations research. Although intellectual insurgents pushed increasingly direct and explicit conceptualizations of racism, social scientists more accommodating to white racial reaction cleared the field for the return of race relations scholarship to its old ways of racism evasiveness—as well as for a stronger form of racism denial in which even the word "race" would be largely banished from scholarship and social policy discourse.

Explanations of the demise of the civil rights movement range from its own success or it simply running out of steam to white racial backlash and repression. The latter cause is supported by the highly racialized political events that marked the transition between the 1960s and the 1970s. In 1968, the watershed year in 1960s social activism, both Richard Nixon and George Wallace exploited and fueled the white racial backlash to further their presidential ambitions. Nixon, the Republican candidate, won with the help of highly racialized appeals to European American Southern segregationists previously loyal to the Democratic Party that included a "law and order" crackdown on African American protest and opposition to racially ameliorative public policies like open housing and forced busing to promote school integration. After his election, Nixon crafted a "southern strategy" package of racially charged policies and platforms for his reelection in 1972 that has served as the centerpiece of the Republican election hopes to the present day. His successor, Gerald Ford, continued most of Nixon's backlash policies. Even after African Americans gave a big assist to the election of Democrat Jimmy Carter as president, Carter appointed African Americans to various posts, but did not address the issues important to most African Americans. During the 1970s the Ku Klux Klan nearly tripled its membership, and toward the end of the decade there were significant setbacks in the courts to affirmative action as a means of ensuring that qualified African Americans and Latino/a Americans be admitted into institutions of higher education and be hired for well-paying jobs. Yet, although African American militancy declined, African Americans were able to solidify many gains of the civil rights movement. There was a significant increase in the number of African American elected officials; numerous conferences, organizations, and institutions were established; and affirmative action resulted in major gains in college enrollment and professional employment.[23]

By the late 1970s, some African American intellectuals and activists fretted about what they took to be ominous signs that the nation's racial history of a century earlier was repeating itself. Just as the first reconstruction following the abolition of slavery ended with a long period of intense racial repression, so now would there be another prolonged period of white racial hostility following the demise of the civil rights movement? However, the 1970s proved to be more complex and ambiguous than simply a period of repression and decline. Moreover, the academic race relations publications lagged behind the racial events of the larger society in a way that produced a pattern of extremes more pronounced than what was happening more generally with race relations in the larger society. Although some of the most racially insurgent work was published in the early 1970s after African American militancy had reached its peak, some of that decade's most racially accommodating scholarship would come closer to the end of that decade after the white racial backlash had begun to recede somewhat. In the late 1970s there was also the persistence of the systemic racism perspective.[24]

One of the most influential and best known white-backlash scholars was Harvard University sociology professor and future U.S. senator Daniel Patrick Moynihan. While African American activists and intellectuals pushed for systemic change, Moynihan lit the fuse of intense racial conflict with his 1965 U.S. Department of Labor report on changing African American family structures in which he concluded that at "the heart of the deterioration of the fabric of Negro society is the deterioration of the Negro family." When placed in historical and political context, it is evident that Moynihan chose his facts and drew his conclusions largely to provide Johnson with a way out of his commitment to African Americans and to escape the white political backlash it had cost him.[25]

As he progressed in his transformation into one of the nation's most influential neo-conservatives, Moynihan had an even more shocking recommendation for his next presidential boss, Richard Nixon: that in regard to race relations Nixon adopt a policy of "benign neglect."[26] It is no accident that such policies redirecting attention from systemic white racism were proposed at a time when the civil rights movement was losing steam but an end to the ensuing white backlash was nowhere in sight. No other sociologist would have as much influence in both academic race relations study and social policy until near the end of the decade when William J. Wilson published *The Declining Significance of Race*. In between those two racially reactionary publications there was important insurgent race relations scholarship that went relatively ignored.

Joel Kovel's *White Racism: A Psychohistory*

As you have seen, the urban racial rebellions of the late 1960s provoked even a presidential commission to conclude that it was white racism that was at the heart of the nation's racial conflict. While the words "white racism" went far beyond what the racially cautious profession of sociology was prepared to articulate, still other voices outside of the discipline were not so restrained. A case in point was the publication in 1970 of Joel Kovel's *White Racism: A Psychohistory*.

The fact that he was no mainstream American social scientist was clearly evident in Kovel's scholarship, as was the significance of both recent and earlier historical events. His training was in medicine, with specialties in psychiatry and Freudian psychoanalysis. With his radicalization in the 1960s by the U.S. involvement in the Vietnam War and the rise of other sources of social turbulence, Kovel's politics and writings also became heavily influenced by Karl Marx and the Neo-Marxist psychoanalysts Norman O. Brown and Herbert Marcuse. Kovel's eclectic method, which combined the insights and methods of "history, depth psychology, sociology and the study of culture" with those of the "great works of literature," focused on racism as a highly organized system of oppression. Both the historical events driving Kovel's analysis and the centrality of social structure to it are explicit early in *White Racism*. "Our racial crisis has made us realize that white racism in America is no aberration, but an ingredient of our culture which cannot be fully understood apart from the rest of our total situation."[27]

One of Kovel's most significant contributions to racism studies is psychohistory as "a theory of cultural change" that matches particular periods of U.S. historical and economic development to their specific cultural and psychological manifestations of racism. The first of these three types, dominative racism, was most characteristic of the era of slavery in the antebellum South and entailed "direct physical oppression and sexual obsession" fueled by resentment from the European American petit-bourgeois and working class. The second type, aversive racism, more common in segregated Northern enclaves, entailed an emotional "coldness and the fantasy of dirt." And finally, meta-racism—the most recent and advanced form—was described as being impersonal in its nature, existing largely "without psychological mediation" and being "carried out directly through economic and technocratic means." Here *meta* did not actually mean *beyond* or *after* racism, but rather a movement beyond its personal, belief-centered manifestation. For Kovel,

From the Civil Rights Movement to The Declining Significance of Race 77

meta referred therefore to the *meta*morphosis of racism beyond its more overt, intentional, and belief-driven manifestations to what today remains largely hidden as institutionalized or systemic racism. It is a form of racism that in its shift "from human to nonhuman agencies" has become so institutionalized and covert that human prejudice and agency are no longer needed. For example, today racial inequality is perpetuated through the apparently color-blind, impersonal workings of the economy. But Kovel avoided a common pitfall of those who advocate an institutionalized racism approach by making it clear that he was not suggesting that it "works without human hands." Instead, "it is a very human process, even to the degree of mystification which is applied to make the economy seem a natural force instead of the expression of class conflict." It is in this way that "racist oppression occurs today through the seemingly automatic laws of the economic system."[28]

Unfortunately, in his attempt to bring class agency into his metaracism, Kovel engaged in the type of conceptual colonization common among Marxist treatments of racism as a mere offshoot of class-based oppression. As Kovel put it, "it is well known that behind the racist system is one of class oppression, and that the immediate occasion for the creation of mutually hostile ethnic groups organized in a racist hierarchy has been the strategy— whether consciously articulated is not to the point—of dividing and weakening the working class in its struggle against capital." Unfortunately such extreme contextualization was not enough to save Kovel's provocative book from its additional fates of conceptual minimization and underdevelopment. Despite his assertion that racism is an integral part of the American "cultural order" that has helped maintain its stability, Kovel remained content to treat racism largely as an irrational set of beliefs.[29]

African American Insurgency Finds a Sociological Voice: Robert Blauner's *Racial Oppression in America*

Every institution of American society was in some way impacted by the civil rights movement; the social sciences were no exception. By the 1970s words like racism, domestic colonialism, and racial oppression were publishable fare as American social science, struggling to reestablish its credibility and relevance in the field of race relations, became more receptive to the conceptualizations of the racially oppressed. One of the most influential examples of such movement translation and legitimation work done by a prominent European American sociologist is Robert Blauner's 1972 *Racial Oppression in America*. Blauner—who became radicalized in his racial thinking after the Watts rebellion of 1965—made his system-challenging politics clear in his book's "may his death be avenged" dedication to the African American revolutionary George Jackson who, many Leftists believed, was murdered the previous year by San Quentin prison guards after being set up for a bogus prison break.[30]

In his critique of race relations theory, Stephen Steinberg, one of Blauner's students, characterized *Racial Oppression in America* as not only an example of the "'scholarship of confrontation'" and "a canon of antihegemonic discourse," but also—as indicated by the words racial oppression in its title—being representative of a paradigm shift in race relations research. The influence of Blauner's book is somewhat ironic considering that there was nothing particularly new about his essays or his thinking. They were largely an articulation of ideas about racial and class oppression through the domestic colonialism lens popular among African American intellectuals and activists of that time. His contribution was therefore not as an intellectual architect but as a carrier, translator, and legitimizer of radical African American thought. While those ideas provided Blauner with a fountain of timely and relevant knowledge, as a European American sociology professor at the prestigious University of California at Berkeley he, in turn, infused them with the legitimacy of elite social science.[31]

In one of the book's eclectic essays, Blauner outlined four essential elements of a viable alternative to the "sociology of race." First, in an apparent challenge to the conceptual extenuation of race relations scholarship ranging from mainstream academicians like Park to radical Marxists who assumed that race and ethnicity are largely epiphenomena of larger and more enduring social forces that will disappear as those forces of modernity evolve, Blauner rejected "the view that racial and ethnic groups are neither central nor persistent elements of modern societies." Second, he dismissed the then-commonly held conceptual colonization and conflation assumption that "racism and racial oppression are not independent dynamic forces but are ultimately reducible to other causal determinants, usually economic or psychological." Next, Blauner criticized the conceptual minimist view that "the most important aspects of racism are the attitudes and prejudices of white Americans." Finally, he rejected the conceptual obfuscation of social scientists and others who deployed the "*immigrant analogy*" to deny the significance of racial oppression through its insistence "that there are no essential long-term differences—in relation to the larger society—between the *third world* or racial minorities and the European ethnic groups."[32]

Like Carmichael and Hamilton, Blauner's greatest contribution to racism studies was his dissemination and legitimation of the view long held by African Americans that racism is systemic and should be studied directly and explicitly. Blauner made this clear in his choice of the book's theme as "the central and independent role of racial oppression in American life." According to Blauner, what social science therefore needs is to move beyond what I refer to as its conceptual extenuation and conflation to "a model of American society and its social structure in which racial division and conflict are basic elements rather than phenomena to be explained (or explained away) in terms of other forces and determinants." Blauner also stressed the need for a systemic approach to racism in his chapter titled "Race and the White Professor," where he explained, "The liberal professor tends to define racism in a much more restricted sense than do people of color and white radicals today.... The third world definition of racism tends to be broader and more sociological. It focuses on the society as a whole and on structural relations between people rather than on individual personalities and actions." Later Blauner emphasized that "racism is a system of domination as well as a complex of beliefs and attitudes."[33]

The main language-centered shortcoming of Blauner's internal colonialism theoretical approach is conceptual underdevelopment, which is due to two factors. First, there is the inherent limit of the internal colonial analogy as an explanation of racial oppression in nations like the United States. Then there is Blauner's failure to advance his theory beyond what he came to see as the "faddish," "mechanical," and "dogmatic" colonial analogy that lacked a viable solution to racial oppression. That failure was due in part to the fact that in light of the much too impersonal conceptualization of institutionalized racism, he came to question the value of social theory altogether. Another reason Blauner gave for not developing a more adequate theory of racial oppression seemed based in careerism-driven racial accommodation. Just as in the publication of *Racial Oppression* Blauner benefited from being at the right place at the right time, he later suffered career consequences for his "'bad boy' book." Blauner recalled that after being "burned professionally by my embrace of the colonial perspective . . . a part of me felt that it would be safer to ground my future work in the concrete life experiences of real people, downplaying the bigger questions in a charged field such as race relations, where the lines between theoretical analysis and political advocacy easily get fuzzy." Thus at the peak of the civil rights movement's militancy, Blauner stressed the colonial analogy of African and African American freedom struggles. However, as those struggles receded, he returned to the sociological mainstream and its culture of poverty explanation of the African American condition.[34]

The Death of White Sociology?

In the early 1970s African American sociologists also rode the currents of racial insurgency into more militant places than they had dared to venture before. In 1973, just five years prior to the publication of William J. Wilson's racially accommodative classic, *The Declining Significance of Race*, Joyce Ladner, a former civil rights activist whose previous work on impoverished African American women safely fit within the confines of the culture of poverty perspective, published a collection of essays she edited under the provocative and hyperbolic title, *The Death of White Sociology*. Through its militant rhetoric, that book seemed to offer a manifesto for linguistic racial confrontation congruent with the spirit of African American intellectual insurgency in the larger society. For example, to set the stage for those essays Ladner began with an epigraph from Lerone Bennett's *The Challenge of Blackness* that stressed the urgency of African Americans moving beyond white conceptualizations.

> It is necessary for us to develop a new frame of reference which transcends the limits of white concepts. It is necessary for us to develop and maintain a total intellectual offensive against the false universality of white concepts. . . . We must abandon the partial frame of reference of our oppressors and create new concepts which will release our reality. . . . We must say to the white world that there are things in the world that are not dreamt of in your history and your sociology and your philosophy.[35]

Unfortunately that anthology suffered from conceptual underdevelopment both in its premature pronouncement of the death of white sociology and by the fact that it did not offer a viable alternative.

Other books published that same year by African American sociologists were less inclined to engage in such a broadside against the profession. In his book, *Racial Conflict in American Society*, Joseph Himes expanded the ideas about the positive social functions of racial conflict he had previously published in article form; and racism remained a significant enough topic for William J. Wilson to react against in his book *Power, Racism, and Privilege*.[36]

The White Backlash Pushes Race-Relations Scholarship Back to The "Negro Problem"

The Emergence of William J. Wilson's Sociological Backlash against the Conceptualization of Systemic Racism

One of the first things evident in Wilson's *Power, Racism, and Privilege* is the influence of Pierre van den Berghe, who by that time had taken a sharp rightward turn in his racial and career politics. Wilson studied at the University of Washington, where van den Berghe was employed when he published *Race and Racism*, and seemed to have followed at least nominally in van den Berghe's methodological footsteps in the preface of *Power, Racism, and Privilege*, which rooted the book in Wilson's "growing interest in comparative and historical race relations." Wilson also thanked van den Berghe for comments and suggestions; cited him fifteen times, mostly in notes, in the book's index; and included *Race and Racism* and two other van den Berghe publications in his list of references.[37]

Like van den Berghe's, Wilson's scholarship has closely followed the nation's racial mood. The first sentence of the first chapter of *Power, Racism, and Privilege* stated that "few fields in the social sciences have received the degree of attention from both scholars and laymen as has race relations."[38] But just five years later, as race relations waned as a national issue and there was a growing white backlash against affirmative action and, with his help, a return to a focus on low-income African Americans themselves as the nation's black underclass problem, Wilson's career would soar due to the extraordinary attention he received from the racially accommodative title of his next book, *The Declining Significance of Race*.

In *Power, Racism, and Privilege* Wilson examined the issue van den Berghe raised as to whether, because it draws so heavily from other sociological specialty areas, race and ethnic relations is actually its own specialty area. Consistent with this conceptual extenuation view, Wilson blamed the narrowness of the race and ethnic relations approach for its failure. He noted, for example, that to understand racism we must comprehend power and to know power we must understand racism. Unfortunately, Wilson's narrow and faulty conceptualization of each concept made it impossible for him to account for their interrelationship. As justification for rejecting the very robust, oppression-centered Marxist view of power, Wilson embraced the theory work of Hubert Blalock that replaced the Marxist emphasis on "'power struggle'" with a more nuanced conceptualization of "'power contests.'" By removing power from notions of group hierarchies and oppression, Wilson deradicalized the concept and made it fit the pluralist view of power that would come to dominate much of the theory work in the field, including Michael Omi and Howard Winant's racial formation theoretical conceptualization of a world without systemic racism, and the post-modernist view of scholars like David Theo Goldberg who, like Omi and Winant posited many different "racisms" by several racial groups.[39]

With his weak conceptualizations of racism and power Wilson shifted the focus away from an active and dynamic process of racial *oppression* to a more static view of racial *stratification*, conceived of largely as a residual of past racist practices plus the insufficient human capital possessed by ghetto residents who are isolated and trapped in a web of self-perpetuating pathological behavior. This was accomplished by a perspective that is sufficiently ahistorical in its misunderstanding of both the nature of "race" and of race-based oppression to make both appear to have no beginning and to be natural and inevitable. In a section titled "Power and the Origin of Racial Stratification," Wilson claimed that "racial domination and exploitation have occurred repeatedly throughout history" and that "usually when two distinct racial groups have established contact and have interacted for a continuous period, one group ends up dominating the other."[40] Through these claims that racial stratification is natural and inevitable he rationalized the conceptually misdirected focus of much contemporary research on "race" and socioeconomic status that attempts to explain the relatively low position of African Americans outside of the sociohistorical context of race relations, per se, through stratification research that often entails little more than running "race" as a variable.

Wilson's choice of the term racial stratification rather than racial oppression is also significant in that the former—viewed principally through a human capital deficiency lens—is an example of conceptual misdirection that keeps the focus on the characteristics of what is assumed to be a largely static and pathological African American underclass, while the latter stresses the more dynamic and exploitative nature of race relations. This is consistent with Wilson's oppression-evasive definition of power and his conceptual colonization of racism as but one, largely antiquated, aspect of contemporary racial stratification. Reflecting this focus, much of today's sociological analysis of "race" is limited to trying to explain racial differences in socioeconomic status and mobility devoid of any theory work that locates such dissimilarities within the racialized group relations that actually produce them. Once again, through this process of conceptual misdirection away from systemic racism, a sociologist reduced the nation's systemic white racism problem to its "Negro problem."

Chapter 3 of *Power, Racism, and Privilege* bears the same Race and Racism title as Pierre van den Berghe's book. Following closely what was racially prudent at the time, Wilson noted that it was the Kerner report that thrust racism into the national discourse. That statement also provided cover for Wilson to use such a controversial but book-selling word, in its title, which he quickly began to deconstruct of its analytical power. Wilson began his critique of the term racism by citing a study that was critical of the Kerner report's failure to specify precisely what it meant by racism. From there he went on to complain about "the recent tendency to expand the term 'racism' to so many different categories that a precise conceptual and empirical application becomes difficult." Wilson specifically cited the need to distinguish racism from discrimination, prejudicial attitudes, and ethnocentrism. All of this ultimately justified his acceptance of the conceptually minimist definition of racism as essentially a set of beliefs, and more specifically an ideology.[41]

After making it clear that he viewed racism as merely an ideology, Wilson then described it as a phenomenon that has much broader scope. To Wilson racism—or perhaps more appropriately put racist ideology—can take two forms as a justification for social inequality—the biological and the cultural—and can operate at three social levels—the institutional, the collective, and the individual. Furthermore, those different levels can be placed along a continuum from the relatively loosely organized individual-level racism to the highly structured institutionalized racism. But, again, if we stay true to Wilson's actual definition of racism, what can be highly, moderately, or loosely structured is not racial oppression, but only its ideological justification. Under this shaky logic, racism can be conceived to be normative, but not systemic. To someone who believes that racism is systemic, Wilson's tiny conceptualization of racism makes about as much sense as reducing capitalism to a set of dominant stratification beliefs—an ideology that explains and justifies who gets what and why. Unfortunately Wilson was not inclined to move that far ahead of mainstream sociology. Adding to this conceptual confusion is the fact that he does acknowledge, in making another point, the existence of "a system of racial stratification." For Wilson, not only isn't racist ideology the core of racism as a system of "race"-justified oppression; in his view, a racial stratification system can actually exist largely independent of racism, however defined. By applying van den Berghe's notion of an evolutionary shift from paternalistic to competitive racism, Wilson imagined racial stratification without much racism, even as he very narrowly defined it. As he put it, "although racial stratification is still quite prevalent in the United States, racism as a line of defense against black encroachment is not nearly as heavily relied on as it was in the late nineteenth and early twentieth centuries." Wilson's conclusion that racism and racial stratification are not synonymous represents their relationship as being at most that of two overlapping circles. Consequently, even after the end of racism (i.e., racist ideology), a system of racial stratification may remain in place. Under this reasoning Wilson provided a way for sociology to continue its studies of "race," now as a concoction of stratification without hierarchy, by avoiding not only the increasingly popular but contentious term *racism*, but even the discipline's traditional focus on "race relations." Apparently Wilson concluded that, fed by radical African American intellectuals and activists and even the politically mainstream Kerner report, the conceptualization of racism had been allowed to grow much too big for its sociological britches. Wilson was content to have the system of racial stratification, with racism as the racist ideology that held it together and fueled it being increasingly less needed for its operation, remain not only conceptually underdeveloped but largely invisible.[42]

Through his *Power, Racism, and Privilege* book Wilson separated racism from racial stratification, while in his *Declining Significance of Race* book, which I examine later, he established racial stratification as a usually unnamed specialty area that allows for an essentially racism-blind and victim-centered analysis of the condition of impoverished African Americans. In this way Wilson justified for policy elites a conceptual-misdirection-driven retreat from the specter of systemic white racism that African Americans had forced onto the national agenda and a return to a focus on the immediate social environment, attitudes, and behavior of the African American poor themselves.[43]

Oliver C. Cox's *Race Relations*

A cursory glance at the receptions of Cox's *Caste, Class, and Race* and of William J. Wilson's *The Declining Significance of Race* might easily give the impression of Cox as a courageous and persecuted truth teller and Wilson as a well-rewarded, career-driven, racial accommodationist. But a closer look at evolution of the ideas of these two African American sociologists reveals more similarities than differences. This is evident when we compare the LRA ideological viewpoints articulated in Cox's last book, *Race Relations*, and Wilson's first book, *Power, Racism, and Privilege*.

Race Relations: Elements and Dynamics was published in 1976, twenty-eight years after *Caste, Class, and Race*, two years after Cox's death, and three years after the publication of Wilson's *Power, Racism, and Privilege*. Because *Race Relations* was written after the modern civil rights movement of the 1960s, Cox should have been able to see that history had proven him wrong in two of the basic assumptions of *Caste, Class, and Race*: the impossibility of productive African American insurgency and the inevitability of a successful class revolution in the United States. But like many other sociologists then and now, Cox did not let reality stand in the way of his ideology-driven theories.[44]

While Cox's *Caste, Class, and Race* was radical, at least as a powerful class-centered polemic, *Race Relations* proved to be, like Wilson's *Power, Racism, and Privilege*, sociologically mainstream and racially reactionary to the perceived excesses of the black power phase of the civil rights movement Cox had failed to foresee. In *Race Relations* Cox proposed "a distinct theory of race relations" at a time when African American insurgency had freed ample space for the use of more hierarchically explicit terms like racism and racial oppression. With his focus on race relations theory, Cox framed his scholarship in a way that might facilitate his escaping the bitter cold of sociology's hinterlands for the elusive warmth and acceptance of the profession's mainstream. In describing the goal of this, his last book, Cox seemed less intent on fostering revolution than he was in filling in some conceptual gaps for "concerned teachers." While Cox stated that he continued to "regard the economics of race relations as crucial," his new book—like Wilson's *The Declining Significance of Race*—focused more on the plight of the African American poor than on race *relations* per se. And like Wilson, Cox apparently assumed that impoverished African Americans were different in their behavior and aspirations than poor people generally in capitalist societies. In the development of his "distinct" race relations theory, with its focus on the pathological culture and need for assimilation of the racially oppressed, Cox seemed now to be less a radical disciple of Marx and more a student of the conservative French sociological pioneer Emile Durkheim.[45]

Neither Cox's *Caste, Class, and Race* nor his *Race Relations* was primarily concerned with hierarchical race relations. While the focus of the former was class conflict, the main concern of the latter was the need for the cultural assimilation of impoverished African Americans. With that emphasis, *Race Relations* engaged in racism evasion through both conceptual colonization and conceptual misdirection. Toward the end of his life Cox, like other class-centered scholars of that time, had become an adherent of the increasingly popular culture of poverty perspective on intergenerational poverty. In this way, what the civil rights movement had framed as a problem of systemic racism and Neo-Marxists had colonized as a class problem became once again essentially a "Negro problem." Following Park's race relations cycle theory, Cox concluded that the solution to that problem was racial assimilation. While Cox saw color as a temporary obstacle to the assimilation of African Americans, he believed that process would persist until it was completed. From his peculiar blend of Marxist, Durkheimian, and Parkian theory, Cox concluded that it was just a matter of time before racism ran its course as a part of a worldwide trend to capitalism-driven cultural assimilation. Therefore, more in line with the racial accommodationist philosophy and conceptual-extenuation reasoning of Booker T. Washington than that of the radical racial and class oppression tradition of W. E. B. Du Bois; and once against rejecting any significant role for African American insurgency, the focus should be not on challenging racism or capitalism but on preparing individual African Americans to take full advantage of racism's inevitable demise. For, as Cox concluded in his apparent ultimate embrace of capitalism as a progressive transformative force, "the principal hope for the Negroes' cultural inclusion in American society centers about their success as businessmen."[46]

Advocates of the Systemic Racism Approach

As the 1970s progressed, the divide persisted in the discipline between those who accepted and those who rejected the conceptualization of systemic racism pushed forward by the civil rights movement. Two of the leading proponents of the systemic racism perspective were the European American sociologists David Wellman and Joe Feagin.

David Wellman

Wellman began his 1977 book, *Portraits of White Racism*, with a critique of the limitations of scholarship that focused on prejudiced individuals as an explanation of a phenomenon that to him was obviously systemic in nature. Although his systemic racism perspective was heavily influenced by Robert Blauner, who headed the research grant project Wellman directed for him in the mid to late 1960s, its conceptualization was also severely limited by

Wellman's attempt to remain true to the project's rather narrow attitudes-centered focus. Wellman used the case histories of five European Americans interviewed as part of that larger study to argue that racism could not be comprehended outside of culturally sanctioned beliefs that justify white racial privilege. The irony of Wellman's broad systemic racism approach is therefore that—reflecting the nature of the data he had to work with—his conceptually minimist definition of racism as beliefs was actually quite small.[47]

In explaining why he found prejudice to be an inadequate explanation of white racism, Wellman cited its failure to account for "the pervasiveness and subtlety of racist beliefs in American life." As part of his alternative explanation, Wellman gave us a sort of backhanded definition of racism when he said that "racism can mean culturally sanctioned beliefs that, regardless of the intentions involved, defend the advantages whites have because of the subordinated position of racial minorities." A problem with Wellman's conceptualization of racism is that apparently it *can mean* other things as well. The definition just quoted also shares with the institutional racism perspective the questionable assumption that the existence of racism can simply be inferred from certain racial group differences. And also embedded within that assumption is the view that any beliefs that serve to justify the racial status quo are inherently racist.[48]

The way Wellman backs into his rather sketchy systemic racism approach, which is much larger than either his data or his conceptualization of white racism, is through his premise that rather than being aberrant, beliefs that justify the racial status quo are, indeed, both normative and ideological. That is, white racism cannot be reduced to irrational prejudice. Instead, the beliefs binding the system of racial oppression together are "culturally sanctioned, rational responses to struggles over scarce resources." Wellman is at his best in advancing our understanding of systemic racism when he steps away from his attitudinal data. In a footnote he attributes to Robert Blauner and the African American scholars and intellectuals W. E. B. Du Bois, Harold Cruse, Stokely Carmichael, and Charles Hamilton this "alternative perspective" of viewing racism as being systemic. The systemic racism perspective is important if for no other reason than that it is an accurate articulation of the dominant African American experience and view of racism. In my racism classes I cite this excerpt from *Portraits of White Racism* as an example of how students should be able to conceptualize racism once they comprehend its systemic nature.

> I view racial stratification as part of the structure of American society, much like class division. Instead of being a remnant from the past, the social hierarchy based on race is a critical component in the organization of modern American society. The subordination of people of color is functional to the

operation of American society as we know it and the color of one's skin is a primary determinant of a person's position in the social structure. Racism is a structural relationship based on the subordination of one racial group by another. Given this perspective, the determining feature of race relations is not prejudice toward blacks, but rather the superior position of whites and the institutions—ideological as well as structural—which maintain it.[49]

Note how in making his views compatible with the perspective held by most African Americans Wellman actually changed his definition of racism. Racism was no longer just the set of beliefs that so neatly fits his data set.

Wellman later explained that he was not really presenting conflicting definitions of racism but three different dimensions or faces in which racism manifests itself. In addition to the "'personal prejudice'" component social scientists stress, which Wellman considered to be too limited, racism also manifests itself "ideologically" and "institutionally" in systemic practices. Although Wellman's approach stressed the latter two of these, his study's primary definition of racism was beliefs manifested within these three dimensions. As Wellman put it, "racist beliefs simultaneously include and reflect many facets of life in a racially divided society: ideological, institutional, and personal."[50]

In addition to conceptual minimization, another major problem in Wellman's book is conceptual underdevelopment due to the lack of fit between the attitudinal-level data his study must explain and the actual size and scope of racism as a real-world phenomenon. Consequently, from a racism studies perspective, some of Wellman's strongest empirical contributions are weak conceptually, while his strong conceptual work often rests on a weak empirical foundation. Still, Wellman made a significant contribution to racism studies on those occasions when he stepped back far enough from his attitudinal data and small, research-centered definition of racism to envision racism as being systemic as he did in his characterization of racial stratification cited above, where Wellman confidently asserted that "racism is a structural relationship based on the subordination of one racial group by another."[51]

Joe and Clairece Feagin's Discrimination American Style

Toward the end of the 1970s the split between a systemic racism approach and a backlash against studying racism at all was evident. Emblematic of this split was the publication of two books in 1978: Joe Feagin and Clairece Booher Feagin's *Discrimination American Style: Institutional Racism and Sexism* and William J. Wilson's *The Declining Significance of Race*. Today Joe Feagin is the most prolific and influential scholar of systemic racism, while his wife and sometimes coauthor, Clairece Booher Feagin, is also an accomplished author of children's books. The Feagins began their book with this acknowledgment of the nation's "pulling back" from its concern about racial and gender-based oppression: "As this goes to press, concern over discrimination against nonwhite minorities and women has receded substantially into the background. The publicly expressed concern of the 1960s over such matters seems to have evaporated."[52] The times had changed quickly. As you will see, while once again Wilson was racially in sync with the changing times, the Feagins were not.

While doing graduate studies at Harvard, Joe Feagin was influenced by a course he took on African Americans from Thomas Pettigrew and by Gordon Allport's lectures on the social psychology of prejudice. Later, after accepting a position at the University of California at Riverside, he was exposed to radical ideas, including the writings of Karl Marx. Then still later, while at the University of Texas at Austin, his thinking about racial oppression was shaped by the work of W. E. B. Du Bois, Oliver C. Cox, and other African American intellectuals and activists. Feagin's conceptualization of systemic racism was also swayed by his year as Scholar-in-Residence at the U.S. Commission on Civil Rights, where his perspective was further influenced by African American, Latino/a American, and feminist scholars. It was research he did then that served as the basis for the book he coauthored with his wife Clairece four years later. Yet another fuel source for their book's explicit racism and sexism foci was the recent militancy of the civil rights movement and the growing voice of African American and feminist activists and intellectuals who insisted that both phenomena were not only important but systemic. In brief, it was these factors that enabled the book and Joe Feagin's later systemic racism work to break free of the linguistic shackles of the relatively conservative sociological mainstream.[53]

Like other racism-centered scholars at that time, the Feagins began their work by clearing the conceptual field upon which their study would be built. First they uprooted the then-still dominant prejudice-centered race relations paradigm along with the legacy of a pair of Parkian assumptions. To this end they stated that prior to the late 1960s the prevailing explanation of discrimination was prejudice, a conceptually minimist view that was coupled with the "optimistic" and conceptually extenuating assumption that prejudice was "an archaic survival of an irrational past which could and would disappear as this society became more industrialized, rational, and progressive," and people of color—what the Feagins awkwardly referred to as "nonwhite minorities"—became assimilated into society's mainstream. What they exposed there was the confluence of psychology and social psychology, the popular tendency to reduce racism to individual-level racial bigotry, and the evolutionary and assimilationist assumptions of Park's race relations cycle theory. After uprooting these conceptual weeds, the Feagins began to build their movement toward a systemic racism perspective through their conceptual work on a more general theory of discrimination.[54] Although such an approach fit the historical pattern of sociologists not focusing directly and explicitly on racism and took them into some dangerous terrain when it came to the pitfalls of conceptual conflation, it did lay the foundation for later work specifically on systemic racism.

The Feagins pointed out that since the 1960s three new theoretical explanations of discrimination had emerged: the institutional racism approach of Carmichael and Hamilton, the internal colonialism perspective brought to sociology by Robert Blauner, and the interest theory of Wellman and others. By centering their analysis of discrimination on both institutional racism and sexism, the Feagins made clear that their concern was not just racial or gender *relations* but with group hierarchies and their negative consequences for subordinated groups—in a word, oppression. This is evident in their definition of discrimination as "*actions or practices carried out by members of dominant groups, or their representatives, which have a differential and negative impact on members of subordinate groups.*"[55]

To flesh out their theory of discrimination, the Feagins created a typology based on the two dimensions of scale and intent—that is, the extent of its embeddedness within larger organizations and the extent to which discrimination is intentional. From the various combinations of scale and intent the Feagins derived four types of discrimination: isolate discrimination, small-group discrimination, direct institutionalized discrimination, and indirect institutionalized discrimination. By isolate discrimination the Feagins meant intentionally discriminatory acts carried out by individuals against members of subordinated racial and gender groups that are not condoned by the norms of the larger organization or society. An example is a racially bigoted police officer who, in violation of department policies, routinely brutalizes African American prisoners in his custody. Small-group discrimination entails the same level of intent but greater organizational embeddedness, which the Feagins defined as "intentionally injurious actions taken by a small group of individuals acting against members of subordinate groups without the support of the norms prevailing in a larger organizational or community context." Here they cited the example of Klan members bombing an African American church. By direct institutionalized discrimination the Feagins meant discriminatory actions that are both intentional and have a high degree of organizational support. Such actions would include widely accepted racially discriminatory laws, policies, and practices like those characteristic of the systems of Jim Crow in the American South and of Apartheid in South Africa. Finally, by indirect institutionalized discrimination—the type they were most interested in—the Feagins denoted acts that revealed a low level of intent but a high degree of organizational embeddedness. Such actions discriminated against people of color through the quiet everyday operations of organizations and institutions even though they were not intended to do so. Two examples are racial disparities in health care provision and in the criminal justice system.[56]

In addition the Feagins delineated two, more specific, forms of indirect institutionalized discrimination. Side-effect discrimination entails discrimination within one organization or institution that resulted in racially disparate outcomes in another organization or institution. An example is housing discrimination that resulted in a child living in a neighborhood with poor schools, which later in turn affected her ability to find a good job. So although there may not have been direct discrimination in the employment or educational arenas, intentional racial discrimination in housing ultimately determined the fate of that child there as well. By past-in-present discrimination the Feagins meant "apparently neutral practices in an institutional (organizational) area that systematically reflect or perpetuate the effects of intentional discriminatory practices in the past in that same institutional (organizational) area." For example, African Americans who have faced job discrimination in a particular occupation in the past may later find themselves facing a "last hired, first fired" predicament when job layoff decisions were made based on employee seniority.[57]

By explaining the multi-institutional scope and flow of racism, the Feagins not only demonstrated the sociological utility of institutionalized racism theory but also fleshed out the beginnings of a sociologically grounded theory of systemic racism that has proven essential for the emergence of racism theory and racism studies. Aside from the conceptually obfuscating tendency to use such problematic terms as "black," "white," and "minorities" uncritically, the Feagins' ideas tended to be linguistically sound. They suffered mainly from conceptual underdevelopment. They offered no definitions of race and racism that allowed them to contextualize their origins, nature, dynamics, and persistence. And while they sketched out the broad contours of the interconnectedness of racism in various institutional arenas independent of intent, much remained to be conceptualized about the specifics of how such systemic racism works. To that end the Feagins must explain the centrality of white racial identity to (and its mobilization within) the specific operations of racial discrimination. This would entail systematic examination of the links between "race" as an ideological construct, white racial identity, and the various organizational and institutional structures and processes of white racial privilege.

The changed racial climate the Feagins referred to in their preface proved far more receptive to the publication that same year of William J. Wilson's *The Declining Significance of Race*—a book that for many otherwise progressive sociologists delivered a knockout punch to the insurgent systemic racism perspective.[58]

William J. Wilson's *The Declining Significance of Race*

If one book epitomizes Stephen Steinberg's "scholarship of backlash" against the racially confrontational scholarship of the 1960s and 1970s, it is Wilson's *The Declining Significance of Race*. The book's argument is that "race relations in America have undergone fundamental changes in recent years, so much so that now the life chances of individual blacks have more to do with their economic class position than with their day-to-day encounters with whites." Like Cox's *Race Relations*, Wilson's *The Declining Significance of Race* was part of a paradigm shift from what Steinberg referred to as a race relations perspective to one of "the 'political economy of race,'" with the aim being to better account for the combined impact of racial and class dynamics on those deemed least likely to have benefited from the civil rights movement, the African American poor. Congruent with their radical antecedents including Cox's *Caste, Class, and Race*, through the language-centered racism-denial practice of conceptual misdirection these academically, politically, and policy mainstream studies returned sociological scholarship away from racial hierarchies to its more traditional and accommodative focus on the "Negro problem"—comprising the presumed myriad of social and cultural pathologies of impoverished, ghetto-bound African Americans. Also, like those earlier studies, they tended to be plagued by a "class"- (now usually socioeconomic status) centered conceptual colonization. Moreover, *Race Relations* and *The Declining Significance of Race* also suffered from the conceptual conflation of "class" with "race" such that it is impossible to determine which factor is decisive and how.[59]

The basic theoretical argument for *The Declining Significance of Race* was laid out eleven years earlier in Pierre van den Berghe's *Race and Racism*—which in turn was heavily influenced by the race relations cycle theory work of Robert Park. As in his previous book, Wilson dutifully acknowledged comments and suggestions from van den Berghe, who had by that time shifted his racial politics markedly to the right.[60]

As justification for his conceptual conflation of "race" (as African American specific cultural pathology) with "class," Wilson seemed to take at least a momentary swipe at the conceptual colonization of race by class-centered scholars, when he asserted that "when black and white relations are viewed from a broad historical perspective, a uniform reliance on class to explain all forms and degrees of racial conflict can be as misleading as a uniform reliance on race." Unfortunately, consistent with the racism-evasive linguistic practices of conceptual obfuscation and conceptual misdirection, what Wilson meant by "race" remained a mystery, with the bulk of his study's focus suggesting that rather than a concern with contemporary race relations his main interest was the culture of impoverished African Americans. And when race relations were referred to, it was through the use of racially accommodative terminology like "black and white relations" and "racial conflict" that keep hidden their hierarchical and asymmetrical nature rather than straightforward language like racism, racial domination, or racial oppression.[61]

Contrary to Wilson's own conceptual conflation, debates over his alleged declining significance of race argument tend to be framed in a false dichotomy of "race" versus class. Although Wilson did not explicitly make this claim, he fueled that confusion by suggesting a direct correlation between the rise in the importance of "class" and a decline in the significance of "race" in determining the life changes of low-income African Americans. Not only does such either/or analysis make no sense for poor African Americans, but it ignores the fact that Wilson's main concern was with neither "race" (as in race relations or more specifically racism as an oppressive system) nor class. Many scholars falsely assume that by "race" Wilson meant the declining significance of racism as compared to the increasing significance of class-based inequality, when in fact he made reference to neither. In his declining significance of race argument, by "race" Wilson referred to past racist beliefs whereas by "class" he meant nothing that remotely resembled the conceptualization of the term that stresses economic, political, and social domination through accumulated wealth and class consciousness.

With this misunderstanding, many of Wilson's ostensibly class-centered progressive supporters seem comfortably confused that it is really Wilson and themselves who are doing the radical and profound class stuff as opposed to the politically myopic and reactionary race politics of those who still cling to the racism side of that debate. Nothing could be further from the truth than the fanciful notion that Wilson has done a racism versus class dynamics study. In Wilson's book contemporary racism is absent from the analytical equation; in fact, the index contains only one reference to the word racism—and that citation refers the reader to the listings under racial beliefs systems, suggesting that to the extent Wilson was concerned about the declining significance of racism it was with his conceptually minimist view of the waning importance of racial belief systems, not with racism as a highly organized system of oppression. While that index listed "racist society," which Wilson defined as "a society in which the major institutions are regulated by racist ideology," the term was not only limited to ideology but was used to refer to America's *past* in which "race" *was* the decisive factor in determining the life chances of African Americans. As I noted earlier Wilson does not actually include a large and robust conceptualization of class in his analysis. Instead, unlike scholars whose view of class is in line with the influential work of Karl Marx, he limited his focus to socioeconomic status, as conceived by Marx's more conservative contemporary Max Weber. This is evident in Wilson's definition of class as "any group of people who have more or less similar goods, services, or skills to offer for income in a given economic order and who therefore receive similar financial remuneration in the marketplace." Finally, Wilson took a human capital approach that uncritically accepted the structure-functionalist view of social stratification that people are rewarded fairly according to what they contribute to society and ignores the significance of unearned wealth. Wilson's narrow occupation-centered and economics- and power-evasive definition of class accepted the class structure as being open and fair and placed the analytical focus on neither racial nor class oppression, but on the assumed human capital deficiencies of individual impoverished African Americans.[62]

Rarely has a sociology book stirred as much controversy as *The Declining Significance of Race*. This is especially interesting given its rather pedestrian argument about the increasing significance of economics in shaping the life chances of African Americans. The economic thrust of the civil rights movement was clear in the twin jobs and freedom focus of the 1963 March on Washington. Indeed, after the movement had won important victories it was widely recognized that the next battleground would be economic inequality as indicated by the frequently raised complaint of "what good is it to integrate a Woolworth's lunch counter if you don't have the money to buy a hamburger?" When Martin Luther King Jr. was assassinated in 1968, he was in Memphis to support a strike of sanitation workers, and the following year his planned Poor People's Campaign was executed without him. Recall also that an important goal of the institutional racism perspective I discussed earlier was to acknowledge and explain the changing nature of race relations with its generally more subtle means of sustaining the racial status quo economically and in other ways.[63]

So what was the real source of the controversy over Wilson's book? It was, of course, the book's *Declining Significance of Race* title. That title provided ideological fuel for a growing white backlash against affirmative action and other race-specific measures to address the relatively low socioeconomic status of African Americans. By doing so it provoked a huge racial split in praise and condemnation by European Americans and African Americans both within the discipline of sociology and in the larger society. Had Wilson's publisher used the title of the first draft of his manuscript, *The Transformation of Race Relations*, or some other less provocative title, would it have sparked the same controversy? And with a title that did not so readily feed the white racial backlash, would Wilson have been elected President of the American Sociological Association, been recruited to Harvard University, become recognized as the nation's leading expert on the persistence of African American poverty, become so successful as a research grant recipient from mainstream American foundations, and received the prestigious and financially bountiful MacArthur Fellowship? Those are just a few of Wilson's many career bonuses that followed the publication of his book with its title that proved so appealing to the nation's white power structure. Perhaps coincidentally, the most successful court ruling against affirmative action to date, commonly known as the Bakke case, was made the same year the book was published. Wilson's title and content provided specific ideological fodder for the anti-affirmative action movement by questioning the value of affirmative action except for what he characterized as the relatively privileged African American middle class. To this end Wilson claimed that relatively affluent African Americans were increasingly disengaging themselves along class lines from the plight of impoverished African Americans—a division he argued was exacerbated by affirmative action. Finally, it was not only *what* Wilson said that was so ideologically appealing but *who* said it. Under any title, would Wilson's book have received the same recognition had it not been written by a prominent and seemingly progressive African American sociologist? I don't think so![64]

Wilson's books not only legitimatized the discipline's retreat from its civil rights movement mandate to examine systemic racism directly and explicitly, but also its shift of focus away from race *relations*, period. With Wilson's successful conceptual conflation of "race" with low-economic status through his argument that there was no longer an understandably very high level of poverty among African Americans due to their status as a racially oppressed group, but rather a somehow distinct phenomenon of self-generating African American poverty, the analytical focus was now safely returned to the most racially accommodative topic of all: the cultural pathology-driven social and economic problems of African Americans as a "race."

The Declining Significance of Race had, and still has, profound public policy implications. By calling into question the utility of racism cognizant, sensitive, and targeted public policy it provided ideological justification for the nation to continue its move in a direction of racial benign neglect not seen since the years following the Moynihan report. It also embroiled the discipline of sociology into a fruitless decades-old debate about the relative importance of "race" versus "class." Indeed, within sociology graduate programs throughout the United States the debate was rigged with "race" versus "class" PhD qualifying exam questions that threatened to slam shut the career gates of any graduate student who in effect refused to declare in writing his or her rejection of the civil rights movement's call for a direct and explicit examination of systemic racism, as the discipline moved its specialty area of race relations away from the study of *relations* at all and back to its long-standing primary focus on the nation's "Negro problem." A generation of sociologists-in-training were also forced to engage Wilson's declining significance of race in theses, dissertations, and publications before teams of evaluators, usually European American and largely biased toward Wilson's ideological point of view. Wilson's book was so successful in not only diverting sociologists' attention from systemic racism but in conflating the problem of white racism with that of black poverty that for all practical purposes neither race relations nor poverty and inequality continued to exist as distinct areas of sociological focus.

Through its effective use of numerous language-centered racism denial practices, *The Declining Significance of Race* provided a powerful ideological fuel source for racism-evasive social science and public policy. Of the twelve forms of such practices identified in table 1.1, Wilson effectively deployed at least seven of them—conceptual colonization, conflation, minimization, misdirection, obfuscation, rejection, and underdevelopment. And when such linguistic practices are used together, their powers of racism evasiveness can increase exponentially. For example, through conceptual colonization Wilson reframed the nation's serious white racism problem as an assumed to be much larger and more important issue of socioeconomic status. This was accomplished in part through the conceptual conflation of "race" and "class" to a point that contemporary race relations became devoid of any real analytical power. Taking racism out of the analytical equation was also facilitated by the conceptual minimization of racism to a now-past racist belief system. These linguistic practices also facilitated a shift in focus away from systemic racism through conceptual misdirection back to the pre–civil rights movement emphasis of the "Negro problem." Moreover, Wilson's "race" focus aided the conceptual obfuscation of his study by his use of the term in such a vague and imprecise way that it was virtually meaningless. Finally, the conceptual rejection of clear and explicit racism-specific language resulted in Wilson's ideas remaining so conceptually underdeveloped that they were unable to account for the centrality of current institutional and systemic racism in impacting the lives of impoverished African Americans. After all, one can't analyze what one can't see, and it is impossible to "see" what goes unnamed.

The Declining Significance of Race was a significant setback for racism studies in at least three ways. First, it made clear that the post–civil rights movement structures of the discipline, research funding, and public policy were once again firmly aligned against racism-centered explanations of the social and economic conditions of African Americans and other racially oppressed people. Second, the reaction to the book caused the discipline to get caught up in an intellectually and social-policy stifling debate of "race" versus "class" and a rejection of racism scholarship that has contributed significantly to the underdevelopment of racism theory. Finally, as Stephen Steinberg has noted, it effectively beat back, at least temporarily, the challenge of the institutionalized racism perspective the civil rights movement had forced into the national discourse such as the white racism-centered findings of the Kerner report.[65]

While it may have been Wilson's intention to check what he saw as the excesses of the systemic racism perspective, the impact of his book was much greater than that. Its effect was essentially like that of Wilson tossing a live grenade into American race relations scholarship and walking away. After that explosion there was little left whole. As you will see in the next chapter, its African American underclass, post-modernist, critical race theory, attitudinal research, running "race" as a variable, and systemic racism remains are a poor excuse for a coherent paradigm of racialized group relations.

CONCLUSION

In this chapter I continued my linguistic racial accommodation and confrontation centered critique of the most influential race-relations theory scholarship and racial policy discourse by focusing on the decades of the 1960s and the 1970s, which encompassed both the modern civil rights movement and the then-new scholarship of the white racial backlash. A theme that emerged in that scholarship since the 1960s civil rights struggle is the battle between the linguistic racial confrontation-focused systemic racism view of racial oppression popular among African Americans and their civil rights movement and the post-movement approaches that proved more responsive to the racism-evasive and racially accommodative mood ushered in by the white racial backlash.

With pressure from the civil rights movement the 1960s saw more scholarship and other racial discourse that viewed race relations as being characterized by racial conflict and conceptualized as racism. As race relations became more honest and straightforward during the tumultuous 1960s, so did the language used to describe it. In addition there was greater awareness of how such language expands and contracts in response to changes in race relations. Not only was conflict brought back to the center of race relations scholarship but so were words like black power, domestic colonialism, racism, and even white racism. Unfortunately these challenges to the linguistic racial order of things often suffered from the conceptual minimization of definitions of racism that were much too small to capture its full scope as a systemic phenomenon, the conceptual extenuation that assumed that as society evolved racial issues would simply dissolve, the conceptual conflation of racism with other forms of social stratification, the conceptual obfuscation of imprecise and meaningless language, and the confusing meanings of the emerging systemic racism lexicon that often remained conceptually underdeveloped as it was all too often simply made to fit the language of the then existing scholarly and popular racial discourse.

During the 1970s race-relations research took two opposing forms: the scholarship of insurgency and of backlash. For the insurgent scholarship early in the decade like Joel Kovel's book on white racism, Robert Blauner's writings on racism as domestic colonialism, and the Feagins' early work on institutionalized racism, the main problem was conceptual underdevelopment: the need to flesh out the details of how racism worked as a highly organized system of oppression. Although William J. Wilson's work, which in keeping with the white racial backlash shifted race relations scholarship away from racial oppression to socioeconomic status and cultural pathology, benefited from most of the linguistic-centered racism denial practices, especially important were his conceptual colonization of "race" to "class," or more precisely socioeconomic status; conceptual minimization of racism by treating it largely as an ideology; and the conceptual misdirection of analysis away from systemic racism to the social isolation and lifestyles of the African American poor.

In chapter 4 I examine the deployment of various language-centered racism denial practices from the 1980s through the present to expose the impact of the institutionalized legacy of the white racial backlash on linguistic racial accommodation and theoretical fragmentation in contemporary social science and popular race relations discourse.

Chapter Four

Theoretical Fragmentation

The White Backlash and Its Legacy of Failure

> Humpty Dumpty sat on a wall,
> Humpty Dumpty had a great fall;
> All the king's horses
> And all the king's men
> Couldn't put Humpty Dumpty together again.[1]

Humpty didn't just fall. He was pushed! By the late 1970s, what remained of that mess of broken eggshell and yolk was a sociological mainstream that had, in the face of an increasingly institutionalized white racial backlash, retreated to its pre–civil rights position as the keeper of a minuscule, ideology and attitudes centered definition of racism. On the fringes remained fragments of a theoretically emaciated conceptualization of systemic racism, theoretically pretentious exercises in critically examining "race," the running of race as a variable in theoretically shallow quantitative research, poststructuralist analyses of the meanings of various racial projects to change or maintain existing race relations, and the restriction of conceptualizations of racism to what fits the methodology and data of attitudinal research. But so far, no one in sociology has been able to put Humpty Dumpty back together again.

LINGUISTIC RACIAL ACCOMMODATION FROM THE 1980S TO THE PRESENT

In the two previous chapters I examined various language-centered racial accommodation practices and their underlying racism-evasive assumptions during the first century of American sociology and through the crucial decades of African American protest and white backlash of the 1960s and 1970s, respectively. In this chapter I do the same for the decades of the 1980s to the present. As usual, before I begin my review of the literature of each period I briefly establish its historical context. But first, here is a brief overview of race relations and their linguistic racial accommodation (LRA) implications during that entire period.

An Overview of Race Relations and LRA since the 1980s

An examination of the three and a half decades from the election of Ronald Reagan as a racially reactionary president through the second term of Barack Obama as the nation's first African American president is a study in contrasts. It is a period of both great progress and great challenges for the nation's racially oppressed—one that echoes the sentiment about racial progress in the United States often expressed by African Americans and other people of color as entailing a step backward for every two steps forward. It is not surprising that a time of such great expectations and frustration began and ended with strong racial tensions, as changing racial demographics played themselves out in national politics and in the police and vigilante killings of African Americans, which were echoed by the weak treatment of race relations and racism in sociology and the other social sciences. Although there is now more explicit discussion of racism, the conceptualization of that term took a decisive turn away from the linguistic racial confrontation of the 1960s and 1970s back to the default option of linguistic racial accommodation common during the pre–civil rights movement era. As a consequence of that big step backward, as was true for the civil rights movement, American sociology proved incapable of explaining the racial madness that is exploding all around it.

The Reagan Backlash of the 1980s

The early face of the 1980s bears a close resemblance to the recent urban unrest over the police and vigilante killings of African Americans. In December of 1979 it was the city of Miami, where Arthur McDuffie, a father of two, while in police custody with his hands cuffed behind his back, was kicked and beaten into a coma with the aid of flashlights that cracked his skull. As usual, the officers were acquitted of all charges and, as is not uncommon, all hell broke loose as area residents took to the streets seeking justice they felt they did not and could obtain in the courts.[2]

Unlike most of the urban civil unrest of the 1960s, when rage was directed against property and the police and those killed or injured tended to be African Americans, this time the initial attacks were against scores of European Americans who were dragged from their cars as they attempted to drive through African American neighborhoods. Eight were beaten or burned to death and many more were injured. Over the following two days, more than fifty buildings were destroyed and another two hundred and forty were damaged. On the second and third days, the battle's racial tide shifted as the police, security guards, and European American vigilantes killed nine African Americans. President Carter visited the area weeks later and met with enraged local leaders and residents, some of whom booed and threw trash as his limousine left the neighborhood.[3] What a welcome to the 1980s—just two years after the publication of William J. Wilson's *The Declining Significance of Race*!

With the presidential election less than six months away, the racial unrest in Miami advanced Ronald Reagan's campaign strategy. Reagan was forthright in his appeal to white racial animus when he launched his presidential campaign in Philadelphia, Mississippi with a call for "states' rights." That small town was known nationally only as the site of the murders of three civil rights workers sixteen years earlier; and "states' rights" was a well-known rallying cry for Southern states to defend segregation and to turn a blind eye to attacks on civil rights workers. Reagan's highly racialized platform was blatant enough to win him the endorsement of a Ku Klux Klan organization, which boasted that it "reads as if it were written by a Klansman." With Reagan's election as president, the Republican Party (the party of Lincoln) finally realized "the full-fledged emergence of a dominating racist coalition" it had first sought in the 1960s through its Southern strategy, which had sought to rally to its fold racially bigoted Southern Democrats through the appeal of racial code words like "law and order," "welfare," and "busing." As a candidate, Reagan added to that lexicon a new code word, "welfare queen" and as president he rolled back decades of efforts at desegregation, enforcement of civil rights laws against discrimination, and the amelioration of the effects of past racial discrimination.[4]

The fear of "black" criminality was crafted into the racial trump card played by Reagan's vice president, George H. W. Bush, in his successful run for the presidency. The most memorable and probably the most effective action of his campaign against the Democratic nominee, Massachusetts governor Michael Dukakis, was the "Willie Horton" advertisement. William Horton was an African American prisoner in Massachusetts who was charged with, while on a weekend furlough, kidnapping a woman and her fiancé and raping her. After changing Horton's first name to Willie to make it sound more sinister, the Bush campaign exploited the incident to paint Dukakis as being both pro–African American and soft on crime. Like Reagan, after he took office in 1988 Bush created more racial tension by continuing an unrelenting attack on affirmative action and through new tough anticrime legislation that disproportionately targeted African American youth.[5] It is not surprising that within this decade of racial backlash there was an assault on the concept of systemic racism.

Omi and Winant's *Racial Formation in the United States*

In 1986 Michael Omi and Howard Winant published *Racial Formation in the United States*, arguably the most influential race and ethnic relations book since *The Declining Significance of Race*. Omi and Winant's ideas were built upon their supposition that the postmodern civil rights movement era required a poststructuralist theory—one that was more compatible with the broad-based, multi-issue, but still economics-centered progressive social movement they wanted rather than the dominant ethnicity-based theory and its class-focused and nation-based theory challengers of the 1960s. Like Wilson and other class- or socioeconomic status-centered scholars and activists who engaged in conceptual colonization, their goal was to develop a progressive democratic movement that, by ultimately going beyond "race" and racism, would appeal to the majority of Americans. Consequently, their own racial formation theory was more driven by the authors' liberal coalitional movement ideology and strategy than their own interest in racial oppression and the facts regarding its prevalence, persistence, nature, workings, consequences, and eradication.[6]

Omi and Winant were fully aware of the reactionary social and historical context in which they conceived their theory. In regard to race relations, they described the 1960s as a decade of movement, the 1970s as one of quiescence, and the 1980s as a time of backlash. However, they seemed not to have appreciated the differences between the confrontationist inclination of much of the scholarship of the early 1970s and the accommodationist tendency of that of the late 1970s. In addition, they seemed unaware of how the race relations of the 1980s may have tempered their own work. They were especially blind to how it may have facilitated their retreat from scholarship that analyzed racist structures characteristic of much of the insurgent literature of the late 1960s and early 1970s (e.g., domestic colonialism and institutional racism) to a poststructuralist reduction of racism to largely individual-level bigotry and of race relations to fairly open and power pluralistic struggles over various racial projects like the cultural nationalism pushed by some African Americans.[7]

Unlike the racism theories that emerged from the civil rights movement in the late 1960s and early1970s, or even earlier race relations theories, the main focus of Omi and Winant's theory was the ever-changing politics and meanings of "race." As they put it, "our theory of *racial formation* emphasizes the social nature of race, the absence of any essential racial characteristics, the historical flexibility of racial meanings and categories, the conflictual character of race at both the 'micro-' and 'macro-social' levels, and the irreducible political aspect of racial dynamics." Defining racial formation as "the process by which social, economic and political forces determine the content and importance of racial categories, and by which they are in turn shaped by racial meanings," they maintained that "crucial to this formulation is the treatment of race as a *central axis* of social relations that cannot be subsumed under or reduced to some broader category or conception." Omi and Winant therefore argued that rather than being treated as a "fixed, concrete and objective" "*essence*," race should be understood as "*an unstable and 'decentered' complex of social meanings constantly being transformed by political struggle.*" A third key concept for racial formation theory was the racial state, which in their approach assumed that the state does not simply intervene as a mediator of racial conflict but that it was "inherently racial" and moreover was "itself increasingly the pre-eminent site of racial conflict." Through these and other conceptualizations, the major contribution Omi and Winant offered to race relations and racism theory was a dynamic approach to the politics of racial categories and conflicts. Not central to their "race"-centered analysis was the concept of racism, which in a note they limited to "those social practices which (explicitly or implicitly) attribute merits or allocate values to members of racially categorized groups solely because of their 'race.'"[8]

In their book's second edition, Omi and Winant acknowledged that racial formation theory was indeed intended "to reformulate the concept of racism"—a concept that they, like Wilson, argued was overly expanded during the heat of the civil rights movement. In a new section entitled "What is Racism?" Omi and Winant stated that they did not like the focus on institutional and systemic racism for a number of reasons, including their belief that the conceptual "'inflation'" of racism resulted in "a deep pessimism about any efforts to overcome racial barriers" because "an overly comprehensive view of racism" could function as "a self-fulfilling prophecy." Under this essentially "it doesn't make us feel good" line of reasoning against a large and robust definition of racism, the authors chose instead a conceptually minimist and power-pluralistic notion of multiple racisms, which also included what they cast as "racism" against European Americans. Apparently they did not give much consideration to *who*, racially, would feel good or bad by having their racial experiences, worldviews, and movements affirmed or denied by those opposing definitions. Their conclusion that the mere acknowledgment that racial oppression is systemic is somehow disempowering to the oppressed reveals an amazing blindness both to how social oppression works and to the lessons of the successes of the civil rights movement and other liberation struggles throughout history. Finally, despite the existence of much research in many fields that suggest otherwise, they decided to retain the notion that race should be treated as being conceptually distinct from racism rather than its ideological core.[9]

In their third edition of *Racial Formation in the United States* Omi and Winant stated that, although each chapter had been radically revised, because their book had so well stood the test of time, its core argument remained intact. One difference that is quickly noticeable, however, is its language—both the more frequent use of the word racism and its pairing with race—which suggested that what they now offered as their contribution to "racial theory" was not just a theory of race, or more specifically racial formation, but of race and racism. Indeed, their stated goal was now "to develop an overarching perspective on both race and racism." Unfortunately, their increased interest in racism seemed largely intended to subsume it under their conceptualization of race. Making race much larger and more sociologically significant than racism, as they put the latter back in its more manageable, pre–civil rights movement place, entailed some fancy and logic-trampling analytical footwork. For example, despite their earlier acknowledgment that "the construction of race and racial meanings" "is not benign," they go so far as to suggest that the race concept can indeed be a good thing. Once again reflecting their fundamental misunderstanding of the origins, nature, and functions of race, they removed the concept from its specific historical and geographic context as a justification for colonial and slavery-based exploitation and went so far as to declare that "'making up people,'" placing people into racial categories, is something we all do as "part of a universal phenomenon of classifying people on the basis of real or imagined attributes." Thus they not only defended and praised race, but engaged in the linguistic racial accommodation practice of conceptual colonization by boldly reducing racism to but one component of the assumed larger and more sociologically significant conceptualization of race.

> Powerful as racism is, it does not exhaust race. It does not crowd out antiracism or eliminate the emancipatory dimensions of racial identity, racial solidarity, or racially conscious agency, both individual and collective. Indeed race is so profoundly a lived-in and lived-out part of both social structure and identity that it *exceeds and transcends* racism—thereby allowing for resistance to racism. Race, therefore, is *more* than racism; it is a fully fledged "social fact" like sex/gender or class. From this perspective, race shapes racism as much as racism shapes race.[10]

Again, it is their racially liberal, historically blind, and bogus assumption that the race concept is essentially benign and not necessarily hierarchical that causes Omi and Winant to write things that are so greatly at odds with what we now know about both race and racism. If race is a benign concept, and one without a historical beginning, and therefore no possibility of an end, then we can indeed imagine a world in which racialized groups still exist, but there is either no racism or so little racism that it is merely one of many different competing racial projects. Such a specious argument could only be believed if we were to completely ignore what the latest and most credible historical, anthropological, and natural science research tells us about the origins, nature, and functions of the race concept. Although researchers in many disciplines other than sociology (e.g., African American scholars like anthropologist Audrey Smedley and evolutionary biologist Joseph L. Graves)[11] are at the forefront of this "no race" understanding, too many sociologists just won't let it go.

Despite Omi and Winant's implicit criticism and their aim to move the field beyond more explicit analyses of systemic racism, the proponents of systemic racism theory were slow to respond. One of the first critiques from this perspective came from David T. Wellman. In the second, 1993, edition of *Portraits of White Racism* Wellman argued that racial formation theory "fails as a theory of racism" because it is racism evasive in its focus on race as an ideology rather than racism as a system. Although Omi and Winant are likely to respond that developing a theory of systemic racism, a notion they rejected, was never their intent, the specifics of Wellman's critique merit our attention, especially his concerns about racial formation theory largely ignoring oppression-centered issues like hierarchy, power, and privilege. In making his case, Wellman asserted that

> ironically, although *race* is central to the American experience in Omi and Winant's account *racism is not*. Racial formation is a theory of racial meanings, not racial privilege. They analyze neither the social location occupied by European Americans, nor the benefits associated with that location. Conceptually speaking, then, racism is not a crucial element in their theoretical formulation. It is defined almost as an afterthought.[12]

In brief, Wellman criticized Omi and Winant's racial formation theory because white racial privilege is not central to its perspective; it reduces the problem of racial oppression largely to linguistic and discourse issues; aside from its work on the racial state it is for the most part disconnected from political and economic structures; and racism and racial oppression are not at its analytical core.[13]

Only recently—more than two and a half decades after the publication of Omi and Winant's first edition—did Joe Feagin respond in a comprehensive manner to that challenge to the wisdom of the very existence of racism studies. Feagin and his coauthor, Sean Elias, laid out the following specific criticisms of racial formation theory from a systemic racism theory perspective: its failure to address "whites' centrality in societal racism"; its "one-sided emphasis on 'meanings of race'" rather than on struggles over racially structured institutions, power, and material resources; its overemphasis of the state relative to other sources and sites of racial oppression, conflict, and change; its pluralist view of competing racial projects in their "oxymoronic" notion of a "'racial democracy'"; its overly optimistic view of the racial progress made in the United States; and its "dismissal of much critical black thought as radical."[14]

Racial formation theory—essentially an anti-systemic racism theory—achieves much of its racially accommodative function through extremely racism-evasive language. While subtle and indirect in their approach, as I noted earlier, Omi and Winant engaged in what ultimately amounted to conceptual colonization. By theoretically capturing the issue of racial oppression and through conceptual minimization reducing it to individual racial bigotry, they seemed to hope to transcend the troublesome notion of systemic racism to realize their own political vision of a multi-issue, but economics-dominant, progressive social movement. Indeed, consistent with their poststructuralist and pluralistic conception of power, these authors rarely used relational terminology. Instead, by referring to the body of work they critique and contribute to as "racial theory," Omi and Winant engage in conceptual rejection as they avoid theorizing about *relationships*, be it race relations, racial oppression, or racism. Instead they seem to be more comfortable with the conceptual misdirection embedded in the use of terms like "racial minorities" and with the conceptual obfuscation inherent in the use of phrases like "the centrality of race" and "the issue of race."[15]

Despite the serious flaws in Omi and Winant's conceptualization of race and racism, as is evident by their use of language like "structures of domination," their theory work does make some important contributions to our understanding of systemic racism. Chief among these is their conceptualization of the racial state as its political apparatus, together with their very dynamic approach to racial politics. Omi and Winant not only help us to understand the nature, function, and workings of the racial state and its key role in the coordination of systemic racism, but also provide revealing insights into how its structures and dynamics change, both as a stimulus and as a response to the changing dynamics of race relations during different historical periods characterized by various mechanisms of racial control like colonization, slavery, Jim Crow, and today's economic neoliberalism. This fluid conceptualization of race relations can also incorporate the effects of various challenges from the racially oppressed.[16]

Unfortunately racial formation theory rejects two core premises of racism studies: the myth of race and the reality of racism. Omi and Winant appear to be blind to the facts that, first, race is not only an erroneous, but an inherently racist concept[17] and that, second, racism is an important social phenomenon that cannot be reduced to mere racist practices and should be conceptualized both directly and explicitly. Consequently they reject efforts to abolish the race concept as the ideology at the heart of systems of racial oppression just as they criticize the very concept of racism as being both inflated and outdated. To the extent that they refer to racism, they deflate its meaning by both reducing it to but one component of an assumed much larger concept of race and referring to many "racisms." Finally, when they do use the term racism, which they view as being non-systemic in nature, they do so in a way that does not distinguish between the racial bigotry of individuals and racism as a well-organized feature of highly racialized societies. In brief, while dismissing the very notion of racism studies, despite its social constructionist premise, racial formation theory actually reifies race—its major concern—by treating it as a valid social science concept that is not to be challenged, but upon which research projects and careers may be built. As you have seen, a key goal of racial formation theory is to discount and bypass the concept of systemic racism that Omi and Winant see as being troublesome to their progressive majoritarian movement strategy. When it comes to addressing the myth of race and the reality of racism, Omi and Winant's racial formation theory gets things backward, treating contemporary racism largely as an inflated if not anachronistic myth while the race concept—social construction or not—is assumed to be real. At the core of this analytical illogic is their fundamental misunderstanding of both concepts.

Critical Race Theory

While politically moderate and liberal social scientists were realigning themselves with the rightward movement of the nation, another group of scholars pushed forward from the left margins of one of its most powerful and conservative institutions: the American legal system. Although that movement traces its origins to the 1970s when legal scholars and activist lawyers grew concerned with what they saw as the demise of the civil rights movement as a driver of progressive change, critical race theory (CRT) scholars did not hold their first national conference until the last year of the 1980s. With intellectual roots in critical legal studies, radical feminist theory, radical European intellectuals like Antonio Gramsci and Michel Foucault; leaders of radical African American and Latino American thought like Sojourner Truth, Frederick Douglass, W. E. B. Du Bois, Martin Luther King Jr., and Cesar Chavez; as well as others from the black power and Chicano movements, critical race theory was built on the following basic tenets. First, consistent with a systemic racism perspective, racism is assumed to be "ordinary, not aberrational." Second, racism as a social system serves multiple functions for the racially dominant group. Third, the race concept and racial categories are assumed to be social constructions, not biologically based essences. Fourth, the racialization of a particular group may differ over time given the needs of the dominant racialized group, and the consequences of racialization are different for each group. Fifth, each individual has multiple social group memberships (e.g., a heterosexual, low-income, African American woman) and "potentially conflicting, overlapping identities, loyalties, and allegiances." And finally, people with different racialized group experiences (e.g., Native Americans, African Americans, Latino Americans, and Asian Americans) have "a unique voice of color" that should be heard that reflects their own "presumed confidence to speak about race and racism."[18]

The following are prominent themes that characterize the work of CRT scholars. The conceptual themes of *"interest convergence, material determinism, and racial realism"* refer to CRT's rejection of the approach of racial "'idealists'" who reduce racism to attitudes, ideas, and other mental and linguistic constructions for a "'realists'" view that racism exists because it creates and sustains material and other benefits for the racially dominant group. Another CRT theme is its *"critique of liberalism,"* which rejects liberalism and its strategies like color-blindness for addressing the nation's serious problem of systemic racism. Finally, the CRT theme of *"structural determinism"* assumes that "our system, by reason of its structure and vocabulary, is ill equipped to redress certain types of wrong." This suggests, for example, that professional, discipline, funding, and department structures that discourage the use of straightforward language like racism, white racism, racial oppression, and the racially oppressed are incapable of providing straightforward and honest analyses of such phenomena.[19]

CRT scholars have used storytelling to bring forth the voices of the racially oppressed. Its power is evident in the work of one of the movement's founders, Derrick Bell. His *Faces at the Bottom of the Well: The Permanence of Racism* used parables to argue that racism is a permanent feature of the structure of American society. In this way Bell's book, and the CRT movement more generally, challenged the poststructuralist sociologists like Omi and Winant who tried to move the discipline back to a time when the concept of systemic racism had not been pushed to the center of its race relations discourse.[20]

Ironically, given its name and its language-focused theme of structural determinism, CRT often makes uncritical use of the term "race" and other race-related terminology (e.g., "black," "white," "minorities") and system-maintaining language. In addition, although CRT rests on its assumption of systemic racism, CRT has done little—apart from useful insights into how racism works within the law—to build the theory needed to explain its workings. As CRT theory has spread, it is often used so loosely as to give theoretical credence to any "critical" examination of "race." Not only do many of those who identify themselves as critical race theorists often ignore its basic assumptions and themes, but they use the pretense of doing critical race *theory* as a way to justify work that, while it may fit an overall power/conflict perspective, is largely atheoretical in its lack of analytical details. As is true for systemic racism theory, critical race theory remains more a set of conceptual assumptions than an actual theory. Consequently, like its conceptual base of systemic racism, CRT's major weakness is conceptual underdevelopment.[21]

Jaynes and Williams's *A Common Destiny*

In 1989 there was still more evidence that mainstream American social science was moving backward when it came to understanding race relations. The National Academy of Sciences published a book, touted as a second Myrdal study, that detailed facts about the status of African Americans drawn from its more than thirty commissioned papers. *A Common Destiny: Blacks and American Society* was like *An American Dilemma* in that it received funding from the Carnegie Corporation and other major foundations, and that it was largely data-driven with even less in the way of race relations theory, and no effort to understand the nature, causes, and workings of racial oppression. This is evident in the fact that race relations were not included among the topics of its five "working panels." Aside from a lone chapter on racial attitudes and behavior, the book dealt primarily with the socioeconomic status of African Americans, the victims of racial oppression, while steering clear of race *relations*-focused analyses, especially systemic racism explanations. Once again, through the process of conceptual misdirection, the focus was safely on the "Negro problem," not the issue identified by the Kerner report two decades earlier as systemic white racism.[22]

The "New Democrats," the Criminal Justice System, and Racial Oppression in the 1990s

President George H. W. Bush's Democratic Party opponent in the 1992 presidential election was "New Democrat" Bill Clinton. As a leader of that party's regressive reform movement, Clinton concluded that the failure of the Democratic Party in national elections was due to the widespread perception that it was too liberal—more specifically, that it was too much in favor of big government, too beholden to African Americans and other people of color, anti-business, too soft on crime and timid on defense, and unable to reach European Americans in the South. While showing himself to be comfortable around and friendly to African Americans, in his campaign Clinton carefully avoided topics that might be perceived as benefiting them, while promising to "'oppose racial quotas'" and to support "'welfare reform.'"[23]

As president, Clinton continued to be adept at appearing to advance African American aspirations while effectively maintaining the racial status quo. African American voters were rewarded through largely symbolic appointments of African Americans to cabinet-level and other key positions while highly racialized substantive federal policies were crafted to fit the wishes of racially conservative European Americans. Such policies included welfare reform based on racist stereotypes like lazy, sexually promiscuous, dishonest, and welfare-dependent black "welfare mothers"; a rejection, ostensibly influenced by Clinton policy advisor William J. Wilson, of race-specific solutions to inner-city poverty; and anticrime initiatives that disproportionately labeled young African American males as criminals and channeled them into the criminal justice system.[24]

In the 1990s racism manifested itself quite visibly throughout the criminal justice system in various forms including not only mass incarceration, but racial profiling and racially targeted police harassment, brutality, and fatal shootings. In March of 1991, four Los Angeles police officers were captured on video viciously beating Rodney King, a plainly subdued African American motorist who had tried to elude them in a high-speed car chase. A year later, again following the pattern that had been repeated in Miami and many other cities, all hell broke loose in the nation's second-largest city after the police officers were acquitted. During six days of civil unrest forty-two people were killed and seven hundred buildings were destroyed, with property damage totaling more than a billion dollars. And that was just the beginning of a decade of intense conflict between African Americans and the police. This was especially true in New York, the nation's largest city, where protests in response to outrageous police behavior like the sadistic sodomizing of Abner Louima and the firing of a fatal barrage of bullets that riddled Amadou Diallo's body when his wallet was mistaken for a weapon, often inflamed by the racially divisive rhetoric of Mayor Giuliani, made the city appear to be on the verge of a racial breakdown.[25]

In 1996 the verdict of not guilty in the trial of the African American football star O. J. Simpson, who was charged with the killing of two European Americans—his ex-wife and a man she was dating—intensified racial tensions for many years to come. That trial and verdict exacerbated a dramatic shift in racial attitudes that was evident two years earlier in a survey that showed less concern about the problems facing the racially oppressed, increasing hostility toward immigrants, and for the first time in the seven years the poll was conducted a majority of European Americans agreeing with the notion that equal rights had been pushed too far.[26] As was true for the 1970s and the 1980s, the impact of such retrenchment of concern about racial matters was evident in the nation's race relations scholarship.

West's *Race Matters*

In the 1990s, even progressive African American intellectuals seemed to adjust their discourse to keep in line with the nation's new political and public-policy center. A case in point is Cornel West's popular and well-received book, *Race Matters*. By engaging in the same conceptual conflation of racism and poverty and equating culture as a structure equal to those two in affecting the life chances of low-income African Americans, philosophy Professor West joined many conservatives, moderates, and liberal social scientists in blaming much of African American poverty on what was assumed to be African American–specific pathology; what used to be referred to as simply the "Negro problem." Ignoring the fact that in capitalist societies throughout the world poverty has the same effect in lowering aspirations and in generating crime, hopelessness, and other social problems regardless of the racialized ethnicity of the poor, West, in his essentially culture of poverty argument, went so far as to conclude that "the most basic issue now facing black America" is its own "*nihilistic threat to its very existence.*"[27]

Eduardo Bonilla-Silva's ASR Article

In the racially intense political environment of the 1990s, even the extremely racism-evasive *American Sociological Review* published an article that actually contained the word *racism* in its title. That action might seem like a bold move on the part of *ASR*, the flagship journal of the American Sociological Association. However, the "racism" that the ASA allowed was not the large and robust, systemic racism African Americans had forced into the national discourse through social protest. Instead, the article's focus was on *rethinking* racism through a compromise that would, through contextualization, make it appear bigger than it had been treated in most of the racism as attitude or ideology-centered scholarship, but still allow it to remain much smaller than the experientially based knowledge of the racially oppressed that the phenomenon they endure daily is, indeed, systemic. By repackaging, and thus relegitimating what is essentially an old, less challenging, and more manageable sociological conceptualization of racism, it had an effect that was actually conservative and system sustaining.

In the abstract to that 1996 article, "Rethinking Racism: Toward a Structural Interpretation," Eduardo Bonilla-Silva, who has identified himself racially as a "black" Puerto Rican, promised to fill a void by introducing "*a structural theory of racism based on the notion of racialized social systems.*" After identifying racism as the "central topic" for those who would understand whatever it was that he meant by "racial matters," Bonilla-Silva complained that most who study racism treat it as "a purely ideological phenomenon." But then Bonilla-Silva himself adopted what the critical race theorists argue is a racial "idealist" viewpoint, a perspective Bonilla-Silva criticized, by restricting his own definition of racism to ideology: "I use the term *racism* only to describe the racial ideology of a racialized social system." In doing so, he rejected both the materialist orientation of the racial "realist" view of CRT scholars and the civil rights movement's victory in having racism be recognized as a system or social structure. Instead Bonilla-Silva was content to reduce racism to being "only part of a larger racial system." In the end, his attempt to reduce rac*ism* to just the ideology of a racialized social system is as credible as someone insisting that capital*ism* and colonial*ism* are merely the ideological components of those systems of economic and political exploitation.[28]

Based on the erroneous assumption that ideology on the one hand, and an oppressive system on the other, can credibly be viewed as being sufficiently distinct to make such a distinction, Bonilla-Silva tried to convince the reader that his article, building on the work of institutionalized racism, internal colonialism, and racial formation theories, offered a significant new contribution by making explicit the connecting arrow between the two. In brief, his thesis suffered from the logical fallacy of seeking to make a distinction without a difference.[29]

The reader is left wondering if there really is a meaningful difference between what others deem as systemic racism and Bonilla-Silva's conceptualization of racialized social systems as "societies in which economic, political, social, and ideological levels are partially structured by the placement of actors in racial categories or races" that involve "some form of hierarchy that produces definite social relations between the races" and between systemic racism and his definition of "the racial structure of a society" as "the totality of . . . racialized social relations and practices." Both seem to suggest that racialized societies and their racial categories —which are, as Bonilla-Silva acknowledged, always hierarchical in nature—are inherently racist. If so, why not simply use the term racist social system or systemic racism? Otherwise we are left pondering how a *racialized* social system could exist without being *racist*. Finally, since by racism Bonilla-Silva means only racial ideology, wouldn't it be less confusing to refer to his theory as a structural theory of racial ideology?[30] As a *"structural theory of racism,"* Bonilla-Silva's article suffers from conceptual minimization and underdevelopment.

An equally important and closely related flaw in Bonilla-Silva's work is his convenient misunderstanding of the race concept. As I noted earlier, unless one assumes, like Omi and Winant, that the concept of race is benign—that it is not inherently hierarchical and therefore intrinsically racist—it is illogical to presume, as do Wilson and Omi and Winant, that a "racialized social system" could exist without being more precisely a *racist* social system. And if a racialized social system is by definition a racist social system, then what we have is simply systemic racism that, like other oppressive systems, is justified by its ideological core component—in this case the race concept. By ignoring that simple fact, along with the hard-fought lessons of the civil rights movement, Bonilla-Silva's theory work neatly fits the politics of linguistic racial accommodation.

What is ironic and perplexing about Bonilla-Silva's work is that he obviously employs a systemic racism perspective. This is evident by his acknowledgment of the influence of the "institutionalist" and internal colonialism theories. It is also evident in much of his language (e.g., "racialized social system," "racial system" "racial structure," "racial practices" that are "embedded in normal operations of institutions," and *systematic* discrimination") and by his own assertion that in his approach "racism is viewed as systemic." But still he refuses to define racism as more than a structurally embedded ideology. It is as if he is a town crier whose job it is to warn his fellow citizens of the return of a monster that has wreaked havoc on their village for centuries. However, that rather simple task is made nearly impossible because, although he dutifully shouts out a description of some of the ugly details of the monster's appearance, he refuses to call its name.[31] Through his conceptual minimization of racism Bonilla-Silva helped shrink the concept back to the relatively tiny size most social scientists allowed it to have prior to the modern civil rights movement and its push for the institutionalized and systemic racism perspectives.

Carter A. Wilson's *Racism: From Slavery to Advanced Capitalism*

Ironically, a book published the same year as Bonilla-Silva's *ASR* article, which was written by an African American political scientist, made an impressive and sophisticated case that racism is indeed systemic. Unfortunately, both within the discipline of sociology and elsewhere, Carter A. Wilson's *Racism: From Slavery to Advanced Capitalism*—which built on ideas expressed in Joel Kovel's *White Racism*—has been largely ignored. A Google Scholar search I did on June 11, 2015 revealed only 69 citations for Carter A. Wilson's *Racism* compared with 1334 citations for William J. Wilson's *The Declining Significance of Race*. This suggests that in explaining the low socioeconomic status of African Americans, 90 percent of whom experience poverty at some point in their adult lives, William J. Wilson and other sociologists successfully shifted much of the focus away from systemic racism factors like housing and job discrimination, and racism in the educational, criminal justice, and health care systems back to the less controversial, victim-centered, and more racially accommodative subculture of the African American "underclass." The reason that even progressive scholars of color do not cite Carter A. Wilson's well-crafted book on racism is likely the simple fact that it does not reflect their scholarly interests and needs—which happen to fit closely those of their professional disciplines, and of the larger society and its white power structure. It is not that they can't find a good book on racism theory. It is more likely that they don't even look.[32]

Although Carter A. Wilson's book offered a comprehensive, historically rooted, and multidimensional theory of systemic racism that accounted for the macro-level economic, political, and cultural changes in how racism manifests itself, like other systemic racism theories, in some important ways, it remained conceptually underdeveloped. For example, in addition to not accounting for relevant gender dynamics, it also failed to specify the structures, processes, and institutional transactions through which racism operates at any particular time.

President Clinton's Race Initiative

In 1997 President Bill Clinton announced his administration's race initiative, which some ambitious sociologists and other race relations–focused social scientists imagined to be their *American Dilemma* moment. They were badly mistaken. Although that undertaking did essentially subcontract out to another organization the sponsorship of some socioeconomic status studies, its centerpiece was not research, theory, or policy, but instead the promotion of interracial dialogue. The initiative's report did, however, reflect the social science of much of the pre- and postmodern civil rights movement era in that its focus was not on racism as a highly organized system of oppression but racism once again reduced to, as one critic put it, "the level of individual beliefs and actions." In this way Clinton's race initiative "effectively nullified the concept of institutionalized racism" which, along with the phrase white racism, was given credence by the Kerner report. What had changed in the nearly three decades between? It was most likely politics that accounted for that conceptual minimization. The Kerner report was initiated by President Johnson while American cities burned, whereas the Clinton initiative was begun after national politics had shifted decisively to the right—perhaps as an effort by Clinton, during his second term, to shore up his legacy as a racial healer who was sensitive to the needs of African Americans, his most loyal supporters.[33]

The work of the President's Advisory Board on Race—established by an executive order on June 13, 1997—also suffered from its conceptual rejection of terms like racism and racial oppression and reference to racial hierarchies, and from its conceptual obfuscation in that the word race is used so loosely as to be almost meaningless. Note the racism-evasive language in the executive order's goals and objectives (italics mine). The main function of the advisory board was to "advise the President *on matters involving race and racial reconciliation*" including the following tasks:

> Promote a constructive national dialogue to confront and work through challenging *issues that surround race.*
>
> Increase the Nation's understanding of our recent history of race relations and the course our Nation is charting on *issues of race relations and racial diversity.*
>
> Bridge *racial divides* by encouraging leaders in communities throughout the Nation to develop and implement innovative approaches to calming racial tensions.
>
> Identify, develop, and implement solutions to problems in areas in which *race has a substantial impact*, such as education, economic opportunity, housing, health care, and the administration of justice.[34]

Theoretical Fragmentation: The White Backlash and Its Legacy of Failure 115

While it is certainly not unusual for the language of the executive branch of government to be sufficiently vague to seek to build the broad-based consensus thought necessary to ensure its political palatability,[35] the conceptually obfuscating language italicized above is both racism evasive and racially accommodative in that it says little to suggest that systemic white racism is a problem.

The goal of the Clinton initiative was neither to study racial problems—however defined—nor to develop policy recommendations to address them but, rather, simply to organize fifteen months of national dialogue about "race." This ultimately entailed "conversations" through various types of forums involving "approximately 17,000 people in 39 States and 89 cities." With the Right wing's strong offensive against affirmative action and civil-rights related policies in the 1990s, even that caused controversy. The head of the initiative was John Hope Franklin, the noted African American historian who had previously chaired a working panel for the research project published as *A Common Destiny*. Franklin complained in a foreword to a publication containing that report, published more than a decade later, that President Clinton remained silent while the board came under attack for not including staunch conservatives on the panel and barely mentioned its appointment in his lengthy autobiography. Apparently there was not even enough interest in what was widely viewed as a failed effort of little consequence for a commercial publisher to print its report. Clearly this was no Kerner report.[36]

In his introduction to that Yale University Press publication of the report released twelve years after Clinton announced his "race" initiative, Steven F. Lawson expressed curiosity as to why Clinton failed to follow through on even the rather modest recommendations of the racially accommodative report, which included: "strengthen civil rights enforcement," "improve data collection on racial and ethnic discrimination," and "strengthen laws and enforcement against hate crimes." Lawson surmised that, "written to appeal to unity and reconciliation, the text was carefully constructed to avoid confrontational language or cast[ing] blame." After observing that it called for neither major new programs like the War on Poverty nor significant new legislation, he stated that "the core of its recommendations concerns education and healing" and continued dialogue. Lawson quoted the *New York Times* conclusion that the recommendations were "modest" and broke "little new ground." He placed that failure in its political and racial context, with his observation "that politicians and the public did not more eagerly embrace such a moderate and largely inoffensive approach suggests a great deal about the racial attitudes and complacency that existed and that continue to do so." That complacency was also evident in Franklin's cover letter to Clinton, in which he twice referred to the report Clinton had apparently committed himself to write and deliver to the American people. President Clinton, whose time was increasingly consumed in dealing with his sex scandal involving the intern Monica Lewinsky and the resulting impeachment proceedings, and growing concern about a possible war with Iraq, wrote no such report and drew up no "work plan" of policy proposals.[37]

Smelzer, Wilson, and Mitchell's America Becoming

Clinton's race initiative, with the President's Council of Economic Advisors, also sponsored the publication of twenty-eight papers presented at a conference that met at the National Research Council in October of 1998. Those papers, with William J. Wilson as one of their three coeditors, were published by the National Academy of Sciences as *America Becoming: Racial Trends and Their Consequences*. Like *A Common Destiny* and *An American Dilemma*, it largely comprised factual information about the social, economic, and political conditions of non–European American racialized groups. But unlike the Myrdal study, neither *A Common Destiny* nor *America Becoming* had an overarching theoretical framework about racial relations in the United States that attempted to tie those many facts together.[38]

Unlike the Kerner Commission report, Clinton's executive order for his President's Advisory Board on Race gave the impression that to the extent the nation had a racial problem it was in no way hierarchical group relations. Instead, through conceptual misdirection, the problem was portrayed as being one largely of inadequate communication between socially, politically, and economically equal racial groups. While both Myrdal's study and the Kerner report reflected a liberal consensus on the centrality of individual-level racial prejudice and institutionalized white racism respectively, *A Common Destiny* and the *One America in the Twenty-First Century* report of Clinton's race initiative and its *America Becoming* offspring helped complete the conceptual misdirection project of Moynihan, William J. Wilson, and others that took the focus of social-science research off racism.

In her rejection of the popular view that Clinton's "race" initiative was a colossal failure, Claire Jean Kim argued that it was, indeed, quite successful in recasting current racial discourse and policies away from the racial liberalism ushered in by *An American Dilemma* during the postwar period to the cultural pathology focus that dominates the study of the African American poor today.

> Clinton's race initiative repudiated this liberal orthodoxy, essentializing racial/cultural differences and arguing that the race problem consisted not of White racism but of the threat these differences posed to national unity. This recasting of the American Dilemma reflected two major ideological developments of the post-civil rights era: the growing liberal-conservative consensus on the need to move beyond a focus on racism and race in public policy and the spread of multiculturalist ideas and rhetoric.[39]

This is the political context in which American social science began to abandon the systemic racism perspective. That environment persists, as President Obama made clear in his 2008 speech on "race" in Philadelphia when he indicated that he found the idea that racism is endemic in America to be offensive. Then and now, the political message is clear to sociologists and other social scientists: a large and robust conceptualization of racism as being systemic is, once again, officially off limits.

Racial Politics in the New Millennium

In a practice they have pursued in every presidential election since then, during the 2000 presidential campaign Republicans intensified their efforts to, in the name of ensuring voting integrity, suppress the votes of African Americans and other groups (e.g., the poor, Latinos, and students) who have traditionally been inclined to vote Democratic. The nation took a sharp rightward turn the following year, after terrorist attacks in the United States on September 11 by Islamist extremists from Saudi Arabia and other middle-eastern countries. Those attacks were followed by a rise in highly racialized animus toward people of middle-eastern ancestry including Arab Americans and other ethnic groups mistaken for middle-easterners.[40]

Less than a year after his reelection, George W. Bush faced and failed a challenge that literally brought to the surface for the world to see the persistence of racial and economic inequality in the United States. For days after New Orleans's poorly designed, built, and maintained levees broke in the wake of Hurricane Katrina, while President Bush vacationed at his ranch in Texas, the world saw seemingly countless media images of dark-skinned people clinging to rooftops, with no food and no clean water. It was as though the most affluent nation on the planet had neither boats, nor helicopters, nor trained personnel, to rescue those too poor to flee the city. For many African Americans throughout the country, a more plausible explanation was articulated by hip-hop artist Kanye West, who proclaimed during a nationally televised fundraiser that "George Bush doesn't care about black people!" Apparently most African Americans agreed, as indicated in a poll a month and a half later that showed Bush's approval rating among African American had dropped to just 2 percent.[41]

Republicans soon found that they did not have just an African American problem; Latino Americans and other advocates for immigrants took to the streets that following year to protest what appeared to many observers to be racist immigration policies. For years the Republicans had been pushing tough and highly racialized policies regarding what they framed as a problem of "illegal aliens." By the mid-2000s Latinos in the United States pushed back through social protest that had grown too large to ignore. These included annual May Day rallies in support of immigrants. In 2006 a million and a half people (including 400,000 in Chicago alone) participated in May Day rallies in dozens of cities nationwide to pressure the U.S. Congress to grant legal status to the nation's undocumented immigrants.[42]

Racial tensions came to a boil in the small town of Jena, Louisiana, in 2007 after an African American student sat under the "White Tree" at the local high school—a tree that by tradition was reserved exclusively for European American students. The next day a trio of nooses appeared on that tree—a symbol African American residents of that town saw as a threatening turf marker of the long history of lynchings of African Americans in the American South. It did not take long for those racial tensions to boil over into violence when a European American boy was beaten by six African American teenagers. Instead of the African American youth being charged with assault and tried as juveniles, the local district attorney charged them with attempted murder and made clear his intention to try them as adults. Protests against those severe charges reached their climax with the convergence of 10,000 mostly young, African American people from across the nation on Jena, which had a population of only 3000. Those efforts were successful in pressuring the local authorities to reduce the charges against the defendants to what was more in line with what the protesters considered to be their actual actions.[43]

The year after the Jena Six movement, 2008, there was a presidential election that proved historic for African Americans. While Barack Obama's election may have caused some Americans to become unrealistically optimistic about the nation's racial progress, a Gallup poll taken about a year after that historic event suggested that little had actually changed. It found no significant increase in the percentage of Americans who believed that race problems would eventually be resolved (56 percent), although a one-day Gallup poll conducted the day after Obama's election had found a spike of optimism to 67 percent. The more normal 56 percent figure was virtually identical (55 percent) to when the question was first asked in 1963 during the peak of the civil rights movement. Indeed, for African Americans optimism dropped in 2009 compared to the previous year. As is typical for such polls, there was a huge racial divide, with most European Americans expressing the belief that the nation's racial problems would eventually be worked out, while most African Americans disagreed.[44]

Contrary to the hard-pushed declining significance of race and the coming of a post-racial America argument, civil rights issues were abundant and clearly visible in the early years of the 2010 decade. An Associated Press poll conducted in 2012 found that racial prejudice had actually increased since President Obama's election four years earlier and that a majority of Americans now expressed negative feelings toward African Americans.[45] In the highly racialized Republican Party primary, Newt Gingrich frequently referred to President Obama as the "food stamp president." During an Iowa caucus campaign appearance, Rick Santorum reportedly told a largely European American audience that he did not want to "make black people's lives better by giving them somebody else's money." Racist comments in Ron Paul's newsletters during the 1980s and 1990s came to light, and shortly before the New Hampshire primary some of his supporters released a video revealing that rival Republican candidate Jon Huntsman had adopted two children from Asia. Later in his presidential campaign Mitt Romney resurrected the old highly racialized Republican standard of "welfare" by falsely accusing Obama of relaxing welfare reform restrictions.[46]

As was true following his 2008 election, there were racist reactions to Obama's reelection. For example, only minutes after Obama's reelection an estimated 550 students at the University of Mississippi shouted racial slurs and taunted other students. There was a similar outpouring of anger and hatred hundreds of miles away at Hampton-Sydney College in Virginia, where some of an estimated forty students not only shouted racial slurs but threw bottles, set off fireworks, and made threats of physical violence outside that college's Minority Student Union. Racist reactions were not limited to college campuses; social media like Twitter and Facebook were flooded with racist postings.[47]

Barely a month after President Obama's second inauguration, a trial verdict threatened to throw the nation into years of racial division not seen since the O. J. Simpson acquittal. That tension began with the fatal shooting of seventeen-year-old Trayvon Martin, an unarmed African American youth, by twenty-eight-year-old George Zimmerman, a neighborhood watch volunteer of European American and Latino American descent. Despite numerous questions raised regarding the validity of Zimmerman's account of the shooting as self-defense, it took more than six weeks of protests, both nationally and locally in Florida, for that state to even bring charges against him. And although Zimmerman did indeed racially profile Trayvon Martin with animus, had no business carrying a gun or engaging anyone while on neighborhood watch, and failed to obey a police dispatcher's order not to follow Martin, the jury—which contained only one person of color—found him innocent of all charges. After that verdict, the mood of African Americans soured, as indicated by protests in cities throughout the nation and by a *Wall Street Journal*/NBC poll that found that most African Americans (54 percent) strongly disagreed with the notion that in America people are judged by the content of their character rather than by the color of their skin. Another 25 percent somewhat disagreed, for a total of 79 percent of African Americans who disagreed with that statement. And President Obama was not immune to that fallout. His approval rating among African Americans dropped ten points from the previous month to a still solid, but less impressive 78 percent.[48]

President Obama was moved by the reaction to the Trayvon Martin shooting to do something he had previously avoided; launch a racially specific program of action. In February of 2014, he announced his "My Brother's Keeper" initiative, targeted at helping African American and Latino American boys and young men. The rationale for the program paralleled some of the racially specific culture of poverty framed appeals the president had previously made for African American males to be socially responsible, but this time he also tepidly suggested that racial discrimination had limited their life chances, although he never actually used those words or the word racism. In setting the stage for that subtle communication, President Obama acknowledged the presence of the parents of Trayvon Martin and of Jordan Davis, another Florida teenager killed by a European American man in the same state. In that speech President Obama identified "boys and young men of color" as an example of "groups that have had the odds stacked against them." He also mentioned "disparities" in the "criminal justice system that have hit the African American and Latino communities especially hard." And he highlighted the high rates of school suspensions for African American and Latino youth.[49] Those were relatively strong words for a president who had been inclined toward racism evasiveness during much of his two administrations.

Unfortunately, the slayings of unarmed African American youth continued. Here are just a few examples. Less than two weeks after President Obama's reelection, Jordan Davis, whom I mentioned earlier, joined Martin as another unarmed seventeen-year-old African American male who was shot by a European American man in Florida, in this instance for playing music too loud. Like George Zimmerman, the defendant, Michael Dunn, expressed strong animus toward young African American men. Indeed, he encouraged his lawyers to build his stand-your-ground-law defense around his alleged fear of dangerous African American "thugs." Less than a year later in Charlotte, North Carolina, a European American police officer shot twenty-four-year-old Jonathan Ferrell ten times when, after an automobile accident, Ferrell sought help by knocking on the door of a suburban resident. In an eerily similar killing less than two months later, Renisha McBride was shot in the face with a shotgun at close range by a European American man in Dearborn Heights, Michigan after she ran onto his porch seeking help following an automobile accident.[50]

In July of 2014 on Staten Island, New York, Eric Garner, a forty-three-year-old African American father of six under arrest for selling "loosies" (untaxed cigarettes), was videotaped as police officers pinned him to the ground, one of them administered a department-banned chokehold, and they ignored his numerous pleas that he could not breathe. The New York City Medical Examiner ruled Garner's death a homicide. A month later the nation became embroiled in yet another intense racial crisis when a European

American police officer in the St. Louis suburb of Ferguson, Missouri, killed Michael Brown, an unarmed African American teenager, in what to many was an execution-style shooting. The situation was inflamed by many actions of the police, including leaving Brown's body in the street for many hours, not releasing the name of the officer who killed him until nearly a week later, the seemingly indiscriminate use of smoke bombs and tear gas against protestors, the deployment of weapons and other equipment usually reserved for military combat, the detention of journalists, and the release of a video of Brown apparently robbing a store that many area residents saw as an attempt to justify his killing by tarnishing his reputation. Such actions fueled weeks of protests, shootings, looting, violent confrontations with the police, and hundreds of arrests. Following more than a hundred days of protest in front of the headquarters of the Ferguson Police Department, a grand jury rendered its decision in a process that many saw to be rigged by a pro-police district attorney who had a reputation for unfairness among local African Americans. When it was announced that the grand jury declined to indict the officer who killed Michael Brown on any of the five possible state charges, violence erupted again in Ferguson and there were protests in cities across the United States. Two days after Brown was killed, Ezell Ford, a twenty-five-year-old mentally ill African American man, was fatally shot by the Los Angeles police, whose account of the shooting differed radically from that of neighborhood witnesses. A week after the decision of the grand jury not to bring charges in the killing of Michael Brown, a grand jury in Staten Island also declined to indict the police officers who killed Eric Garner. Once again racial tensions spiked and protests broke out in cities across the nation. A group concerned about such killings reported that in the United States, in that one year alone, the police killed at least fifty-six unarmed African Americans.[51]

As one newspaper article put it in reference to the racial impact of those killings, "in city after city, 2014 became a year in which the nation's lingering racial fissures burst open." Not surprisingly, a poll conducted in mid-December revealed that most Americans (57 percent) considered race relations to be bad. That trend of increased racial tensions continues. In April 2015 a North Charleston, South Carolina police officer was caught on video as he fatally shot Walter L. Scott in the back eight times as he fled by foot following a traffic stop for a broken taillight. After violent unrest broke out in Baltimore later that same month following the death of Freddie Gray from a mostly severed spine while he was in police custody an NBC News/*Wall Street Journal* poll found that 96 percent of Americans expected more racial unrest that summer with most (54 percent) anticipating that it would happen in a metropolitan area near them. And all that happened before an angry white supremacist, who told a group of African Americans at a bible study group that he had to kill them because blacks raped white women and were taking over the country, killed nine people in that Charleston, South Carolina church.[52] Neither space nor time limitations permit inclusion of other examples of racism to the time of the publication of this book, so I will stop here in mid-2015, as this manuscript enters its production process. I think you get the picture. In the United States such racial madness continues, with no end in sight, as it seems that increasingly America's racial status quo is being protected by angry "white" men with guns. Unfortunately such racial events, which have so profoundly shaken and shaped the consciousness of new generations of African Americans and other racially oppressed people, have been largely ignored in both the substantive and theory work of American sociology. Once again the discipline has proven itself to be at best irrelevant.

More of Bonilla-Silva's Tiny Conceptualization of Racism

In 2001, Eduardo Bonilla-Silva's *White Supremacy and Racism in the Post–Civil Rights Era* expanded upon his interests in the changing nature of "racism" and his racialized social system theory. That book's main argument was that as the needs and structures of racialized social systems change, so does the dominant racial ideology that supports them. For example, extending his *ASR* article's argument, including its assumption that racism is just ideology, Bonilla-Silva reasoned that there has been a shift from the overt and biologically based racial ideology of the Jim Crow era to the more covert, culturally focused "color-blind" racism of today's post–civil rights movement era. Although Bonilla-Silva asserted that his book's "basic contention is that racism should be conceptualized in structural terms," he again settled for a conceptualization that limited racism to its ideational component—an approach he again criticized, while being content with simply contextualizing it.[53]

That Bonilla-Silva's conceptual focus is not systemic racism is clear from the victim-focused subtitle of his Introduction: "Why Are Racial Minorities Behind?" It is not surprising that in making room for what he saw as his work's contribution he began by criticizing the dominant race and ethnic relations paradigm. What is disappointing is his attempt to do so by using the language of that paradigm (e.g., the uncritical acceptance of color-race terminology like "race," "blacks," "whites"; the conceptual misdirection of "racial minorities"; and the conceptual obfuscation of phrases that give the word race agency like "due to race"). And, after offering a scathing critique of the limits of attitudinal research, Bonilla-Silva ultimately confined his theoretical approach to what can be measured through an attitudinal research agenda.[54]

These and other criticisms also characterize *Racism without Racists: Color Blind Racism and the Persistence of Racial Inequality in the United States*, a book Bonilla-Silva published two years later—recently released in its fourth, 2014, edition—that emphasized the institutional racism perspective's focus on the covert, but not its conceptualization of racism as being an oppressive system. Because he shrank racism to its ideology, Bonilla-Silva confused the color-blind ideology that sustains systemic racism (by justifying that nothing substantial needs to be done to address it) with what he called color-blind racism. Consistent with the poststructuralists he did not embrace, he seemed to believe that there are different racisms that emerge at different times rather than a transformative system of racial oppression that persists because it is adept at manifesting itself in different forms consistent with its survival needs at a particular time and under a particular set of circumstances. In Bonilla-Silva's view, each new racial ideology or attitude can be viewed as a new racism. Another problem is his confusion of racial bigotry (e.g., his conceptual minimist use of the term "racists" to refer to individuals) with racism, which is in fact a system of oppression.[55]

Using the terminology of a systemic racism perspective, Bonilla-Silva did acknowledge that people of color still face "*systemic* discrimination," and that in contrast to most European Americans, who reduce racism to prejudice, "for most people of color racism is systemic or institutionalized." And certainly Bonilla-Silva realized that when African Americans complain that they cannot get ahead because of the way "the Man" has things set up, they are not simply referring to racial ideologies or attitudes that are systemically embedded. But in the end, even with his work to structurally contextualize racism, his attempt to shrink the concept of racism to what he considered to be a more sociologically manageable size through his own tiny conceptualization of it as "a sociopolitical concept that refers exclusively to racial ideology that glues a particular racial order," combined with his failure to treat the race concept as an inherently racist ideology, did not allow him to use the term *systemic racism* to refer to what racism clearly is: a system of oppression that is justified by the ideology of race.[56]

Although Bonilla-Silva complained about racism evasiveness in society, much of his own language is racism evasive. For example, the first chapter of *Racism without Racists* quoted Albert Memmi's book *Racism* as its epigraph: "there is a strange kind of enigma associated with the problem of racism. No one, or almost no one, wishes to see themselves as racist; still, racism persists, real and tenacious." Yet Bonilla-Silva entitled that chapter "The Strange Enigma of Race in Contemporary America"—a linguistic switch-up that is indeed a "strange kind of enigma." Another example is found in the section "Key Terms: Race, Racial Structure, and Racial Ideology," where Bonilla-Silva introduced the concepts that are central to his analysis, and the concept of racism is not included. The book's index cited page 102 for Bonilla-Silva's definition of racism, and on that page his "structural definition of 'racism'" was mentioned, but racism was not actually defined.[57]

After reducing racism to its ideological component, Bonilla-Silva found himself needing a larger, more substantial concept. In the end he turned to the sufficiently vague and non-controversial conceptual catch-all of "race." The book's actual focus is how color-blind ideology (which in the social sciences is often operationalized as racial *attitudes*) is central to the operation of the United States as a highly racialized social structure. His conceptually minimist approach, like that of William J. Wilson, Omi and Winant, and others, is much too small to encompass the reality of racism as a system of oppression. In his failed attempt to solve that problem Bonilla-Silva tried to jerry-rig the racialized social system onto his racism as ideology approach to give it more breadth and depth. Where he made his mistake is that he confused the part of the answer his work provided in helping us to understand racial ideology and attitudes with the whole of systemic racism. Still, Bonilla-Silva made an important contribution in helping us to understand how such ideologies and attitudes operate in highly racialized democracies where, because of conflicting ideals like equality, racism is often kept covert.

Bonilla-Silva has more recently provided an autobiographical account of his evolution as a sociologist and reflected on the strengths and weaknesses of his "racialized social system approach." In that article he revealed that neither his community activism as a student in Puerto Rico nor his graduate school courses and dissertation were in the area of race relations. Instead, his interest was class relations. Consistent with the Marxist tradition of conceptual colonization, which saw racism as an ideology used to justify exploitative class relations, in the formative years of his thinking about race relations Bonilla-Silva came to see racism as only an ideology. That approach was also a good fit with a grant that afforded him access to lots of attitudes-centered data and for his later publication in the *American Sociological Review*. Although Bonilla-Silva has refined his theory work on race and racism and does study the phenomena as being important in their own right, he has retained its treatment of racism as ideological beliefs.[58]

In the Reflections section of that article, whose title seems to place Bonilla-Silva's work in the camp of critical race theory, which in fact is critical of his idealistic approach to the conceptualization of racism, he lamented not having "spent more time explaining that racism as ideology ('prejudice') is also material and consequential." Once again the language of the systemic racism approach is evident (e.g., "racism is systemic"), although he still would not call it by its name, systemic racism. Bonilla-Silva also offered insightful criticisms of Omi and Winant's work, especially their underdevelopment of their key concept, "race." Finally, of particular relevance to this study is his discussion of his *"racial grammar"* concept as a determinant of what is allowed into and what is kept out of racial discourse.[59]

Bonilla-Silva seems to be in the middle of a rapid renovation of his conceptualization of racism. It remains to be seen, however, whether his construction work goes beyond just adding a new façade with some brightly painted systemic racism words. While retaining much of his old problematic thinking about racism as *only* ideology (e.g., his conceptualizations of "color-blind racism" and "the 'new racism'"), in an article Bonilla-Silva had published online in late May 2015 he not only stressed that it "should be conceived in materialist rather that [sic] idealist fashion" but actually referred to racism as "a form of social organization." Moreover, he expanded his view of "the 'new racism'" beyond ideology to include a "set of mostly subtle, institutional, and seemingly nonracial mechanisms and practices." Instead of one incredibly narrow definition of racism he now seems to have two, sometimes conflicting, conceptualizations: one of racism *as* ideology, the other of racism *as* a social structure not limited to ideology. Even that change may be more apparent than real, however, because it is not clear that Bonilla-Silva has actually moved much beyond his original and primary focus on racism as ideology. For example, this is how he explained the evolution of his scholarship. "Like Marx and Engels, I regret the one-sidedness in my earlier work, but hope that my later work on racial ideology . . . is evidence of my belief of the centrality, and indeed, materiality of ideology in the making of race in our lives." And apparently he also still sees racism as *producing* "a *racial structure*" rather than having evolved from an ideology to *being* a *racist* structure, while elsewhere in that same article he stated that "racism is the product of racial domination projects" like colonialism and slavery—a "form of social organization" that once it emerged "became embedded in societies." So it is not clear if he now means more than his treatment of "racism as ideology" as, indeed, being systemic when he refers to "systemic racism" and asserts that "racism has always been systemic" in the United States. With this lack of clarity about the simple fact that racism is a highly organized system of oppression with the race concept as its ideological core, in his conceptualization of racism it is not clear whether Bonilla-Silva now embraces a large and robust systemic definition of racism consistent with the understanding of systemic racism held by most racially oppressed people. Consequently the reader is left wondering if we can rightfully conclude that his view of racism has now evolved and expanded to the point where he unambiguously conceptualizes racism as being much larger than his very clear and emphatic *ASR* article definition of racism as *only* "the racial ideology of a racialized social system . . . that is . . . only part of a larger racial system." Hopefully we will get a clearer view of Bonilla-Silva's ideas as he finds a way to move them beyond this conceptual fog. I believe that the easiest and simplest path forward is for him to acknowledge that his earlier definition of racism is much too small for the intellectual and analytical tasks at hand.[60]

In brief, despite his contributions to our understanding of systemic racism, and the evolving nature of his ideas, Bonilla-Silva still has yet to adequately address the major flaw of his work—his tendency to reduce racism from what it is—a highly organized *system* of "race" justified oppression—to its mere *ideological component*.

Unlike the work of other scholars that is doomed as racism theory by their basic racism-evasive assumptions, because Eduardo Bonilla-Silva's foundational ideas are so deeply rooted in the systemic racism perspective, he has three options if he would like to have it not only continue to be taken seriously within highly careerist and racially evasive American sociology, but to be accepted as being true to the real-life experiences of the racially oppressed. He can: (1) *expand his definition of racism* so that it is clear that he considers racism to be a system of "race" justified oppression; (2) *make it clear that the focus of his research and conceptual work is racial ideology and attitudes,* not racism; or (3) *emphasize that his is a partial theory of systemic racism,* one that focuses only on its ideological component.

More on Joe Feagin's Underdeveloped Systemic Racism Theory

Unfortunately advocates of the systemic racism perspective, myself included, have yet to flesh out the details necessary for it to retain its credibility, especially as many manifestations of race relations become increasingly subtle and complex. We are all guilty of conceptual underdevelopment. One of the big disappointments in this regard is Joe Feagin's 2006 *Systemic Racism: A Theory of Oppression*. When I first read the title I thought that finally Feagin—the leading exponent of systemic racism theory and probably the world's most prolific racism scholar—had succeeded where others have failed. But despite Feagin's promise to "develop a theory of systemic racism," he said little more about systemic racism than what he has already written elsewhere. Aside from a few nuggets like the chapter in which he noted that "from a systemic racism perspective, U.S. society is an organized racist whole with complex, interconnected, and interdependent social networks, organizations, and institutions that routinely imbed racial oppression" and his work on racial framing, the book is largely a substantive history of racial oppression in America.[61]

In that book Feagin defined the "white racial frame" as "an organized set of racialized ideas, stereotypes, emotions, and inclinations to discriminate." He stressed that such frames are institutionally embedded such that "consciously or unconsciously" they are "expressed in the routine operation of racist institutions of this society." Thus, racist social systems are built and defended through the white framing of all things racial. Feagin seemed to imply that "racist ideology"—as "an interrelated set of cognitive notions, understandings, and metaphors that whites have used to rationalize and legitimate systemic racism"—is a component of the broader concept of the white racial frame. Feagin also brought into his analysis here and in his 2010 book, *The White Racial Frame*, the counter-frames of the racially oppressed and others who challenge the usually dominant white racial frames and the systemic racism they support. Six of his *Systemic Racism* book's nine chapters examine slavery, legal segregation, and "contemporary racial realities" separately through the eyes of African Americans and then through those of European Americans. More useful would have been a historically rooted theoretical explanation of the interrelated structures and processes of contemporary systemic racism that built upon his earlier insightful writings on the different types of institutionalized racism, how such racism in the past impacts the racially oppressed today, and how racism in one institutional arena results in significant racial disparities in other contemporary institutions. By focusing so much on racial frames—which seem to be little more than an expanded social-science notion of ideology—Feagin ends up fostering the type of conceptual minimization he abhors. Moreover, with the ascendance of the hierarchies-evasive pluralist view of power within American sociology, the concepts of framing and counter-framing can conveniently be misconstrued to imply a state of power pluralism. These and other problems could have been overcome if Feagin's theory of systemic racism and the role of racial frames within it had been more fully fleshed out.[62]

With such refinement, Feagin's work on white racial frames could be a good place to bring into systemic racism theory the important scholarship on the race concept in general as that system's core ideology and, more specifically, some of the key findings of whiteness studies to explain the centrality of white racial identity to, and its mobilization within, the structures and processes of racial discrimination. An understanding of white racial identity as an organizing principle of systemic racism would entail synthesizing and expanding upon both the micro- and macro-levels of analysis literatures in racism studies and whiteness studies in a systematic exploration of the links connecting race as an ideological construct, white racial identity, and the various structures and processes of white racial privilege.

Unless the systemic racism perspective is further refined, it may well experience the fate of institutionalized racism theory. Or, if it persists, it may prove to be no more useful in explaining the workings of contemporary racial oppression than critical race theory, which shares many of the same assumptions and also remains conceptually underdeveloped. The problem with systemic racism theory is not its expansion of our conceptualization of racism, as William J. Wilson, Omi and Winant, and Bonilla-Silva complain; the problem is the failure to identify the working of its key structures and processes. For example, if everything is racism, then for all practical purposes nothing is racism and there is no need to look for evidence of obvious racist actions. Consequently social structure is privileged while human agency goes largely ignored and little or no effort is made to find the hands at the throttle of racist machinery. In *Welfare Racism* Kenneth Neubeck and I exposed so many hands there that it is impossible for the reader to credibly deny either the systemic nature of welfare racism or the key role of human agency. We found those many hands at the throttle because we did what many scholars do not do today: we looked for them.

To remain viable, systemic racism theory must be more fully developed. If we are to adequately comprehend the organization and workings of systemic racism more work is needed to "connect the dots."

As you have seen, the way American sociology spent much of its time, talent, publication space, and energy during the racially intense period since the 1980s is not impressive. While progressive social scientists have expended much time and effort reacting to the racism-evasiveness of color-blind ideology, in the absence of an effective progressive movement that goes beyond periodic protests, they have been unable to craft an effective intellectual vision to explain what is happening racially in the United States. Hopefully that will change with what may be the emergence of a new civil rights–centered progressive movement. Meanwhile intellectual ineptitude continues to be fueled by the failure of the old race and ethnic relations paradigm, which left race relations scholars fragmented and marginalized into different intellectual camps at various levels of conceptual underdevelopment. With the exception of the rather sketchy contours of systemic racism theory, those various approaches tend to have no overarching explanation of race *relations* at all, much less racism theory. Moreover, scholars have increasingly bought into the racism-evasive notion that today's racism is so complex as to be poststructural. Consequently, as American sociologists have sought more subtle concepts and other analytical tools to explain what they assume to be the increasingly covert and indirect operations of racism, they have largely ignored the more blatant acts of overt racism that, as I have shown, continue to explode all around us. Instead, American sociologists have engaged in racism-evasive endeavors like more debates over whether the condition of low-income African Americans is due mostly to "race" or to "class"; theorizing about the arrival of a mythical postmodern, poststructural, and racism(s) and power-pluralistic age with no dominant oppressive structures like racism at all; the conceptual pretense that any "critical" examination of whatever "race" is, no matter how theoretically shallow, is indeed a "theory"; and the intellectually myopic pretense that the totality of racism can be captured through what is essentially a racial attitudes methodological and theoretical lens.

CONCLUSION

As you have seen, the race relations scholarship in the United States from the 1980s to the present suffers from theoretical fragmentation. While there has been a continuance of insurgent systemic racism and critical race theory perspectives that remain conceptually underdeveloped, other scholarship produced during this period is more racially accommodative and can be characterized largely by conceptual obfuscation or conceptual minimization. Contributing to this theoretical fragmentation is a societal and social-science backlash against the systemic racism perspective African Americans pushed to the center of racial discourse through their civil rights movement. That backlash has included the conceptual colonization of racism by scholars more interested in "class" and poverty related issues; the conceptual conflation of "race" with "class"; the conceptual misdirection to the victims of racial oppression in search of a culture-centered explanation of African American–specific poverty; the conceptual minimization of racism back to a focus on beliefs, attitudes, and ideology; the conceptual obfuscation associated with an increasing reference to "race" as if that word, in and of itself, had some magical analytical power; the conceptual rejection of terms like racism and racial oppression; and the conceptual underdevelopment of critical race theory and systemic racism theory.

In chapter 5 I examine how racism has been defined in American social science and the racial origins and implications of those definitions. After placing social-science definitions within their larger social context, I examine trends in race relations studies. I also stress the urgent need for more constructive, language-centered, criticism to move racism studies beyond its current state of conceptual underdevelopment. I then categorize and critique some influential definitions of racism.

Chapter Five

Defining Racism

Beyond Mini-Racism and the "Race" as Agency Concept

> The power of the white world is threatened whenever a black man refuses to accept the white world's definitions.
> James Baldwin, 1963[1]

The power of any people resides in their ability to define themselves and their circumstances. By definition, the oppressed are less able to do so. That does not mean, however, that they are powerless, or that they do not give voice to what is important to them in the private, relatively safe spaces of their lives. And it does not preclude the possibility that at times they become bold enough to publicly challenge the hegemonic definitions of things with those of their own. This has certainly been the case when it comes to defining the racial condition of African Americans and other racially oppressed people in the United States. Today, even when referring to the same incident, European Americans are likely to deploy the language of "race" whereas those who are racially oppressed are most likely to, when they can, put forth the word racism. As you will see in this chapter, even when the term "racism" is used by both groups, it is likely to be given radically different meanings. For example, although within the permissible parameters of the white power structure racism is typically limited to the bigoted attitudes and behavior of a lone individual, it can also be defined, more consistently with the perspective of the racially oppressed, in a way that is large and robust enough to encompass the entire system of racial oppression.

In this chapter I continue my analysis of how American sociologists and other social scientists have conceptualized racism by focusing specifically on how they have defined racism.

CONCEPTS AND DEFINITIONS IN THE SOCIAL SCIENCES: THEIR MEANING AND SIGNIFICANCE

In the introduction to his book *Racism: A Very Short Introduction* Ali Rattansi cautioned that "racism is not easy to define."[2] This "racism is complex" argument, common among postmodernists, justifies conceptual obfuscation that is not only false but stifling to racism-targeted scholarship, discourse, and public policy. The "complexity" of racism is largely political—and by that I do not simply mean that the conceptualization of racism is subject to much political contestation. Such politicized complexity is rooted in the fact that in highly racialized democracies like the United States those individuals, groups, organizations, and institutions that are invested in both maintaining the racial status quo and touting the national ideals of democracy and egalitarianism encourage, whether consciously or unconsciously, the conceptual confusion and imprecision that keeps the topic sufficiently vague as to remain largely invisible.

What Concepts and Definitions Are and What They Do

Consistent with the sociology of knowledge literature I reviewed in chapter 1, back in 1930 Herbert Blumer noted that there is a reciprocal relationship between perception and conception. Not only does one's perception of things affect how they are conceived, but one's conception of things helps to shape one's perceptions of them.[3] This reciprocal relationship is central to what I refer to as the double whammy of racism-evasive politics—that is, the vicious cycle in which the politics of denial causes the misconceptualization of race relations and that misconceptualization, in turn, justifies and otherwise fuels more denial. Further, it suggests that once a phenomenon is conceptualized in a certain way (e.g., as "race" and therefore the "Negro problem") within sociology and the other social sciences, it becomes very difficult for it to be perceived differently (e.g., racism as a systemic problem), much less to be conceived differently (e.g., as systemic racism). Blumer's observation also helps us to understand why certain phenomena, once accepted as so real by the social sciences that they become reified (e.g., the race concept), are so difficult to abandon even in the face of abundant disconfirming empirical evidence.

In his discussion of the "verbal character" of concepts, Blumer revealed the largely ignored function they can serve in facilitating discourse that leads to social change. First, he noted that "by reason of its verbal or symbolic character, the concept may become an item of social discourse and so permit the conception that it embodies to become common property." Next, "in becoming social property it permits others to gain the same point of view and employ the same orientation. As such it enables collective action." For example, relevant to this study, I might say that it is the verbal character of concepts as expressed through their key symbol of words that enables the racially oppressed to articulate and struggle to place their concern about systemic racism on the national social-policy agenda. Building on his point about how the scientific concept can facilitate the collective action needed for social change, Blumer noted that it "enables one to circumvent problems of perceptual experience"—for example, by allowing European Americans to see racism through the eyes of those who experience it. Of course, scientific concepts (e.g., the race concept) have also served the hegemonic ideological function of justifying racial oppression and thus maintaining the racial status quo. Consequently conceptual battles have historically been at the center of the dialectical relationship between oppressors and the oppressed.[4] In this study I conceptualize that battle as being between linguistic racial accommodation and linguistic racial confrontation.

Blumer also made an observation that should raise a caution flag for social scientists who argue that, when it comes to race relations, popular, commonly understood terminology should be used. That observation also helps us understand why there is such an emotional outcry among the general public of the racially dominant group—one that may in turn cause social scientists to become conceptually shy—when common sense conceptualizations of things (e.g., "race") are challenged (e.g., by the word racism). As Blumer put it, "it is not, perhaps, unfair to say that common-sense concepts are in the nature of stereotypes. Their meaning is just taken for granted, their character just naturally sensed. To question them is unthought-of; indeed, to question them is to evoke emotion." In stark contrast, as Arthur Stinchcombe so eloquently and succinctly stated about the chief ideal of social science concepts, "the first requirement for a concept is that it accurately reflect the forces actually operating in the world."[5]

The meanings, functions, and power of concepts are ultimately determined by their definitions. To work effectively, a definition must make clear not only what it includes but what it excludes; that is, effective concepts both specify and delimit. For example, a definition of racism that includes most forms of social oppression (e.g., oppression based on ethnicity, gender, sexual orientation, and mental and physical disability) is no definition at all. The same is true of the casual use of "race," or "the race issue." Both examples fail to meet even the popular definitions of a definition found in, for example, *Merriam-Webster's Collegiate Dictionary*: "a statement expressing the essential nature of something," and "the action or the power of describing, explaining, or making definite and clear." Of course, what is included in or excluded from a concept—especially a social concept—is a value judgment, with the values of those with the power to define things most likely to prevail. In his analysis of the functions of definitions in the social sciences, Richard Popkin tied these two characteristics of definitions together by defining social science definitions as "limited concepts which serve as value judgments about a related or seemingly related group of phenomena." Finally, in his article on the same topic, N. S. Timasheff broke down these linguistic structures even further by noting that "definitions consist of words, and words are symbols representing ideas or facts, that is, singled-out states of knowable reality."[6]

Figure 5.1 sums up the literature I have reviewed thus far on the significance, functions, and relative locations of perceptions, conceptions, definitions, and words as the key linguistic components of ideology. Beginning with its largest outer rim, you can see that popular perceptions like those of the nature of race relations are gross and unrefined relative to its three inner circles. Such perceptions are made manageable through conceptions like white racial superiority or systemic racism. Those conceptions or concepts are delimited and refined through definitions. Finally, definitions are constructed with words that are also used to name the concepts defined. In that figure we have represented what is essentially the linguistic anatomy of ideology that either sustains or challenges the racial status quo. With that illustration we can once again appreciate the fact that when it comes to understanding and challenging oppressive systems like racism, words matter.

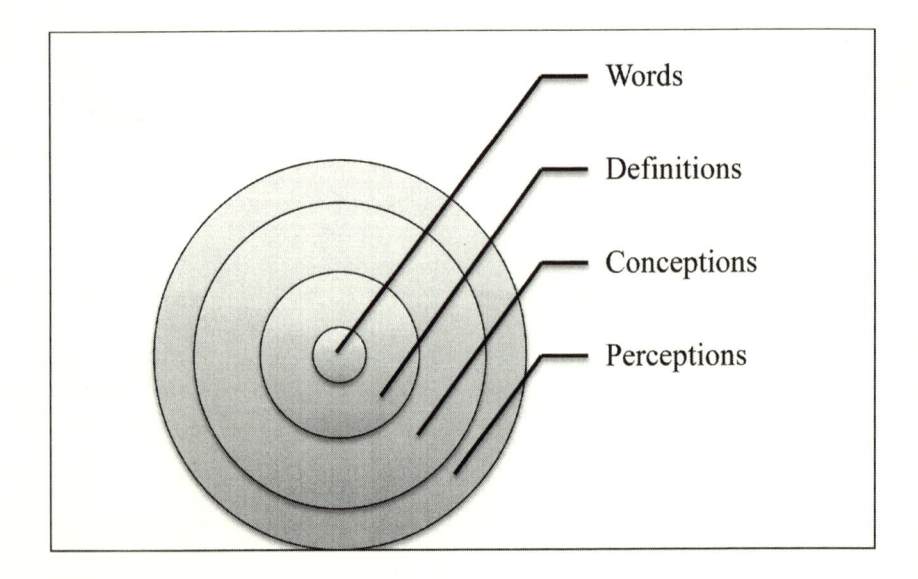

Figure 5.1. The Linguistic Anatomy of Ideology: Perceptions, Conceptions, Definitions, and Words

Defining Racism: Beyond Mini-Racism and the "Race" as Agency Concept 135

AGAIN, WORDS MATTER

One of the reasons that it is so difficult to have honest and productive discussions about systemic racism in the United States and other highly racialized societies is that, by definition, the racially accommodative language most commonly used is simply not up to the task. This is clear in figure 5.2, where the term race is so ambiguous as to be meaningless and the popular conception of racism as no more than individual-level racial bigotry leads to nothing but emotionally charged name-calling and finger-pointing about *who* is the "racist." Clearly if we are to have a productive dialogue, one with systemic racism as the core concern of the racially oppressed, we will first need a less racism-evasive and more precise set of concepts, definitions, and words to work with. Otherwise, as the cartoon captures so succinctly, any attempt to discuss the problem is likely to result in little more than name-calling and finger-pointing.

Now that I have established the importance of concepts, definitions, and words in both reflecting and shaping our perceptions of our racialized world I will briefly discuss three concepts—two old and one new—that can help us

Figure 5.2. "National Dialogue on Race" Cartoon. *Source: Robert Englehart, The Hartford Courant, July 20, 2010*

comprehend why the ostensibly simple and straightforward task of defining racism is so complicated.

RACE, RACISM, AND THE "RACE" AS AGENCY CONCEPT

Race

Although some scholars trace the Western intellectual roots of the race concept back to the sixteenth century, it did not enter into popular usage until the nineteenth century, when it was deployed as an ideology to justify European colonialism, slavery, and capitalism as systems of economic exploitation and profit making based on the treatment of human beings as less than—or not at all—human. Once established, the notion of race in by then highly racialized societies like the United States became as commonplace as water is to fish; and, like fish and their relationship to water, it was not something many people questioned. Even political progressives assumed that the term race was a socially benign reference to biological facts, and that only its misuse was problematic. In recent decades, however, scientific findings have radically challenged our understanding of the race concept. Advances in biology and breakthroughs in DNA research have revealed the notion of biologically based races to be bogus, requiring sociologists to at least parenthetically acknowledge that race is a social construct, a human invention, and a falsehood. Moreover, recent anthropological and historical research has stressed that race is not only a social construction, a human invention, and an untruth, but it is indeed an ideology—a lie that was fabricated to justify a system of "race"-based exploitation.[7] Today the race concept is so discredited that scholars who do quantitative research in which they run race as a variable often spend more time explaining what race is not than what it is. Ironically, in disciplines that rely on conceptual and methodological precision, today the greatest use of the term *race* seems to be in enabling social scientists to be sufficiently vague and non-controversial for mainstream research funders, journals, and other publications to continue supporting their study of the victims of racial oppression rather than the highly organized racialized group *relations* such oppression entails.

Racism

As I mentioned in chapter 2, the term racism was probably first coined in 1938 in a book of the same name by German sociologist and sexologist Magnus Hirschfeld. Because Hirschfeld did not actually define the term, it is left for the reader to interpret its meaning based on whatever criterion he or she may choose. For example, in my search for an explicit conceptualization of racism I found a statement in which Hirschfeld identified the goal of his book as "to examine the racial theory which underlies" the Nazi "doctrine of race war." Taken by itself, that goal statement suggests that Hirschfeld engaged in what I refer to as conceptual minimization by limiting racism to a theory (or ideology) deployed to justify the actions of the Nazis. However, using a more interpretative content-centered approach to discern Hirschfeld's conceptualization of racism, Feagin and Elias concluded that his overall approach is systemic in nature.[8] In this chapter I eschew such interpretations in favor of explicit definitions of racism.

From Hirschfeld on it is clear that closely related to the content of such definitions is their magnitude, with that size expanding and contracting consistent with historical changes in race relations. Simply put, in the United States conceptualizations of racism grow larger in response to African American social protest and they shrink as a reaction to white racial backlash.

The Rise and Fall of Big Racism

In the early 1990s Robert Blauner wrote a magazine article to explain why it is that African Americans and European Americans so often talk past one another in discussing racial incidents and issues. To that end his essay provided provocative insights into both the history and consequences of language battles in the United States over definitions of racism. Through his definition of language as "a system of implicit understandings about social reality" and his assertion that "racial language encompasses a worldview," Blauner laid out his assumptions about the systemic nature and ideological functions of language. Later, in tracing the history of the contested "meaning of racism" in both social science and the larger society of which it is a part, Blauner noted that in the 1940s the term was limited to what he referred to as the "ideological racism" that justified white racial supremacy. However, "by the 1950s and early 1960s, with ideological racism discredited, the focus shifted to a more discrete approach to racially invidious attitudes and behavior, expressed in the model of prejudice and discrimination." By the mid-1960s, with its conceptualization of institutional racism, the civil rights movement forced the issue of racial oppression front and center. Blauner also observed that in the 1960s and 1970s what he considered to be another definition of racism was pushed forward. "'Racism as atmosphere'" denoted the fact that people of color may feel uncomfortable in organizations and institutions designed by and for European Americans. Yet another conception of racism that was championed during that time is what Blauner referred to as "'racism as result,'" an example being the underrepresentation of people of color in society's key institutions and positions. Finally, by the late 1970s, with the white backlash fully in place, racism was increasingly articulated as "'reverse racism'"—that is, as racial discrimination against European Americans due to racially ameliorative policies and practices like affirmative action.[9]

Blauner noted that eventually even racial liberals like British sociologist Robert Miles became critical of what they saw as "inflation" of the racism concept. While acknowledging the important role of the white racial backlash in the push back toward a smaller conceptualization of racism, Blauner concluded that conceptual inflation was indeed a problem: "while institutional racism exists, such a concept loses practical utility if every thing and every place is racist." Blauner is right about his last point. As I noted earlier in this chapter, a key function of conceptual definitions is to delimit. Therefore a sure-fire way of imploding any concept is to make it include everything. Indeed, conceptually, if everything is racism then nothing is racism.[10]

While I agree with Blauner that conceptual problems played a significant role in the demise of racism as a big concept, which in the institutional racism perspective included what he referred to as "racism as atmosphere" and "racism as result," I would emphasize the effect of conceptual underdevelopment more than conceptual inflation. Unfortunately Blauner failed to comprehend that the true nature of that "inflation" had nothing to do with the actual size of racism. The radical, racial-oppression-centered conceptualization of Carmichael and Hamilton was not the failed institutional racism perspective of later racial liberals who denuded the concept of not only its focus on oppression but of any hint of human agency and any need for systemic change beyond various diversity projects to make existing social structures more sensitive to the needs of racial and other "minorities."[11]

The notion that racism was institutionalized and impersonal gave such diversity bureaucrats and institutional-reform-minded scholars license to engage in the conceptual slothfulness of simply accusing institutions of being racist because they yielded racially disparate outcomes, without the hard work of specifying the machinery through which such racial inequality is actually generated and reproduced. It was those advocates of this racially liberal view of institutional racism that made the concept unworkable. And it was unworkable not because this conceptual balloon was too large or "inflated," but because it seemed to be pumped up with no conceptual or theoretical substance. So, ironically, part of the reason for the failure of the institutional racism perspective, despite its great potential, is that this apparently radical conceptualization provided diversity-focused professionals and social scientists with a convenient escape route through which they could just declare the institutional existence of the thing without doing the hard intellectual, political, ethical, and emotional work of specifying how it works and why. Without such conceptual work, in the end their notion that the mere existence of quantifiable racial differences is indicative of institutionalized racism is no more convincing to the general public than the arguments of racial bigots that they are proof of white racial supremacy. Such a lack of analytical specificity also worked well in the emergence of what I refer to as the "race" as agency concept.

The "Race" as Agency Concept

In contrast to the original race essentialist conceptualization of race, the "race" as agency concept does not overtly view race as a biological categorization of human beings according to physical traits as well as cognitive and social attributes like intelligence, character, and morality. Neither does it treat race as a social construction, or more specifically as I do as the core ideology of a system of "race"-justified oppression. This new conceptualization of race also does not explicitly address race-based hierarchy, power differences, or exploitation. Instead, "race" has now been transformed into a strange social power-eviscerated conception that is assumed to somehow have agency of its own either as an issue or as an entity or process that actually does things.

When, for example, the word "race" is combined with the word "issue," that term is assumed to express action, at least indirectly, in that it refers to matters that are yet to be resolved. Similarly, when the word "race" is followed by the word "question," it can be seen as acting through its call for answers. Indeed, any noun can be used to express action if presented in a way that suggests that it does something. So when social scientists refer to "the race issue," "the issue of race," "the race question," "the question of race," or simply to "race" as if it has agency (e.g., "because of race," "due to race," "the effect of race," "race does" or "race does not"), they give race a new meaning and power that appears to be quite different from that of its discredited conceptualization as a biology-based category of people who belong to one of assumed inherently unequal groups. Yet ironically, by granting race such false independent agency, this new social-science fiction confuses and camouflages the real human agency that drives racism as a highly organized system of "race" justified oppression. That is, this "race happens" perspective falsely assumes that it is race, whatever it may be, that does things, not humans who operate the machinery of systemic racism to acquire and sustain privilege, with race as its ideological core. So still, despite these apparent differences, like the original race concept it assumes that deep down there must be something problematic, pathological, and inferior about the racialized group that has been singled out for scrutiny. Indeed, this apparently "new" race concept is simply a more subtle and sophisticated manifestation of the more traditional conceptualization of race; one that by its ability to avoid any reference to group *relations*, much less *hierarchies*, is even better equipped to serve the needs of systemic racism in highly racialized democracies that claim to have moved beyond both "race" and racism.

Not all of the race as agency scholarship, however, is so theoretically malnourished. Building on the symbolic interactionist theoretical perspective and more specifically racial formation theory, Matthew Hughey has articulated another, subjective, version of the race as agency conceptualization by defining race as a process. After referring to something much smaller and more specific in scope—racial identity formation—he then went far beyond *racial identity formation* when he radically expanded the *race* concept itself and gave it agency, not just as a thing, but as a social process. In a hyper-ambitious definition I find to be emblematic of the conceptual inflation and fuzziness of much of the new sociological scholarship on race, he wrote, "race is not a static event but a process of patterned events that demonstrate a larger cultural system that continually reracializes certain objects, habits, rituals, words, and people." In the face of such obvious theoretical zealotry even the most basic social-science precepts like the need for conceptual clarity, simplicity, and precision don't stand a chance.[12]

Such reasoning allows scholars to remain blind to certain inconvenient truths about the nature of social inequality. With this blindness to the non-subjective components of social structures, there seems to be no limit to the level of abstraction to which they take their conceptualizations of "race," while essentially ignoring its very real and materialist origins, functions, and consequences. Through what might be described tongue in cheek as their own particular "Keep Race Alive!" movement, Omi and Winant, and now Hughey, keep such race-centered scholarship perpetually thriving by redefining race as a never-ending process of the often competing meanings of various racial identities and projects.

Figure 5.3 illustrates what I call the "race" as agency concept, a trend in what is usually conceptual non-definition and obfuscation that emerged as a result of the convergence of four factors in the post–civil rights movement era: the continued white backlash against the civil rights movement and its very explicit reference to racism, racial oppression, and even white racism; the fragmentation of race and ethnic relations theory, and its subsequent de-emphasis of racial *relations*; the rise of a quantitative social science and its positivistic methodological philosophy; and the power-evasive use of the passive voice.

The final essential ingredient for the rise of the "race" as agency concept is what June Jordan referred to as "the irresponsible language of the passive voice"—an emotionally, politically, ethically, and intellectually lethargic and detached grammatical style that seems to assume that "stuff" just "happens." In exposing its inefficacy, Jordan put forth the following questions about the power-evasive use of the passive voice. "Is someone really saying those words? Is any real life affected by those words? Should we really just relax into the literally nondescript, the irresponsible language of the passive voice? Will the passive voice lead us safely out of the action? Will the action and the

[Diagram: Four boxes with arrows pointing to a central circle labeled "The 'Race' as Agency Concept". The boxes are: "The White Racial Backlash", "The Demise of Race *Relations* Theory and the Rise of Theoretical Fragmentation", "The Power-Evasive Use of the Passive Voice", and "The Rise of Positivistic Research Methods".]

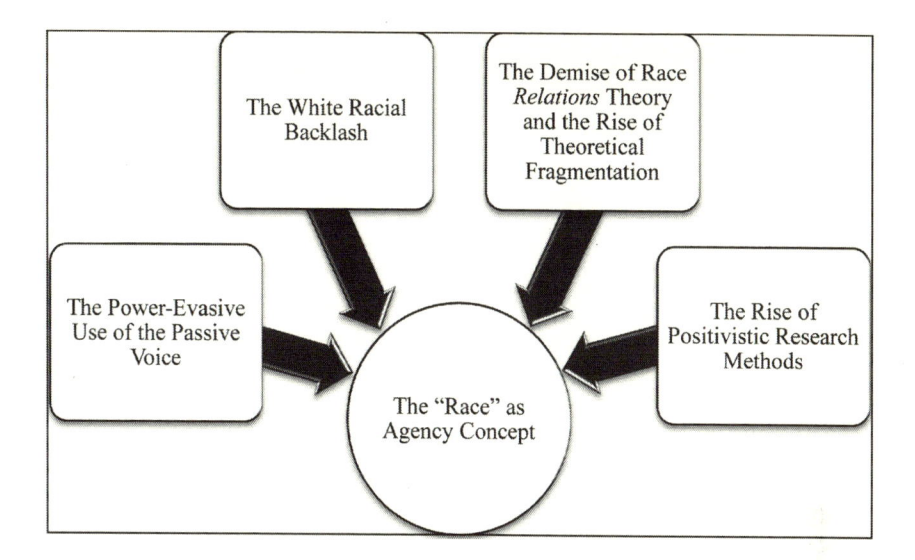

Figure 5.3. The Rise of the "Race" as Agency Concept

actors behind it leave us alone so long as we do not call them by their real names?"[13] The use of the passive voice is attractive to many social scientists because it makes their analysis and conclusions appear to be objective and value neutral when, as Jordan made clear, its actual power-evasive effect is quite the opposite.

The contemporary use of race as a non-defined and ambiguous concept provides a way for social scientists to nominally talk about race relations without implying that European Americans are a part of the analytical frame, let alone observing that that frame includes not only group relations but also group inequality and privilege. I believe that the increasing popularity of the "race" as agency concept is not in spite of the fact that it is ambiguous and trivial, but *because* that ambiguity and triviality allows social scientists and other elites to safely appear to be engaging in erudite discourse on one of the nation's most serious problems—asserting, for example, that they "view race critically"—while effectively saying nothing.

This "race" as agency trend is but one manifestation of racism-evasive linguistic practices that have emboldened even otherwise progressive sociologists to actually ridicule the need for clear and precise conceptualizations of racism and that have given quantitative sociologists the green light to simply run "race" as a variable.

Another troubling trend that hinders the conceptualization of racism is the accommodative stance justified by what I call linguistic racial realism.

LINGUISTIC RACIAL IDEALISM VERSUS LINGUISTIC RACIAL REALISM

Taken out of the context of my larger linguistic racial accommodation and confrontation argument, the terms linguistic racial realism and linguistic racial idealism could be confusing. For example, one might assume that linguistic racial realism—as a language-based portrayal of race relations as they really are—would be what the racially oppressed and their supporters would want, as opposed to linguistic racial idealism, which might seem to portray a fanciful and idealized conception of race relations. But within the context of my larger conceptualization of linguistic racial accommodation and confrontation, being a linguistic racial realist, like being a racial realist, is to be a pragmatist who is "realistic" in accepting the linguistic racial status quo, whereas being a linguistic idealist entails challenging the existing linguistic racial order by calling systemic racism by its name. I briefly defined linguistic racial realism as it relates to race relations scholarship as the extreme and misguided pragmatism of accepting popular racially accommodative terms. Similarly, I defined linguistic racial idealism as what emboldens scholars to reject and confront such accommodation by having the temerity to speak plainly by using straightforward words like racism and racial oppression. Linguistic racial idealism and confrontation are most likely to flourish in environments that encourage constructive criticism.

The Need for Constructive Criticism as a Challenge to Linguistic Racial Realism

The lack of constructive criticism—by which I mean criticism that accepts the work as having value and offers suggestions for improving it—in both race and ethnic relations and racism scholarship is an important reason that linguistic racial realism and other forms of racial accommodation have gone unchallenged for so long. For example, in chapter 4 I noted that it took Joe Feagin more than two and a half decades to respond in detail to Omi and Winant's racial formation theory, which in its conceptualization of "race" and racism functioned as a torpedo aimed at systemic racism theory. There are many reasons for the lack of sufficient criticism in these specialty areas to keep their conceptualization sharp and provocative: the professional marginality of those specialties and many if not most of the academicians who study them, the lack of grant money and other opportunities to support the critical mass of high-quality scholars needed for conceptual competition and debate, the racial marginality of many of its scholars who feel heat coming from so many places that they are reluctant to cause any additional stress for themselves and their fellow scholars from racially oppressed backgrounds or for progressive European American scholars who share their concerns, the existence of friendship networks among such scholars that may seem threatened by criticism, and so on.

Such constructive criticism, I argue, should begin at home. It would be helpful for each scholar to reflect on his or her own work and publicly state its limitations so that others can advance it. The best way to view such useful criticism is not as individual career races with winners and losers, but instead as a relay marathon team in which we pass on from generation to generation our contribution to the essential work in the enduring struggle against racial oppression. That relay team metaphor also suggests that beginning such criticism at home should mean including those who share the same political domicile, such as committed antiracists on the Left.

Critical engagement among influential scholars on the political Left is essential for the following reasons. First, their opinions matter to me and many other progressives they influence, so to critically engage them is to honor them and their work. Second, I think that if there are to be effective challenges to what I refer to as linguistic racial accommodation, I expect those challenges to come from the radical Left, not from liberals, moderates, or the Right. Third, I believe the Left has been intimidated by the Right's charges of political correctness, academic elitism, and the unfounded fear that the Right is trying to take the race concept away from us in order to bolster its racism-evasive color-blind ideology. To the latter point, let me say that I see no evidence that racially conservative European Americans are ready to relinquish their "whiteness" and the race concept, whether to maintain ideological consistency or for any other reason. Fourth, I believe that since the white racial backlash was fully institutionalized in the 1980s the Left has been largely reacting to the Right's ideology and agenda—instead of crafting its own long-term radical offensive in its own words. And finally, once the pressure of the civil rights movement stopped, most of the Left dropped its direct and explicit focus on systemic racism and returned to its strategy of dealing quietly with racial matters under the assumed larger umbrella of a majoritarian economic justice movement. That strategy failed, as it has done so many times in American history.

Now for the Good News

Today we may be witnessing the emergence of a majoritarian progressive movement around civil rights—one that also encompasses the issue of economic justice. This new broad-based civil rights movement coalition may consist of women concerned about recent infringements on their reproductive rights; gay, lesbian, and transgender Americans fighting for their civil rights; Latino/a Americans alarmed about immigration racism; African Americans upset about racism in the criminal justice system and voter suppression; Muslim and Arab Americans tired of being racially profiled at airports and of the police infiltration of their mosques and neighborhoods; Asian Americans burdened with the high rate of physical assaults against them; and people trapped in a cycle of poverty who have experienced a highly organized political assault on their rights to such necessities as food, clothing, shelter, and health care. Such a movement would also fit well the growing international movement for human rights.

Hopefully, this is not just wishful thinking on my part. There are some rays of hope, including, for example, the "Moral Mondays" movement that was first organized in North Carolina by a coalition of NAACP, clergy, and other progressive leaders and organizations. That movement, which emerged to protest extreme right-wing legislative actions seen as being harmful to the civil rights and economic well-being of African Americans, poor people, women, and other vulnerable groups, has spread to other states both in the South and elsewhere throughout the United States. Within electoral politics, such a broad-based coalition promises to make it increasingly difficult for extreme right-wing candidates to win high office. If effective social theories are to be attuned with viable social change possibilities, it is those broad-based civil and human rights and economic justice movements that racism theory should be crafted around.[14]

To continue my challenge to the conceptually stifling culture of non-criticism, I will now share with you a brief debate I had with a colleague, whom I respect and admire, that illustrates my conceptualizations of linguistic racial realism and linguistic racial idealism. Our relationship not only survived that debate but has grown stronger since then.

Linguistic Racial Realism and the Reluctance to Use the Word Racism

In 2002 Stephen Steinberg published an article in *New Politics* that caught my eye because of its reference to the opposition I faced when I first proposed teaching my white racism course at the University of Connecticut. In that article Steinberg made what I considered to be a strong case for using the term "racial oppression" instead of "race relations." In a letter published in that periodical I welcomed that step forward but cautioned that Steinberg's argument should not be used as an opportunity to place yet an additional nail in the coffin of the word *racism*, a term African Americans have fought so hard to bring to and keep at the center of the nation's racial discourse. This is what I had to say in making the distinction between racial oppression and racism.

> The term racial oppression is fine for describing the actions and consequences of racism as a system. However, we also need a name for that system itself. That name is racism. This is consistent with Marxist scholars who use capitalism to refer to the system of economic oppression. There is no confusion about

the fact that capitalism refers to an economic SYSTEM and not just a set of beliefs. The "confusion" about the meaning of the term racism is political, not conceptual. This can be seen in the fact that while it is the term of preference of racially exploited people it is fiercely disallowed by the white power structure. In both cases both sets of terms are useful (i.e., capitalism and economic oppression and racism and racial oppression). We are dealing here with an *and/both* situation, not *either/or*.[15]

Next came Steinberg's response, whose core I quote here. Please pay attention to the linguistically pragmatic reason he gives for opposing my definition of racism as a system of oppression. While Steinberg made it clear that he had no objection "to the use of the term 'racism,' especially when it is given institutional anchorage, as in the claim that the United States is 'a racist society,'" he went on to argue that

it is not quite accurate to say that racism is to racial oppression as capitalism is to economic oppression. As Cazenave knows, "racism" has been so eviscerated by reductive reasoning that the term is commonly understood to refer, not to structures and institutions, but to disembodied beliefs and attitudes that need to be rooted out, presumably through education and good will. No such confusion exists with respect to capitalism: what comes first to mind are political and economic institutions that wield great power.[16]

Steinberg certainly is right in saying that the common view of racism in the United States is reductionist and not systemic. This is clear in my always-handy *Merriam-Webster's Collegiate Dictionary*, which gives two definitions of racism: one as a race essentialist belief and the other as racial prejudice and discrimination.[17] Where we disagree is the degree to which, when it comes to racism and other forms of oppression, progressive antiracist scholars and activists should operate *within* the prevailing linguistic framework. As Steinberg is well aware, systems of oppression are held together in large part by the dominant ideologies that encompass and express the perceptions, concepts, definitions, and words of those who would maintain the status quo. Consequently it is common for the oppressed to pack their own perceptions into the concepts, definitions, and words with which they construct their own challenging or counter ideologies. Throughout African American history and social thought, the condition of African Americans has been viewed as being both hierarchical and systemic. And since the civil rights struggle of the 1960s the preferred term of African Americans for that oppressive system has been racism. Through that struggle terms like racism, racial oppression, and even white racism were forced into the national discourse, just as since the white racial backlash to that movement they have been increasingly disallowed. Many progressives believe that for scholars to reach a larger audience they should be practical by using commonly accepted terminology. They are, like Steinberg was in his letter, linguistically realistic in this regard. As a linguistic idealist I could not disagree more. I think that since racial hegemony is held together at its core by words, the words that construct and maintain systems of oppression (e.g., "race") must be challenged by the words (e.g., racism) of those who suffer that oppression.

With this example to help clarify the difference between linguistic racial realism and linguistic racial idealism, let's take a look at another case of linguistic racial realism by another influential progressive scholar I hold in high regard.

Linguistic Racial Realism and the Uncritical Acceptance of the Race Concept

Patricia Hill Collins is one of the most rightfully appreciated and progressive African American sociologists of our times. As an intellectual concerned about multiple forms of oppression, Collins is definitely a words person. Indeed, at least three of her books—*Black Feminist Thought*, *Fighting Words*, and *Black Sexual Politics*—contain glossaries. Moreover, as one of the most influential scholars for young generations of progressive sociologists, what she says about words can matter as much as the words she says. Although Collins defines racism as being systemic, not only does she use the highly problematic color-race terms "Black" and "White," she takes to task those scholars who place the word *race* in quotes to emphasize that it is a social construction rather than a biological fact that should not be reified through its indiscriminate use. Indeed, she goes as far as to deem that practice both elitist and paternalistic, asserting that it is "yet another example of exclusionary language available to the privileged (and morally superior) few." She then gives two additional reasons for rejecting that practice. "First, why select 'race' for quotation marks and not 'gender' or 'sexuality'? What is it about 'race' that makes it more constructed than other systems of power? Second, despite its constructed nature, the effects of 'race' remain real for millions of people."[18]

I reject the logics of all three arguments. First, Collins committed the logical fallacy of ad hominem by essentially labeling those who problematize the race concept by placing it in quotes as being elitist and paternalistic, and the logical fallacy of irrelevant appeals by justifying a particular practice by appealing to its popularity. She also committed the logical fallacy of the double standard through the divergence between her criticism and her own linguistic practices such as problematizing the words White and Black by capitalizing their first letters when they are used to refer to racial/ethnic designations and by unapologetically and appropriately using such uncommon—and therefore elitist?—terms in her own books like paradigm, intersectionality, discourse, and hegemonic femininity. In support of her second point—after suggesting that the mere assumption that race is a social construction somehow makes its uncritical use problematic to the critics of that practice—she also committed the logical fallacy of two wrongs make a right by arguing, within her logic, that because other terms that refer to social constructions are not written with quotes, that is a valid reason for not doing so with the word *race*. She is also wrong in her assumption that race is no more constructed than gender or sexuality. Whereas gender and sexuality refer to phenomena that include but are not limited to ideology, the race concept originated only as an ideology used to justify "race" based oppression. Finally, to make her third and final point, she committed the straw person logical fallacy by falsely suggesting that scholars who merely chose to problematize the race concept are, by doing so, somehow arguing that race as a social construction (or ideology, as I would say) is not real in its consequences.[19] While I certainly do not consider myself to be linguistically elitist, racially paternalistic, or blind to the insidious consequences of "race," I belong to the category of scholars Collins criticized who stress that to use the word race uncritically is to reify it—a concept that I believe is not only inherently racist but is nothing less than the core ideology holding together systems of racial oppression.

This new manifestation of linguistic racial realism shares the same political roots as the "race" as agency conceptualization I discussed earlier, including the accommodation of progressive social scientists and activists to the white backlash against direct and explicit discussions of racism and racial oppression. Examples of the "race" as agency concept in Collins's work include her reference to the "issue of race" in discussing different categories of social issues, her use of the phrases "treat race" and "race continues to be" in her discussion of race as a consensus issue, and her phrase "race itself plays an important part" in reference to its relationship to hegemonic femininity.[20] When I examine the impact of quantitative methods on conceptualizing and defining racism in the next section, it should be clear how common such language is for those scholars who run "race" as a variable—something that Collins, as a theoretician, generally does not do, although she does seem to have been influenced by the racial language of their positivistic methodology. I suspect that what many progressive scholars insist is merely their effort to be pragmatic in allowing their message to reach as large and as influential an audience as possible is, for all practical purposes, no different from accommodating their message racially so that it will be more widely accepted. In academic circles it is well known that when we academicians, many of whom are quite precise in our scholarly terminology, don't want to deal with something that is controversial or unpleasant, we show great skills at verbal obfuscation.

Well-intentioned progressive scholars like Eduardo Bonilla-Silva, Stephen Steinberg, Patricia Hill Collins, and myself are often caught between the rock of authenticity and the hard place of accessibility to power. Because of the militant denial of systemic racism in highly racialized democracies like the United States, to communicate effectively in challenging racism, scholars often feel that we must dance a delicate dialectic of the two. If we ignore the issue of accessibility we may speak the "truth" of linguistic racial idealism, but few people outside of the proverbial "church choir" will hear it. If, on the other hand, we strive too much for accessibility through a strategy of linguistic racial realism, we may actually reify the words and concepts from which the ideological core of systemic racism is built and maintained. In this study I admittedly push closer to the authenticity of linguistic racial idealism than the accessibility of linguistic racial realism. I do so because, as you have seen, it is my premise that the field has been seriously underdeveloped by scholars working within existing linguistic frameworks, which tend to be racially accommodative. This inclination toward linguistic racial realism is especially prevalent among those academics who use quantitative research methods.

THE RISE OF QUANTITATIVE RESEARCH METHODS: FROM STUDYING RACE RELATIONS TO RUNNING "RACE" AS A VARIABLE

One of the most extreme conceptual consequences of the white racial backlash and its linguistic racial accommodation is the tendency of today's quantitative social scientists to simply "run race" as a variable in search of racial differences. This entails the use of computer-based statistical analysis to discern the relationship between "race" and other social indicators with no real attempt to conceptualize the meaning of those findings by locating them within the context of racialized group relations. Other culprits behind this trend are the breakup of the race and ethnic relations paradigm and the rise of quantitative research methods.

When "race" is merely "run" as a variable—with little regard for its conceptual meaning and no overarching theory to explain its workings—it is typically treated as an independent actor, apart from any actual race relations context. For example, "race" as a measure of racial differences can be used as an indicator of racial inferiority or superiority; a pathological or positive racial subculture; a variable to be eliminated once other assumed to be more important factors are controlled for; or a usually weak, indirect, and always inconclusive test of racism, which itself is rarely measured.

Quantitative research methods came to dominate the social sciences as the interest in race *relations* (what might best be referred to as racialized group relations) faded. Their growing influence helped exacerbate not only that trend but ultimately the ascendance of the "race" as agency conceptualization that also encourages today's uncritical and under-conceptualized statistical analysis of "race" as a variable. Those changes combined with the end of the modern civil rights movement to remove any incentive for methodologists to develop techniques for studying racialized group relations. Consequently, we have now reached a point where today it is not uncommon in sociology departments, after hearing a guest lecturer or job candidate report on a study that entails a statistical analysis of "race," to devote half an hour or so to having members of the audience offer the presenter their own Rorschach-like interpretation of what "race" is and what they think the presenter's research results actually mean, if anything. Such cavalier treatment of "race" as a variable in the twenty-first century is both conceptually and methodologically indefensible. Sociology, psychology, and other so-inclined disciplines cannot continue along this path and expect to be taken seriously—especially not in an era when the natural sciences continue to devastate the validity of the race concept. Not only does running "race" as a variable often produce little more than sociological nonsense, it promotes victim analysis, perpetuates racist stereotypes, and ultimately helps reify the race concept—the ideological core of systems of race-justified oppression.[21]

Ironically, it is just this type of race as a variable research, which produces the lowest yield conceptually and consequently has the least ability to explain society's big questions, that has the greatest legitimacy through the pretense that it is social "science." This was evident when in June of 2015 I did a JSTOR electronic search of the publication records of the discipline's most respected journals, which are now predominantly quantitative. From its founding in 1936 sociology's most prestigious journal, the *American Sociological Review* (*ASR*), published only one article with the word racism in its title—the article by Eduardo Bonilla-Silva I reviewed in the previous chapter—and no articles with titles containing the term racial oppression. The same numbers are true for the *American Journal of Sociology* (*AJS*), which was founded in 1895. Finally, *Social Forces* (*SF*), which was established in 1922 and has had from its beginning more focus on race relations, managed to publish only five articles with the word racism in their titles and none with titles containing the term racial oppression. Although, as I noted earlier, the term racism was not coined until the late 1930s and some of those journals' overlooking of racism from then to the 1960s can be attributed to the tendency of the discipline to define racism as largely a psychological phenomenon (e.g., as a set of beliefs or attitudes), what is also interesting and supports my "race" as agency argument is that the last articles with the words race relations in their titles appeared in *ASR* in 1976, in *AJS* in 1975, and in *SF* in 1993; the *SF* article I just mentioned—along with one other in 1990—are the only ones in that journal since 1972 to have race relations in their titles. The two *SF* articles published in the 1990s both referred to race relations during earlier time periods, with the 1990 article entailing a comparison of the emergent 1990s to the 1960s and the 1993 article focusing on the two decades of 1870–1890. The various sets of figures I have examined here suggest that even before the publication of William J. Wilson's *The Declining Significance of Race*, quantitative researchers in the discipline were moving away from dealing with the nation's racial problems as a relational phenomenon and had mostly returned to the default option of treating it as the "Negro problem"—a trend in tune with that of American society in general. Today most of the race and ethnic relations articles appearing in those journals have titles like these taken from *ASR*: "Race, Instruction, and Learning," "Race, Class, and Consciousness," and "Race and Socioeconomic Segregation." These trends reflect racial discourse changes within the larger society. For example, in his analysis of "racialized discourse" in *New York Times* articles from 1987 through 2004, Matthew Hughey found a decline in the number of times racial group relations was mentioned from 292 times in 1987 to zero in 2004. Moreover, such a decline is clearly not an indication of improving race relations. This is evident in that during a period that Hughey identified as one of white backlash (1993 through 1998) there were only two mentions of racial group relations in that, the nation's most respected, newspaper.[22]

Feagin and Vera have blamed this failure of American sociology to address the causes, nature, consequences, persistence, and workings of systemic racism—and society's big questions in general—on a trend beginning in the 1940s toward what they refer to as "'instrumental positivism.'" By "instrumental" Feagin and Vera meant that "it limits social research to only those questions that certain research instruments and techniques will allow," and by "'positivism'" they referred to the fact that "it commits social scientists to research approaches generally mimicking those of the natural sciences." They noted that by the 1970s most major sociology departments had committed themselves to instrumental positivism. Quoting Abigail Fuller, the authors indicated that instrumental positivism, or abstract empiricism as it is sometimes known, reflected a "larger 'positivistic culture'" in which "knowledge is fragmented, specialized, and divorced from its historical and social context, and as such, is robbed of its critical functions." Regarding the knowledge, power, and language implications of instrumental positivism, Feagin and Vera concluded that "as a rule, those wanting to do acceptable sociology will certainly need to use the discipline's mainstream vocabulary and place their ideas and findings within the conceptual horizons enforced by the discipline's gatekeepers, such as the mainstream editors, editorial boards, and peer reviewers of the major journals." Such "accommodation," which also includes conforming to the demand of funding agencies, "has resulted in only a limited array of acceptable research topics being studied."[23] It is an understatement to say that systemic racism is not on that list of approved topics.

In that very same decade of the 1970s, sociology's most prestigious journals stopped publishing articles on race relations and began issuing those that, with very little if any conceptual explanation of what was happening racially in the larger society either currently or historically, used sophisticated sampling and other statistical techniques as they "ran" their emerging conception of "race" as a variable that somehow means something and does things. This created a real conundrum for those scholars whose ideas and work do not fit the agenda of the nation's political and economic mainstream. For example, to ensure the generalizability of its findings, quantitative social science research relies on large and representative data sets. Collecting such data is expensive. Consequently social scientists depend on either grant funding, which is rarely available for controversial topics like racism, or on existing data sets that are not likely to contain items specifically dealing with racism. Without such "scientific" data, social scientists are rarely able to publish in prestigious and overwhelmingly quantitative journals like *ASR*, *AJS*, and *SF*—which, as you have seen, hardly ever include articles on topics like racism. Finally, due to the problem of "methodological individualism," even when scholars are able to publish in such positivist journals about controversial topics like racism, they are not likely to study social structures because survey and census data are compiled from the responses of isolated individuals. Consequently a study of racism is likely to be based on how individual respondents answer a few items intended to measure racial attitudes rather than an analysis of racist social structures. Rather than the conceptualization of "race" and racism determining how they are measured, increasingly it is their measurement that determines their conceptualization. Such biases in mainstream sociology journals have resulted in a split within the discipline between sociologists who tend to publish in such journals and those generally more critical scholars who tend to use qualitative research methods and are more likely to publish their work in book format.[24] So the vicious cycle continues as social scientists conveniently, but erroneously, pretend that the major bias in social science comes from problems with the techniques they use to collect or analyze data, while ignoring the major source of such bias: the questions that—for political and economic reasons—go unasked, and therefore unanswered. Such trends also impact how racism is defined.

DEFINING RACISM

When it comes to conceptualizing racism in a straightforward way, American social science often resembles a surrealistic world where none of the usual rules of facts and logic apply. Although for space and other reasons I have limited the focus of this book to social science in the United States, that should not suggest that the same confusion does not exist in other highly racialized democracies. The tangle in British sociology, for example, is so great that, as an outsider unfamiliar with the intricacies of British racial culture and politics, I would not even know where to begin to try to straighten it out. For instance, as I noted earlier, a basic rule of the social sciences is that one should try to define one's concepts as simply, clearly, and precisely as possible. Even for non-positivists that seems to be reasonable enough. But for the British postmodernist sociologist Ali Rattansi, even the need for simple, clear, and precise definitions is a point of contention. And as if to make this point, his Oxford University Press book *Racism: A Brief Introduction* provides the most muddled explanation of "race" and racism I have read. In the end, after challenging existing definitions of racism, Rattansi does not define the term himself. The focus of his book seems to be little more than an "it's all very complex and confusing" defense of conceptual obfuscation. On the opening pages, he asserted:

> My research and writing in this area have been particularly concerned to move discussions of racism away from over-hasty definitions, lazy generalizations, and sloppy analysis. In particular, it is my view that public and academic debates should move away from simplistic attempts to divide racism from non-racism and racists from non-racists. At the risk of exaggeration, I would suggest that one of the main impediments to progress in understanding racism has been the willingness of all involved to propose short, supposedly watertight definitions of racism and to identify quickly and with more or less complete certainty who is *really* racist and who is not.[25]

By setting up his racists-versus-non-racists straw argument, Rattansi draws attention away from three essential facts about racism. First, racism is systemic, not merely personal. Second, at the core of racial and other forms of oppression lie asymmetrical power relations. And finally, language plays a key role in both sustaining and challenging the racial status quo. Only by uprooting the conceptualization of racism from its social, political, and economic moorings could Rattansi dare to reduce the problem of defining racism to its presumed complexity.

A good example of the opposite, highly contextualized, approach to defining racism issues is the argument by Ashley Doane, a European American sociologist, that in the United States there exists a power-asymmetric "central rhetorical struggle" within "racial discourse" over the "'contested concept'" of racism. In explaining why such discourse "does not occur in a vacuum," Doane stated that it is instead "shaped by the changing structure of racial conflict and racial ideologies in the larger society." He noted that due to the successes of the civil rights movement and other major social transformations like changing demographics, there is now relatively little normative approval for overtly expressed racism. Moreover, due to its covert and institutionalized nature, contemporary racial oppression is especially vulnerable to the ideology of systemic racism theory with its demand for large-scale, yet specific, social analysis and change. On the other hand, "to the extent that individual definitions of racism become dominant, what emerges is a social world in which it is difficult to challenge or even envision institutional racism." Doane concluded that despite the counterchallenge of the movement toward a systemic racism perspective in some academic and activist circles, fueled by the supremacy of color-blind ideology, it is now the smaller—individual attitudes and behavior centered—definition of racism that prevails and is ascending.[26] It is within this politically reactionary environment that even a highly trained social scientist like Ali Rattansi can confidently insert an issue as absurd as "who is *really* racist" into the center of racism studies discourse through a publisher as distinguished as Oxford University Press.

Contrary to Rattansi and other postmodernist scholars, I take what they would likely consider to be the radical and extreme position that racism can and should be defined simply, clearly, and precisely.

Influential Definitions of Racism

In addition to categorizing the various definitions of racism taken from the literature I reviewed in the previous three chapters, I reveal their assumptions about the nature of racism and identify their language-centered racism-denial practices that in one way or another discount its scope, persistence, and consequences. I also include other recent definitions of racism taken from other sources such as popular racism-focused textbooks.

I am struck by how much of the literature is plagued by the language-centered racism denial practice of conceptual non-definition—the use of terms like race and racism without defining them. Unfortunately, Magnus Hirschfeld, the scholar who coined the term racism, got things off to a bad start by not explicitly defining it. Indeed, only about half of the scholarship I reviewed since the 1938 publication of his *Racism* contains explicit definitions of racism. That is why you will find that much of the literature I examined in previous chapters is not represented here. Having made this point about the tendency not to define racism, I now turn our attention to what is actually there.

Existing definitions of racism fall into three major conceptual categories:

1. Racism defined as a set of beliefs or ideology (B/I),
2. Racism as racially discriminatory behavior and practices (RDB/P), and
3. Racism as systemic racism (SR).

These categories are not mutually exclusive. For example, properly conceived the systemic racism definition also encompasses racism defined as a set of beliefs or ideology and racism defined as racially discriminatory behavior and practices.

Of the sixteen scholars whose definitions I review in this section, six fit exclusively the Beliefs or Ideologies category, two fit exclusively the Racially Discriminatory Behavior and Practices category, and only three, including my own, fit exclusively the Systemic Racism category. Three scholars fit both the Beliefs or Ideologies and the Systemic Racism categories, and the definitions of two scholars fit both the Racially Discriminatory Behavior and Practices and the Systemic Racism categories. Let's take a closer look at these definitional categories and the specific definitions under each. As figure 5.4 shows, these five single or combined categories of racism definitions fit a continuum from the least to the most systemic. That is, they extend from beliefs/ideology (B/I) to racially discriminatory behavior and practices (RDB/P) to beliefs/ideology and systemic racism (B/I-SR) to racially discriminatory behavior and practices-systemic racism (RDB/P-SR) to systemic racism (SR), which again encompasses the other definitions included in that continuum.

The Dominant Definition of Racism Then and Now: Racism as Beliefs or Ideologies

Despite what may have been a much larger conception of racism, because Hirschfeld stated the goal of his book as the examination of the "racial theory" beneath the Nazi "doctrine of race war," he may have given others the impression that a much smaller beliefs- or ideology-ism-centered conceptualization of racism was in order—what I refer to as the *mini-racism* perspective. The largest single number of definitions of racism then and now fit the category of Beliefs and Ideologies. This was certainly the case for anthropologist Ruth Benedict's publication of *Race and Racism* four years later, when she defined racism as "an unproved assumption of the biological and perpetual superiority of one human group over another," a "doctrine," "an ism," "a belief," and "the dogma that one ethnic group is condemned by nature to congenital inferiority and another group to congenital superiority." As even Benedict's conceptually minimist language suggested, any complete definition of racism must contain within it its conceptualization of race. Unfortunately, as you may recall from chapter 2, like most of her contemporaries, and despite her reference to "ethnic groups" in her definition of racism, Benedict conceptualized race as referring to real and essential biological differences between different groups of peoples.[27] Within those conceptualizations of race and racism, Benedict was content to treat racism as an

B/I   RDB/P   B/I-SR   RDB/P-SR   SR

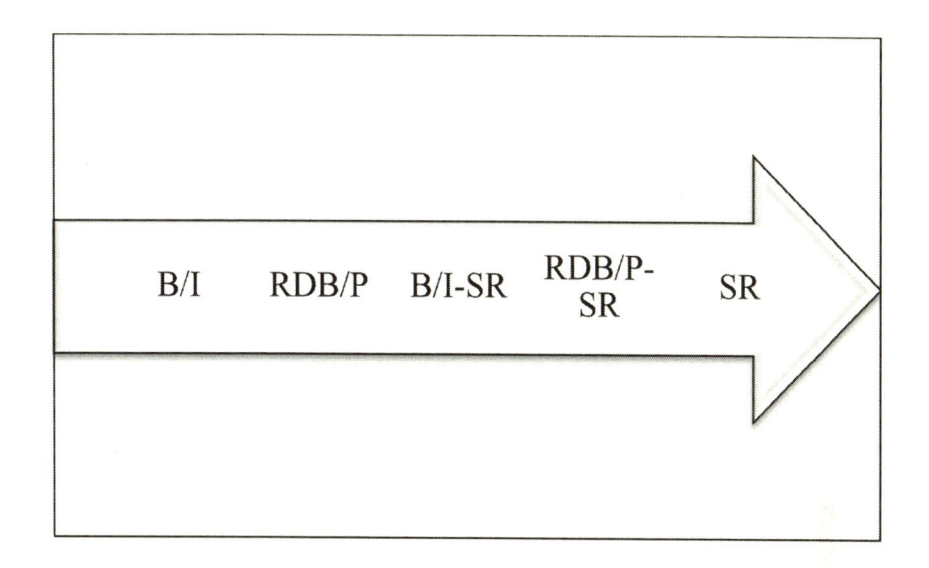

Figure 5.4. Continuum of Categories of Racism Definitions by the Degree to Which They View Racism as Being Systemic

isolated ideology or set of beliefs, rather than viewing the race concept as the ideological glue that held systems of race-justified oppression together.

Regrettably, it was Benedict's approach to defining racism that became and remains dominant in American social science. Two and a half decades later, after the civil rights movement shoved a large and robust view of racism back into the national discourse, in his book of the same title sociologist Pierre van den Berghe also defined racism in a conceptually minimist way as "any set of beliefs that organic, genetically transmitted differences (whether real or imagined) between human groups are intrinsically associated with the presence or the absence of certain socially relevant abilities or characteristics, hence that such differences are a legitimate basis of invidious distinctions between groups socially defined as races."[28]

In chapter 3 I mentioned van den Berghe's influence on William J. Wilson's conceptual work. Like van den Berghe before him, in his 1973 book, *Power, Racism, and Privilege*, Wilson took a beliefs/ideology focused approach to racism that also suffered from conceptual minimization in his definitions of racism as "a philosophy or ideology of racial exploitation" and "as an *ideology of racial domination or exploitation that (1) incorporates beliefs in a particular race's cultural and/or inherent biological inferiority and (2) uses such beliefs to justify and prescribe inferior or unequal treatment for that group.*" Wilson took the same approach with the identical result in his 1978 book, *The Declining Significance of Race,* when he defined racism as "racial belief systems," that is, "the norms or ideologies of racial domination that reinforce or regulate patterns of racial inequality."[29]

Between the publications of those two Wilson books, Oliver C. Cox, a scholar many see as the antithesis of Wilson in his non-accommodative spirit and focus on the systemic nature of the economic oppression he saw as being the foundation of what he referred to as racial animus, also defined racism in a conceptually minimist way as a set of beliefs and ideology. In *Race Relations* Cox surmised that racism "explains and justifies racial exploitation and prejudice; it shows why white dominance over peoples of color is proper and inevitable."[30]

While scholars like Wilson and Cox seemed to accommodate themselves linguistically and theoretically to the white racial backlash, the political Right showed no interest in meeting them halfway. Right-wing ideologues like Dinesh D'Souza instead took the next big step by not only officially declaring *The End of Racism*, but blaming the relative low socioeconomic status of African Americans on their cultural pathology and, while claiming that white racism was no longer a significant factor impacting the life chances of African Americans, highlighting "black racism" against European Americans and other ethnic groups.[31] With social science's re-endorsement of a mini definition of racism as racially bigoted beliefs and ideologies, right-wing ideologues could reduce any remaining discourse on racism to no more than the type of "who is a racist?" name-calling illustrated in figure 5.2.

This was the racially reactionary political environment in which the following year, 1996, Eduardo Bonilla-Silva criticized the tradition of defining racism in a conceptually minimist way while doing exactly that through his definition of racism as "only" "the racial ideology of a racialized social system" rather than as that system itself—with, as I would suggest, the race concept as its core ideology. The apparent influence of this movement is evident in the glossary of the third edition of Christopher Bates Doob's racism textbook, where he defined racism as "the belief that actual or alleged differences between different racial groups assert the superiority of one racial group."[32]

There is nothing about doing research on beliefs and ideologies that requires acceptance of such a tiny (or mini) definition of racism. Beliefs and ideologies are society-wide "social facts" that exist prior to the birth of most of the individuals who internalize them through a process of intergenerational socialization. In setting out the contours of the sociological method, Emile Durkheim made it clear that such social facts could not be reduced to the mere attitudes and behaviors of individuals.[33] Following the lead of psychologists and the restraints of traditional survey research methods, most sociologists who do research based on attitudinal data conveniently forget that important point about beliefs and ideologies as social facts and simply shrink their definitions to the mini-racism size that best fits their research methodology and career ambitions. Moreover, rather than simply acknowledge that their work and the data that supports it address only a relatively small, although important, component of racism, they succumb to the temptation to inflate the importance of their scholarship through incredible claims that racism encompasses only the work they do. In these and other ways, rather than expand their sociology to fit social reality, they shrink social reality to fit their sociology.

Racism as Racially Discriminatory Behavior and Practices

In a note in their first, 1986 edition of their book *Racial Formation in the United States*, Omi and Winant defined racism as "those social practices which (explicitly or implicitly) attribute merits or allocate values to members of racially categorized groups solely because of their 'race.'" This definition of racism as racially based social practices, while larger than the actions of a single individual, served their conceptual minimization purpose of shrinking what they considered the then-far too big systemic racism conceptualization down to size so that racial concerns would not dominate or derail what they believed to be a much larger and more important progressive movement coalition. By the third edition of their book, however, they had advanced their racism shrinkage project beyond the need to even define the term.[34]

Critical race scholars ultimately settled on a similar conceptualization of racism as racially based social practices, but for a very different, equally practical (as opposed to theoretical) reason. In the glossary of their 2012 primer, *Critical Race Theory*, Delgado and Stefancic defined racism as "any program or practice of discrimination, segregation, persecution, or mistreatment based on membership in a race or ethnic group." Although one of the assumptions of CRT is that racism is systemic, in their definition these CRT legal scholars choose to focus on what they can remedy in the courts, racially discriminatory behavior. But because actual intent is so difficult to prove they often find themselves relying on exposing patterns of disparate racial outcomes reminiscent of that rather weak correlational argument that has plagued institutionalized racism theory. So in this way their theorizing is limited by their legal practice, just as the theory work of social scientists is often restricted by their social movement ideals or research methodology. Their definition of racism also reveals that in addition to this conceptual minimization, these critical race theorists conceptually conflated racism with ethnicity-based discrimination.[35]

Racism as Both Beliefs or Ideology and Systemic Racism

Joel Kovel conceptualized racism as taking two forms and as operating at two levels. In *White Racism*, he defined racism as a "set of beliefs" and as "the tendency of a society to degrade and do violence to people on the basis of race."[36] It is the latter, racism as a social tendency, definition that treats racism as systemic. Although Kovel offered a historically grounded and multidimensional racism theory, it remained conceptually underdeveloped in that the institutional and inter- or trans-institutional (i.e., systemic) workings of racism remained unspecified.

Two years later, in his book *Racial Oppression in America*, sociologist Robert Blauner defined racism in a variety of ways, including his gender-awkward definition of "a historical and social project aimed at reducing or diminishing the humanity or manhood (in the universal, nonrestrictive meaning of the word) of the racially oppressed." In addition to being a social project, Blauner saw racism as being "a principle of social domination by which a group seen as inferior or different in alleged biological characteristics is exploited, controlled, and oppressed socially and psychically by a superordinate group." Finally, in his most succinct definition Blauner addressed what he saw as both the systemic nature of racism and its ideological core by defining racism as "a system of domination as well as a complex of beliefs and attitudes."[37] I think the later definition is powerful not only for its succinctness but for its completeness. From my perspective, aside from explicitly including racially discriminatory behavior and practices, all that remains undone is the location of the race concept at the very center of that ideological core with some specification of what it, along with racial beliefs and attitudes, do for systemic racism; something like "racism is a system of domination, justified by an ideological complex of racial beliefs, attitudes, and practices, with the race concept as its core." Without such specification of how these various components of systemic racism work Blauner's conceptualization of racism remains underdeveloped.

Blauner's student David Wellman also conceptualized racism both as beliefs and ideology and as a system of oppression. In his attitudinal research–based book, *Portraits of White Racism*, Wellman defined racism as "culturally sanctioned beliefs which, regardless of the intentions involved, defend the advantages whites have because of the subordinated position of racial minorities" and "white racism" as "a culturally sanctioned, rational response to struggles over scarce resources." Moving beyond that study's attitudinal data Wellman also defined racism as "a structural relationship based on the subordination of one racial group by another."[38] But, like that of Blauner and other scholars who combined the beliefs and ideology and the systemic racism conceptualizations of racism, Wellman's work remained not only conceptually undersized but underdeveloped, especially in fleshing out the specific ways in which systemic racism operates.

Racism as Both Racially Discriminatory Behavior and Practices and Systemic Racism

Stokely Carmichael and Charles Hamilton's *Black Power*, which was published as the civil rights movement reached the peak of its militant black power phase, provided the first major conceptual bridge between the approach of racism as discriminatory behavior and practices and that of systemic racism. After defining racism as "the predication of decisions and policies on considerations of race for the purpose of *subordinating* a racial group and maintaining control over that group," Carmichael and Hamilton stressed that such racism takes two forms: "individual racism and institutional racism." "The first consists of overt acts by individuals" while "the second type is less overt, far more subtle, less identifiable in terms of *specific* individuals committing the acts," and "originates in the operation of established and respected forces in the society." Those two types of racism operate at different levels of society and with different degrees of visibility, with the latter being referred to as institutional racism—the most rudimentary form (or component) of systemic racism.[39] Despite the major advances Carmichael and Hamilton made with their conceptualization of institutional racism, by confusing racial bigotry with racism their notion of individual racism encouraged the very conceptual minimization they challenged. In addition, their larger conceptualization of institutional racism remained conceptually underdeveloped in explaining how racism worked at that level, much less at the interrelated institutional or systemic level.

For a very short period of time, some agencies of the federal government and other organizations in the United States were inclined to see racial discrimination as a social problem that should be conceptualized and addressed. As I noted in chapter 3, Joe Feagin's approach to racism was influenced by a year he spent in the mid-1970s as Scholar-in-Residence with the U.S. Commission on Civil Rights. That experience was captured in a book he coauthored a few years later with his wife, entitled *Discrimination American Style: Institutional Racism and Sexism*. In that book the Feagins engaged in a bit of conceptual colonization by not providing their own definition of institutional racism, but instead treating it as one form of the assumed broader concept of institutional discrimination. They did, however, offer some important guideposts as to how the specific structures and processes of institutional racism and systemic racism work. To this end the Feagins noted that racism as direct racial discrimination in one contemporary institution can affect what occurs as indirect racial discrimination in another ("side-effect discrimination") just as direct racial discrimination in the past can lead to indirect racial discrimination in the present ("past-in-present discrimination"). While they provided a good beginning for both intra-institutional and trans-institutional (i.e. systemic) analyses, the outlines of their workings remained sketchy and conceptually underdeveloped, as did the key role of ideology in their operation.[40]

Racism as Systemic Racism

In his more recent work, Joe Feagin has taken an explicit systemic racism approach. In the second edition of their *White Racism* textbook that was first published in the mid-1990s, Feagin, Vera, and Batur defined "'white' racism" as "a centuries-old system intentionally designed to exclude Americans of color from full participation in the economy, polity, and society," and "racism" as "a *system* of oppression of African Americans and other people of color by white Europeans and white Americans."[41] But unfortunately, once again, Feagin and his colleagues have done little to flesh out the mechanics of the specific institutional and ideological components of systemic racism. While working within a general systemic racism conceptual framework, the focus of their work has been largely substantive. Consequently the systemic racism perspective has remained not only conceptually underdeveloped but undefended from attacks from those inclined to change the focus from racism to the behavior of the African American poor themselves, poststructuralists, ideology- or attitudes-centered researchers, and others hostile for various reasons to a large and robust conceptualization of racism.

With much of American social science theory moving back to its small, premodern civil rights movement conceptualization of racism, some of today's most explicit embracing of the systemic, or what is sometimes referred to as the structural, racism perspective has come from non-academic antiracists. For example, in the third (2011) edition of *Uprooting Racism*, social justice activist and writer Paul Kivel defined racism as "the institutionalization of social injustice based on skin color, other physical characteristics and cultural and religious difference." He continued by noting that "white racism is the uneven and unfair distribution of power, privilege, land and material goods favoring white people." Or, as he put it, "another way to state this is that white racism is a system in which people of color as a group are exploited and oppressed by white people as a group."[42] Kivel's approach to systemic racism suffers from both conceptual conflation and conceptual underdevelopment. His first definition seems more like a definition of ethnoracism, conflating racism and ethnicity, and his definitions overall do little to show the crucial institutional and ideological workings of racism as a highly organized system of oppression.

I also take a systemic approach to conceptualizing and defining racism. In keeping with this approach, I define racism most simply as "a highly organized system of 'race' justified oppression." That is an abbreviated version of the following definition I crafted for my article with Darlene Maddern on the controversy over my white racism course: "racism is a highly organized system of race-based group privilege that operates at every level of society and is held together by a sophisticated ideology of color/race supremacy."[43] My most recent and elaborate definition of racism includes brief explanations of its key concepts of system, ideology, and race. Racism is a highly organized *system* of social oppression comprising all of the interrelated institutions and organizations of society and justified by the *ideology* of *race* as the existence of biologically distinct and inherently unequal categories of people. Notice how I incorporate ideology into my definitions of racism as its key ideational component without actually reducing racism to an ideology. And by specifying "biologically distinct," I mean to make clear that this definition does not include ethnicity and ethnicism, which I believe should be conceptualized and defined as their own interrelated, but sufficiently distinct, phenomena.

CONCLUSION

As you have seen in this chapter, struggles to break free of the racially accommodative shackles of linguistic racial realism have profound implications for the pursuit of a more honest linguistic racial idealism that allows for defining racism in a way that is serious enough to rescue us from such conceptual madness as engaging in fruitless "you are a racist" name calling and finger pointing; incredibly tiny definitions of racism; and the discursive and analytical absurdity of the "race" as agency concept.

Definitions are affected by our perceptions of the world just as they, in turn, steer those perceptions. This is especially true for the politically contentious phenomenon of racism since its very definition is a key component of the linguistic anatomy of the ideology that either sustains or challenges the racial status quo. The best single predictor of the existence, size, and robustness of definitions of racism in highly racialized democracies like the United States is the current state of race relations. The normal state of affairs is denial, during which racism goes largely unseen and undefined. And when seen, it is usually conceptualized as being so tiny and insignificant as to reflect the irrational sentiments of only a relatively few socially deviant and marginalized individuals. However, when the racial order is challenged by the protests of the racially oppressed, it is capable of adapting to that pressure by grudgingly allowing the issue of racism into social discourse. And if that protest is too loud to ignore, as it was during the widespread and violent unrest of the mid and late 1960s, the racial order may, at least momentarily, tolerate a large systemic view of racism. But once that pressure subsides, social scientists are only too willing to shrink the conceptualization of racism back to its more manageable mini-racism size or, beyond that, to an even more conceptually confusing notion of "race" itself as an agent of action that neatly resets American race relations scholarship to its default setting focus on the "Negro problem."

The popular acceptance that racism is a highly organized "race"-justified system of oppression requires a large and robust conceptualization whose advocates aren't afraid not to mince their words, regardless of the negative career and other political consequences. Such understanding necessitates not only courage but the willingness and ability to do the theory work needed to specify the institutional and ideological workings of systemic racism at every level. The antiracist struggle cannot be successful with even another ten thousand substantively focused studies that document the many manifestations of systemic racism. As I noted earlier, at the core of all systems of oppression are words. It is through the use of such words that the social theories and other ideologies that maintain such systems are built. And it is only through solid intellectual work that social scientists who intend to not only challenge but to dismantle such systems can be effective. At the center of such an effort must be the crafting of the large and robust conceptualizations of systemic racism needed to teach people of goodwill exactly what this beast is and how it might best be slain. This is what the civil rights movement pushed for and what racially reactionary social scientists, many of whom see themselves as progressive, push against.

With the exception of Joe Feagin, the most influential American sociologists in the area of race and ethnic relations today—William J. Wilson, Michael Omi and Howard Winant, and Eduardo Bonilla-Silva—all share, to use Omi and Winant's terminology, a common "race project." That is to shrink the concept of racism back down to a more manageable, post–civil rights movement, size for the profession and the larger structure of racialized group relations of which it is a part. That goal was achieved largely through the linguistically centered racial accommodation denial practice of conceptual minimization. With the reestablishment of that sociological canon, the conceptually underdeveloped work of Feagin's systemic racism camp and the advocates of a more systemic racism-friendly critical race theory would be tolerated as conceptual outliers, but rarely engaged intellectually. Marginalized outside the nation's acceptable mini-racism racial canon, conceptually such scholarship all too often suffers a fate equivalent to death in academia. It is ignored.

In chapter 6 I examine the theoretical implications of abandoning linguistic racial accommodation as I use my experiences in teaching about systemic racism as conceptual guideposts for theorizing about racism as a highly organized system of "race"-justified oppression.

Chapter Six

Confronting Racially Accommodative Language by Conceptualizing Racism as a System of Oppression

> If we lived in a democratic state . . . we would not tolerate the language of the powerful and, thereby, lose all respect for words, *per se*. We would make our language conform to the truth of our many selves and we would make our language lead us into the equality of power that a democratic state must represent.
> June Jordan[1]

Words matter! One word, a single word, can cause a radical paradigm shift in how racism is perceived, conceptualized, defined, analyzed, and addressed. Here is an example. One day I read an op-ed newspaper essay in which an African American sociologist challenged the stereotypes that so often obstruct the job-seeking efforts of young African American men. While I was pleased that the essay made its point so eloquently, I also felt a profound sense of loss for what it did not attempt, and therefore could not achieve: a fundamental challenge to the racial order that could have been raised with a change of one word. By referring to "racial" stereotypes, the author kept the focus on the characteristics of the young African American men and raised an issue of whether such stereotypes were accurate or inaccurate. I lamented what could have been accomplished had that well-intentioned and progressive sociologist simply replaced the single word "racial" with the word *racist*. With that one word change, the focus would have been removed from defending the character of those victimized by racial stereotypes and placed instead on the racist system that created them in the first place and the racial bigotry of the potential employers who internalized those stereotypes and executed them in their hiring practices. The tendency to use the expression "racial stereotypes," I believe, actually legitimizes and reifies such stereotypes by raising them to the level of unresolved issues that merit social-science debunking. Calling them *racist* stereotypes would have resulted, instead, in shifting the essay's analytic spotlight to the racist origins and functions of the stereotypes themselves, the system they serve, and the people they benefit. I refer to such a shift as linguistic racial confrontation (LRC).

LINGUISTIC RACIAL CONFRONTATION

As the African American poet and activist June Jordan asserted in this chapter's epigraph, sometimes intolerance can be a good thing. This is especially true when it comes to the refusal to accept injustice and the language with which it is built and maintained. Implicit in her words is the fact that if language is to be true and just, it must be made to be that way. It must be made to be "a democratic language," not "the language of the powerful that perpetuates that power through the censorship of dissenting views."[2] Such democratic language would not privilege the racism-evasive terminology of the powerful like "race," "the race issue," and "minorities," but would welcome the words of the oppressed, like systemic racism and racial oppression. Jordan's challenge amplifies the famous Frederick Douglass quotation I referred to in this book's introduction chapter, which speaks so eloquently to the experiences of African Americans and other oppressed people in the United States: "power concedes nothing without a demand."[3] As both of those accomplished wordsmiths were well aware, especially potent is the power of words. The focus of this chapter is not the linguistic racial accommodation (LRA), which as I have shown helps maintain the racial status quo, but its political opposite, the linguistic racial confrontation (LRC) that challenges that established order.

Figure 6.1 illustrates that dialectical relationship between linguistic racial accommodation and linguistic racial confrontation in language usage at a particular point in time. The dynamics of that inherently unequal power struggle determine the extent to which the prevailing racial discourse either sustains or challenges the racial status quo. It is the state of race relations during a given historical period that determines the balance of linguistic power between the two, with the dominant default status being the generally more robust linguistic racial accommodation. For example, both prior to and after the more militant phase of the African American freedom struggle, when American cities burned, the words white racism have been disallowed in most racial discourse.

My White Racism course is a case in point of that dialectical tension.

```
            LINGUISTIC
              RACIAL
          ACCOMMODATION
              ▼
  ═══════════════════════════════
              ▲
   LINGUISTIC
     RACIAL
  CONFRONTATION
```

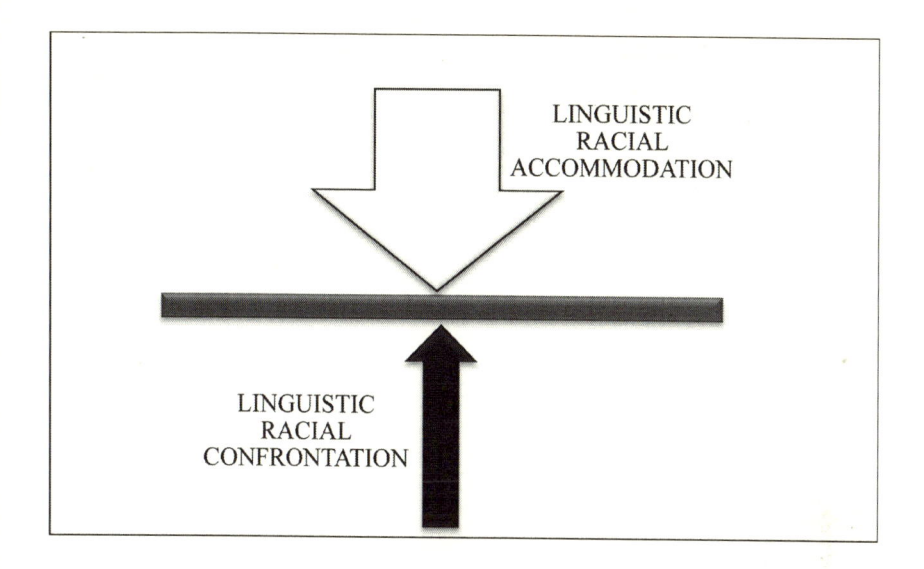

Figure 6.1. The Dialectical Relationship between Linguistic Racial Accommodation and Linguistic Racial Confrontation that Determines the Prevailing Racial Language at a Given Point in Time

TEACHING ABOUT SYSTEMIC WHITE RACISM

In this book's prologue I recounted that the title of my White Racism course, with the course's root assumptions that the race concept is bogus and racism is systemic, provoked a linguistic racial confrontation that challenged two of this society's most basic discursive rules of race relations: first, that "race" be treated as real and, second, that racism, to the extent that it is acknowledged at all, be perceived as tiny in scope and insignificant in its impact.

The first of those linguistically realist LRA discursive rules that led some to be offended by my White Racism title is rooted in the race-essentialist assumption that, despite all of the popular talk about America being a color-blind society and social-science teachings on race as a social construction, race/color categories like "white" and "black" are real and must be respected as such. Its linguistically idealistic LRC opponent is the course's premise that, because race is at best a now scientifically discredited myth, it is impossible for the title to be offensive to the "white race," because there is, indeed, no white race to offend or to defend.

Conformity to the second linguistically realistic discursive rule requires that to be allowed into racial discourse racism must undergo a linguistic racial accommodation process of conceptual minimization that reduces it to its widely accepted mini conceptualization of racism as bigoted attitudes and behaviors of a relatively few individuals who are out of sync with society's current norms of racial tolerance and harmony; in short, that racism is no more than racial bigotry. The course is offensive to those who accept that definition because it singles out white people as racists, implying that non-white individuals are never bigoted. Its linguistically idealistic LRC challenge is the view that because racism is indeed systemic, individuals are not the course's focus.

The conclusion that white people should be offended by the White Racism course title because it unfairly singles them out as white racists can be reached only if the logic of the LRC challenging assumptions is ignored. Those LRC assumptions are, simply stated, that the "race" concept is bogus and that racism is systemic. In contrast, the reasoning of the LRA dominant assumptions can be stated equally as simple: that "race" is real and an essential determinant of who we are, and racism is only racial bigotry.

Overview of Linguistic Racial Idealism Focused Course Content

In an edited book chapter I gave an overview of my White Racism course and stressed the central place of linguistic racial confrontation in it. There I explained that the course is important not only because "it is one of the most straightforward and honest courses taught anywhere on the topic of—what for political reasons alone is generally and confusingly framed as—'race,'" but also "because it places the chief beneficiaries of racial oppression, not its 'minorities' victims, at its analytical core." I also stressed that such a recasting of the "historical 'Negro problem'" in the United States "as what it actually is, a systemic white racism problem" required a rejection of the failed yet still dominant race and ethnic relations paradigm in American sociology.[4]

Because the two basic assumptions upon which my White Racism course is based are the no-race premise and the fact that racism is systemic, central to that course are the conceptualizations of "race" and racism. In doing that conceptual work, I launch an LRC challenge to their opposing and dominant LRA assumptions by discussing with my students a *Hartford Courant* op-ed essay in which I argued that, contrary to the prevailing tendency in American society to treat race as reality and racism as a myth or falsehood, addressing this nation's serious racial problems requires us to do exactly the opposite. That is, we must both reject what I refer to as "the Myth of Race" and accept "the Reality of Racism."[5] Consistent with my observation about the dueling linguistic racial realism-grounded LRA assumptions of those who opposed the course and the linguistic racial idealism-driven LRC premises of those who supported it, the two lessons I tell my students I want them to take away from the course are (1) the fact that the "race" concept is bogus and (2) the difference between racism and racial bigotry. With that knowledge, they can fully appreciate why a course titled White Racism is in no way offensive to "white" people. If racism refers to social structures rather than individual people, and if there are no white or other races of people, then not only is there no reason for the course title to be deemed offensive; there are no people who could legitimately take offense.

The Course's No-Race Premise and More

It is this discursive battle, revolving around the course's no-race premise, that contains within it a somewhat humorous irony. Although its White Racism title was deemed by some "white" people to be offensive to the white race, the course is built on the assumption that the very concept of race is bogus. I make this point with a bit of drama in one of the course's early lectures. First I ask my students to envision the opponents to the course on the curricula and courses committee as "comedic Musketeers who thrust their swords high into the air as they loudly proclaim, 'On guard! We must defend the white race!'" Then I whisper to my students "a 'secret,' which if it had been known prior to the course being approved would have been even more upsetting to those who opposed the course title." This secret is that "the course is built on a 'no-race' premise." To support that point, I note that "based on the best historical, anthropological, and human genome evidence available it categorically rejects the notion that there are biologically distinct races of people." Finally, I conclude by stating that because "there is no 'race,' 'black,' 'white' or otherwise," "there is no white race to offend or defend."[6]

But I go much further than the widely accepted racially liberal view that race is a social construction. To make my point that race is nothing less than the core ideology binding together systems of "race"-justified oppression, I discuss with my students their chapters' readings from Audrey Smedley's important study of the history of the race concept in North America. The findings of that African American anthropologist provide an LRC challenge to LRA language. For example, she concluded that race is not just a social construction, it is a "worldview" used to justify exploitation: "race is a cosmological ordering system that divides the world's peoples into what are thought to be biologically discrete and exclusive groups. The racial worldview holds that these groups are by their nature unequal and can be ranked along a gradient of superiority-inferiority." Smedley then noted that because of their stratification function, some of the beliefs that comprise race as a worldview are, indeed, ideologies. She therefore had no problem with the interchangeable use of the words *worldview* and *ideology* in reference to the race concept.[7]

Smedley's provocative history of the origin and evolution of the race concept in North America has profound implications far beyond racial liberalism and its push for racial-equality focused reforms, with the race concept left intact. It certainly challenges Michael Omi and Howard Winant's increasingly extreme defense and expansion of what they portray as a natural, inevitable, and in some ways good, race concept. It also puts to rest any implication of Eduardo Bonilla-Silva's work that a "racialized" social system could exist that is not, indeed, a *racist* system. Moreover, Smedley's study convincingly demonstrates that because that conception assumes that different racialized groups are inherently unequal, the very notion of "racial equality" is oxymoronic. Consequently all efforts to redeem the race concept under the banners of reform efforts for racial equality are doomed. The profound LRC conclusion I draw from Smedley's work has radical implications for how social scientists and others treat the language of race. That conclusion, which I share with my students, is simply this. The very concept of "race" is *inherently* racist. As I noted in an essay published in the newsletter of the Association of Black Sociologists, "'race' should be problematized—and ultimately relinquished—not only because it is *confusing* (e.g., as to which individuals today fit which categories), but because it is *erroneous*, and most importantly, because it is *injurious*."[8] By ignoring, or not taking seriously, the latest advances in our understanding of the race concept from academic disciplines other than sociology, otherwise progressive scholars like Omi and Winant, Bonilla-Silva, and Patricia Hill Collins fail to appreciate how much the uncritical use of the inherently racist race concept serves to reify race as the core ideology of racism as a highly organized system of "race"-justified oppression.

Speaking about "race"-justified oppression, although I am critical of much of Pierre van den Berghe's work, I find his insight into the political origins of racialized thinking to be useful to my understanding of the origin of racism. In my class I summarize this in a PowerPoint slide entitled "Pierre van den Berghe—on the Relationship between Egalitarian Ideals and the Development of Racism."[9] I then pose the following question, "How is slavery justified in a society built on the assumption that all human beings are created equal?" The answer is, "Simple. People of African descent are not human." That is followed by this explanation. "So, ironically, the ideal of equality played a major role in the development of racism, as it does today in its maintenance" as a rationale for opposing any "race"-specific efforts to address racial inequality issues. I then explain that although racism began with the creation of unequal racial categories and other ideologies that justified slavery, it quickly became institutionalized to include racist policies, procedures, and practices that permeate the entire American social system. Even after slavery was abolished, racism as a highly organized "race"-justified system of oppression continued, as it does today. Let's take a closer look at the other core assumption of the course: that racism is, indeed, systemic.

The Course's Racism Is Systemic Assumption

I also use a bit of humor to make my point about the second key assumption of the course: that racism not only exists, is pervasive, and is devastating in its social consequences, but is, indeed, systemic. To remind my European American students that I am teaching a course on systemic racism and not a class on racially bigoted individuals that they should take personal offense to, I periodically tell them, "I am not talking about your mama!" In making this point, I stress that I am a sociologist, not a psychologist; and as a sociologist it is my job to examine social structures, not the attitudes and behaviors of individuals. Both the course's social structuralist perspective and its treatment of race as an ideological construction are made clear in the language of the course description section of its syllabus.

> In the United States, as well as throughout much of the world today, people designated as "white" are the socially dominant racialized group. The highly organized system of racial oppression which maintains their privileged position is systemic white racism. This course explores white racism as a central and enduring social structure around which the United States and other modern societies are organized and evolve.[10]

A Sampling of Course Lecture Notes

More on the Course's Social Structural Emphasis

In an early lecture in which I explain why it is important to focus specifically on "white" racism, I also make clear the course's systemic racism focus. I state that as a sociologist my concern is with understanding social structures—how societies are organized and why they and their key components persist or change. I also note that, unlike what is generally assumed, racism is a group and societal-level phenomenon—what Emile Durkheim referred to as a "social fact," one that cannot be reduced to the prejudice and behavior of individuals. Therefore, while it is true that there are racially prejudiced African Americans, Latino/a Americans, Asian Americans, and Native Americans, the focus of the course is systemic racism, not just the attitudes and behaviors of racially bigoted individuals. Consistent with that focus, white racism can be defined as a "race"/color-justified system of group privilege. To make this point I refer to a *Hartford Courant* commentary in which I argue that America is racist to its core due to its racist historical foundations, its core racist values, and the overlapping racist institutions that comprise its social system. Therefore, to say that America is racist to its core is simply to say it is racist in its social structure.[11] Of course, that conclusion has profound implications far beyond piecemeal racially liberal analysis and reform. It implies that effective change must reach beyond examining "race" and white privilege critically and increasing diversity on college campuses and in the workplace. Early in the semester I make my radical antiracist position and goal clear by asserting that as a highly *structured* (i.e., organized) feature of U.S. society, systemic white racism can be expected to continue indefinitely, unless there is *fundamental* (i.e., structural) change. As support for this perspective I refer to "the permanence of racism" thesis of critical race scholar Derrick Bell, and like Bell serve my LRC notice that I have no intention of remaining within the relatively safe LRA boundaries of white liberal thought and language.[12]

Defining White and Racism

As is clear from the course's title, its two key concepts are *white* and *racism*; thus it is positioned at the conceptual nexus of two emerging interdisciplinary specialty areas—whiteness studies and racism studies—both of which have profound language implications. In class I note that, because there are individual people of color who are lighter in skin color than most European Americans and because science no longer supports the legitimacy of the race concept, whiteness is clearly not just a color or a race. While many American social scientists today acknowledge that whiteness is a social construction, most Americans still uncritically accept race/color terminology despite insisting that the United States is a color-blind nation. Moreover, the language differences over the meaning of whiteness reach far beyond a question of what is accepted on campus and off campus.

Within academia there are two very different conceptualizations of whiteness as a social construction. The first is the racially liberal perspective of whiteness as racial privilege supported by Peggy McIntosh in the late 1980s with her cogent metaphor of unpacking the "invisible backpack of white privilege."[13] I refer to that perspective as being racially liberal because it accepts white racial identity and designation uncritically and requires "white" people only to acknowledge and perhaps challenge some of the unfair benefits they receive because of it. Otherwise, as is true for racial liberalism generally, it leaves the color-based system of group privilege intact, although hopefully a bit less onerous. Conferences held based on this racially liberal view of whiteness would have their participants leave with the LRA language of white and whiteness "unpacked," as McIntosh might say. Because I believe that race/color terminology is the ideological core of racial oppression, I find this to be a tragic failing.

In my class I challenge this racially liberal perspective on whiteness with a radical alternative deeply rooted in the African American social thought of intellectuals like W. E. B. Du Bois, James Baldwin, and Toni Morrison.[14] This perspective on whiteness requires students to do much more than, depending on the idiom du jour, "unpack" white racial privilege or critically examine or "interrogate" race. Indeed, with its assumption that one cannot both uncritically accept white racial identity and work effectively against white racism, it treats the concept of a "white" antiracist as oxymoronic. Under the leadership of scholar/activists like Noel Ignatiev, David Roediger, and Theodore Allen; movement names like the New Abolitionists; and periodicals like *Race Traitor*; this perspective challenges European Americans to do nothing less than to abolish race and whiteness as they continue to engage in a radical antiracist struggle.[15] I offer that serious LRC challenge to my students.

The second half of the course title is, of course, racism. In chapter 5 I discussed the systemic approach to defining racism I use in my classes and writings. In my White Racism class I point out that while some scholars have viewed racism as a set of *beliefs* and others as racially discriminatory *behavior*, I define it as a *system* of "race"-justified oppression. I then note that my systemic definition of racism is, indeed, large enough to encompass racist beliefs and behavior. As an example of the multidimensional nature of systemic white racism, I share with my students Feagin, Vera, and Batur's definition of white racism as "the *socially organized set of practices, attitudes, and ideas that deny African Americans and other people of color the privileges, dignity, opportunities, freedoms, and rewards that this nation offers to white Americans.*"[16]

I also take the opportunity of defining racism to introduce a new way of distinguishing between systemic white racism on the one hand, and bigotry on the part of African Americans and other people of color on the other. As I noted earlier, making such a distinction is crucial because one of the ways European Americans deny the seriousness of white racism is by insisting that it is no different from that of "black racism" or the "racism" of members of any other racial group. First, I introduce the popular racism-requires-power argument by briefly discussing Feagin and Sikes's definition of racism as "racial prejudice backed by power and resources." I then criticize that definition for being both simplistic and outdated in its assumption that African Americans and other people of color lack the power and resources to discriminate. For example, I point out that certainly President Barack Obama had the power to discriminate as do African American mayors, CEOs, and school superintendents, to mention just a few.[17]

Influenced by Feagin, Vera, and Batur's argument that because racism is a group-level phenomenon it is not appropriate to refer to black racism, I formulated for my students a level-of-organization explanation of what distinguishes white racism from so-called black racism. Here is the argument I draw from.

> In its fullest definition, racism is a *system* of oppression of African Americans and other people of color by white Europeans and white Americans. There is no black racism because there is no centuries-old system of racialized subordination and discrimination designed by African Americans that excludes white Americans from full participation in the rights, privileges, and benefits of this society.[18]

But after having said all that, Feagin, Vera, and Batur returned to the old power-based analytical framework. They did stress, however, that the power to discriminate required for racism is systemic and therefore goes beyond "sporadic instances of people of color discriminating against whites."[19] I am able to avoid confusion about what power is and who has it by focusing instead on the *levels of organization* at which both white racism and African American racial bigotry operate.

Figures 6.2 and 6.3 illustrate that in terms of its sociological scope, the organization of systemic white racism is much larger than that of the racial bigotry of some African Americans and other people of color. Moreover, I should note that the relative sizes of these two figures grossly understate the vast differences in magnitude between phenomena that occur at the societal and institutional organizational levels and those limited to the formal organizational, primary group, and individual levels.[20]

A closer look at figures 6.2 and 6.3 begins with the three levels of social organization systemic racism and racial bigotry share. That examination reveals that although there are both African American and European American racial bigots, white racism and African American bigotry are not socially equivalent phenomena. This fact is evident as we let our eyes scan the fourth and fifth levels of figure 6.2 and compare the five levels of organization for systemic white racism to the relatively small three levels for racial bigotry shown in figure 6.3. Racial bigotry occurs at three levels: the individual (e.g., bigoted individuals); the primary group level (e.g., a small group of young men who hang out together and mark their territory with racist graffiti); and the formal organizational level (e.g., white nationalists and bigoted black nationalists). I then make it clear to my students that in both figures racial bigotry exists and should be treated as a serious social problem with horrific consequences for its victims and their loved ones, in some cases going so far as to include murder. Although I do not discount the existence or consequences of bigotry among the racially oppressed, I do acknowledge that some racial bigotry by African Americans and other people of color may be reactive to systemic white racism, and that as such it does not usually have the added power of being attached to a larger system of racial oppression.

In brief, I make a distinction in the sociological *scope* of African American bigotry compared to systemic white racism, which includes but cannot be limited to the racial bigotry of European Americans. By sociologi-

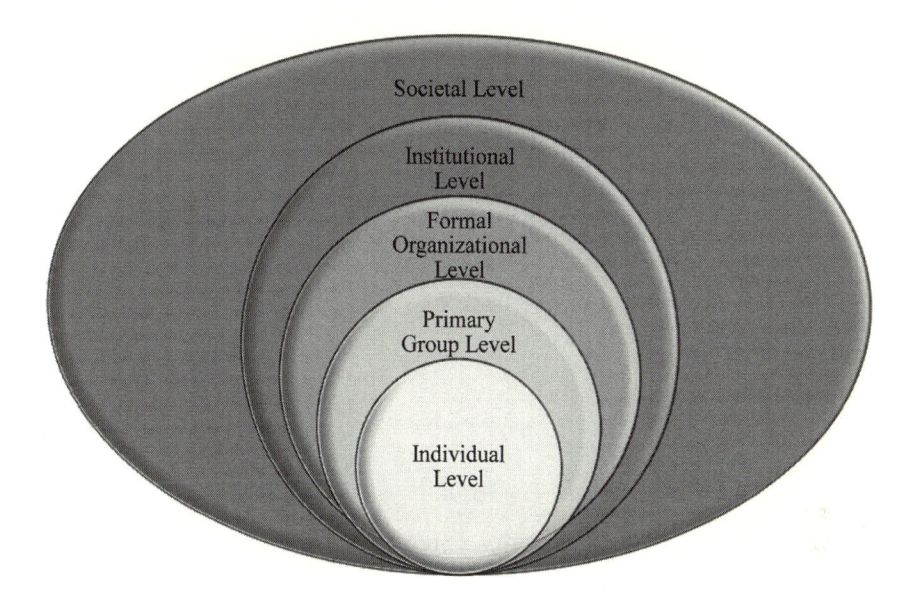

Figure 6.2. Levels of Organization of Systemic White Racism of Some African Americans and Other Peoples of Color

cal scope I simply mean the social terrain occupied by the two phenomena. In making this point to my students I note that systemic white racism (figure 6.2) includes European American bigotry at the individual, primary group, and formal organizational levels but then continues on to two additional levels: the institutional and the societal or systemic levels. Examples at the institutional level include racism embedded in politics, education, and the mass media. I then explain that all of a society's interrelated institutions and other organizations, plus the "race" concept and other racist ideologies, constitute its social system, which operates at the societal level. Finally, I conclude my explanation of that figure by stating that, as a highly organized feature of society, racism at that societal level adversely affects tens of millions of racially subordinated people on a regular basis. It can operate quietly without individuals expressing overt racial hostility, and its consequences include all of the negative effects of racial bigotry plus the highly institutionalized greatly reduced life chances of its many victims (e.g., ghettoization, poverty, high levels of stress-related illness, poor health care access, and lower life expectancy). I conclude by noting that both Joe Feagin and I view white racism as a systemic phenomenon—one that cannot be reduced to the level of individual prejudice—and for that reason we sometimes use the terms *systemic racism* and *systemic white racism*. I also tell my students that

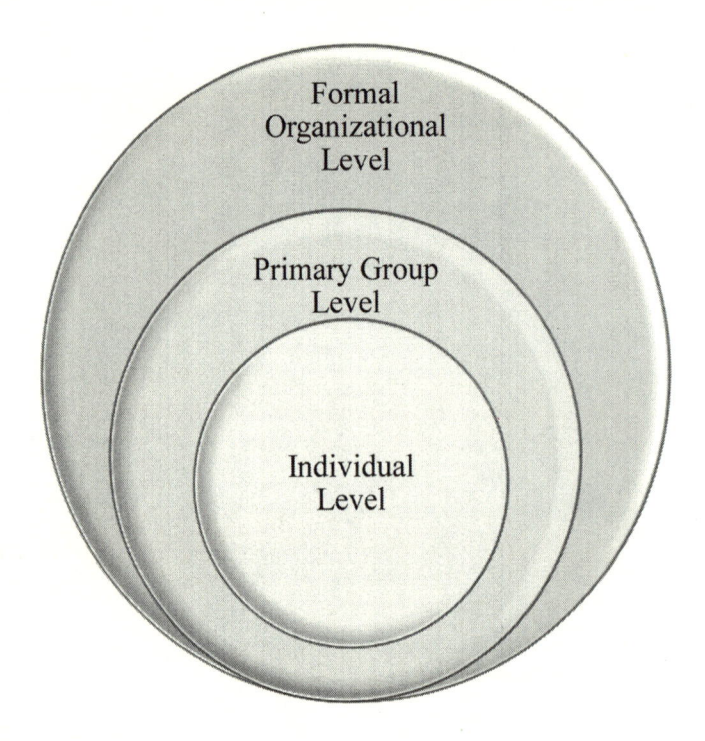

Figure 6.3. Levels of Organization of Racial Bigotry of Some African Americans and Other Peoples of Color

since all racism by my definition is systemic, when I use the single word *racism*, the fact that racism is both systemic and "white" is implied.

As I noted many times in this book, one of the most effective racism-evasive tactics is to reduce racism from being systemic to the relatively small size of racial bigotry. When this is done, racism discourse becomes personal and emotional, with fighting words like "white racists" being treated as no more of a social problem than "black racists." Moreover, any challenge to racist actions can be taken as a personal assault as attention is deflected away from those actions and their consequences. In addition, this type of language confusion makes it nearly impossible to understand how non-bigoted people, even those of color, can create racist images or engage in racist actions without themselves being overtly racially bigoted. Examples include a career-driven Puerto Rican writer who writes screenplays for a Latino American comedy that are loaded with racist stereotypes and an African American store clerk who has been trained to racially profile other African Americans.

I advise my students to always use the term *racist* to refer to actions (e.g., racist police misconduct) and structures (e.g., racist social system) and the products they generate (e.g., racist attitudes and racist culture), and to *never use the word racist to refer to individuals*. The appropriate term for an individual who is racially bigoted is *racial bigot*. This simple language shift alone could have a significant impact in cutting through system-sustaining linguistic racial accommodation. Of course, that language change will not happen just because it should. What makes and keeps such language muddled is power; making it clear requires the ability to change racial power relationships, at least enough so that the white power structure will concede to that measure of linguistic racial confrontation.

Finally, I synthesize what I taught my students about whiteness and racism into the definition of white racism as "the organization of white racial identity in the acquisition and sustenance of white racial privilege." With the help of that definition I conclude that the necessary and sufficient conditions for the occurrence of systemic white racism are white racial *identity* and privilege-seeking social *organization* based on that identity. Or, as I express it formulaically in a PowerPoint slide, White Racism = White Racial Identity + White Racial Privilege.

Still More on the Systemic Nature of Racism

To make my case about the systemic nature of racism in the strongest credible language possible, I distribute and discuss with my students copies of a *Hartford Courant* commentary in which I answer the question "Is America Racist?" in the affirmative by arguing "Yes. America Is Racist to Its Core." I like to share that essay with my students because, although its America-is-racist-to-its-core argument may initially seem over the top, as a sociologist, or a social structuralist as I sometimes refer to myself to my students, I am easily able to make that case because to say that America is racist to its core is to simply state what is demonstrably true: that it is racist in its social structure. I rely on three pillars of support for that bold LRC assertion: the nation's racist historical foundation and legacy; its white supremacist beliefs; and the racist organization and operation of its social institutions.[21]

In laying out the racist historical foundation and legacy part of my argument to my students, I stress that as a historical sociologist I believe history is profoundly more important than the lessons it offers as mistakes for us humans to avoid repeating. Instead I insist that when it comes to oppressive social structures, unless history is changed in some fundamental way, *it is* the present. To make this part of my America-is-racist-to-its-core argument, I show a PowerPoint slide of a three-story house named "Racist Social Structure." The foundation of that house is labeled PAST. Its main floor is the PRESENT, and its second floor is the FUTURE. In this way I help my students to understand the point I illuminate in the essay with the help of some examples of the racist experiences of Latino/a Americans, African Americans, and Asian Americans: that "contemporary white racist attitudes and practices are built upon this nation's legacy of past white-racist views and actions."[22]

As a segue to my second point—about the centrality of white supremacist beliefs, I quote my essay that "key to this historical legacy are white supremacist values and ideologies that often manifest themselves in white racist stereotypes." Then I mention that such "stereotypes are key building blocks in the ideological justification of white supremacist beliefs and practices." Finally, to make my point about the essential role of racist institutions, I note that "social science research documents that white racism is central to the structure and operation of every institution of American society." [23]

I conclude that essay by stressing the radical implications of my America-is-racist-to-its-core argument for those who would eradicate racism. "In brief, white racism is a systemic problem, not a problem of a few racial bigots. Since white racism is a core feature of the organization and evolution of American society, it will persist unless society is changed in a fundamental way. Its eradication requires systemic solutions that fundamentally challenge both 'white' racial identity and privilege."[24]

I display another PowerPoint slide (see figure 6.4) to illustrate how these three major components of systemic white racism fit together. At the very bottom of the figure is the historical foundation upon which present and future racist structures rest. Then notice the five major interrelated institutions that, together with the many other institutions and organizations, make up much of its current social structure. In addition to not including all social institutions and organizations, the figure makes no attempt to assess their relative power and influence. Finally, "race" and other racist ideologies (including racist stereotypes, images, and language) provide the societal-level cognitive glue that binds the racist social structure together.

Through these lectures my students better appreciate why they should embrace explicit and direct terminology like white racism and racial oppression while avoiding the use of conceptually obfuscating and misdirecting words like "race" and "minorities."

Of course, my White Racism course and its key concepts do not exist in a theoretical vacuum. Many of those underlying assumptions are evident from the LRC words those theories so often use—like conflict, power, oppression, ideology, fundamental, structural, systemic, and of course racism—as well as those LRA terms they avoid, like the uncritical use of "race," "black," "white," and "minority groups." Indeed, my racism courses, this study, and the observations of other scholars suggest a list of criteria for a comprehensive theoretical perspective on systemic racism.

```
                    Economy

     Politics                     Education

        ←── "Race" and Other Racist Ideologies

      Religion                    Family

            ⇑              ⇑
  Racist Historical Foundation and Legacy
```

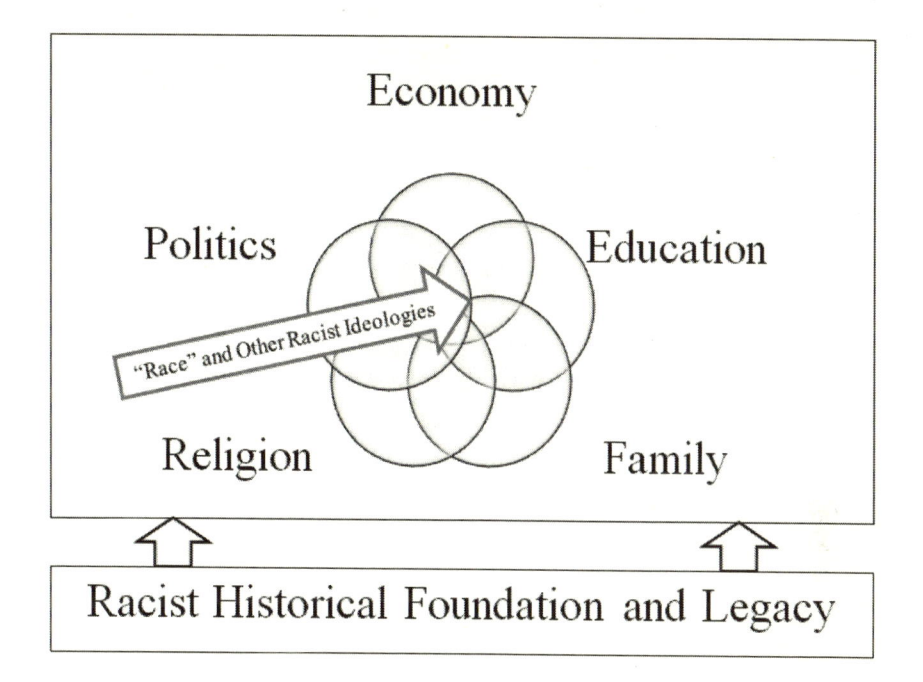

Figure 6.4. The Racist Social System and Its Historical Foundation and Legacy, Interrelated Major Institutions, and Core Ideologies

SYSTEMIC RACISM DISCOURSE UNCHAINED: CRITERIA FOR A COMPREHENSIVE THEORETICAL PERSPECTIVE

The View beyond Linguistic Racial Accommodation

Imagine that a spaceship full of explorers from another planet has just landed on Earth. They quickly dispatch a team of scientists to collect as much data as possible on the planet, including the social life of its human inhabitants. What types of conceptual tools would they need to describe and explain what they observe about the racial order of the United States and Earth's other highly racialized societies? And how might the concepts they construct and the theories they organize them into to make sense of what they see differ from those crafted by the natives who operate within the fetters of highly institutionalized linguistic racial accommodation restraints? Now imagine what such a conceptual framework or theoretical perspective on systemic racism might look like if its Earthling exponents could somehow free themselves from the bondage of linguistic racial accommodation.

Once again I must acknowledge that no scholar has done more in articulating a vision of the systemic racism perspective than has Joe Feagin. Unlike myself, Feagin is optimistic about what he sees. "Today, we are in the early stages of developing a major new conceptual paradigm on U.S. racial matters, with a new array of conceptual and interpretive tools and a growing number of social scientists, legal scholars, and others starting to realize the old 'race relations' paradigm's limits." [25] As I discussed in earlier chapters of this book, what is also known as the race and ethnic relations paradigm was discredited in the 1960s with its failure to predict the civil rights movement. Now, more than a half century later, the main trend within sociology has been—following Wilson's lead—to focus increasingly on the assumed cultural deficiencies of the African American poor; uncritically jump on Omi and Winant's postmodernist racial formation bandwagon, which was designed to lead us away from focusing on racial oppression toward a power-pluralistic view of numerous racisms and racial meanings–driven projects; do work with little theoretical content under the façade of ostensibly engaging in serious "critical race theory" scholarship; like Bonilla-Silva, shrink the definition of racism closer to its pre–civil rights movement size; treat "race" as a self-operating agent that somehow has the power to do things on its own without human agency; or simply run "race" as a variable with little if any conceptualization of what race is, how it is used, by whom, and why. Yes, there is lots of provocative work being done under the banners of critical race theory and systemic racism theory, but, as I have shown, that scholarship is still conceptually underdeveloped and marginal in its influence on the discipline.

Unlike Feagin, I don't believe that what we currently see unfolding in what he calls a new paradigm is capable of seriously challenging the dominant racism-evasive tendencies of highly professionalized and careers-driven social science, let alone of society more generally. I think that much of the progress toward the development of a viable systemic racism theoretical framework has either been beaten back by the sociological mainstream or has stalled due to its own inadequate conceptual work. Moreover, I believe the challenge Feagin envisions is only possible through a strong radical antiracism movement, one that emboldens progressive scholars to do serious intellectual work on racial oppression in opposition to highly institutionalized LRA forces. The ultimate goal of such a *radical* antiracism movement and its requisite intellectual work must be nothing less than the *destruction of systemic racism*—not just persuasion of the racial order to be more diverse and accepting of "minorities." We can't just wait for Feagin's radical vision to naturally unfold. Against all odds, we must *make it happen* by *forcing* changes in existing power relations. And at the center of such change must be our transformation of our language.

If Feagin's vision is to gain enough traction it must free itself from the theoretical quicksand in which it is currently mired. What do those aspirations suggest as the criteria for a comprehensive theory of systemic racism?

According to Feagin, "those working in this contemporary paradigm are attempting to develop a better theory of racial oppression, one that shows racial oppression's deep structures, assesses its dimensions and reproductive processes, and demonstrates how both inertial forces and change forces have shaped it over time." For this to happen, Feagin sees the need for innovative conceptual work that is congruent with "the counter-mainstream tradition of scholars of color such as W.E.B. DuBois and Oliver C. Cox." Within that tradition Feagin would surely include the work of civil rights movement intellectuals like Carmichael and Hamilton, which enlarged the concept of racism and pushed the topic of systemic racism to the center of national discourse.[26]

My theoretical work here is unambitious. I simply make suggestions as to how the contours of a comprehensive systemic racism theoretical perspective can be more fully developed from what I consider to be its current anemic state. While I identify the requisite components of a robust theoretical perspective, I make no effort to connect the dots toward the development of empirically verifiable, propositions-based, substantive theory. Finally, I will not propose strategies and tactics for a viable antiracist movement. Those important tasks remain for other scholars and other books.

I begin this work with an overview of social theory.

Social Theory: An Overview

Building on figure 5.1, which illustrates the linguistic anatomy of ideology as consisting of—in descending order—perceptions, conceptions, definitions, and words, figure 6.5 shows that those four factors also constitute the essential building blocks used in theory construction.

While my primary interest in this book thus far has been in the workings of words, definitions, and the perceptions they reflect in the conceptualization of racism, it is also important to briefly examine their impact on how racism is and should be theorized. A good place to begin in establishing the importance of such theory work is by defining what a theory is.

What Is a Theory?

In *The Structure of Sociological Theory* Jonathan Turner defined theories as "concepts organized into groups of statements." That definition works well with this book's focus on the conceptual level of analysis and also fits figure 6.5's representation of concepts as essential building blocks in theory construction. That focus and assumption are further supported by the following assertions by Turner regarding the structural components of theory in a later edition of that book: "concepts are the building blocks of theory," "concepts are constructed from definitions," and "a definition is a system of terms." Finally, the centrality of language to theory construction and how such lan-

```
                    Theory Construction
         ─────────────────────────────────────
                       Perceptions
              ───────────────────────────
                        Concepts
                  ─────────────────
                       Definitions
                      ─────────
                         Words
```

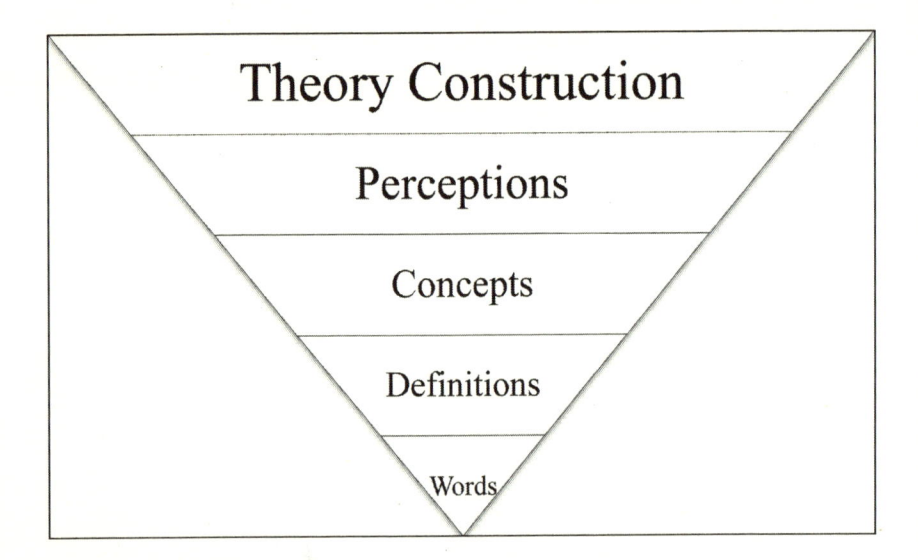

Figure 6.5. Theory Construction and Its Building Blocks: Perceptions, Concepts, Definitions, and Words

guage reflects one's relative social location and experiences is stressed by Nicholas Mullins's simple, but for this study insightful, observation that "theories provide a bridge between language and experience."[27]

Different Types and Levels of Theory

For my purposes, the chief distinction regarding different types and levels of theories is the one I made earlier between substantive theory, which I will not attempt here, and my much less aspiring focus on a theoretical perspective, or what is also known even more modestly as a conceptual framework. In distinguishing the two, Nicos Mouzelis defined substantive theory as "a set of interrelated substantive statements trying to tell us something new, something we do not know about the social world, which statements can be tentatively proved or disproved by empirical investigation," and a conceptual framework as "a set of tools that simply facilitate, or prepare the ground for, the construction of substantive theory." He cautioned, however, that the two overlap and that the distinction between them is relatively new. Indeed, such a distinction barely existed in classical sociology. It came much later as theory became a specialty area once sociology became highly professionalized. Mouzelis emphasized, however, that today the goal of most sociological theory "is not to fashion substantive theories" to be judged by their "empirical verifiability," but instead "to construct sets of conceptual tools" to be judged by their "heuristic utility."[28] I believe that racism theory is so conceptually underdeveloped that a rush toward the development of substantive theory could set it further back. So instead, the immediate focus of racism theory work should be the more adequate fleshing out of a viable theoretical perspective.

Theoretical Perspectives

Through their specific language, which articulates their underlying assumptions about how society works, theoretical perspectives provide "a general perspective or orientation for looking at various features of the social world."[29]

In sociology there are three major competing theoretical perspectives: structural-functional theory, conflict theory, and symbolic interaction theory. Each seems to bring useful tools to the analysis of racism and other social phenomena. For example, in my White Racism class I note that structural-functional theory can be used to explain the persistence of racism in terms of the economic, political, and the social status/prestige functions it serves as a highly organized social structure for those European Americans who benefit from it. Conflict theory explains racism as a system of privilege-generating oppression that is established and maintained through the power of the dominant racialized group and altered through successful challenges from racially oppressed groups. Finally, symbolic interactionist theory accounts for the centrality of meanings (e.g., "race," "whiteness," and racist images and stereotypes) in the social construction and maintenance of racial hierarchies.

Each of these three perspectives has its limitations. With its emphasis on social consensus as what holds societies together, structural-functional theory is more inclined to focus on how race relations are stabilized through the widespread acceptance of the norms of the existing racial order. Consistent with that concern about consensus and social stability is its interest in how different racial groups get along within the existing normative order. It is the conflict theoretical perspective that best accounts for the role of power and conflict in how systems of racial oppression are set up, sustained, and changed. However, with its emphasis on power, conflict, and social change, the conflict theoretical perspective has a more difficult time explaining the everyday workings of social structures and processes when such forces are not obviously at play. Finally, due to its concentration on subjective meanings, the symbolic interactionist perspective is not very adept at explaining the more materialist or "objective" social inequality manifestations and workings of social structures.

One might therefore deduce that the best way to understand a social phenomenon like racism is simply to combine elements of each theoretical perspective into one approach that contains the advantages of them all, without their respective limitations. Unfortunately, crafting such a synthesis is problematic because each theoretical perspective rests on its own set of assumptions about how society works, and those assumptions tend to be incompatible. In their introductory sociology textbook Margaret Andersen and Howard Taylor identified for each perspective its general view of society, basic questions, and major criticisms. The structural-functional theoretical approach (what they refer to as functionalism) views society as being "objective," "stable," and "cohesive." Conflict theory sees it as "objective," "hierarchical," and "fragmented." And symbolic interactionist theory perceives society as being "subjective" and "imagined in the minds of people." The structural-functional theory view of the "basis of social order" is "consensus among public on common values," compared to "power" and "coercion" for those taking a conflict perspective, and "collective meaning systems" and "society created through social interaction" for adherents of the symbolic interactionist approach. While structural-functional theory views inequality as being "inevitable" and indeed "functional for society," conflict theory roots it in a "struggle over scarce resources," and the focus of symbolic interactionist theory is "inequality demonstrated through meaning of status symbols." Whereas structural-functional theory identifies the "source of social change" as "social disorganization and adjustment to achieve equilibrium" and assumes that "change is gradual," conflict theory explains change as deriving from "struggle" and "competition," and the symbolic interaction theoretical perspective sees it as being driven by an "ever-changing web of interpersonal relationships and changing meaning systems." Finally, Andersen and Taylor identified the major criticism of the structural-functional theory approach as "a conservative view of society that underplays power differences among and between groups," whereas critics of conflict theory charge that it "understates the degree of cohesion and stability in society," and the symbolic interaction approach has been criticized because of its "weak analysis of inequality" and its tendencies to "ignore material differences between groups in society" and to overemphasize "the subjective basis of society."[30]

Each perspective also has its own orientation to racial language, and its own excuses for not treating it with the seriousness it deserves. Although one might assume that the structural-functional theory perspective is best equipped to explain the persistence of racially accommodative language because of the sustenance function it serves for racist social structures, with its focus on consensus and social stability, it takes racial accommodation for granted to the point that it is not viewed as being problematic. One might also assume that both conflict theory and symbolic interactionist theory would be useful in showing how racist social structures are both organized and challenged through language. However, with its concentration on objective social structures, the conflict perspective is likely not to emphasize factors like language that are often treated as if they are purely subjective, and many adherents of the symbolic interactionist theoretical perspective are extreme in their treatment of social structures as being subjective. Consequently, consistent with the poststructuralist trend in American sociology, these approaches tend to discount the more objective manifestations of social structures and the centrality of language to them and to treat symbolic conflict (e.g., over racial meanings) as being much more pluralist than it actually is.

Those three major theoretical perspectives also provide the basic assumptions of other smaller and more substantively focused sub-categories of theoretical perspectives. For example, in my Racism Theory graduate seminar I identify the following racism-related theoretical perspectives that all accept the basic premises of conflict theory: institutional racism, internal colonialism, systemic racism, racial state theory, the neo-Marxist theory of racial oppression, critical race theory, and critical whiteness studies. The black feminist perspective is another theoretical framework that encompasses a racism lens that I have found very useful in my teaching and scholarship for its ability to account for gendered racism.

The systemic racism approach is the substantively focused conflict theoretical perspective I believe offers the most promise as an explanation of and challenge to racial oppression. According to Feagin, systemic racism refers to "the core racist realities" that "are manifested in each of society's major parts." To make this point he uses the metaphor of a hologram: "if one breaks a three-dimensional hologram into separate parts and shines a laser through any part, the whole three-dimensional image is projected from within one part. Like a hologram, each part of U.S. society—the economy, politics, education, religion, the family—reflects the fundamental reality of systemic racism."[31]

FROM BREAKING CHAINS TO BUILDING THEORY: THE CRITERIA OF AN EFFECTIVE THEORETICAL PERSPECTIVE ON SYSTEMIC RACISM

So what does an effective theoretical perspective need to include to capture the complex multifaceted reality of systemic racism?

Criteria Suggested by the Existing Literature

There is perhaps no better articulation of the challenge and promise of sociology than C. Wright Mills's *The Sociological Imagination*. It is there that Mills laid out the formidable analytical task of any credible theoretical perspective with his provocative observation that "neither the life of an individual nor the history of a society can be understood without understanding both." Mills lamented the elusiveness of such a perspective when he observed that "yet men do not usually define the troubles they endure in terms of historical change and institutional contradiction." This is so, he observed, because "they do not possess the quality of mind essential to grasp the interplay of man and society, of biography and history, of self and world." Consequently "they cannot cope with their personal troubles in such ways as to control the structural transformations that usually lie behind them." Mills concluded that to see their social world in this way, they need the "quality of mind" he referred to as "the sociological imagination." To meet the challenge and promise of Mills's sociological imagination, a viable theoretical perspective on systemic racism must therefore be historical in its method, systemic in its scope (e.g., to account for "institutional contradiction"), and able to explain multiple levels of social phenomena (i.e., individuals in their relevant social and historical context).[32]

The sociological imagination is also useful in placing the theories individuals hold and share about how their social world operates within their appropriate sociohistorical context. When this is done, it quickly becomes clear that social theory work is inherently political. Indeed, in many instances the only real difference between social-science-based social theory and political ideology is the pretense that the former is derived from a value-free social science. For example, liberal social theory accepts the social system as being basically good and suggests only some minor reforms to sustain that system by helping it work more smoothly and thus avoid major system-threatening challenges. A liberal social science response to a program of racial internment might be to conduct periodic quality of life surveys to ensure that camp internees receive adequate food, water, clothing, heat, fans, ventilation, sanitation, health care, and recreation. A radical approach, in contrast, would be to study that internment program and the larger system of racial oppression of which it is but one component to discover any weaknesses that can be helpful in the development of strategies and tactics for escape and ultimately the destruction of both. In brief, whereas racially liberal theory accommodates itself to the demands of the white power structure, radical antiracism theory exists solely to destroy it.

Joel Kovel made this point about the importance of theory work that, as I would put it, flees the intellectual plantation of linguistic racial accommodation for the battleground of linguistic racial confrontation, when he identified the goal of his *White Racism* book as "to contribute toward a theory that resists compliance with racist society—one that presses not for the reforming of racism, but its overthrow." For this to happen "requires a break with the framework provided by normal social science, precisely because it is the function of such discourse to keep our understanding of society piecemeal and fragmented." Again, an effective theory of systemic racism must have as its chief political value and goal not the amelioration of systemic racism and its core ideology of race, but their destruction.[33]

Geographer David Harvey has also stressed the importance of scholars making explicit the usually hidden political context of their theory work: "social science formulates concepts, categories, relationships and methods that are not independent of the existing social relationships. As such the concepts are the product of the very phenomena they are designed to describe." Harvey identified three types of social theory based on the political functions they serve: status quo theory, revolutionary theory, and counterrevolutionary theory. Caste theory is an example of status quo theory, whereas systemic racism theory and its institutional racism precursor are cases of revolutionary theory, and Wilson's declining significance of race thesis is a classic example of what Harvey refers to as counterrevolutionary theory.[34] One of the reasons systemic racism theory remains so underdeveloped is the success of the counterrevolutionary theories, which have taken up so much time, space, talent, and other resources within professionalized social science study and discourse.

The chief exponent of a large and radical theory of systemic racism is Joe Feagin. Although much of Feagin's work has been substantive rather than theoretical in its main focus, as I noted earlier, he has identified what he considers to be the criteria of an effective theory of systemic racism. For example, in making his case that such an approach must be large in its scope, oppression focused, and historical, Feagin insisted that, unlike the dominant race and ethnic relations perspective, it provided "a full recognition of the big picture—the reality of this whole society being founded on, and firmly grounded in, oppression targeting African Americans (and other Americans of color) now for several centuries." For Feagin, based on the assumption that "U.S. society is an organized racist whole with complex, interconnected, and interdependent social networks, organizations, and institutions that routinely imbed racial oppression," its focus must be on the systemic nature of racism. Such an approach must also be able to account for how "this system has changed somewhat over time in response to pressures within the societal environment." In their race and ethnic relations textbook, Joe and Clairece Feagin identified the following six "themes" that "a comprehensive theory of racial oppression" should encompass: *"initiation," "mechanisms," "privileges," "elite maintenance," "rationalization,"* and *"resistance."*[35]

Building on what I discussed in the previous section, as well as what I have stressed elsewhere in this book based on my own ideas and those of the many other scholars whose thoughts I have drawn from, here is my list of what I think such a theoretical perspective must do.

My Criteria List for a Comprehensive Theoretical Framework to Explain Systemic Racism

These two dozen criteria are organized around the following six themes I have stressed in this book. Such a theoretical framework must be systemic racism and oppression specific, able to treat "race" as its core ideology, comprehensive, dynamic, theoretically compatible and useful, and language focused.

Systemic Racism and Racial Oppression Specific

1. Focus directly and explicitly on systemic racism.
2. Explain racial oppression (i.e., the asymmetrical power *relationship* between racialized ethnic groups rather than focus on a single group).

Treat "Race" as the Core Ideology of Systemic Racism

3. View the race concept as the core ideology of systems of "race"-justified oppression.
4. Centrally locate white racial identity and privilege within its analysis.

Comprehensive (Multidimensional and Multilevel)

5. Define racism as being systemic.
6. Explain how racism is organized or structured.
7. Be comprehensive and multidimensional in its focus on all of the major components of systemic racism.
8. Explain both overt and covert forms of racism.
9. Explain systemic racism at the macro, meso, and micro levels of analysis.
10. Account for both social structure and human agency, and their interactions.
11. Account for both the "objective" and "subjective" dimensions of social structures, and their interactions.
12. Explain individual, primary group, and organizational level racial bigotry within the larger context of systemic racism.
13. Include methods that are both historical and nationally comparative.
14. Account for systemic racism as a global phenomenon.

Dynamic (Processes, Methods, and Change Focused)

15. Explain the origins of systemic racism.
16. Account for the methods and processes of systemic racism; including its organizational and institutional transactions.

17. Account for both the persistence of racism and for changes in the forms its manifests under different sociohistorical conditions.
18. Explain how systemic racism is successfully challenged and how it can ultimately be destroyed.

Theoretical Compatibility and Usefulness

19. Be compatible with the basic assumptions of the conflict theoretical perspective.
20. Be useful in the development of substantive theory.
21. Fit harmoniously with intersectional scholarship while being able to go analytically deep with its own primary focus on systemic racism.

Language Focused

22. Recognize the centrality of language in the operation of and challenges to both the "objective" and the "subjective" dimensions of systemic racism.
23. Explain the role of linguistic racial accommodation in the maintenance of systemic racism and the effect of linguistic racial confrontation in challenging and destroying that system.
24. Be honest in its use of language—with no regard for the political, career, and other negative consequences of not working within the white power structure's acceptable parameters of racially accommodative language.

CONCLUSION

I have stressed elsewhere in this book that to honestly address their systemic racism problems, highly racialized societies like the United States must be pushed beyond their linguistically racial accommodative tendency to treat the placement of people into racial categories as a commonly and uncritically accepted reality and racism as largely a myth to the opposite linguistically racial confrontational view that it is, indeed, race that is a socially devastating myth (as in untruth) and racism that is the pressing reality that must be addressed. In this chapter I sketched the contours of what a linguistically honest theoretical perspective on racial oppression might look like if somehow its exponents were able to break free of the intellectual shackles of racially accommodative language like "race" and embrace the racially confrontational conceptualization of systemic racism.

I am not naïve, however, about the relationships among language, power, and voice—who gets to say what, and using what words. I realize that if a viable systemic racism theoretical perspective actually breaks its chains, it will not be because doing so is right. Systemic racism is not right, yet it has managed to not only endure, but to flourish for centuries, with substantial support from the social sciences. An honest discussion of racism in the United States is dependent on a change in racial power relations. But racially progressive intellectuals cannot simply wait for such macro-level changes to happen, as they did in the late 1960s when even a federal government commission was forced to mouth the words white racism as this nation desperately tried to restore peace to its many burning cities. Radical antiracist scholars and activists are honor- and duty-bound to deploy linguistic racial confrontation to, as June Jordan so eloquently put it, "make our language conform to the truth of our many selves."[36]

In this book's next chapter I bring my analysis to its conclusion by summarizing the lessons learned in this study about language-centered racism denial practices, as well as the challenges remaining, for those who are committed to building racism studies and racism theory that are capable of conceptualizing racism directly and explicitly in the language of the racially oppressed.

Conclusion

Lessons Learned and Challenges Remaining: Toward a More Honest Conceptualization of Racism

> Be skillful in speech, that you may be strong...
> words are braver than all fighting; a wise man is
> a school for the magnates, and those who are aware
> of his knowledge do not attack him.
> *The Teaching for Merikare*[1]

Once upon a time in a beautiful and bountiful land far far away there lived a powerful and ruthless king who was well served by his talented and loyal wizard. Through the wizard's magic the king, who was small, bald, and quite ordinary, was made to appear to be so towering, handsome, and godlike that no mere mortal could imagine challenging his power or, indeed, would want to. For many years, under the wizard's spell, the common folk—simple peasant farmers—remained quiet as almost everything they owned was taken from them as taxes to feed the seemingly bottomless coffers of their insatiably greedy king, who was said to be of a fairer-skinned and more deserving breed of men. But as the wizard grew old and his powers diminished, some of the people began to see quick glimpses of who their monarch actually was and what he was really up to. As word of what they had seen spread throughout the kingdom, those normally gentle peasants rose up in revolt and drove the wicked king and his sycophant wizard into exile. One day, long after the king died, the now hungry, cold, and weary wizard struggled to make his way back home to the kingdom. When he arrived at its mighty drawbridge, the wizard frantically performed numerous magic tricks for the people with the hope that they would once again be awestruck by his mighty powers and realize how much they still needed him. He turned puppies into frogs, bats into tiny dragons, and rabbits into ducks. But this time the people were not moved. They scoffed at his puny and pathetic magic and he was never again allowed inside the walls of what was now their new democratic nation.

In this conclusion chapter I examine the lessons of this study that can help the racially oppressed and their allies muster the strength to, when necessary, turn away the social science and other wizards of linguistic racial accommodation and to insist, instead, that their own words and the pain and wisdom they express be heard by society's intellectual and policy magnates. After I summarize this study's major findings I conclude with a few parting words toward the development of a radical and linguistically confrontational racism studies.

SUMMARY OF THIS STUDY'S MAJOR FINDINGS

As Thomas Pettigrew noted, American sociology has historically played both a critical and a supplicant role when it has come to its conceptualizations of the nation's racial order. In this study you have seen that more often than not that role has been as a supplicant server of power—white power. That posture of conformity has been accomplished through the use of various linguistic racism denial practices.

During its first century (1850–1950) a cyclical pattern was institutionalized involving this nation's racial structure, career rewards and punishments, academic racial knowledge, racially accommodative language, and language-centered racism denial practices. To this day, that vicious cycle still ensures that the linguistic racial accommodation within sociology and the other social sciences sufficiently matches that of the larger highly racialized society of which they are a part.

Beginning in the mid-nineteenth century the language-centered racism denial practice of *conceptual misdirection* justified then existing race relations as being rooted not in racial oppression but, instead, in the assumed biological inferiority of people of color. Later, in the 1920s, the practice of *conceptual extenuation* offered the ideological balm that race relations would change naturally over time with other changes in the social structure, with no need for human intervention. In the 1930s *conceptual realism* ruled as a language-centered racism denial practice that accepted the racial status quo as a given—a set of social arrangements that could not and should not be changed. Then in the 1940s, the *conceptual idealism* that racism could not persist because it was incompatible with America's democratic and egalitarian values provided a new palliative against those who might argue for the need for fundamental change. During that same period radical class-focused scholars, who eagerly awaited what they saw as an inevitable proletariat revolution in the United States, deployed the practices of *conceptual conflation* of racial oppression with class-based oppression and *conceptual colonization* of racism by their class interest that discounted race relations as a mere nasty residue of exploitative class relations. Closing out that century, in the 1950s the language-centered racism denial practice of *conceptual minimization* reduced race relations to psychologists' interests in the prejudice of bigoted individuals.

Due to its extreme posture of linguistic racial accommodation, the race and ethnic relations paradigm of American sociology proved itself incompetent in predicting the major transformation in race relations that culminated in the modern civil rights movement. As the discipline entered its second century, however, there emerged a measure of hope that it might be better able to align its analytical lens with what was actually happening racially within the United States. Unfortunately, although there was some effort in the 1960s and 1970s—mostly by some highly marginalized sociologists—to catch up with the civil rights movement and its emphasis on social conflict as a means of change and on racism as being systemic, that was relatively short lived. The scholarship of that period suffered from not only *conceptual underdevelopment* but also *conceptual minimization*, *extenuation* of racism to assumed larger social forces and trends, *conflation* with social class issues, *colonization*, and *obfuscation* through the use of terminology that was so vague as to be meaningless.

By the late 1970s American sociologists were working hard to redirect the focus away from racial oppression as the cause of the problems facing the African American poor, and later to treat racial conflict as little more than highly subjective and pluralistic contests over racial meanings and projects, or to shrink the scope of the racism concept back to its tiny, but now contextualized, pre–civil rights movement size. Those efforts were greatly facilitated by the rise of quantitative research methods; the growing influence of the poststructuralist movement within the discipline; the desire of some progressive scholars to shift attention away from racial oppression-centered movements to what they saw as larger and more progressive and economics-centered struggles; the resurgence of the culture of poverty perspective on the "black underclass"; and the return of focus on attitudinal research. With its *conceptual misdirection, colonization, conflation, obfuscation, rejection* of the use of racism specific terminology, *minimization*, and *underdevelopment*, William J. Wilson's *The Declining Significance of Race* best captured the power of that white backlash.

As sociology has accommodated itself in these and other ways to the white power structure's rejection of any notion of systemic racism and to its insistence that democratic America is indeed color-blind, it has broken into a number of ineffectual and underdeveloped theoretical factions. Concurrently, neither the number nor the intensity of language-centered racial accommodation practices have diminished and they have become increasingly more sophisticated, with the practices of *conceptual misdirection, minimization,* and *underdevelopment* now all being prominent, and with *conceptual colonization, rejection,* and *obfuscation* still having their impact.

In this study you have seen how early sociologists proffered racist theories of African American inferiority that justified slavery, Jim Crow, and other forms of racial oppression and established the tendency that continues to treat the "Negro problem" as their discipline's analytical focus rather than the system of racial oppression that has caused African Africans so many problems, social and otherwise. Because of this complicity, the discipline was so ignorant of the role of racial conflict in the origins, maintenance, and changing of that system that it failed to see the coming of the modern civil rights movement. Then, under the intense pressure of urban rebellion and burning cities, with concepts like institutional and systemic racism the profession finally allowed the language of the racially oppressed into its analyses. However, with the coming of the post–civil rights era and its institutionalized white backlash, progressive sociologists of all racialized backgrounds crafted theories of "race" and the African American condition that helped put those large and robust definitions back in their place. Simultaneously they also helped change the topic altogether to the assumed bad behavior of the African American poor; created a postmodernist fantasy world in which systems of racial oppression were replaced with new racisms, multiple racisms, and racial identity and meaning projects; and shrunk the definition of racism to a point that it became so small and effete that it could explain little more than the persistence of racist attitudes in a society ruled by color-blind ideology. Once again, with the help of their largely compliant social sciences, the scales of the racial language dialectic in the United States and other highly racialized societies have been tipped to a default position of linguistic racial accommodation.

In this study I also demonstrated how various developments in American race relations have, in turn, shaped how racism is defined within the social sciences—definitions that have with a few notable exceptions been kept both small and underdeveloped. To that end I have shown, for example, how the size of such definitions actually expand and shrink in response to African American insurgencies and white racial backlashes, respectively. I also paid close attention to the limits placed on the conceptualization of racism by the ascendance of quantitative research and the emergence of a trend of treating "race" as a phenomenon that is assumed to have agency within itself independently of human actions—except maybe the assumed pathological behavior of impoverished African Americans. Then I showed that what appeared to be a diverse assortment of influential sociologists with different substantive focuses and theoretical approaches all worked separately toward a common goal: to shrink the definition of racism back to the pre–civil rights movement's incredibly small size that is less controversial and thus more manageable for both the social sciences and the larger racial order of which they are a part. While acknowledging that the systemic racism perspective still survives and provides the framework for many racism-centered studies, I concluded that it remains woefully underdeveloped and marginal in shaping the theoretical direction of the discipline.

Building on those findings, I made specific suggestions toward the advancement of racism studies and its theory by sharing some of the conceptual work I have done in my racism-focused classes and by providing a list of criteria for the crafting of a more fully developed theoretical perspective for the study of racism as a highly organized system of "race"-justified oppression.

CONCLUSION: LESSONS LEARNED TOWARD THE CONSTRUCTION OF AN INTELLECTUALLY RADICAL AND LINGUISTICALLY CONFRONTATIONAL RACISM STUDIES

There are both sobering and hopeful lessons to be learned from this study for the advancement of the forces of linguistic racial confrontation against those of linguistic racial accommodation.

Some Sobering and Some Hopeful Lessons

Perhaps the most sobering lesson of this analysis is the fact that it is power—not what is right and reasonable—that determines if and how racial oppression is conceptualized in the social sciences and the larger society. When it comes to racialized group relations, the social sciences have distinguished themselves to a much greater degree as followers than as leaders. I am not saying that sociology and the other social sciences have no power. They do possess power. But as you have seen, that power rests primarily not in what they produce as "science" in helping us to understand the workings of racialized group relations, but in what they construct as language-centered ideology that either supports the racial status quo or challenges it.

Can sociology and the other social sciences be changed in such a way that they distinguish themselves as being less the protectors of the racial status quo and operate more as agents for fundamental change? The answer is yes and no. In theory, it could begin to happen with such minor reforms as the establishment within the American Sociological Association of a section specifically on racism with its own journal that focuses exclusively on racism, with a special emphasis on the building of racism theory. However, even such modest changes within that highly entrenched bureaucracy would prove difficult any time in the near future given its current external racial environment and its internal professional politics and vested interests.

There could be some changes within the discipline if what appears to be the emergence of a broad-based majoritarian civil rights movement around issues as diverse as women's reproductive rights; voting rights; racist police and vigilante killings; stand your ground laws; gay, lesbian, and transgender rights; immigration racism; and violence against Asian Americans proves to be more than a mirage in a desert of despair. The changing racial demographics of the United States and other highly racialized societies could provide additional fuel for change. However, it is unrealistic to expect such changes within sociology and the other social sciences to be major and enduring. History has shown us that they possess an impressive ability to respond with only token and temporary adjustments to embarrassing social realities they can no longer credibly ignore.

Fortunately, another important lesson of this study is that we need not wait for change to come from either the social sciences or from the larger societies of which they are a part. There are scholars like Joe Feagin who push hard against existing political currents. The publication of this book by a prominent press, and the fact that you took the time to read it, indicate that the struggle is far from over. It continues, not just during times when massive social protests force the white power structure and its intellectuals to listen to the words of the racially oppressed, but any time some scholar during more ordinary times such as now shows the temerity to subvert that order through his or her own linguistic racial confrontation.

Hopefully, even during the worst of times, there will continue to be intellectual subversives who know how much words matter and, against all odds, muster the courage to speak truth to power in their own words. In brief, we can be the change we seek. To this end we must do our small part to *force* a change in the way we are allowed to speak about racial oppression as we struggle, with the help of others, to bring about the larger changes in power relations that will make the powerful listen to the words of the racially oppressed. Such change begins, of course, with our having the audacity to speak our own truths. To reach a better place we must be willing to leave the relatively snug harbor of linguistic racial realism and accommodation and venture out into the turbulent and often uncharted seas of linguistic racial idealism and confrontation. At stake is whether America's white racism problem is honestly recognized as being just that or will continue to be framed, with the help of its social-science wizards, in racism-evasive ways such as the "Negro problem" of African American pathology and inferiority.

I hope this book will inspire at least a few scholars and activists to keep the faith in conceptualizing racism more consistently with the daily experiences of the racially oppressed and less accommodatively for those powerful forces that are inclined to deny its very existence. May we all sleep well tonight knowing that, because we are not powerless, there are, indeed, limits to how far we will bend over to assume the uncomfortable and degrading position of linguistic racial accommodation.

I end this study with just two words, the same two words with which I began it; a mantra that I believe cannot be repeated enough by those of us who have committed ourselves to comprehend and dismantle racism and other highly organized systems of oppression. It is in these two words that we find revealed the most important single lesson of this study. Words Matter!

Epilogue

Unfinished Business in Confronting Racially Accommodative Language

> I know one thing we did right
> Was the day we started to fight,
> Keep your eyes on the prize,
> Hold on.[1]

In this one book I have only been able to scratch the surface of the many problematic ways linguistic racial accommodation (LRA) manifests itself in the social sciences and elsewhere as a form of system-sustaining racism evasiveness. Below are a few more examples I think are important that do not neatly fit the organizational flow of this book's previous chapters. As you will see, they are all in serious need of effective linguistic racial confrontation (LRC).

THE MINORITY GROUP CONCEPT STANDS ITS GROUND

What is most revealing about the power behind the LRA concept of minority group is its persistence. That racism-evasive term remains popular despite the fact that it has been largely discredited on social science grounds like conceptual clarity, precision, and validity, as well as by the insightful arguments of those who have found their various unique ethnic and other social identities, histories, and experiences smothered under its alien, blanket, and deleterious characterization of them.[2] The persistence of the minority group concept aptly demonstrates the staying power of linguistic racial accommodation even when it is patently illogical and highly contested. The specific language-centered racism denial practice that helps account for its persistence is conceptual misdirection. The concept of minority group misdirects the focus away from systemic racism and onto "minority" group victims of that oppression and their assumed pathological behavior, which is at least implied to be the real cause of their many social problems.

One of the reasons the term minority is so inept in conceptualizing racism is that its origins are literally foreign to the sociohistorical context of racial oppression in the United States and elsewhere. This lack of sociological imagination is rooted in the persistence of the dogmatic and racism-evasive insistence of influential American sociologists that any explanation of racial oppression must have a theoretical and substantive scope that goes well beyond racism itself. In keeping with this pressure for what I call conceptual extenuation, the concept was originally used in the early twentieth century to refer to the situation of "national minorities"—groups living in European countries in which their own ethnic nationality did not comprise the numerical majority of the population. Over time the word national was dropped as the idea was expanded to include racial oppression in the United States and eventually other groups that would fit into the popular definition of a minority group crafted by Louis Wirth in 1945 as "a group of people who, because of their physical or cultural characteristics, are singled out from the others in the society in which they live for differential and unequal treatment, and who therefore regard themselves as objects of collective discrimination."[3]

From its very beginning the notion of minorities was plagued with problems. Chief among them is the issue of the meaning of the word minority. Though its original usage was limited to groups in Europe who constituted numerical minorities, once the term became popular and institutionalized, its expansion to other situations was defended by reasoning that in European colonies like India or South Africa, the majority of a nation's population could be described as a minority group regardless of the fact that the numerical minority was actually the socially dominant group. Consequently today sociology professors typically find themselves prefacing their lecture on the concept with the awkward and time-consuming task of first explaining what it is not, and then justifying its continued use by clarifying that minority group status refers to a group's power relationship rather than to its population size.

Wirth's definition could have, with only a slight modification and no confusion, referred to a socially oppressed group. All that was needed was reference to the oppressor group and its interests and specification of the nature of the oppression. Interestingly enough, although Wirth did include the term "dominant group" elsewhere within his terminology, there was usually no attempt to juxtapose words like minority-majority or dominant-subordinate. Such juxtaposition would have spelled out the asymmetrical, and therefore oppressive, nature of those group power relationships. Even

Wirth's use of the term dominant group did not last long, as sociologists and other policy elites began to focus exclusively on minority group problems within the same blaming-the-victim sociohistorical and power vacuum as they did in reference to America's archetypal "Negro problem." With this odd construction, the minority group idea was systemically elusive in its ability to infer the existence of an oppressive social system without naming it or identifying its key structures, functions, workings, and beneficiaries.[4]

Such obvious and unnecessary conceptual confusion has caused some scholars to conclude that minority group is both a euphemism for the more honest, but forbidden, term social oppression, and a dominant-group ideology that functions to take the focus off racial and other specific forms of social oppression. Along these lines, in his critique of the minority group concept, Barton Meyers went beyond specifying its numerous problems and placed it in international perspective as an ideology that was developed and refined by American sociologists to protect their nation's expanding global power and influence. Rebellions of potentially insurgent groups at home or abroad could be averted through the dissemination of the minority group concept's key ideals of national loyalty, political consensus, and cultural assimilation. In this way, U.S. national and international interests would not be threatened by groups able to muster international support for their insurgent movements. This peacekeeping function was also served by the expansion of the concept of minorities to the point of almost meaninglessness, facilitated by the conflation of racially and ethnicity based oppression; with the term minority group serving as the bridging concept for the new emerging race and ethnic relations paradigm.[5]

Consistent with this view of the ideological origins of the minority group concept and with my arguments about linguistic racial accommodation and confrontation, David Nibert rooted the genesis and staying power of the term minority group as a "social scientific euphemism" in the fact that "the mainstream culture of the United States precludes the characterization of certain groups in society as 'oppressed.'" He observed that "despite the widespread use of the concept by oppressed people, sociologists have been reluctant to call 'minority groups' oppressed because such a perspective is outside the range of accepted political discourse." Nibert placed that language battle within a sociology of sociology perspective by quoting Robert W. Friedrichs—who, in turn, appeared to be mindful of Kenneth Burke's dramatistic approach to the study of language and its concept of terministic screens I discussed in chapter 1. Friedrichs cautioned that "the very linguistic tools [social scientists] select act as a screen through which filter only those aspects of experience that are consistent with the conceptual scheme used" and that beyond serving as screens "the linguistic instruments we use . . . set limits to the very questions we can ask."[6]

Insurgency of the oppressed is built on grievances. Any idea that justifies treating all ostensibly similar phenomena as the same under one general concept or theory dampens those specific group grievances, their sociohistorical context, and their resultant forms of collective consciousness and action. In this way a broad social conceptualization that encompasses so much (e.g., racialized group membership, gender, sexual orientation, and disability status) that it has no real power to delimit anything serves as a system-maintaining ideology of issue evasiveness that makes social movement activity against social oppression unlikely. As a mobilization slogan "Workers of the world unite!" could work, whereas "Minorities of the world unite!" just doesn't cut it.

A major reason for the continued popularity of the term minority is the fact that it has been highly institutionalized as part of the diversity ideology and management strategy of schools, governments, corporations, and nonprofit organizations. African American sociologist Doris Wilkinson, for example, has revealed her own "indoctrination in sociological reasoning and forced compliance with editorial stipulations."[7] Organizations find the minority concept attractive because it allows them to reduce any racial or other social oppression problems to the need to recruit more minorities and to devise better means for their institutional assimilation. Through conceptual obfuscation and misdirection most change efforts can then be targeted at the minorities as the problem rather than at themselves as institutions. With their crafting of the minority concept, American sociologists helped develop the race and ethnic relations paradigm that from its beginning has been plagued by numerous problems, not the least of which is the powerful language-centered racism denial practice of conceptual conflation.

As you have seen, there is no valid reason for the continued use of the words "minorities" or "minority groups." A clearer, more precise, and more honest use of language is simply to use the words oppressed or oppressed groups and to specify the nature of the oppression they face (e.g., the racially oppressed or racially oppressed groups).

THE FOLLY OF CONCEPTUAL CONFLATION, AT HOME AND ABROAD

As I have discussed, conceptual conflation is the muddling of racism with another form, or multiple forms, of social oppression. Specific examples are its confusion with ethnicity, class, or gender. William J. Wilson did racism studies a great disservice when, instead of just focusing on the high rates of poverty among African Americans, he called into question the very systemic racism that makes such poverty so prevalent, thereby shifting the social-science and public-policy focus back to a culture of poverty analysis of the

African American poor that conflated their "race" with their impoverished condition. Ironically, while touting "the declining significance of race," Wilson's work has actually increased the focus on the "race" of African Americans—defined as cultural pathology—as the explanation of their relatively high poverty rates.

Decades later, two African American sociologists warned of such racism-evasive conflation of "race" with class. In his article "Anything but Race: The Social Science Retreat from Racism," Melvin Thomas examined social-science research in the United States in the wake of Wilson's success in discounting systemic racism as an explanation of African American poverty. After revealing his own difficulty in staying focused on racism in that article's "Anything but Race" title, Thomas laid out how African Americans' relatively high rates of poverty are blamed on low-income African Americans themselves despite the overwhelming evidence that racism is the real culprit. This is done by the "ideological defenses of 'white privilege'" provided through the "'popular,'" but weak, alternative theoretical explanations of "social class, cognitive ability, lack of work ethic or morality, human capital deficits, spatial mismatch, and family structure." The irony of Thomas's "anything but race" argument is that he may be technically correct in using the word "race" there because racism-evasion has gotten to the point where today it is increasingly uncommon for there to be an explicit analysis of "race," whatever it is assumed to mean. Ironically again, however, the alternative explanations he lists typically entail research where "race" is run as a variable when quantitative methods are used or, when the study is based on qualitative ethnographic methods, the focus is exclusively on an African American sample. In any case, studies using both methodologies imply that there is something racially pathological about impoverished African Americans. In his book chapter "Race and Class: Why All the Confusion?" Johnny E. Williams is explicit in identifying the problem as one of conflation. While acknowledging that racially and class-related issues are not only interrelated but feed off one another, Williams argued that many "class issues . . . are concealed in racial terms" and that "those with various types of power have vested interests in creating and sustaining the confusion" by "conflating race and class."[8] That certainly seemed to have been the case for the high rates of African American poverty, which have seen no significant public or social policy initiatives since William J. Wilson helped reframe the issue from the racially contentious one of systemic racism to an assumed less politically controversial socioeconomic status and culture issue.

This trend toward conceptual conflation is also evident in the work of sociology graduate students. I remember the paper of a graduate student who, through the use of the term "ethnoracial," thoroughly blurred any meaningful distinction between the workings of racial oppression and subjugation based on ethnicity. While she probably considered her use of the ethnoracial concept to be innovative and bold, I found it to be hopelessly muddled in conceptual conflation. That student may have been misled by the many well-regarded scholars who, through a range of conceptualizations like ethnoracial, ethnclass, and intersectionality, encourage such work without even a footnote on the problem of conceptual conflation. Indeed, I found the same problem to be true for an accomplished scholar whose analytical and conceptual skills I regard highly.

In her important study of everyday racism in the Netherlands, Philomena Essed, a social scientist of African Surinamese descent, offered a bountiful chest of analytical tools, including the concept of gendered racism, which heavily influenced my own study of welfare racism with Kenneth Neubeck. In my racism theory graduate seminar I mention that the main problem I have with Essed's study was her tendency toward conceptual conflation, a problem that at times made it nearly impossible for me to determine whether a particular case example she gave was driven primarily by racism or the ethnicity-based oppression she referred to as ethnicism. As she acknowledged, this is especially true when she discussed the more subtle expressions of bigotry.[9]

As Essed's work revealed, the ramifications of the conceptual conflation of racism and ethnicity-based oppression are international and extend well beyond American poverty policy debates and academics. It is, indeed, a reason that the United Nations has so often failed to address either problem effectively. That failure is most evident in its inability to engage some of the world's most powerful and highly racialized nations to discuss the problem of systemic racism. As I noted previously, American social scientists crafted the minority group concept with an eye toward managing not only what was happening at home with their own nation's system of racial oppression, but other racial and ethnic conflicts worldwide that might threaten U.S. economic and political interests. Early on, the UN approach to such conflicts mirrored certain features of the failed minority group concept, including its conflation of racism with ethnicity-based oppression.

Conceptual conflation, and its closely related language-centered racism denial practice of conceptual inflation, are evident in the 1963 "United Nations Declaration on the Elimination of All Forms of Racial Discrimination," which defined racial discrimination as "discrimination between human beings on the ground of race, colour or ethnic origin." These flaws are even more evident in the difference between the long and short form of the title of the UN's ill-fated 2001 conference in Durban, South Africa. The brief title of that conference was the World Conference against Racism, as shown on a logo image on the conference website. The longer title, which appeared right beside it, was the World Conference against Racism, Racial Discrimination, Xenophobia and Related Intolerance. And listed beneath that expanded title were the issues of "trafficking in women and children," "migration and discrimination," "gender and racial discrimination," "racism against indigenous peoples," and "protection of minority rights." From its website it appeared that in the worst tradition of the umbrella concept of minority group, the conference could encompass almost any social inequity-related issue. In this way conceptual conflation led to conceptual inflation, which entailed defining racism so broadly, by including nearly every other form of social oppression, that the term became meaningless. Unfortunately, by doing so, instead of purchasing the coalition-fueled peace its planners may have hoped for, they allowed the conference to be held hostage by the intense ethnic conflict at its Durban meeting between some Arab and Jewish groups that culminated in a walkout by the United States and Israel.[10] With the United States and other important nations boycotting subsequent conferences due to their objections to what their leaders saw as its anti-Semitism in equating Zionism with racism, it seems likely that those nations, which all have serious systemic racism problems, will continue to have an excuse to steer clear of such meetings until there is peace in the Middle East—the likelihood of which, given the millennia of conflict in that region, is not encouraging. Once again we see that, rather than achieving the well-intentioned goal of building bridges, conceptual conflation just creates a mess, both analytically and politically.

Aside from the politics involved, the solution to what seems to be this terribly complex problem is actually quite simple. The United Nations should make it clear in its definition that racism is systemic and is limited to "race"-justified oppression. Then it could more manageably organize both racism-centered meetings and other forums to address other important social issues.

NEW RACISM AND MANY RACISMS? OR JUST THE SAME OLD RACISM EVASIVENESS TUMBLING DOWN A SLIPPERY SLOPE?

As you have seen, the numerous serious flaws of the still-popular concept of minority group and the related problem of conceptual conflation have contributed to the abandoning of the reality of racism as a systemic form of oppression civil rights activists and intellectuals fought so hard to have recognized, for ideology-driven social-science sophistry that would be laughable if not for its serious social consequences.

Scholars who cannot acknowledge that racism is, indeed, a system of oppression sometimes justify their attempts to slay what they seem to perceive as the frightening analytical beast of systemic racism theory by arguing that the concept is so inflated that it will surely cause its advocates to tumble down a slippery conceptual slope.[11] Although there is more than a kernel of truth in this point, I strongly reject the solution of simply slaying the seemingly unruly creature. A more measured remedy is to just do the conceptual work needed to fully flesh out its analytical structures and processes. As I have stressed earlier in this book, I see the main problem of the systemic racism perspective as one of its conceptual underdevelopment, not inflation. Ignoring the reality of systemic racism creates even more slippery slopes for those who attempt to travel difficult analytical terrain while intoxicated by their own racism evasiveness.

Not far down these slopes can be found the notions of "new racism" and "many racisms." Both are examples of the types of sociological silliness that have to be constructed to fit what the profession is politically willing and equipped to do to retain its footing as it descends back down into its imaginary world where racism is not systemic. The idea of a fundamentally new and different general racism and multiple forms of racism—as opposed to the same old racism simply manifesting itself in diverse ways (e.g., dominative racism or aversive racism) or within different institutional components of society (e.g., as cultural racism, welfare racism, or immigration racism) as it is adjusted to changing sociohistorical conditions—seems to be attractive to many racially accommodative sociologists. Fueling this attraction for the new and terrific is, of course, the career-building claim that one has discovered or conceptualized something previously unknown.

The notions of new or multiple forms of racism are central to the work of influential scholars like Omi and Winant, David Theo Goldberg, and Eduardo Bonilla-Silva. The ahistorical tendency of sociology is one reason that such newness claims usually go unchallenged within that discipline. Another reason is that today there seems to be little critical sociology of sociology to call out such assertions for often being little more than what conservative sociologist Pitirim Sorokin deemed the profession's latest "fads and foibles," or what others have periodically described as simply being "old wine in new bottles."[12] The focus on new and many racisms works especially well for those who, because of their methodology and substantive interests, find it professionally inconvenient to see the truth of racism as a systemic form of oppression, and instead depict it as being nothing more substantial than periodically changing racial ideologies and attitudes. Finally, this new racism perspective neatly fits the postmodernist assumption that the old, objective, and materially based social structures no longer exist.

The many racisms argument is especially debilitating, not only because it—like the new racism perspective—denies the existence of racism as a systemic form of oppression, but because it also justifies one of the most effective forms of racism evasiveness by shrinking its size down to the scope of the racial bigotry of individuals, thus allowing any attempt at discourse about racism to degenerate into a finger-pointing shouting match over who is a racist person. Once again, like its new racism cousin, this many or multiple forms of racism racism-evasive practice is aided by the poststructuralist intoxicant that equates African American, European American, Asian

American, and Native American "racisms" by denying the existence of racism as an enduring, in numerous ways objective, and still very consequential social structure. The apparent logic of this specious argument is built upon the acceptance of a pluralist view of both power and racism that makes it nearly impossible to see racism as being the asymmetrical and highly organized form of oppression it is.

I offer a simple rebuttal to the warning that treating racism as a system of oppression leads us down an analytical "slippery slope." If one's analysis is historically grounded and rooted in the assumption that racial oppression is systemic, then there is no need for conceptualizations like new racisms and many racisms. The work of Joel Kovel and Carter A. Wilson I discussed earlier assumes that because racism is a system of oppression it persists by taking new forms as it adapts to changing sociohistorical conditions. That is, although racism is expressed in different psychocultural manifestations during different historical eras, its ultimate source is the one, old but ever adapting, system of racial oppression—not new and many racisms. Things become unnecessarily complicated, however, for scholars who, wittingly or not, embrace the basic tenets of the poststructuralist perspective that reject the existence of objective and materialist social structures while accepting the pluralist view of power. Then, in order to traverse the slippery slope of explaining covert racism, which the institutional and systemic racism perspectives are better equipped to handle, ideologies and attitudes-centered researchers find themselves needing to assert that what we have now are many new racisms that require ever new, more subtle and more complicated postmodernist explanations. In this view, every new manifestation of racial ideologies or attitudes qualifies as a new racism, and since racism is a characteristic of individuals, not social structures, every group has its own racists and racisms.

BREAKING FREE OF DISCIPLINARY RESTRAINTS BY FLEEING THE PLANTATION OF PROFESSIONALIZED SOCIOLOGY

As you have seen, linguistic racial accommodation is heavily enforced through the very academic disciplines that pride themselves on their socially critical analysis. One of the first things that scholars who are committed to understanding and eliminating oppression learn is that the goal of human liberation often runs counter to the ambition of building and sustaining a professional academic discipline. That is, their primary work is eliminating social oppression, not advancing their own careers or a particular—usually system-sustaining—social-science discipline. Taking a radical anti-oppression stance means therefore that one does not stay in one's place, discipline-wise or in any other way. Instead, we must go boldly through all doors that might lead us to our goal of human liberation. For example, many sociologists feel no sense of urgency about addressing the race concept in any way that goes deeper than labeling it a social construction because they are either ignorant of, or simply ignore, the profound implications of the huge breakthroughs in comprehending its origins, validity, and functions that have been made in diverse fields such as anthropology, history, and evolutionary biology. By learning to eschew disciplinary boundaries, radically progressive scholars can also escape the intellectually stifling impact of their particular LRA linguistic strictures.

If the goal of our work is human liberation, then sociology and other academic disciplines must be viewed as tools. To the extent that such devices are useful in exposing and ultimately ending oppression, they should be used. When they prove themselves useless and otherwise culpable in bolstering oppressive systems, they should be abandoned. So, ironically, to achieve C. Wright Mills's challenge of the sociological imagination, we may need to move beyond sociology—or at least sociology as a profession.

OVERCOMING THE DEMISE OF SYSTEMS AWARENESS AND THE RISE OF SYSTEMS BLINDNESS

In his popular self-help book *Focus: The Hidden Driver of Excellence*, Daniel Goleman devoted an entire chapter and more to the systems blindness he saw as impeding the ability of individuals to focus their intellect and emotions to achieve their highest human potential. I believe that Goleman's concern also accurately captures the challenge facing racism studies. A major obstacle to our ability to see and understand racism as a highly organized system of "race"-justified oppression is the demise of "systems awareness" and the rise of "systems blindness" in American social science generally, and especially within sociology's race and ethnic relations specialty area.[13]

In this book I have examined numerous reasons behind various efforts to shrink the conceptualization of racism from the large system's perspective forced into the national discourse by the civil rights movement. Prominent among these are the linguistic racial accommodation of career-oriented sociologists in response to the institutionalized legacy of the white racial backlash, efforts to make conceptualizations of racism fit attitudinal-size data, the ahistorical nature of race relations research and theory, and the rise of post-structural theories that depict today's racism as being too subtle and complex to be understood as an oppressive social structure.

Another explanation is more biographical. As Philomena Essed has stressed, "knowledge of racism" is learned through one's life experiences—an observation that fits snugly with Goleman's insights into the rise and demise of "systems awareness." To make his point, Goleman gave examples of how throughout much of human history the ability of people to survive the often harsh vicissitudes of nature depended on knowledge that was passed down from one generation to the next about its workings as an ecological system relevant to such matters as to when to plant crops or how to navigate oceanic waters. Goleman expressed concern that with the availability of modern technology like computers and GPS, much of that knowledge is in danger of being lost. I am fearful that the same fate of "'systems blindness'" may await the post–Jim Crow era generations of "race" and racism scholars. Survival under overt systems of racial oppression like slavery, colonialism, Jim Crow, and Apartheid required the development of keen systems analytical skills that last a lifetime, even after racial oppression assumes less overt and more subtle forms. Unfortunately, once new generations of scholars who are increasingly removed from either direct or indirect experiences of such overt forms of oppression assume that such skills are no longer necessary, they may be encouraged, through means I have outlined in great detail in this book, to develop systems blindness, which in turn causes whatever systems awareness skills they do possess to atrophy. To overcome that analytical and organizational impediment, we need to do more work toward the building of what Goleman referred to as "systems literacy."[14]

It is ironic that, at a time when there seems to be diminishing interest in systems analysis within the social sciences, there is a huge growth in such attention in science, technology, business, and nonprofit social change organizations—fields with major stakes in understanding and shaping massive societal change. Apparently the choice of so many American social scientists to remain largely systems blind has nothing to do with the relevance and usefulness of a systems perspective.

THE PROMISES AND CHALLENGES OF EMERGING DEVELOPMENTS IN RACISM STUDIES

Everyday Racism and Micro-Aggressions

I already mentioned Philomena Essed's important research on everyday racism. Joe Feagin and his coauthors are among those who have also made contributions in this area.[15] Scholarship on everyday racism and racism-focused micro-aggressions are significant emerging developments in racism studies because of their trailblazing methodological premise, with profound LRC implications, that the accounts of the racially oppressed matter. The high prevalence and frequency of such incidences, whether big or small, also make it difficult to deny that racism is anything but routine, and thus systemic. The challenge of this approach is to develop macro-level theories that can place those events in their larger sociohistorical context as well as concepts and reliability and validity measures that will force even skeptics to treat those accounts with the gravity they deserve. Admittedly this is not just a social-science concepts and methods issue. Ultimately it is the mobilization of power that forces the voices of the oppressed to be heard by those who are accustomed to ignoring them.

Going Deep with Intersectionality

Despite its importance and promise, the misuse of intersectionality has all too often resulted in scholarship that analytically is a mile wide and an inch deep. This expression of concern is not intended to in any way denigrate the idea of intersectional scholarship or the significant contributions that intellectual movement has made, especially to feminist theory. The basic assumption of intersectional scholarship—pushed with great success by feminist scholars of African descent like Kimberlé Williams Crenshaw, Patricia Hill Collins, Philomena Essed, and Cheryl Townsend Gilkes—that one form of oppression does not operate independent of other forms is well founded. Such knowledge also has profound social movement implications as has certainly been true for poor women of color who have simultaneously fought racism, gender-based oppression, and class exploitation through organizations like the National Welfare Rights Organization and ACORN.

So let me make myself clear. *The concept of intersectionality is useful, important, and necessary. When used appropriately, it can make significant contributions to our understanding of social oppression.* My beef is not with the use of that important analytical tool, but with its racism-evasive *misuse*—especially when it is employed in place of in-depth analysis of systemic racism to justify shallow treatments of "race"—whatever that is—in favor of more privileged forms of oppression. I also don't like the abuse of that concept by some professors who use the idiom of intersectionality to bestow upon themselves an expertise about racial oppression they have not earned by actually reading its literature, much less by conducting research and teaching in the field. And I object to the arrogance young scholars may endure from such shallow intersectional "race" experts when they are sent strong signals that research on racial oppression is legitimate only if it gives whatever they deem to be substantial weight to other oppression-related factors. That is an intellectually oppressive misuse of the concept of intersectionality that sets up yet additional gatekeepers for those who would do racism studies—gatekeepers who allow such research only if it meets their own intersectionality checklist and priorities. The intellectually stifling impact of such intolerance can be increased exponentially when combined with the dogmatism of poststructuralist theorists who glibly dismiss any attempt to focus primarily, although not exclusively, on any form of oppression by labeling it as being a "total" or "totalistic" approach. Finally, without proper safeguards, the intersectionality ideology can exacerbate the serious problems of conceptual conflation, conceptual colonization, and conceptual minimization that have severely limited our social-science understanding of racial oppression. Care should be taken, therefore, to ensure that the intersectionality movement does not provide an intellectual safe haven for conflict-aversive racial liberals who misuse its otherwise liberating ideology to make the topic of racial oppression smaller, and therefore more politically and emotionally manageable, for those with other, assumed to be more important, fish to fry.

For me the issue is not *whether* we address the fact of multiple, overlapping forms of oppression—surely we must—but *how*? Superficial analyses of intersectionality, like much of the multivariate research done by quantitative researchers in search of interaction effects, don't go deep enough. No matter how suggestive their statistics are, they offer no substantial theoretical explanation of multiple forms of oppression. Going deep analytically and politically means focusing, primarily but not exclusively, on one form of social oppression to account for its specific origins, nature, structure, processes, workings, changes, persistence, and consequences, while making clear its connections to other forms of oppression. A good model for how such scholarship can be done is some of the qualitative historical research on punitive public-assistance policies and practices in the United States. Frances Fox Piven and Richard Cloward's *Regulating the Lives of the Poor*, with its main focus on class; Mimi Abramovitz's *Regulating the Lives of Poor Women*, with its major emphasis on gender; and Kenneth J. Neubeck and my *Welfare Racism*, with our chief concern with racism all go deep analytically in explaining their key subject matter without losing sight of the intersectionality of those three important forms of oppression. Backed by the success of such scholarship, young scholars should feel confident in making assertions like "Although my study will also examine other overlapping forms of oppression like ____ and ____, its main focus is ____."

Unconscious Racism and Implicit Racial Bias

There is both good news and bad news in the study of racism. Psychology is back. Prior to the intensification of the civil rights movement in the late 1960s, the influence of psychology helped keep the focus of sociology and other social-science disciplines on the attitudes and behaviors of prejudiced individuals and off racially oppressive social systems. But psychology does have its place. For example, as Joe Feagin has indicated, there is an emotional component of racism that includes strong negative feelings like "hate, fear, guilt, repulsion, and greed" that must be taken into account in explaining racist behavior. Moreover, as Joel Kovel and later Carter A. Wilson explained, different sociohistorical periods of racism have their own psychocultural manifestations of the phenomenon, like the emotionally charged and often largely unconscious form of aversive racism. Clearly there are some aspects of racism, like Thomas Jefferson's lengthy relationship with his slave

Sally Hemings despite his description of people of African descent as aesthetically repulsive, that can't be explained through pure rational self-interest.[16] There are certainly motives for racism that are not as rational as economic exploitation.

Indeed, some insightful psychological studies reveal that there is much to racism that is unconscious. Recent psychological research on unconscious racism, and the racism-centered work on what some scholars refer to more generally as implicit bias, make a powerful case as to why racist attitudes, emotions, and behavior persist. There is also at least an implicit assumption in this research that if such unconscious racial bias is so prevalent, its origins must go beyond the aberrant attitudes and behaviors of a relatively few psychologically abnormal or socially deviant individuals. This psychological research on unconscious racism and implicit racial bias has produced significant breakthroughs in our understanding of racism and promises to give us even more.

However, I harbor three concerns about research on unconscious racism and implicit racial bias, or the interpretation thereof. First, it can reduce systemic racism to an individual level of racial bigotry. Second, it may excuse bigotry as being unconscious and therefore unintentional, and not something anyone can be held accountable for. Third, because it treats bigotry and other manifestations of unconscious bias as being naturally engrained in our biology as human beings, the notions of unconscious racism and implicit racial bias can easily be used to circumnavigate the need to view racism as a form of social oppression.

Although I believe that such obstacles can be overcome through multidisciplinary theory and research that locates unconscious racism and implicit racial bias within the larger context of systemic racism, I am not optimistic that this will happen to any significant degree. Unfortunately, from a linguistic racial accommodation perspective, there are probably more incentives for psychologists to keep their unconscious racism and implicit racial bias research far removed from the actual macro-level realities of racial oppression. To the extent that such scholarship releases racism from its sociohistorical moorings, it should remain popular among racism-evasive people of European descent and attractive to potential funding sources and publication outlets.

Historically Grounded Cross-National Research

Another area of racism research that offers both promise and risk is nationally comparative historical research. One promise is that such research will help us to better understand what all systems of race-based oppression hold in common, as well as what needs to be understood that is unique to a particular region or nation and its historical development. It can also help us to better comprehend the political, economic, cultural, and other factors that fuel the globalization of racism as a phenomenon heedless of national boundaries. Finally, more nationally comparative historical research on systemic racism could expand our knowledge to promote an understanding of racism as a global system of racial domination.

Such an approach is impeded by the need for macro-level theory with a global reach and by the dearth of studies based on nationally comparative and historical research methods. Another impediment is the lack of a common definition of racism—one that could be used as a benchmark for nationally comparative studies as well as for the UN efforts to monitor racist policies and practices in nations throughout the world. Finally, another lesson from the UN debacle I discussed earlier is that nationally comparative historical research on racism must break free of the shackles of conceptual conflation.

May the struggle continue whenever and wherever it is needed as we muster the courage to confront the racially accommodative language upon which the racial status quo is built!

Notes

PROLOGUE

1. John Bartlett and Justin Kaplan, ed., *Bartlett's Familiar Quotations* (Boston: Little, Brown, 1992), John 8:7.
2. Noel A. Cazenave, "From a Committed Achiever to a Radical Social Scientist: The Life Course Dialectics of a 'Marginal' Black Sociologist," *The American Sociologist* (Winter 1988): 349, 351–52.
3. Cazenave, "From a Committed Achiever to a Radical Social Scientist," 347–48.
4. Cazenave, "From a Committed Achiever to a Radical Social Scientist," 352.
5. June Jordan, "Problems of Language in a Democratic State," in *Some of Us Did Not Die: New and Selected Essays of June Jordan* (New York: Basic, 2002), 226–27; Noel A. Cazenave and Darlene Alvarez Maddern, "Defending the White Race: White Male Faculty Opposition to a 'White Racism' Course," *Race and Society* 2, no.1 (2000): 31.
6. Cazenave and Maddern, "Defending the White Race," 27.
7. Cazenave and Maddern, "Defending the White Race," 32–33.
8. Cazenave and Maddern, "Defending the White Race," 34.
9. Cazenave and Maddern, "Defending the White Race," 34.
10. Noel A. Cazenave, "Why I Will Teach a Course on White Racism," *Hartford Courant*, February 18, 1996, C1.

INTRODUCTION

1. Paul Laurence Dunbar, "We Wear the Mask," in *The Collected Poetry of Paul Laurence Dunbar*, ed. Joanne M. Braxton (Charlottesville: University of Virginia Press, 1993), 71.
2. Wendy Brown-Scott, "Plessy v. Ferguson (1896)," in *Civil Rights in the United States*, ed. Waldo E. Martin Jr. and Patricia Sullivan (New York: Macmillan Reference, 2000), 2:600. A plethora of genetic, anthropological, and historical evidence has effectively debunked the notion that there are actually "black," "white," and other biological "races" of people. See for example, Joseph L. Graves Jr., *The Race Myth: Why We Pretend Race Exists in America* (New York: Plume, 2005) and Audrey Smedley and Brian D. Smedley, *Race in North America: Origin and Evolution of a Worldview* (Boulder, CO: Westview, 2012). Therefore instead I will use as appropriate pan-ethnic (e.g., African American, European American, Asian American,

Latino/a American) and ethnic terminology (e.g., Irish American, Italian American, Puerto Rican). While I will not use the word "white" to refer to people of European descent who are sometimes darker in skin color than individuals of color deemed as "black," Asian, or Latino/a, I will use the term to refer to highly racialized social structures like white power structures and events like white backlashes. Similarly I will also use historically rooted terms like black power and black nationalism as appropriate.

3. Stuart McCready, "In Pursuit of Happiness: An Invitation to Discovery," in *The Discovery of Happiness*, ed. Stuart McCready (Naperville, IL: Sourcebooks, 2001), 22.

4. For more on the relationship between Booker T. Washington and Robert Park, see John H. Stanfield, *Philanthropy and Jim Crow in American Social Science* (Westport, CT: Greenwood, 1985), 38–40; Stephen Steinberg, *Race Relations: A Critique* (Stanford, CA: Stanford University Press, 2007), 25–27; and "Booker T. Washington and the Politics of Accommodation," Digital History, University of Houston, http://www.digitalhistory.uh.edu/database/article_display.cfm?hhid=218.

5. "West Indian Emancipation, Speech Delivered at Canandaigua, New York August 3, 1857," in *Frederick Douglass: Selected Speeches and Writings* (Chicago: Lawrence Hill, 1999), 367.

6. "Booker T. Washington and the Politics of Accommodation."

7. Booker T. Washington, "The Standard Printed Version of the Atlanta Exposition Address, Atlanta, GA, September 18, 1895," in *The Booker T. Washington Papers*, ed. Louis R. Harlan, vol. 3, 1889–1895 (Urbana: University of Illinois Press, 1974), 585–86.

8. Booker T. Washington, *Up From Slavery: An Autobiography* (New York: Barnes and Noble, 2003), 118, 136.

9. Andrew Romano and Allison Samuels, "Is Obama Making it Worse? An Exclusive Newsweek Poll Reveals the Persistence of America's Stark Racial Divide," *Newsweek*, April 16, 2012, 41.

10. Bob Herbert, "The Scourge Persists," *New York Times*, September 19, 2009. http://www.nytimes.com/2009/09/19/opinion/19herbert.html?; Rinku Sen, *Colorlines*, October 28, 2010, http://colorlines.com/archives/2010/10/the_most_racist_campaign_in_decades_and_what_it_demands_of_us.html; Associated Press, "Obama Election Spurs Race Threats," MSNBC, November 15, 2008, http://www.msnbc.msn.com/id/27738018/ns/us_news-life/t/obama-election-spurs-race-threats-crimes/; Gillian Flaccus, "GOP Official Apologizes for Obama Chimp Email," *MSNBC*, April 19, 2011. http://www.msnbc.msn.com/id/42656911/ns/politics-more_politics/t/gop-official-apologizes-obama-chimp-email/; ABC News Transcript, "Tea Party Under Fire: Billboard Shows Obama & Hitler," *Good Morning America*, July 14, 2010; Todd Spangler and Cassandra Spratling, "Debate Over Obama's Agenda Marked by Charges of Racism, Denials of Prejudice," *Detroit Free Press*, September 23, 2009; Romano and Samuels, "Is Obama Making it Worse?," 40–41.

11. "Obama's 'Teachable Moment' on Race," *Christian Science Monitor*, July 31, 2009, 8; "Over Beers," July 30, 2009, White House Blog, http://www.whitehouse.gov/blog/2009/07/30/over-beers.

12. Perry Bacon Jr., "In Wake of Police Shootings, Obama Speaks More Bluntly about Race," NBC News, January 3, 2015, http://www.nbcnews.com/politics/barack-obama/wake-police-shootings-obama-speaks-more-bluntly-about-race-n278616; "Transcript: Barack Obama's Speech on Race," NPR, March 18, 2008, http://www.npr.org/templates/story/story.php?storyId=88478467.

13. March 26, 2008 letter from Johnny E. Williams et al. to the Honorable Barack Obama. "Social Scientists' Letter to Senator Obama on Systemic Racism," March 27, 2008, http://www.racismreview.com/blog/2008/03/. Intense opposition was expressed to that letter by some subscribers to the Association of Black Sociologists listserv, who felt that criticism of Obama might hurt his election chances.

14. Scott Wilson, "Obama Deftly Handles Race Remarks," *USA Today*, March 24, 2012, http://www.usatoday.com/USCP/PNI/Nation/World/2012-03-24-bcfloridahateobama_ST_U.htm; Romano and Samuels, "Is Obama Making it Worse?," 41. There has been much debate among African Americans about whether it is fair to criticize President Obama for not speaking out and acting more directly and forcefully on issues of particular importance to African

Americans—including, of course, racism. Arguments in support of his not doing so have included the warning that doing so would be political suicide and the complaint that it is unfair to criticize him for not doing what other presidents before him have also not done. Still another argument he himself articulated in a 2012 interview in a prominent African American magazine is that he "is not the president of Black America," but of all America. Those who believe, as I do, that President Obama could have done more argue that as his most supportive and loyal constituent group, it was reasonable for African Americans to expect him to at least be as sensitive to our needs as he has been to other constituent groups, including Wall Street. We also believe that presidents are not powerless prisoners of majority political opinion. As the expression "all politics is local" implies, effective governance entails the use of skillful means to be responsive to needs of specific constituent groups of various sizes. Finally, we argue that giving an African American president a pass on addressing issues of specific concern to African Americans not only establishes a bad precedent but effectively disenfranchises us from participation in the political process beyond voting, campaigning, and writing checks. As you will see later in this book, during his second term President Obama did on occasion speak out more directly against racial discrimination, especially in response to the large number of killings of African Americans by European American police and vigilantes.

15. Ruth Frankenberg, *White Women, Race Matters: The Social Construction of Whiteness* (Minneapolis: University of Minnesota Press, 1993), 14–15.

16. The 2012 *Newsweek* poll I referred to in an earlier note found that while 60 percent of African Americans responded yes when asked "Is racism a big problem today in America?" only 19 percent of European Americans did so. Romano and Samuels, "Is Obama Making it Worse?,"41.

17. Susan Cain, *Quiet: The Power of Introverts in a World that Can't Stop Talking* (New York: Crown, 2012), 91–92, 296n91.

18. Eduardo Bonilla-Silva, "Rethinking Racism: Toward a Structural Interpretation," *American Sociological Review* 62 (June 1996): 476.

19. Harvard Sitkoff, *The Struggle for Black Equality: 1954–1992* (New York: Hill and Wang, 2008), 219; Noel A. Cazenave, "We Can Still Remove Barriers of Racial Divide to Save Nation," *Hartford Courant*, October 10, 1996, A23.

1. UNDERSTANDING LINGUISTIC RACIAL ACCOMMODATION AND CONFRONTATION

1. Oliver C. Cox, *Caste, Class, and Race: A Study in Social Dynamics* (New York: Monthly Review Press, 1948), 399.

2. Chapter 2 of Davita Silven Glasberg and Deric Shannon's book on political sociology was useful to this organization and review of what they refer to as power structure theories. Davita Silven Glasberg and Deric Shannon, *Political Sociology: Oppression, Resistance, and the State* (Los Angeles: Pine Forge, 2011). See especially their table on page 35. Robert A. Dahl, *Who Governs? Democracy and Power in an American City* (New Haven: Yale University Press, 1961).

3. C. Wright Mills, *The Power Elite* (New York: Oxford University Press, 1956); Glasberg and Shannon, *Political Sociology*, 35.

4. E. E. Schattschneider, *The Semisovereign People: A Realist's View of Democracy in America* (Hinsdale, IL: Dryden Press, 1975), 69; Peter Bachrach and Morton S. Baratz, *Power and Poverty: Theory and Practice* (New York: Oxford University Press, 1970), 4, 8–9, 16.

5. Steven Lukes, *Power: A Radical View* (London: MacMillan, 1974), 19, 34–35. See Glasberg and Shannon, *Political Sociology*, 35 for more on what they refer to as class dialectic theory based on the work of Karl Marx.

6. Lukes, *Power*, 57, including footnote 2; John Gaventa, *Power and Powerlessness: Quiescence and Rebellion in an Appalachian Valley* (Urbana: University of Illinois Press, 1980), xi, 4.

7. Lewis A. Coser, "Sociology of Knowledge," in *International Encyclopedia of the Social Sciences*, ed. David L. Sills, vol. 7 (New York: Macmillan and Free Press, 1968), 1.

8. Coser, "Sociology of Knowledge," 2.

9. Coser, "Sociology of Knowledge," 5. Karl Mannheim, *Ideology and Utopia: An Introduction to the Sociology of Knowledge* (New York: Harcourt, Brace, and World, 1936), 2, 40; Coser, "Sociology of Knowledge," 3.

10. Daniel Littleat, "Sociology of Knowledge: Mannheim," *Understanding Society*, January 12, 2012, http://understandingsociety.blogspot.com/2012/01/sociology-of-knowledge-mannheim.html; Peter L. Berger and Thomas Luckmann, *The Social Construction of Reality: A Treatise in the Sociology of Knowledge* (New York: Anchor, 1967), 3, 37.

11. "Epistemology," *Internet Encyclopedia of Philosophy*, http://www.iep.utm.edu/epistemo/; Steve Fuller, *Social Epistemology* (Bloomington: Indiana University Press, 1988), 3–4; "Social Epistemology," *Stanford Encyclopedia of Philosophy*, http://plato.stanford.edu/entries/epistemology-social/.

12. The first time I heard the word ignorance used as a verb was by my former research assistant, Dena Wallerson. Charles W. Mills, *The Racial Contract* (Ithaca, NY: Cornell University Press, 1997), 18, 96–97.

13. Shannon Sullivan and Nancy Tuana, eds., *Race and Epistemologies of Ignorance* (Albany, NY: SUNY Press, 2007), 1–2.

14. Kenneth Burke, *Language as Symbolic Action: Essays on Life, Literature, and Method* (Berkeley: University of California, 1966), 45, 47.

15. Michel Foucault, *The Archaeology of Knowledge* (New York: Pantheon, 1972), 216, 219; Pierre Bourdieu, *Language and Symbolic Power* (Cambridge, MA: Harvard University Press, 1991), 37, 164, 166.

16. Norman Fairclough, *Language and Power* (Harlow, Essex, UK: Longman, 2001), viii, 1–2.

17. Fairclough, *Language and Power*, 2–3.

18. Fairclough, *Language and Power*, 71, 75. Fairclough borrowed the concept of antilanguage from Michael Halliday.

19. Joe R. Feagin, *Racist America: Roots, Current Realities, and Future Reparations* (New York: Routledge, 2014), xiv; Joe R. Feagin, *The White Racial Frame: Centuries of Racial Framing and Counter-Framing* (New York: Routledge, 2010), 9; Stokely Carmichael and Charles V. Hamilton, *Black Power: The Politics of Liberation in America* (New York: Vintage, 1967), 5.

20. Feagin, *Racist America*, xiv.

21. Feagin, *White Racial Frame*, 7, 18–19.

22. Joel Kovel, *White Racism: A Psychohistory* (New York: Columbia University Press, 1984); Carter A. Wilson, *Racism: From Slavery to Advanced Capitalism* (Thousand Oaks, CA: Sage, 1996), v–vi, x, 173.

23. Wilson, *Racism*, 173.

24. Wilson, *Racism*, 16, 20, 165; Noel A. Cazenave, "Racism: Never New, Just Rediscovered," *Hartford Courant*, March 4, 2012, C1, C3.

2. LINGUISTIC RACIAL ACCOMMODATION FROM SLAVERY TO THE CIVIL RIGHTS MOVEMENT

1. Upton Sinclair, *I, Candidate for Governor: And How I Got Licked* (Berkeley: University of California Press, 1994), 109.

2. Lerone Bennett Jr., *Before the Mayflower: A History of Black America* (Chicago: Johnson Publishing, 1982), 256, 274; James B. McKee, *Sociology and the Race Problem: The Failure of a Perspective* (Urbana: University of Illinois Press, 1993), 28.

3. McKee, *Sociology and the Race Problem*, 23; Joseph R. Feagin, *Racist America: Roots, Current Realities, and Future Reparations* (New York: Routledge, 2014), 54, 57.

4. McKee, *Sociology and the Race Problem*, 22; Thomas F. Pettigrew, ed., "Introduction," in *The Sociology of Race Relations: Reflection and Reform* (New York: Free Press, 1980), xxi; Carter A. Wilson, *Racism: From Slavery to Advanced Capitalism* (Thousand Oaks, CA: Sage, 1996), 109–10.

5. Kenneth O'Reilly, *Nixon's Piano: Presidents and Racial Politics from Washington to Clinton* (New York: Free Press, 1995); James Bradley, *The Imperial Cruise: A Secret History of Empire and War* (New York: Back Bay Books, 2009); Mary J. Deegan, *Jane Addams and the Men of the Chicago School, 1892–1918* (New Brunswick, NJ: Transaction, 1990); Timothy Noah, *The Great Divergence: America's Growing Inequality Crisis and What We Can Do about It* (New York: Bloomsbury, 2012), 13; E. Franklin Frazier, "Sociological Theory and Race Relations," *American Sociological Review* 12, no. 3 (June 1947): 267; McKee, *Sociology and the Race Problem*, 22–23; Mike Forrest Keen, *Stalking the Sociological Imagination: J. Edgar Hoover's FBI Surveillance of American Sociology* (Westport, CT: Greenwood, 1999), 12.

6. Frazier, "Sociological Theory and Race Relations," 265, 267–68; G. Franklin Edwards, "Edward Franklin Frazier," *American Sociological Review* 27, no. 6 (December 1962): 890–92.

7. McKee, *Sociology and the Race Problem*, 36, 38; Alfred Holt Stone, "Is Race Friction between Blacks and Whites in the United States Growing and Inevitable?," *American Journal of Sociology* 13, no. 5 (March 1908): 677, 684.

8. W. E. B. Du Bois, *The Philadelphia Negro: A Social Study* (New York, Schocken, 1967); McKee, *Sociology and the Race Problem*, 31.

9. McKee, *Sociology and the Race Problem*, 84, 96–97; Stephen Steinberg, *Race Relations: A Critique* (Stanford, CA: Stanford University Press, 2007), 55.

10. Anthony M. Platt, *E. Franklin Frazier Reconsidered* (New Brunswick, NJ: Rutgers University Press, 1991), 41, 43–44; "The Garvey Movement and the Harlem Renaissance," *Encyclopedia Britannica*, http://www.britannica.com/blackhistory/article-285192; Claude McKay, "If We Must Die," in *Harlem Shadows: The Poems of Claude McKay* (New York: Harcourt, Brace and Co., 1922).

11. Steinberg, *Race Relations*, 72. According to Steinberg, Park was "the designated 'father' of the Chicago school of race relations." Robert E. Park, "Methods of Teaching: Impressions and a Verdict," *Social Forces* 20, no. 1 (October 1941): 40–41; Robert E. Park, "An Autobiographical Note," in *The Collected Papers of Robert Ezra Park*, ed. Everett C. Hughes et al., vol. 1 (New York: Arno Press, 1974), vii. Lewis Coser stated that Park once told his coworker Ernest W. Burgess that "he learned more from Washington than from any of his teachers." Lewis A. Coser, *Masters of Sociological Thought: Ideas in Historical and Social Context* (New York: Harcourt Brace Jovanovich, 1971), 369. Others scholars who stressed Booker T. Washington's influence on Park include John H. Stanfield, *Philanthropy and Jim Crow in American Social Science* (Westport, CT: Greenwood Press, 1985), 38–43; Barbara Ballis Lal, *The Romance of Culture in an Urban Civilization: Robert E. Park and Ethnic Relations in Cities* (London: Routledge, 1990), 21; and Mary Jo Deegan, *Race, Hull-House, and the University of Chicago* (Westport, CT: Praeger, 2002), 101–2.

12. Everett Hughes, "Preface," in Robert Ezra Park, *Race and Culture: The Collected Papers of Robert Ezra Park*, ed. Everett Hughes et al., vol. 1 (New York: Free Press, 1950), xiii. According to Hughes, "his essays on race relations are, in fact, essays on social processes and social interaction in general." Robert Park, "The Nature of Race Relations," in Park, *Race and Culture*, 104.

13. Lewis Coser identified Park as the most influential member of the Chicago School of Sociology—the sociology department and approach that dominated the discipline during its formative years as a profession in the United States. Coser, *Masters of Sociological Thought*, 357–58. Park's substantive focus also severely limited his model of race relations. For example, in addition to noting the influence of racial accommodationist Booker T. Washington, Barbara Ballis Lal attributed Park's de-emphasis of the role of racism and racial oppression in urban politics to his emphasis on culture, ethnicity, and other subjective processes and his concurrent de-emphasis of power and conflict. Lal, *The Romance of Culture in an Urban Civilization*, 21.

14. Lewis Coser, *The Functions of Social Conflict* (New York: Free Press, 1956), 16–17; McKee, *Sociology and the Race Problem*, 108–9.

15. Robert Park, "The Bases of Race Prejudice," in Park, *Race and Culture*, 232–36.

16. Thomas F. Pettigrew, "Introduction," xxi; "Introduction, Part I, The Nadir: 1895–1915," 4; and "Introduction, Part II, The Beginnings of Change," 48–49 in *The Sociology of Race Relations*.

17. Monroe N. Work, "The Race Problem in Cross Section: The Negro in 1923," *Social Forces* 2 (January 1924): 248.

18. Steinberg, *Race Relations*, 63; McKee, *Sociology and the Race Problem*, 217.

19. Edward Franklin Frazier, "The Pathology of Race Prejudice," *Forum* 70 (1927): 856.

20. It was Frazier's perceived need to make this science claim that resulted in much of his later scholarship staying safely within the restraints of the dominant race relations paradigm. Frazier, "The Pathology of Race Prejudice," 856–58.

21. Frazier, "The Pathology of Race Prejudice," 856–58.

22. Frazier, "The Pathology of Race Prejudice," 861; Platt, *E. Franklin Frazier Reconsidered*, 84.

23. Steinberg, *Race Relations*, 66.

24. Thomas F. Pettigrew, "Introduction, Part III, "Surviving the Great Depression: 1930–1940," in *The Sociology of Race Relations*, 88; Bennett, *Before the Mayflower*, 359–61.

25. Harry Ploski and James Williams, *The Negro Almanac: A Reference Work on African Americans* (Detroit: Gale, 1989), 24–25; Bennett, *Before the Mayflower*, 360–61.

26. McKee, *Sociology and the Race Problem*, 145.

27. Gunnar Myrdal stated that the caste concept "was already in use before the Civil War" and attributed its increasing use to refer to Southern race relations in the United States to the need "to describe the inferior status of the Negro, especially in scientific and literary circles," without making reference to his former slave status. In accounting for its more popular use Myrdal noted the function the "*'white man's theory of color caste'*" served in justifying the opposition of European Americans to racial amalgamation. Gunnar Myrdal, *An American Dilemma: The Negro Problem and Moral Democracy*, vol. 1 and 2 (New York: Harper Torchbooks, 1944), 57–58, 667; "W. Lloyd Warner," *Encyclopedia Britannica Online* http://www.britannica.com/EBchecked/topic/635940/W-Lloyd-Warner; W. Lloyd Warner, "American Caste and Class," *American Journal of Sociology* 42, no. 2 (1936): 234–37.

28. John Dollard, *Caste and Class in a Southern Town* (New York: Doubleday, 1949), cover page, vii, 11, 61n1, 260.

29. Dollard, *Caste and Class in a Southern Town*, 393.

30. Dollard, *Caste and Class in a Southern Town*, 250.

31. E. Franklin Frazier, *The Negro in the United States* (New York: Macmillan, 1967), 673–74.

32. Manning Marable, *Race, Reform, and Rebellion: The Second Reconstruction and Beyond in Black America* (Jackson: University Press of Mississippi, 2007), 13; McKee, *Sociology and the Race Problem*, 222.

33. Marable, *Race, Reform, and Rebellion*, 14; Ploski and Williams, *The Negro Almanac*, 25; Marable, *Race, Reform, and Rebellion*, 26. According to Marable, as part of this "'Red Scare,'" Du Bois's sociological and other writings were actually "removed from thousands of libraries and universities": 18, 26–27.

34. Bennett, *Before the Mayflower*, 365–67.

35. Bennett, *Before the Mayflower*, 367–69.

36. McKee, *Sociology and the Race Problem*, 227.

37. Myrdal, *An American Dilemma*, xxiii. John Stanfield had this to say about the racial inclinations of the Carnegie Corporation at that time: "The Carnegie Corporation was the most racially exclusive of the major foundations and was very supportive of white supremacy in apartheid societies. It dared not allow blacks any decision-making power in areas such as race-relations research and the development of black libraries. According to Carnegie Corporation protocol, black destiny was to be decided by whites only." Stanfield, *Philanthropy and Jim Crow*, 142. In addition, the Schwendingers noted in a section of their book entitled "The Tuskegee Machine" that Tuskegee's president, Booker T. Washington, received a $600,000

gift for that institution from Andrew Carnegie, who approved of Washington's accommodative and gradualist approach to race relations. This suggests that the Carnegie Corporation's funding of Myrdal's study can best be viewed as being consistent with its tradition of promoting racial accommodation. Herman Schwendinger and Julie R. Schwendinger, *The Sociologists of the Chair: A Radical Analysis of the Formative Years of North American Sociology (1883–1922)* (New York: Basic, 1974), 504.

38. Myrdal, *An American Dilemma*, lxxi.

39. Myrdal, *An American Dilemma*, lxi.

40. For more on Park's frequently expressed contempt for social reformers see McKee, *Sociology and the Race Problem*, 108–9.

41. Myrdal, *An American Dilemma*, 1049–51.

42. Myrdal, *An American Dilemma*, 19, 1045.

43. Myrdal, *An American Dilemma*, 1035–40; McKee, *Sociology and the Race Problem*, 245.

44. Myrdal, *An American Dilemma*, 1036–37; William J. Wilson, *The Declining Significance of Race* (Chicago: University of Chicago Press, 1978).

45. Myrdal, *An American Dilemma*, 1038.

46. Myrdal, *An American Dilemma*, lii–lv.

47. Ralph Ellison, "An American Dilemma: A Review," in Joyce Ladner, ed., *The Death of White Sociology* (New York: Vintage, 1973), 83–85, 92, 95.

48. Gunnar Myrdal with Richard Sterner and Arnold Rose, review of *An American Dilemma: The Negro Problem*, by E. Franklin Frazier, *American Journal of Sociology* 50 (May 1945): 555–57; Oliver C. Cox, *Caste, Class, and Race: A Study of Social Dynamics* (New York: Modern Reader, 1970), 466, 468, 509.

49. Cox, *Caste, Class, and Race*, 509–11, 520, 531–32, 534, 536–37.

50. Ruth Benedict, *Race and Racism* (London: Routledge & Kegan Paul, 1983), vii, 96–97. Cox, *Caste, Class, and Race*, 321.

51. Benedict, *Race and Racism*, 537–38.

52. For more on this view see Joe Feagin's "Capitalism and Systemic Racism: Oliver Cox's Pioneering Work," *Racism Review*, October 14, 2013, http://www.racismreview.com/blog/2013/10/14/capitalism-and-systemic-racism-oliver-coxs-pioneering-work/. In summing up Cox's contribution Feagin concluded that "some 65 years ago, Cox vigorously argued that racial prejudice and framing are the results of *concrete social and material contexts*, not some psychological gremlins inherent in all human beings."

53. Myrdal, *An American Dilemma*, 30, 32.

54. Myrdal, *An American Dilemma*, 36–37, 40.

55. Charles P. Henry, "Abraham Harris, E. Franklin Frazier, Ralph Bunche: The Howard School of Thought on the Problem of Race," in *The Changing Racial Regime, National Political Science Review*, ed. Matthew Holden Jr., vol. 5 (New Brunswick, NJ: Transaction, 1995), 53; Charles G. Gomillion, "The Influence of the Negro on the Culture of the South," *Social Forces* 20 (March 1942): 389; Charles S. Johnson, "The Present Status of Race Relations in the South," *Social Forces* 23 (October 1944): 27–28.

56. Marable, *Race, Reform, and Rebellion*, 26, 43; Keesing's Research Report, *Race Relations in the USA 1954–68* (New York: Scribner, 1970), 1; Thomas F. Pettigrew, "Introduction, Part V, The Great Promise: 1951–1960," in *The Sociology of Race Relations*, 180.

57. Bennett, *Before the Mayflower*, 370.

58. Bennett, *Before the Mayflower*, 374–79.

59. McKee, *Sociology and the Race Problem*, 256, 259.

60. John H. Stanfield, "Introduction," in *A History of Race Relations Research: First-Generation Reflections*, ed. John H. Stanfield (Newbury Park, CA: Sage, 1993), xv–xvi.

61. T. W. Adorno, Else Frenkel-Brunswik, Daniel J. Levinson, and R. Nevitt Sanford, *The Authoritarian Personality* (New York: Harper and Brothers, 1950), cover page, vi; "The Holocaust," http://www.history.com/topics/the-holocaust.

62. "Theodore W. Adorno," *Stanford Encyclopedia of Philosophy*, http://www.plato.stanford.edu/entries/adorno; "The Frankfurt School and Critical Theory," *Internet Encyclopedia of Philosophy*, http://www.iep.utm.edu/franfur/; "Frenkel-Brunswik, Else," *International*

Encyclopedia of the Social Sciences, 1968, http://www.encylopedia.com/doc/1G2-3045000434.html; "Else Frenkel-Brunswik," *Psychology's Feminist Voices*, http://www.feministvoices.com/else-frenkel-brunswik/; "Nevitt Sanford, 86, Psychologist Who Traced Roots of Prejudice," *New York Times*, Obituaries, July 11, 1995, http://www.nytimes.com/1995/07/11/obituaries/nevitt-sanford-86-psychologist-who-traced-roots-of-prejudice.html. Senator Joseph McCarthy led what later was widely characterized as a witch hunt for communists in the U.S. government, on college campuses, in the film industry, and in other institutions of American society. Lois Gordon and Alan Gordon, *American Chronicle: Year by Year through the Twentieth Century* (New Haven: Yale University Press, 1999), 473.

63. McKee, *Sociology and the Race Problem*, 278–79; Adorno et al., *The Authoritarian Personality*, 103, 105–6.

64. Gordon W. Allport, *The Nature of Prejudice* (New York: Doubleday, 1954).

65. Allport, *Nature of Prejudice*, x, xii, 437–40.

66. Allport, *Nature of Prejudice*, 315, 383, 468.

67. Allport, *Nature of Prejudice*, 4, 17–18.

68. Allport, *Nature of Prejudice*, 202–3.

69. Allport, *Nature of Prejudice*, xi, 203–6, 476.

70. Allport, *Nature of Prejudice*, 465, 471–72.

71. McKee, *Sociology and the Race Problem*, 282–83, 291.

72. Arnold Rose, "Intergroup Relations vs. Prejudice: Pertinent Theory for the Study of Social Change," *Social Problems* 4 (October 1956): 173–74, 176.

73. R. A. Schermerhorn, "Power as a Primary Concept in the Study of Minorities," *Social Forces* 35 (October 1956): 53–56.

74. E. Franklin Frazier, *Race and Culture Contacts in the Modern World* (Boston: Beacon, 1957), 6.

75. Herbert Blumer, "Race Prejudice as a Sense of Group Position," *Pacific Sociological Review* 1, no. 1 (Spring 1958): 3, 6.

76. Blumer, "Race Prejudice as a Sense of Group Position," 3.

77. Pierre L. van den Berghe, "The Dynamics of Racial Prejudice: An Ideal-Type Dichotomy," *Social Forces* 37 (December 1958): 138.

78. Everett C. Hughes, "Race Relations and the Sociological Imagination," Presidential address read at the annual meeting of the American Sociological Association, Los Angeles, August 1963. *American Sociological Review* 28 (December 1963): 879–90; Steinberg, *Race Relations*, 10.

79. Hughes, "Race Relations and the Sociological Imagination," 879.

80. Hughes, "Race Relations and the Sociological Imagination," 884, 889–90.

81. Hughes, "Race Relations and the Sociological Imagination," 879, 881. With these limitations in mind Steinberg preferred the term racial oppression as a replacement for race relations while Joe Feagin preferred the words racist relations. Steinberg, *Race Relations*, 16, 43–44; Feagin, *Racist America*, 13, 19.

82. Hughes, "Race Relations and the Sociological Imagination," 883.

83. McKee, *Sociology and the Race Problem*, 1–2. Indeed, according to McKee, "not only had they failed to foresee the coming of new forms of racial struggle, they had even denied such a possibility": 2; Steinberg, *Race Relations*, 8–13.

84. McKee, *Sociology and the Race Problem*, 2, 5.

85. McKee, *Sociology and the Race Problem*, 4–5.

86. Stanford M. Lyman, "Race Relations as Social Process: Sociology's Resistance to a Civil Rights Orientation," in *Race in America: The Struggle for Equality*, ed. Herbert Hill and James E. Jones Jr. (Madison: University of Wisconsin Press, 1993), 370–71.

3. LINGUISTIC RACIAL ACCOMMODATION AND CONFRONTATION FROM THE CIVIL RIGHTS MOVEMENT TO *THE DECLINING SIGNIFICANCE OF RACE*

1. John Bartlett and Justin Kaplan, eds., *Bartlett's Familiar Quotations* (New York: Little, Brown, 1992), 443:19.
2. Robin M. Williams Jr., *American Society: A Sociological Interpretation* (New York: Knopf, 1970), 452, 472, 492. Among the fifteen core American values Williams identified are "equality," "democracy," and "racism and related group-superiority themes."
3. Lerone Bennett Jr., *Before the Mayflower: A History of Black America* (New York: Penguin, 1982), 383–84.
4. Bennett, *Before the Mayflower*, 384–85.
5. James H. Cone, *Martin & Malcolm & America: A Dream or a Nightmare* (Maryknoll, NY: Orbis, 1991); Bennett, *Before the Mayflower*, 413, 419, 424–25, 428–29; Harry Ploski and James Williams, *The Negro Almanac: A Reference Work on African Americans* (Detroit: Gale, 1989), 239; Harvard Sitkoff, *The Struggle for Black Equality* (New York: Hill and Wang, 2008), 155, 210.
6. Thomas F. Pettigrew, ed., "Introduction, Part VI, The Civil Rights Movement: 1961–1970," in *The Sociology of Race Relations: Reflection and Reform* (New York: Free Press, 1989), 238.
7. Lewis A. Coser, *The Functions of Social Conflict* (New York: Free Press, 1956); Joseph S. Himes, "The Social Functions of Racial Conflict," *Social Forces* 45 (September 1966): 1–10.
8. Pettigrew, *Sociology of Race Relations*, 238–39. Himes, "Social Functions of Racial Conflict," 2.
9. Himes, "Social Functions of Racial Conflict," 5–6.
10. Pierre L. van den Berghe, "A Francophone African Encounters the Theory and Practice of American Race Relations," in *A History of Race Relations Research: First-Generation Recollections*, ed. John H. Stanfield (Newbury Park, CA: Sage, 1993), 243.
11. Pierre L. van den Berghe, *Race and Racism: A Comparative Perspective* (New York: Wiley, 1967), 2, 8.
12. Van den Berghe, *Race and Racism*, 11–13.
13. Van den Berghe, *Race and Racism*, 15.
14. Van den Berghe, *Race and Racism*, 17–18.
15. Van den Berghe, *Race and Racism*, 18, 21–22.
16. Van den Berghe, "A Francophone African," 249.
17. Stephen Steinberg, *Race Relations: A Critique* (Stanford, CA: Stanford University Press, 2007), 89; Stokely Carmichael and Charles V. Hamilton, *Black Power: The Politics of Liberation in America* (New York: Vintage, 1967), 199; Sitkoff, *Struggle for Black Equality*, 199–200.
18. Carmichael and Hamilton, *Black Power*, vii–x.
19. Carmichael and Hamilton, *Black Power*, 3–4.
20. Carmichael and Hamilton, *Black Power*.
21. The National Advisory Commission on Civil Disorders, *Report of the National Advisory Commission on Civil Disorders* (New York: Bantam, 1968), xi.
22. National Advisory Commission, *Report of the National Advisory Commission*, xvii, 1–2, 10, 32; Stephen Steinberg, *Turning Back: The Retreat from Racial Justice in American Thought and Social Policy* (Boston: Beacon Press, 1995), 79; Noel A. Cazenave, *Impossible Democracy: The Unlikely Success of the War on Poverty Community Action Programs* (Albany, NY: SUNY Press, 2007), 169.
23. Sitkoff, *Struggle for Black Equality*, 211–12; Ploski and Williams, *Negro Almanac*, 214; Manning Marable, *Race, Reform, and Rebellion: The Second Reconstruction and Beyond in Black America, 1945–2006* (Jackson: University Press of Mississippi, 2007), 147, 151, 171; Bennett, *Before the Mayflower*, 437.

24. Bennett, *Before the Mayflower*, 433; Marable, *Race, Reform, and Rebellion*, 112, 146; Ploski and Williams, *Negro Almanac*, 61, 74, 247; Pettigrew, "Introduction, Part VII, Consolidation and Retrenchment: 1971–1980," in *Sociology of Race Relations*, 313.

25. For a copy of that report and an analysis of the controversy it sparked, see Lee Rainwater and William L. Yancey, *The Moynihan Report and the Politics of Controversy* (Cambridge, MA: MIT Press, 1967), 5.

26. Moynihan sent his controversial memo to President Nixon on February 28, 1970. Ploski and Williams, *Negro Almanac*, 56. Nixon ignored Moynihan's advice and instead, as I noted earlier, made white racial reaction a centerpiece of his politics and policies. Sitkoff, *Struggle for Black Equality*, 212.

27. "Joel Kovel the Author, About Joel Kovel." http://www/joelkovel.com/joelkovel.html; Joel Kovel, *White Racism: A Psychohistory* (New York: Columbia University Press, 1970), ix, xxxviii, 3.

28. Kovel, *White Racism*, ix, xi, xiv, 6.

29. Kovel, *White Racism*, xiv, 4.

30. Robert Blauner, *Racial Oppression in America* (New York: Harper and Row, 1972), iv, ix; Marable, *Race, Reform, and Rebellion*, 126–27.

31. Steinberg, *Race Relations*, 19, 90–91. Blauner, *Racial Oppression in America*, vii–viii. Bob Blauner, "But Things are Much Worse for the Negro People: Race and Radicalism in My Life and Work," in *A History of Race Relations Research: First Generation Recollections*, ed. John H. Stanfield (Newbury Park, CA: Sage, 1993), 5, 12; Robert Blauner (1956) Emeritus Professor, UC Berkeley, http://sociology.berkeley.edu/robert-blauner-1956.

32. Blauner, *Racial Oppression in America*, 2.

33. Blauner, *Racial Oppression in America*, 11–12, 256, 276–77, 280.

34. Blauner, "But Things are Much Worse for the Negro People," 15, 17, 20–21, 30.

35. Joyce Ladner, ed., *The Death of White Sociology* (New York: Vintage, 1973), xiii.

36. Joseph S. Himes, *Racial Conflict in American Society* (Columbus, OH: Charles E. Merrill, 1973); William J. Wilson, *Power, Racism, and Privilege: Race Relations in Theoretical and Sociohistorical Perspectives* (New York: Macmillan, 1973).

37. Wilson, *Power, Racism, and Privilege*, vii.

38. Wilson, *Power, Racism, and Privilege*, 3.

39. Wilson, *Power, Racism, and Privilege*, 4, 8–9; Michael Omi and Howard Winant, *Racial Formation in the United States: From the 1960s to the 1980s* (New York: Routledge & Kegan Paul, 1986); David Theo Goldberg, *Racist Culture: Philosophy and the Politics of Meaning* (Malden, MA: Blackwell, 1993).

40. Wilson, *Power, Racism, and Privilege*, 17–18.

41. Wilson, *Power, Racism, and Privilege*, 29, 32.

42. Wilson, *Power, Racism, and Privilege*, 34, 41, 52–53, 191.

43. Steinberg noted that public policy-wise this also entailed a return to Myrdal's advocacy of race-neutral antipoverty policies. Steinberg, *Turning Back*, 67.

44. Oliver C. Cox, *Race Relations: Elements and Dynamics* (Detroit: Wayne State University, 1976), vi.

45. Cox, *Race Relations*, 1–3.

46. Cox, *Race Relations*, 2–3, 38–39, 60, 80, 302. Consistent with Marx's disdain for what he dismissed as a politically useless lumpenproletariat, with the culture of poverty perspective, and with the still more recent and highly racialized notion of the black underclass, Cox sought to "examine the social ramifications" of elements of "lower-class cultural idealism which establish their own vicious circle inimical to efforts toward inclusion in the mainstream culture." At a time when sociology was rapidly moving toward a conflict theoretical perspective in order to catch up with the tumultuous sixties, Cox seemed very comfortable with deploying the structure functionalism rooted in Durkheimian thought against an emergent black nationalism he felt foolishly glamorized the culture of impoverished African Americans.

47. David T. Wellman, *Portraits of White Racism* (Cambridge, UK: Cambridge University Press, 1993), xi–xii, 80.

48. Wellman, *Portraits of White Racism*, xi.

49. Wellman, *Portraits of White Racism*, 29, 54–55.

50. Wellman, *Portraits of White Racism*, 57–58.
51. Wellman, *Portraits of White Racism*, 55.
52. Joe R. Feagin and Clairece Booher Feagin, *Discrimination American Style: Institutional Racism and Sexism* (Englewood Cliffs, NJ: Prentice-Hall, 1978), xi.
53. Feagin and Feagin, *Discrimination American Style*, xiii; Hernan Vera, "Profile of the President Joe R. Feagin: Willing to Take a Stand," American Sociological Association, *Footnotes* (September/October 1999), http://www.asanet.org/about/presidents/Joe_R_Feagin.cfm.
54. Feagin and Feagin, *Discrimination American Style*, 2.
55. Feagin and Feagin, *Discrimination American Style*, 7, 20–21.
56. Feagin and Feagin, *Discrimination American Style*, 28–32.
57. Feagin and Feagin, *Discrimination American Style*, 32–33.
58. Feagin and Feagin, *Discrimination American Style*, xi, 2–3, 30; William J. Wilson, *The Declining Significance of Race: Blacks and Changing American Institutions* (Chicago: University of Chicago Press, 1978).
59. Steinberg, *Turning Back*, 2, 95; Wilson, *Declining Significance of Race*, 1.
60. Wilson, *Declining Significance of Race*, xii.
61. Wilson, *Declining Significance of Race*, ix.
62. Wilson, *Declining Significance of Race*, ix–x, 202. In a note Wilson stated that this occupation-centered definition is a modification of Weber's conceptualization of class.
63. Sitkoff, *Struggle for Black Equality*, 148, 207–8.
64. Joseph R. Washington Jr., ed., *The Declining Significance of Race? A Dialogue among Black and White Social Scientists* (Philadelphia: Joseph R. Washington, 1979), 118.
65. Steinberg, *Race Relations*, 101–3.

4. THEORETICAL FRAGMENTATION

1. John Bartlett and Justin Kaplan, eds., *Bartlett's Familiar Quotations* (Boston: Little, Brown, 1992), anonymous nursery rhymes, Humpty Dumpty, 790:13.
2. Timothy Messer-Kruse, *Race Relations in the United States, 1980–2000* (Westport, CT: Greenwood, 2008), 10–11; Daryl B. Harris, *The Logic of Black Urban Rebellions: Challenging the Dynamics of White Domination in Miami* (Westport, CT: Praeger, 1999), 1, 73–76, 77.
3. Messer-Kruse, *Race Relations in the United States*, 11–12.
4. Harvard Sitkoff, *The Struggle for Black Equality* (New York: Hill and Wang, 2008), 211; Michael Goldfield, *The Color of Politics: Race and the Mainsprings of American Politics* (New York: New Press, 1997), 314; Messer-Kruse, *Race Relations in the United States*, 9, 51–53; Kenneth O'Reilly, *Nixon's Piano: Presidents and Racial Politics from Washington to Clinton* (New York: Free Press, 1995), 359, 365–66.
5. O'Reilly, *Nixon's Piano*, 379, 382, 390–91, 395–96; Goldfield, *Color of Politics*, 314.
6. Michael Omi and Howard Winant, *Racial Formation in the United States: From the 1960s to the 1980s* (New York: Routledge & Kegan Paul, 1986); Sue J. Kim, *Critiquing Postmodernism in Contemporary Discourses of Race* (New York: Palgrave Macmillan, 2009), 29.
7. Omi and Winant, *Racial Formation in the United States*, 2.
8. Omi and Winant, *Racial Formation in the United States*, 4, 61–62, 68, 76, 145n2. In the third and most recent edition of their book they defined racial formation as "*the sociohistorical process by which racial identities are created, lived out, transformed, and destroyed.*" Michael Omi and Howard Winant, *Racial Formation in the United States*, 3rd ed. (New York: Routledge, 2015), 109.
9. Michael Omi and Howard Winant, *Racial Formation in the United States: From the 1960s to the 1990s*, 2nd ed. (New York: Routledge, 1994), 69–73.
10. Omi and Winant, *Racial Formation in the United States*, 3rd ed., vii–viii, 1, 3, 12, 128–29. While the word racism appeared in the index of their first edition of the book twenty-two times, it was included in the third edition thirty-seven times.

11. Audrey Smedley and Brian D. Smedley, *Race in North America: Origin and Evolution of a Worldview* (Boulder, CO: Westview, 2012); Joseph L. Graves Jr., *The Emperor's New Clothes: Biological Theories of Race at the Millennium* (New Brunswick, NJ: Rutgers University Press, 2001); Joseph L. Graves Jr., *The Race Myth: Why We Pretend Race Exists in America* (New York: Plume, 2005).

12. David T. Wellman, *Portraits of White Racism*, 2nd ed. (Cambridge, UK: Cambridge University Press, 1993), 10.

13. Wellman, *Portraits of White Racism*, 9–10.

14. He responded twenty-six years after the first edition of Omi and Winant's book and eighteen years after the appearance of its second edition as *Racial Formation in the United States: From the 1960s to the 1990s*. Joe Feagin and Sean Elias, "Rethinking Racial Formation Theory: A Systemic Racism Critique," *Ethnic and Racial Studies* (April 2012): 9, 14, 15, 17, 19–20, 22. In an earlier and much briefer critique of racial formation theory Feagin concluded that "missing in both the mainstream race-ethnic relations approach and much of the racial formation approach is a full recognition of the big picture—the reality of this whole society being founded on, and firmly grounded in, oppression targeting African Americans (and other Americans of color) now for several centuries." Joe R. Feagin, *Systemic Racism: A Theory of Oppression* (New York: Routledge, 2006), 7.

15. Omi and Winant, *Racial Formation in the United* States, 1st ed., 2, 12,131.

16. Omi and Winant, *Racial Formation in the United States*, 3rd ed., 128.

17. For a well-documented and argued study of the origins of the race concept that supports this position, see Smedley and Smedley, *Race in North America*.

18. Richard Delgado and Jean Stefancic, *Critical Race Theory: An Introduction*, 2nd ed. (New York: New York University Press, 2012), 4–5, 7–10.

19. Delgado and Stefancic, *Critical Race Theory*, 20–21, 26, 31.

20. Delgado and Stefancic, *Critical Race Theory*, 44.

21. For collections of influential critical race theory articles see Kimberlé Crenshaw et al., *Critical Race Theory: The Key Writings that Formed the Movement* (New York: New Press, 1995) and Richard Delgado, *Critical Race Theory: The Cutting Edge* (Philadelphia: Temple University Press, 1995).

22. Gerald David Jaynes and Robin M. Williams Jr., eds., *A Common Destiny: Blacks and American Society* (Washington, DC: National Academy Press, 1989), iv–v, xii–xiii.

23. O'Reilly, *Nixon's Piano*, 409–11, 413; Messer-Kruse, *Race Relations in the United States*, 85–86.

24. Messer-Kruse, *Race Relations in the United States*, 86. National Medal of Science 50th Anniversary, Awardees through the Years, "William J. Wilson (1935–)," National Science Foundation, http://www.nsf.gov/news/special_reports/medalofscience50/wilson_w.jsp.

25. Manning Marable, *Race, Reform, and Rebellion: The Second Reconstruction and Beyond in Black America, 1945–2006* (Jackson: University Press of Mississippi, 2007), 221–23; Noel A. Cazenave, *The Urban Racial State: Managing Race Relations in American Cities* (Lanham, MD: Rowman & Littlefield, 2011), 24, 31, 139–42.

26. Messer-Kruse, *Race Relations in the United States*, 75, 78–79; Richard L. Berke, "Survey Finds Voters in the U.S. Rootless and Self Absorbed," *New York Times*, September 21, 1994, A21.

27. Cornel West, *Race Matters* (Boston: Beacon, 1993), 12. For a detailed critique of West's book see Stephen Steinberg's *Turning Back: The Retreat from Racial Justice in American Thought and Policy* (Boston: Beacon, 1995), 126–34.

28. Eduardo Bonilla-Silva, "Rethinking Racism: Toward a Structural Interpretation," *American Sociological Review* 62 (June 1996): 465, 467.

29. Bonilla-Silva, "Rethinking Racism," 467.

30. Bonilla-Silva, "Rethinking Racism," 469–70, 474, 476.

31. Bonilla-Silva, "Rethinking Racism," 465, 467, 476; Eduardo Bonilla-Silva, *Racism without Racists: Color-Blind Racism and the Persistence of Racial Inequality in America* (Lanham, MD: Rowman & Littlefield, 2014), 74.

Notes

32. Carter A. Wilson, *Racism: From Slavery to Advanced Capitalism* (Thousand Oaks, CA: Sage, 1996); Mark Robert Rank, *One Nation, Underprivileged: Why American Poverty Affects Us All* (New York: Oxford University Press, 2004), 96.

33. Stephen Steinberg, *Race Relations: A Critique* (Stanford, CA: Stanford University Press, 2007), 105.

34. Steven F. Lawson, ed., *One America in the Twenty-First Century: The Report of President Bill Clinton's Initiative on Race* (New Haven: Yale University Press, 2009), Appendix A, Presidential Documents, A1.

35. Noel A. Cazenave, *Impossible Democracy: The Unlikely Success of the War on Poverty Community Action Programs* (Albany, NY: SUNY Press, 2007). See chapter 2 for my analysis of how "sufficiently vague" language was instrumental in the passage of the legislation that authorized and funded the War on Poverty Community Action Programs, 31, 46–47.

36. Lawson, *One America*, xi–xii, 10; Jaynes and Williams, *A Common Destiny*, v.

37. Lawson, *One America*, xxxi–xxxii, xliii, 4; Renee M. Smith, "The Public Presidency Hits the Wall: Clinton's Presidential Initiative on Race," *Presidential Studies Quarterly* 28, no.4 (Fall 1998):782, 784.

38. Neil Smelzer, William J. Wilson, and Faith Mitchell, eds., *America Becoming: Racial Trends and Their Consequences*, Conference Proceeding, Research Conference on Racial Trends in the United States, 1998, vols. 1 and 2 (Washington, DC: National Academy Press, 2001).

39. Claire Jean Kim, "Clinton's Race Initiative: Recasting the American Dilemma," *Polity* XXXIII, no. 2 (Winter 2000): 175, 189–91.

40. Kim, "Clinton's Race Initiative," 236–37; Adam Nagourney and Janet Elder, "In Final Days, Divided Electorate Expresses Anxiety," *New York Times*, November 1, 2004, http://www.nytimes.com/2004/11/01/politics/campaign/01poll.html?; Adam Cohen, "No One Should Have to Stand in Line for 10 Hours to Vote," *New York Times*, August 26, 2008, http://www.nytimes.com/2008/08/26/opinion/26tue4.html?; "9/11 Attacks," http://www.history.com/topics/9-11-attacks; Ethan Bronner, "Mourning Victims, Sikhs Lament Being Mistaken for Radicals or Militants," *New York Times*, August 6, 2012, http://www.nytimes.com/2012/08/07/us/sikhs-mourn-victims-and-lament-post-9-11-targeting.html.

41. Lisa de Moraes, "Kanye West's Torrent of Criticism, Live on NBC," *Washington Post*, September 3, 2005, C1; Dan Fromkin, "A Polling Free Fall among Blacks," *Washington Post*, October 13, 2005.

42. Nadra Kareem Nittle, "Top 10 Events in Race Relations This Decade (2000–2009)," http://racerelations.about.com/od/historyofracerelations/a/Top10EventsinRaceRelationsThisDecade.htm; Randal C. Archibold, "Immigrants Take to U.S. Streets in Show of Strength," *New York Times*, May 2, 2006, http://www.nytimes.com/2006/05/02/us/02immig.html?.

43. Richard G. Jones, "In Louisiana, a Tree, a Fight and a Question of Justice," *New York Times*, September 18, 2007, http://www.nytimes.com/2007/09/19/us/19jena.html?; Richard G. Jones, "Louisiana Protest Echoes the Civil Rights Era," *New York Times*, September 21, 2007, http://www.nytimes.com/2007/09/21/us/21jena.html?.

44. Frank Newport, "Little 'Obama Effect' on Views about Race Relations: Attitudes toward Race Not Significantly Improved from Previous Years," Gallup Poll, October 29, 2009, http://www.gallup.com/poll/123944.

45. Jennifer Agiesta and Sonya Ross, "AP Poll: Majority Harbor Prejudice against Blacks," October 27, 2012, http://bigstory.ap.org/article/ap-poll-majority-harbor-prejudice-against-blacks.

46. Agiesta and Ross, "AP Poll"; Nadra Kareem Nittle, "Racial Controversies During the 2012 Presidential Race," http://racerelations.about.com/od/thelegalsystem/a/Racial-Controversies-During-The-2012-Presidential-Race.htm.

47. Yamiche Alcindor, "Racial Slurs, Protests at Colleges Urge Deeper Look," *USA Today*, November 12, 2012, A5; Patrick Boehler, "Where Did Those Racist Anti-Obama Tweets Come From? Here is the Science," *Time Magazine Newsfeed*, November 9, 2012, http://www.newsfeed.time.com.

48. Lizette Alvarez and Michael Cooper, "Prosecutor Files Charge of 2nd Degree Murder in Shooting of Martin," *New York Times*, April 11, 2012, http://www.nytimes.com/2012/04/12/us/zimmerman-to-be-charged-in-trayvon-martin-shooting; Adam Nagourney, "Demonstrations Greet Acquittal in Martin Killing," *New York Times*, July 15, 2013, 1A; Yamiche Alcindor and Larry Copeland, "After Verdict, Can Racial Rift Be Healed?" *USA Today*, July 15, 2013, 1A–2A; Jansing & Co., MSNBC, http://video.msnbc.msn.com/jansing-and-co/52479834/#52479834; Ravi Somaiya, "Demonstrations across the Country Commemorate Teenager Killed in Florida," *New York Times*, July 21, 2013, 14N; "Obama Trayvon Martin Speech Transcript: President Comments on George Zimmerman Verdict," *Huffington Post*, July 19, 2013, http://www.huffingtonpost.com/2013/07/19/obama-trayvon-martin-speechtranscript_n_3624884.html; "Poll: Blacks' Views on Race Relations Plummet," July 24, 2013, http://www.newsmax.com/US/poll-race-relations-blacks/2013/07/24/id/516761; "Summer of Discontent: Congress at New Low in NBC/WSJ Poll," July 24, 2013, http://tv.msnbc.com/2013/07/24/summer-of-discontent-congress-at-new-low-in-nbcwsj-poll/.

49. Michael D. Shear, "Obama Starts Initiative for Young Black Men, Noting His Own Experience," *New York Times*, February 27, 2014, http://www.nytimes.com/2014/02/28/us/politics/obama-will-announce-initiative-to-empower-young-black-men.html?hpw&rref=politics&_r=0;"Transcript: Obama Announces 'My Brother's Keeper,'" *CNN Politics*, February 27, 2014, http://www.cnn.com/2014/02/27/politics/obama-brothers-keeper-transcript/.

50. Patrik Jonsson, "Michael Dunn Murder Trial: Online, a More 'Thug'-oriented defense (+ Video)," *Christian Science Monitor* February 12, 2014, http://www.csmonitor.com/USA/Justice/2014/0212/Michael-Dunn-murder-trial-Online-a-more-thug-oriented-defense-video; "Police: Cop Shot Unarmed Man in Charlotte Ten Times," MSNBC News, September 16, 2013, http://www.nbcnews.com/news/us-news/police-cop-shot-unarmed-man-charlotte-10-times-v20530870; "No Charges Made in Detroit Shooting of Unarmed Black Teenager," America Aljazeera, November 7, 2013, http://america.aljazeera.com/articles/2013/11/7/no-charges-made-indetroitshootingofunarmedblackteenager.html.

51. Mark Berman, "Investigations, Outrage Follow Police Chokehold and Eric Garner's Death," *Washington Post*, July 21 2014, http://www.washingtonpost.com/news/post-nation/wp/2014/07/21/investigations-outrage-follow-police-chokehold-and-eric-garners-death/; Elahe Izadi, "Medical Examiner Rules Eric Garner's Death A Homicide, Says Police Chokehold Killed Him," *Washington Post*, August 1, 2014, http://www.washingtonpost.com/news/post-nation/wp/2014/08/01/eric-garners-death-was-a-homicide-says-new-york-city-medical-examiner/; Julie Bosman and Emma G. Fitzsimmons, "Grief and Protests Follow Shooting of a Teenager," *New York Times*, August 10, 2014, http://www.nytimes.com/2014/08/11/us/police-say-mike-brown-was-killed-after-struggle-for-gun.html?_r=0; Yamiche Alcindor and Marisol Bello, "Mom: Slain Teen 'Didn't Create Problems,'" *USA Today*, August 12, 2014, 1A; Yamiche Alcindor, Marisol Bello, and Farah Fazal, "4th Night of Furor Leads to Tear Gas," *USA Today*, August 14, 2014, 1A–2A; Cassandra Vinograd and Erin McClam, "Michael Brown Killing: Police in Ferguson Fire Tear Gas Amid Looting," NBCNews.com, August 16, 2014, http://www.nbcnews.com/storyline/michael-brown-shooting/michael-brown-killing-police-ferguson-fire-tear-gas-amid-looting-n182196; "Ferguson: One Person Shot, Seven Arrested in Overnight Violence," NBC News.com, August 17, 2014, http://www.nbcnews.com/storyline/michael-brown-shooting/ferguson-one-person-shot-seven-arrested-overnight-violence-n182481; "National Guard Ordered Onto Streets of Ferguson, Missouri," NBC News.com, August 18, 2014, http://www.nbcnews.com/storyline/michael-brown-shooting/national-guard-ordered-streets-ferguson-missouri-n182826; Yamiche Alcindor and William M. Welch, "No Charges: Protests Spread Across USA after Grand Jury Won't Indict Ferguson Cop," *USA Today*, November 25, 2014, IA; "Violence Erupts: Grand Jury Clears Police Officer," *Hartford Courant*, November 25, 2014, 1A–5A; Thomas Johnson, "Ezell Ford: The Mentally Ill Black Man Killed by the LAPD Two Days after Michael Brown's Death," *Washington Post*, August 15, 2014, http://www.washingtonpost.com/news/morning-mix/wp/2014/08/15/ezell-ford-the-mentally-ill-black-man-killed-by-the-lapd-two-days-after-michael-browns-death/; J. David Goodman and Al Baker, "New York Officer Won't be Charged in Chokehold Case: Grand Jury's Decision in Fatal Encounter Draws Protests—U.S. Opens In-

quiry." *New York Times*, December 4, 2014, A1, A25; Matt Pearce, "Civil Rights Fights Find New Frontier," *Hartford Courant*, March 6, 2015, A3.

52. Matt Pearce, "Analysis: Tensions over Police, Race Rolled across U.S. in 2014," *Hartford Courant*, January 3, 2015, A4; Carrie Dann, "Poll: 57 Percent of Americans Say Race Relations in U.S. are Bad," NBC News.com, December 17, 2014, http://www.nbcnews.com/politics/first-read/poll-57-percent-americans-say-race-relations-u-s-are-n269491; "Baltimore Riots: Poll Finds 96% Expect More Racially-Charged Unrest Nationwide," NBC News.com, May 3, 2015, http://www.nbcnews.com/storyline/baltimore-unrest/poll-96-expect-more-racially-charged-unrest-nationwide-summer-n352276. David von Drehle, "Line of Fire," *Time*, April 20, 2015, 24–28; Timothy M. Phelps and Christopher Goffard, "No Sanctuary: Suspect Sat among Church Victims," *Hartford Courant*, June 19, 2015, A1, A7.

53. Eduardo Bonilla-Silva, *White Supremacy and Racism in the Post-Civil Rights Era* (Boulder, CO: Lynne Rienner, 2001), 11.

54. Bonilla-Silva, *White Supremacy and Racism*, 1, 11.

55. Bonilla-Silva, *Racism without Racists*.

56. Bonilla-Silva, *Racism without Racists*, 8, 74, 221.

57. Bonilla-Silva, *Racism without Racists*, 1, 8.

58. Eduardo Bonilla-Silva, "More than Prejudice: Restatement, Reflections, and New Directions in Critical Race Theory," *Sociology of Race and Ethnicity* 1 (2015): 73–74, 76–77.

59. Bonilla-Silva, "More than Prejudice," 73, 75–76, 78–79.

60. Eduardo Bonilla-Silva, "The Structure of Racism in Color-Blind, 'Post-Racial' America," *American Behavioral Scientist* (May 28, 2015): 1–5, 11, http://abs.sagepub.com/content/early/2015/05/28/0002764215586826.full.pdf+html; Bonilla-Silva, "Rethinking Racism," 467.

61. Feagin, *Systemic Racism*, 2, 16, 25–28.

62. Feagin, *Systemic Racism*, 25, 28, 191, 227; Joe R. Feagin, *The White Racial Frame: Centuries of Racial Framing and Counter-Framing* (New York: Routledge, 2010).

5. DEFINING RACISM

1. James Baldwin, *The Fire Next Time* (New York: Holt, Rinehart and Winston, 1990), 69.

2. Ali Rattansi, *Racism: A Very Short Introduction* (Oxford, UK: Oxford University Press, 2007), 1.

3. Herbert Blumer, "Science without Concepts," *American Journal of Sociology* 36, no. 4 (January 1931): 518.

4. Blumer, "Science without Concepts," 522, 526.

5. Blumer, "Science without Concepts," 524; Arthur L. Stinchcombe, *Constructing Social Theories* (New York: Harcourt, Brace & World, 1968), 38.

6. *Merriam-Webster's Collegiate Dictionary, Deluxe Edition* (Springfield, MA: Merriam-Webster, 1998); Richard Popkin, "The Function of Definitions in Social Science," *Journal of Philosophy* 40, no.18 (September 1943): 491, 493, 495; N. S. Timasheff, "Definitions in the Social Sciences," *American Journal of Sociology* 53, no. 3 (November 1947): 201.

7. Michael Banton and Jonathan Harwood, *The Race Concept* (New York: Praeger, 1975), 11, 13. Banton and Harwood traced the first use of the term race in English to a poem written by William Dunbar in 1508. Audrey Smedley and Brian D. Smedley, *Race in North America: Origin and Evolution of a Worldview* (Boulder, CO: Westview, 2012); Joseph H. Graves Jr., *The Emperor's New Clothes: Biological Theories of Race and Millennium* (New Brunswick, NJ: Rutgers University Press, 2001); Joseph H. Graves, *The Race Myth: Why We Pretend Race Exists in America* (New York: Plume, 2005); Noel A. Cazenave, "Conceptualizing 'Race' and Beyond," *Association of Black Sociologists Newsletter* (February 2004): 4–6.

8. Magnus Hirschfeld, *Racism* (Port Washington, NY: Keenikat Press, 1938), 35; Joe Feagin and Sean Elias, "Rethinking Racial Formation Theory: A Systemic Racism Critique," *Ethnic and Racial Studies* (April 2012): 13.

9. Bob Blauner, "Talking Past Each Other: Black and White Languages of Race," *American Prospect* (Summer 1992): 56–60.

10. Blauner, "Talking Past Each Other," 60.
11. Blauner, "Talking Past Each Other."
12. Matthew W. Hughey, *White Bound: Nationalists, Antiracists, and the Shared Meanings of Race* (Stanford, CA: Stanford University Press, 2012), 12. Hughey followed most directly in the footsteps of Omi and Winant, who explicitly defined racial formation as a "process" and later argued that race should be understood as *"an unstable and 'decentered' complex of social meanings constantly being transformed by political struggle."* Michael Omi and Howard Winant, *Racial Formation in the United States: From the 1960s to the 1980s* (New York: Routledge & Kegan Paul, 1986), 61, 68.
13. June Jordan, "Problems of Language in a Democratic State," in *Some of Us Did Not Die: New and Selected Essays of June Jordan* (New York: Basic, 2002), 226–27.
14. Curt Anderson, "Stand Your Ground Laws: Despite Outcry, Repeals Unlikely," *Huff Post Politics*, July 13, 2013, http://www.huffingtonpost.com/2013/07/21/stand-your-ground-laws_n_3631625.html; Herbert Buchsbaum, "Budding Liberal Protest Movements Begin to Take Root in South," *New York Times*, March 18, 2014, http://www.nytimes.com/2014/03/19/us/protest-disrupts-georgia-senate-session-on-bill-to-block-medicaid-expansion.html?_r=0.
15. "On 'Racism' and Racial Oppression," To the Editors, *New Politics* (Winter 2002): 234.
16. "On 'Racism.'"
17. *Merriam-Webster's Collegiate Dictionary*.
18. Patricia Hill Collins, *Black Sexual Politics: African Americans, Gender, and the New Racism* (New York: Routledge, 2005), 16–17, 352.
19. Collins, *Black Sexual Politics*, 32. *Logical Fallacies: An Encyclopedia of Errors of Reasoning*, http://www.logicalfallacies.info/; "A List of Fallacious Arguments," http://www.don-lindsay-archive.org/skeptic/arguments.html; Bradley Dowden, "Fallacies," *Internet Encyclopedia of Philosophy*, http://www.iep.utm.edu/fallacy/#DoubleStandard.
20. Collins, *Black Sexual Politics*, 47, 49, 199.
21. Tukufu Zuberi, *Thicker than Blood: How Racial Statistics Lie* (Minneapolis: University of Minnesota Press, 2001); Cazenave, "Conceptualizing 'Race' and Beyond."
22. I used JSTOR Arts and Science I Archives Collection to conduct my electronic searches of these journal articles. The numbers reported do not include book reviews. The 1975 *AJS* publication with race relations in its title is not actually a full-length article, but a "Commentary and Debate" critique of two previously published *AJS* articles published more than four years earlier. Matthew W. Hughey, *The White Savior Film: Content, Critics, and Consumption* (Philadelphia: Temple University Press, 2014), 82–83, 187.
23. Joe R. Feagin and Hernan Vera, *Liberation Sociology* (Boulder, CO: Westview, 2001), 31–32, 107–8, 110.
24. Feagin and Vera, *Liberation Sociology*, 117, 120–21.
25. Rattansi, *Racism*, 1–2.
26. Ashley Doane, "What is Racism? Racial Discourse and Racial Politics," *Critical Sociology* 32, nos. 2–3 (2006): 256–58, 267, 269.
27. Hirschfeld, *Racism*, 35; Ruth Benedict, *Race and Racism* (London: Routledge & Kegan Paul, 1983), vii, 3, 97.
28. Pierre L. van den Berghe, *Race and Racism: A Comparative Perspective* (New York: Wiley, 1967), 11.
29. William J. Wilson, *Power, Racism, and Privilege: Race Relations in Theoretical and Sociohistorical Perspectives* (New York: Macmillan, 1973), 31–32; William J. Wilson, *The Declining Significance of Race: Blacks and Changing American Institutions* (Chicago: University of Chicago Press, 1978), 9.
30. Oliver C. Cox, *Race Relations: Elements and Dynamics* (Detroit: Wayne State University, 1976), 26.
31. Dinesh D'Souza, *The End of Racism: Principles for a Multiracial Society* (New York: Free Press, 1995), 240, 411–13, 483, 526. As perhaps a testimony to how keeping things conceptually muddled can support the racial status quo, aside from three book titles the word racism is not listed in the index of D'Souza's 724-page book.

32. Eduardo Bonilla-Silva, "Rethinking Racism: Toward a Structural Interpretation," *American Sociological Review* 62 (June 1996): 467; Christopher Bates Doob, *Racism: An American Cauldron* (New York: Longman, 1999), 262.

33. Emile Durkheim, *The Rules of Sociological Method* (New York: Free Press, 1964), 1–3.

34. Omi and Winant, *Racial Formation in the United States*, 1st ed., 145n2. In the most recent edition of their book they don't actually define racism. Instead, in keeping with their interest in racial projects, they stated that "a racial project can be defined as racist if it *creates or reproduces structures of domination based on racial significations and identities.*" While they did not explicitly define racism as being systemic, Omi and Winant did refer to "*structures of domination*" and explained that "racist projects exist in a dense matrix, operating at varying scales, networked with each other in formally and informally organized ways, enveloping and penetrating contemporary social relations, institutions, identities, and experiences." Finally, in stressing that racism cannot be reduced solely to "explicit beliefs or attitudes" they stated that racism "involves the production and maintenance of social structures of domination." Michael Omi and Howard Winant, *Racial Formation in the United States*, 3rd ed. (New York: Routledge, 2015), 128–29.

35. Richard Delgado and Jean Stefancic, *Critical Race Theory: An Introduction* (New York: New York University Press, 2012), 171.

36. Joel Kovel, *White Racism: A Psychohistory* (New York: Columbia University Press, 1970), x, 3.

37. Robert Blauner, *Racial Oppression in America* (New York: Harper & Row, 1972), 41, 84, 280.

38. David T. Wellman, *Portraits of White Racism* (New York: Columbia University Press, 1993), xi, 54–55.

39. Stokely Carmichael and Charles V. Hamilton, *Black Power: The Politics of Liberation in America* (New York: Vintage, 1967), 3–4.

40. Joe R. Feagin and Clairece Booher Feagin, *Discrimination American Style: Institutional Racism and Sexism* (Englewood Cliffs, NJ: Spectrum, 1978), xiii, 12–15, 30–31.

41. Joe R. Feagin, Hernan Vera, and Pinar Batur, *White Racism: The Basics* (New York: Routledge, 2001), 2–3.

42. Paul Kivel, *Uprooting Racism: How White People Can Work for Racial Justice*, 3rd ed. (Gabriola Island, BC: New Society, 2011), 2.

43. Noel A. Cazenave and Darlene Maddern, "Defending the White Race: White Male Faculty Opposition to a 'White Racism' Course." *Race and Society* 2, no 1 (2000): 42.

6. CONFRONTING RACIALLY ACCOMMODATIVE LANGUAGE BY CONCEPTUALIZING RACISM AS A SYSTEM OF OPPRESSION

1. June Jordan, "Problems of Language in a Democratic State," in *Some of Us Did Not Die: New and Selected Essays of June Jordan* (New York: Basic Books, 2002), 226–27.

2. Jordan, "Problems of Language in a Democratic State," 227.

3. "West Indian Emancipation, Speech Delivered at Canandaigua, New York August 3, 1857," *Frederick Douglass: Selected Speeches and Writings* (Chicago: Lawrence Hill, 1999), 367.

4. Noel A. Cazenave, "Teaching about Systemic White Racism," in *Teaching Race and Anti-Racism in Contemporary America*, ed. Kristin Haltinner (Dordrecht: Springer, 2014), 249.

5. Cazenave, "Teaching about Systemic White Racism," 252.

6. Cazenave, "Teaching about Systemic White Racism," 251; Noel A. Cazenave and Darlene Alvarez Maddern, "Defending the White Race: White Male Faculty Opposition to a 'White Racism' Course," *Race and Society* 2, no. 1 (2000): 43; Audrey Smedley and Brian D. Smedley, *Race in North America: Origin and Evolution of a Worldview* (Boulder, CO: Westview, 2012), 4.

7. Smedley and Smedley, *Race in North America*, 16. I refer to the work of Audrey Smedley specifically because the earlier editions of her book were solo authored. It was not until its fourth edition that her son, Brian, joined her as coauthor. Thus the ideas discussed here are largely hers.

8. Noel A. Cazenave, "Conceptualizing 'Race' and Beyond," *Association of Black Sociologists Newsletter* (February 2004): 5.

9. Pierre L. van den Berghe, *Race and Racism: A Comparative Perspective* (New York: Wiley, 1967), 77–78.

10. Cazenave, "Teaching about Systemic White Racism," 252.

11. Noel A. Cazenave, "Yes. America is Racist to Its Core," commentary, "Is America Racist?," *Hartford Courant*, April 12, 1998, C1.

12. Derrick Bell, *Faces at the Bottom of the Well* (New York: Basic, 1992).

13. Peggy McIntosh, "White Privilege and Male Privilege: A Personal Account of Coming to See Correspondences through Work in Women's Studies," Working Paper 189 (Wellesley, MA: Wellesley College Center for Research on Women, 1988).

14. See for example W. E. B. Du Bois, "The Souls of White Folk," in his *Darkwater: Voices from within the Veil* (Amherst, NY: Humanity, 2003); W. E. B. Du Bois, *Black Reconstruction in America: 1860–1880* (New York: Touchstone, 1995); James Baldwin, *The Fire Next Time, with Connections* (Austin, TX: Holt, Rinehart and Winston, 1990); Toni Morrison, *Playing in the Dark: Whiteness and the Literary Imagination* (Cambridge, MA: Harvard University Press, 1992).

15. Tamara K. Nopper, "The White Anti-Racist is an Oxymoron: An Open Letter to 'White Anti-Racists,'" *Race Traitor* (Fall 2003), http://racetraitor.org/nopper.html; David R. Roediger, *The Wages of Whiteness: Race and the Making of the American Working Class* (London: Verso, 1991); Theodore W. Allen, *The Invention of the White Race*, vol. 1, *Racial Oppression and Social Control* (London: Verso, 1994); Noel Ignatiev, *How the Irish Became White* (New York: Routledge, 1995). For a revealing study of the oppressive white racial identity that binds even white nationalists and "white" antiracists see Matthew W. Hughey's *White Bound: Nationalists, Antiracists, and the Shared Meaning of Race* (Stanford, CA: Stanford University Press, 2012).

16. Joe R. Feagin, Hernan Vera, and Pinar Batur, *White Racism: The Basics* (New York: Routledge, 2001), 17.

17. Joe R. Feagin and Melvin P. Sikes, *Living with Racism: The Black Middle-Class Experience* (Boston: Beacon, 1994), 4.

18. Feagin, Vera, and Batur, *White Racism*, 3.

19. Feagin, Vera, and Batur, *White Racism*, 3.

20. For a discussion of how my level of organization approach can also be applied to an analysis of gender- and class-based oppression, see Davita Silfen Glasberg and Deric Shannon, *Political Sociology: Oppression, Resistance, and the State* (Thousand Oaks, CA: Sage, 2011), 7–12.

21. Cazenave, "Is America Racist? Yes. America is Racist to Its Core," 1C.

22. Cazenave, "Is America Racist? Yes. America is Racist to Its Core," 1C.

23. Cazenave, "Is America Racist? Yes. America is Racist to Its Core," 1C.

24. Cazenave, "Is America Racist? Yes. America is Racist to Its Core," 1C.

25. Joe Feagin, *The White Racial Frame: Centuries of Racial Framing and Counter-Framing* (New York: Routledge, 2010), 9.

26. Feagin, *The White Racial Frame*, 9.

27. Jonathan H. Turner, *The Structure of Sociological Theory* (Homewood, IL: Dorsey, 1974; 1982), 5, 3–4; Nicholas C. Mullins, *The Art of Theory* (New York: Harper and Row, 1971), 7.

28. Nicos Mouzelis, *Sociological Theory: What Went Wrong?* (New York: Routledge, 1995), 1, 3.

29. Turner, *Structure of Sociological Theory*, 1982, 13.

30. Margaret L. Andersen and Howard F. Taylor, *Sociology: Understanding a Diverse Society* (Belmont, CA: Wadsworth, 2000), 28.

31. Joe R. Feagin, "Toward an Integrated Theory of Systemic Racism," in *The Changing Terrain of Race and Ethnicity*, ed. Maria Krysan and Amanda Lewis (New York: Russell Sage, 2004), 206.

32. C. Wright Mills, *The Sociological Imagination* (New York: Oxford University Press, 1959), 3–5.

33. Joel Kovel, *White Racism: A Psychohistory* (New York: Columbia University Press, 1970), lv.

34. David Harvey, *Social Justice and the City* (Baltimore, MD: Johns Hopkins Press, 1973), 12, 125.

35. Joe R. Feagin, *Systemic Racism: A Theory of Oppression* (New York: Routledge, 2006), 7, 16; Joe R. Feagin and Clairece Booher Feagin, *Racial and Ethnic Relations* (Upper Saddle River, NJ: Prentice Hall, 1999), 6th edition, 58–59.

36. Jordan, "Problems of Language in a Democratic State," 226–27.

CONCLUSION

1. Retha Powers, ed., *Bartlett's Familiar Black Quotations* (Boston: Little, Brown, 2013), "The Teaching for Merikare," 2:3.

EPILOGUE

1. Retha Powers, ed., *Bartlett's Familiar Black Quotations* (Boston: Little, Brown, 2013), from a civil rights movement song, 572:11.

2. For some insightful critiques of the concept of minority groups on social science, ideological, ethnic pride, and other grounds, see Barton Meyers, "Minority Group: An Ideological Formulation," *Social Problems* 32, no. 1 (October 1984): 1–15; James B. McKee, *Sociology and the Race Problem: The Failure of Perspective* (Urbana: University of Illinois Press, 1993), 130–32, 273–75; David Nibert, "A Note on Minority Group as Sociological Euphemism," *Race, Gender & Class* 3, no. 3 (1996):129–36; Doris Wilkinson, "Rethinking the Concept of 'Minority:' A Task for Social Scientists and Practitioners," *Journal of Sociology and Social Welfare* 27, no. 1 (March 2000): 115–32; Doris Wilkinson, "The Clinical Irrelevance and Scientific Invalidity of the 'Minority' Notion: Deleting it from the Social Science Vocabulary," *Journal of Sociology and Social Welfare* 29, no. 2 (June 2002): 21–34.

3. McKee, *Sociology and the Race Problem*, 273.

4. McKee, *Sociology and the Race Problem*, 275.

5. Meyers, "Minority Group: An Ideological Formulation," 1–2, 4–5; Nibert, "A Note on Minority Group as Sociological Euphemism," 129; McKee, *Sociology and the Race Problem*, 130.

6. Nibert, "A Note on Minority Group as Sociological Euphemism," 131, 133–34.

7. Wilkinson, "Rethinking the Concept of 'Minority,'" 121.

8. Melvin Thomas, "Anything But Race: The Social Science Retreat from Racism," *African American Research Perspectives* (Winter 2000): 79; Johnny E. Williams, "Race and Class: Why All the Confusion?" in *Race and Racism in Theory and Practice*, ed. Berel Lang (New York: Rowman & Littlefield, 2000), 215, 222. It was Williams's article that sparked my thinking about conceptual conflation.

9. Philomena Essed, *Understanding Everyday Racism: An Interdisciplinary Theory* (Newbury Park, CA: Sage, 1991), 5. In addition to its conceptual contributions, Essed's work is important because her methodology not only is nationally comparative but boldly confronts the social sciences, which have historically been reluctant to accept it, with the fact that the accounts of those who face racism on a regular basis must be taken seriously. Finally, I should also mention here that Essed's book and other writings and the often intense negative reactions

they have received in the extremely racism-evasive Netherlands provide numerous useful insights into the workings of linguistic racial accommodation and confrontation.

10. United Nations General Assembly, Eighteen Session, Agenda Item 43, "Resolutions Adopted by the General Assembly," 1904 (XVIII), "United Nations Declaration on the Elimination of All Forms of Racial Discrimination," http://www.oas.org/dil/1963%20United%20Nations%20Declaration%20on%20the%20Elimination%20of%20All%20Forms%20of%20Racial%20Discrimination,%20proclaimed%20by%20the%20General%20Assembly%20of%20the%20United%20Nations%20on%20November%2020,%201963,%20resolution%201904%20%28XVIII%29.pdf; World Conference on Racism, http://www.un.org/WCAR; Nicole Itano, "No Unity at Racism Conference," *Christian Science Monitor*, September 7, 2001, http://www.csmonitor.com/2001/0907/pls2-wogi.html; Nicole Gaouette, "U.S. Cites Anti-Semitism in Skipping UN Racism Conference," Bloomberg, June 1, 2011, http://www.bloomberg.com/news/2011-06-01/u-s-cites-anti-semitism-in-skipping-un-racism-conference.html.

11. Thanks to Eduardo Bonilla-Silva for sharing with me his "slippery slope" concern about the systemic racism approach in his comments on a draft of this book's prospectus.

12. Michael Omi and Howard Winant, *Racial Formation in the United States: From the 1960s to the 1990s*, 2nd ed. (New York, Routledge, 1994), 72–73; David Theo Goldberg, *Racist Culture: Philosophy and the Politics of Meaning* (Cambridge, MA: Blackwell,1993), 121; Eduardo Bonilla-Silva, "'New Racism,' Color-Blind Racism, and the Future of Whiteness in America," in *White Out: The Continuing Significance of Racism*, ed. Ashley Doane and Eduardo Bonilla-Silva (New York: Routledge, 2013), 271–84; Pitirim Sorokin, *Fads and Foibles in Modern Sociology and Related Sciences* (Chicago: H. Regnery, 1956).

13. Daniel Goleman, *Focus: The Hidden Driver of Excellence* (New York: HarperCollins, 2013), 136–37,141.

14. Goleman, *Focus*, 136–37, 153–54; Essed, *Understanding Everyday Racism*, 8–9.

15. Essed, *Understanding Everyday Racism*; Joe R. Feagin and Melvin P. Sikes, *Living with Racism: The Black Middle-Class Experience* (Boston: Beacon, 1994); Joe R. Feagin, Hernan Vera, and Nikitah Imani, *The Agony of Education: Black Students at White Colleges and Universities* (New York: Routledge, 1996); Annie S. Barnes, *Everyday Racism: A Book for All Americans* (Naperville, IL: Sourcebooks, 2000).

16. Joe R. Feagin, *Racist America: Roots, Current Realities, and Future Reparations* (New York: Routledge, 2014), 44, 70–71, 125–26; Thomas Jefferson, *Notes on the State of Virginia* (New York: Penguin, 1999), 145–46; Neil A. Lewis, "Study Finds Strong Evidence Jefferson Fathered Slave Son," *New York Times*, January 27, 2000, A14.

Index

Abramovitz, Mimi, 209
accommodation, 40. *See also* linguistic racial accommodation; racial accommodation
ACORN, 208
activism, 20, 71, 79, 124, 203
Addams, Jane, 31
Adorno, Theodore, 52–54, 58
affirmative action, 71, 75, 81, 93–94, 101, 115, 137
African Americans, xvii, 108, 169, 204, 213n2; families, xv–xvi, 38, 75; freedom struggles, 3, 60, 79, 164; men, xv–xvi, 110, 120, 163; migration from South to North, 32, 38, 41, 51; women, 79. *See also individual names, specific events, specific topics,* e.g., animus, stereotypes
African American scholars, 35, 40, 46, 50, 52, 61, 86, 105, 142, 190
agency, human, 56, 77, 104, 127–128, 186; *See also under* race: as agency concept
Alabama. *See* Birmingham; Montgomery Bus Boycott; Selma; Tuskegee Institute
Albany, Georgia, 66
Allen, Theodore, 171
Allport, Gordon W., 54–56, 58, 88
America Becoming (Smelzer, Wilson, and Mitchell), 116–117
An American Dilemma: The Negro Problem and Modern Democracy (Myrdal), 42–51, 54, 57, 116, 218n27, 218n37
American Sociological Review (ASR), 111–113, 122, 124–125, 149
Andersen, Margaret, 182
Anderson, Marian, 38
Anglo-Saxons, 31
animus, racial, 30–31, 101, 117, 119–120, 156
"anti-language" concept, 19, 216n18
antiracists, x, xvii, 7, 9, 143, 145, 160, 162, 170–171, 178–179, 188; radical antiracism theory, 184; white, 171, 230n15
anti-Semitism, 52–53, 203. *See also* conceptual inflation
apartheid, 89, 207, 218n37
Arab Americans, 117, 143
Arab racism, 69
Arkansas, 52
Asch, Solomon, 7
Asian Americans, xvii, 108, 119, 143, 169, 176, 194, 204, 213n2
assimilation, 34, 61, 84–85, 88, 199–200
Atlanta, Georgia, 37, 66; "Atlanta Compromise" speech, 3, 46
attitudes, racial. *See* racial attitudes
The Authoritarian Personality (Adorno et al.), 52–54, 58
aversive racism, 21, 76, 204, 209

Bachrach, Peter, 15
backlash. *See* white backlash
Baldwin, James, 131, 170
Baratz, Morton, 15
Batur, Pinar, 160, 172
beliefs: internalized, 156, 163. *See also* ideologies
Bell, Derrick, 108, 170
Benedict, Ruth, 48, 155
"benign neglect" policy, 75, 94
Bennett, Lerone, Jr., 29, 80
Berger, Peter L., 16
Berns, Gregory, 7
bias, mobilization of, 15
bias, racial. *See* racial bias, implicit
bigotry, racial, xvii, 4, 7–8, 15, 20, 34, 36–37, 52, 58, 62–63, 67, 71, 88–89, 101–102, 106–107, 123, 131, 135, 138, 159, 163, 165–166, 169, 171–172, 186, 190, 202, 204, 210; of African Americans and other peoples of color, xvii, 156, 171–172, 174. *See also* conceptual minimization
Birmingham, Alabama, 60, 66, 73
Black Feminist Thought (Collins), 146
black nationalism. *See under* nationalism: black
black power, 61, 66, 71, 73–74, 84, 96, 107, 159, 214n3
Black Power: The Politics of Liberation in America (Carmichael and Hamilton), 20, 71–73, 159
"black racism", xvii, 156, 171–172
blacks/"black," the term, 8, 122, 146, 176, 213n2. *See also* African Americans; *specific topics*
Black Sexual Politics (Collins), 146
Blalock, Hubert, 81
Blauner, Robert, 77–79, 85–86, 89, 96, 137–138, 158
"Bloody Sunday", 66
Blumer, Herbert, 58, 132–133
Bonilla-Silva, Eduardo, 7, 111–113, 122–126, 127, 147, 149, 156, 162, 168, 178, 204, 232n11
Bourdieu, Pierre, 18–19
British sociology, 151–152
Brown, Michael, 120–121
Brown, Norman O., 76

Brown, Sterling, 46
Brown decision, U.S. Supreme Court, 51, 54
Bunche, Ralph, 46, 51
Burgess, Ernest W., 37, 40, 57, 67, 217n11
Burke, Kenneth, 18, 199
Burundi, 69
Bush, George H.W., 101, 109
Bush, George W., 117
"busing", 101

California. *See* Los Angeles; Watts
Canada, 61
capitalism, 3, 21, 46, 69–70, 83, 84–85, 111, 136, 144, 145
careerism, xiv, 33, 79
Carmichael, Stokely, 20, 71–73, 78, 86, 89, 138, 159, 179
Carnegie, Andrew, 218n37
Carnegie Corporation, 42, 44, 52, 109, 218n37
Carter, Jimmy, 74, 101
Caste, Class and Race (Cox), 47, 84–85, 91
caste theory, 38–41, 46–47, 185
Cayton, Kenneth, 46
Cazenave, Noel A., xiii–xix, 127, 202, 209, 249
censorship of language, 25
The Challenge of Blackness (Bennett), 80
Charlotte, North Carolina, 120
Chavez, Cesar, 107
Chicago school of race relations, 32–38, 47, 217n11, 217n13
Christianity, 4
civil rights: activists, 20, 71, 79, 203; laws, 101; murdered workers, 101
Civil Rights Act of 1964, 66
civil rights movement, 4, 41, 44, 51–52, 65–97, 100, 137, 159, 162, 179, 191, 206, 209; failure to predict, 35, 59–63, 178; new movement coalition, 143–144, 194; post-civil rights movement/era, 1, 95, 102–104, 107, 111–114, 116, 118, 122, 129, 140, 143, 148, 152, 155, 160, 162, 178, 191–192, 206
Civil War, 29, 39, 218n27
Clark, Kenneth B., 46

Index

class, 70, 84–85, 95, 102, 104, 200, 208–209, 223n62, 230n20; divisions, 86; dynamics, 16, 91–92; exploitation, 48, 208; inequality, 92; oppression, 77–78, 85, 93; race vs., 92, 94; relations, 47, 49, 63, 124, 191, 201. *See also* conceptual conflation; hierarchies; socioeconomic status
class theory, 15
Clinton, William J., 109; race initiative of, 114–116
Cloward, Richard, 209
Collins, Patricia Hill, 146–147, 168, 208
colonialism, 104, 125, 136, 207; domestic/ internal, 20, 72–73, 77–78, 79, 89, 96, 102, 112, 183
colonization, conceptual. *See* conceptual colonization
colonization, Western, 48, 69, 106
color, people of. *See* people of color
color-blind ideology, 1, 6, 21, 77, 108, 122–125, 143, 153, 170, 191–192
color line, 5
A Common Destiny: Blacks and American Society (Jaynes and Williams), 109
communism, 218n33, 219n62
concepts, 132–135
conceptual colonization, 24, 48–49, 55, 63, 77–78, 82, 85, 91, 95, 97, 102, 104, 106, 124, 129, 159, 191, 208
conceptual conflation, 24, 40, 61, 63, 70, 89, 91–92, 94–96, 110, 129, 160, 191, 200–203, 208, 211, 231n8
conceptual extenuation, 24, 33–34, 42, 62–63, 78, 81, 85, 96, 190, 198
conceptual framework, xviii, 24, 25, 160, 177, 180
conceptual idealism, 24, 41, 42, 63, 190
conceptual inflation, 24, 138, 140, 202–203
conceptual minimization, 24, 34, 48, 52–54, 55–56, 58–59, 63, 69, 70, 77, 87, 95, 96–97, 106, 112–113, 114, 127, 129, 136, 155, 157, 159, 162, 165, 191, 208
conceptual misdirection, xvii, 24, 30, 32, 45, 63, 82–83, 85, 91, 95, 97, 106, 109, 116, 122, 128, 190–192, 198
conceptual non-definition, 24, 140, 153

conceptual obfuscation, 24, 30, 62, 78, 91, 95–96, 106, 114, 122, 129, 132, 152, 200
conceptual realism, 24, 32, 34, 38, 41, 55, 63, 190
conceptual rejection, 24, 62, 95, 106, 114, 129
conceptual underdevelopment, 24, 63, 79–80, 87, 90, 97, 108, 126, 128–129, 138, 160, 191, 204
conflict, 15, 181, 217n13. *See also* racial conflict
conflict theory, 181–183
confrontation, 9, 13–27, 71, 209. *See also* linguistic racial confrontation (LRC)
congressional hearings, 56
Congress of Racial Equality (CORE), 42, 51
consent, manufacturing, 19
conservative professionalization movement, 34
conservatives, political, 40–41, 45, 116, 182. *See also* Republican party; Right, political
CORE. *See* Congress of Racial Equality
Coser, Louis, 34, 67, 217n11, 217n13
counterrevolutionary theory, 185
courage, x, 9, 49, 71, 162, 194, 211
Cox, Oliver C., 13, 20, 47–49, 55, 84–85, 88, 91, 156, 179, 219n52, 221n6
Crenshaw, Kimberlé Williams, 208, 224n21
crime, 6, 101, 109, 111
criminal justice system, 90, 100, 109–117, 120, 143, 194. *See also* "law and order"; police
critical race theory (CRT), 96, 107–108, 111, 124, 127, 128, 157, 162, 178, 183
Critical Race Theory (Delgado and Stefancic), 157
CRT. *See* critical race theory
Cruse, Harold, 86
culture, 57–58, 61, 76, 84, 110, 201, 217n13; mainstream, U.S., 199, 222n46; racist, 175, 204; and subculture, 113, 148. *See also* conceptual conflation; *specific topics*, e.g., poverty: culture of

cycle theory of race relations (Park). *See under* race relations: cycle theory of

Dahl, Robert, 13
Darwinism, 30
Davis, Allison, 46
Davis, Benjamin, Sr., 41
Davis, Jordan, 120
Dearborn Heights, Michigan, 120
The Declining Significance of Race (Wilson), 76, 79, 81, 83–84, 87, 90–96, 101–102, 113, 149–150, 155, 185, 191, 223n62
definitions, 132–135
Delgado, Richard, 157
democracy/democracies, 70; highly racialized, 6, 8, 9, 25–26, 65, 107, 124, 132, 139, 147, 151, 161. *See also* United States
Democratic party, 74, 101, 109, 117
Depression, Great, 38
desegregation, 66, 101
Detroit, Michigan, 42, 73
Diallo, Amadou, 110
disability status, 133, 199
discourse: political, 15, 199; racial, xvi, 2, 8, 13, 16–17, 19, 27, 61, 68, 72, 73, 96, 116, 124, 129, 144, 150, 152, 164–165
discrimination, 70, 82, 89–90, 113, 157; institutional, 89–90, 159; racial, 20, 90, 101, 120, 127, 137, 159, 202–203, 214n14; racism and, 157–159; systemic, 8, 123. *See also specific topics,* e.g., employment, housing
Discrimination American Style (Feagin and Feagin), 87–90, 159
Doane, Ashley, 152–153
Doane, Woody, xi
Dollard, John, 39–40, 53
domestic colonialism. *See under* colonialism: domestic
dominance, linguistic racial. *See* linguistic racial dominance
domination: racial, 30, 81, 92, 125, 155, 211; racism as system of, 79, 158; structures of, 106, 229n34
dominative racism, 21, 76, 204
Doob, Christopher Bates, 156
Douglass, Frederick, 3, 20, 107, 164

Drake, St. Clair, 46
dramatist approach (language theory), 18
D'Souza, Dinesh, 156, 228n31
Du Bois, W.E.B., 5, 20, 31–32, 35–36, 41, 46, 51, 61, 85, 86, 88, 107, 170, 179, 218n33
Dukakis, Michael, 101
Dunbar, Paul Laurence, 1
Dunn, Michael, 120
Durkheim, Emile, 85, 156, 169, 222n46

economic exploitation/inequality/ justice/ oppression. *See under specific topics,* e.g., exploitation: economic
the economy, 77, 160, 183
education, 46, 51, 75, 90, 113, 114, 173. *See also* Du Bois, W.E.B.
1800s, 30–32
elites: policy elites, 83, 141, 199; power elite theory, 14–15. *See also* class; privilege
Ellison, Ralph, 46, 48
Ellwood, Charles, 31
Emancipation, 29, 46
employment, 41, 51, 75, 90, 113, 114, 163, 201
Engels, Friedrich, 125
enslavement, 55
environment, 30
epistemology of ignorance, 17–18
equality, xviii, 3, 42, 70, 110, 124, 163, 167–168, 221n2
Essed, Phelomena, xi, 202, 206, 208, 231n9
ethnicism, 202
ethnicity, 53–54, 70, 78, 102, 111, 133, 157, 160, 199, 200–202, 217n13. *See also* conceptual conflation
ethnic terminology, 213n2
ethnocentrism, 53, 69, 82
eugenics, 30
euphemism, ix, 199
European Americans, 204, 213n2. *See also* whites; *individual names, specific topics and events*
exploitation, 18, 34, 46, 56, 81, 104, 167; class, 47–48, 208; economic, 48, 70, 112, 136, 210; and mobilization of bias, 15; political, 15, 112; race-based, 136,

139, 155–156, 167
exploitation theory of prejudice, 55–56, 58

Faces at the Bottom of the Well: The Permanence of Racism (Bell), 108
Fairclough, Norman, 19
Fair Employment Practices Commission, 41
the family/families, xvi, 183; *See also under* African Americans: families
fascism, 4, 53
fatalism, 41, 44, 54
Feagin, Joe, and Clairece Booher Feagin, 20, 85, 105, 137, 142, 150, 160, 162, 171–172, 173, 177–179, 183, 185, 194, 207, 209, 219n52, 220n81, 224n14; underdeveloped systemic racism theory of, 126–128; See also *Discrimination American Style*
feminist theory/perspective, 49, 88, 107, 146, 183, 208
Ferguson, Missouri, 120–121
Ferrell, Jonathan, 120
Fighting Words (Collins), 146
Florida, 100–101, 110, 119–120
Flowerman, Samuel H., 52
Focus: The Hidden Driver of Excellence (Goleman), 206
Ford, Ezell, 121
Ford, Gerald, 74
Foucault, Michel, 18, 107
framing, concept of, 20, 126–127
Frankenberg, Ruth, 6
Frankfurt School (Institute of Social Research), 53
Franklin, John Hope, 115
Frazier, E. Franklin, 31, 36–37, 40, 46–48, 57–58
freedom riders, 66
freedom struggles, African American, 3, 60, 79, 164
Frenkel-Brunswik, Else, 53, 220n63
Friedrichs, Robert W., 199
Fuller, Abigail, 150
Fuller, Steve, 17
"The Functions of Racial Conflict" (Himes), 67–68

Garner, Eric, 120

Garvey, Marcus, 32
Gates, Henry Louis, 5
Gaventa, John, 15–16
gay, lesbian, and trangender rights, 143, 194
gender, xvi, 17, 88–89, 104, 113, 133, 146–147, 158, 200–203, 208–209, 230n20. *See also* conceptual conflation
gendered racism, 183, 202
genocide, 52, 69
Georgia. *See* Albany; Atlanta
Germany, 52–53, 136–137, 154
ghettoes/ghettoization, 66, 73, 81, 91, 173
Gidding, Franklin, 31
Gilkes, Cheryl Townsend, 208
Gingrich, Newt, 118
Giuliani, Rudolph, 110
globalization of racism, 186, 211
Goldberg, David Theo, 81, 204
Goleman, Daniel, 206–207
Gomillion, Charles, 50, 61
government, 14–15, 19, 21, 30, 41–42, 51–52, 73, 109, 115, 159, 188, 200, 219n62
Gramsci, Antonio, 107
Gray, Freddie, 121
Great Depression, 38
Greensborough, North Carolina, 66
Greenwood, Mississippi, 71

Halliday, Michael, 216n18
Hamilton, Charles, 20, 71–73, 78, 86, 89, 138, 159, 179
Hampton-Sydney College, Virginia, 119
Harlem, 42; Harlem Renaissance, 32
Harvey, David, 185
health care, 90, 113, 114, 144, 173, 183
hegemony/hegemonic ideologies, 9. *See also* linguistic hegemony; white racial hegemony
Herrenvolk democracies, 70
hierarchies, 35, 48, 60, 72, 81, 83–86, 89, 91–92, 104–105, 112, 116, 127, 139, 145, 181–182; racial, 32, 77, 91, 114, 139, 181
Himes, Joseph S., 67–68, 80
Hirschfeld, Magnus, 136–137, 153, 154
Hispanics. *See* Latino Americans; Latinos/as

Horkheimer, Max, 52
Horton, William "Willie", 101
housing, 74, 90, 113, 114
Hughey, Matthew, 140, 150, 228n12, 230n15
human rights, 144
Huntsman, Jon, 119
Hurricane Katrina, 117

idealism, conceptual. *See* conceptual idealism
idealism, linguistic racial. *See* linguistic racial idealism
ideology/ideologies, 159; internalized, 156, 163; language and, 18–19, 21; of race, 123, 160, 184; racism as, 82, 137, 154–156, 157–158; racist, 9, 48, 70, 82–83, 92, 123, 126, 173, 176. *See also specific ideologies,* e.g., color-blind ideology
Ignatiev, Noel, 171
ignorance: "convenience of", 68; epistemology of, 17–18; the IPA Syndrome, 17; used as verb, 17, 216n12
"illegal aliens", 117
immigrants, 5, 30, 110, 117–118; "immigrant analogy", 78; immigration racism, 143, 194, 204
India, 198
individual racism, 72–73, 159
inequality, 15, 95; class-based, 92; economic, 30, 93, 117; group, 141; racial, 32, 63, 77, 117, 138, 155, 168; social, 70, 82, 140
injustice, 160, 164
Institute of Social Research (Frankfurt School), 53
institutional racism, 20, 72–73, 86, 89, 93, 102, 123, 137–138, 153, 159, 183, 185
instrumental positivism, 150
insurgency, 21, 42, 50, 51, 61, 67–68, 74, 77–79, 84–85, 96, 199–200
integration, 52, 60, 66, 74
internalized beliefs, ideologies, and stereotypes, 156, 163
internment, racial, 184
intersectionality, 70, 146, 202, 208–209
intolerance, 13, 164, 208

Introduction to the Science of Sociology (Burgess and Park), 40
IPA Syndrome, 17
"issue of race". *See* conceptual obfuscation; race: "issue" of

Jackson, George, 78
Jaynes, Gerald David, 73
Jefferson, Thomas, 209
Jena, Louisiana, 118
Jim Crow system, 39, 51, 68, 89, 106, 122, 192, 207
jobs/job-seeking. *See* employment
Johnson, Charles S., 46, 50–51, 61
Johnson, Lyndon B., 73, 75, 114
Jordan, June, xvi, 140, 163–164, 188
justice, 2, 114; economic, 66, 143–144; racial, 41; social, 160

Karr, Alphonse, 65
Katrina, Hurricane, 117
Kennedy, John F., 66
Kerner, Otto, 73
Kerner Commission report, 73–74, 82–83, 95, 109, 114–116
Kim, Claire Jean, 116
King, Coretta Scott, 66
King, Martin Luther, Jr., 66, 93, 107
King, Rodney, 110
Kivel, Paul, 160
knowledge, 26; knowledge theories, 16–18, 22; power elite theory and, 14; sociology of, 16–17
Korean War, 51
Kovel, Joel, 20, 76–77, 96, 113, 157, 184, 205, 209
Ku Klux Klan, 30, 74, 89, 101

labor, 41, 47, 57, 75
Ladner, Joyce, 79–80
Lal, Barbara Ballis, 217n13
language, 18; and challenging the racial status quo, 152, 161, 193, 211; concepts and definitions, 132–135; ideology and, 18–19, 21; power and, 18–19, 26, 164. *See also* linguistic racial accommodation; linguistic racial confrontation; racially accommodative language; racism-evasive language;

words; *specific topics*, e.g., censorship
language-centered racism denial. *See under* racism denial
language theories, 18–19, 22
Latinos/as; Latino Americans, 5, 75, 88, 107–108, 117, 119–120, 143, 169, 174, 175, 213n2
"law and order", 74, 101
Lawson, Steven F., 115
Left, political, 78, 143. *See also* Democratic party; liberals; progressives
Levinson, Daniel J., 53
liberals, political, xiv, 9, 56, 73, 79, 107–108, 116, 184, 209. *See also* Democratic party; Left, political; progressives
liberal social theory, 184
Lincoln, Abraham, 101
linguistic-centered racism denial practices, 97
linguistic hegemony, 21
linguistic insurgency. *See* insurgency
linguistic racial accommodationism, xiv–xvi, 2, 9, 33, 84–85, 102, 217n13. *See also* racial accommodationism
linguistic racial accommodation (LRA), ix–x, xiv–xvi, xvii–xviii, 2, 7–8, 11, 143, 148, 170, 175, 178, 187, 190–193, 195, 197, 205–206, 210; alternative to, 25–27; *An American Dilemma* on/as, 49–51; in American sociology, 29–59, 62–63, 190; confronting, 9–10, 13–27, 36, 68, 100, 133, 142, 197, 199, 232n10; confronting, by conceptualizing racism as system of oppression, 10–11, 163–188; confronting, unfinished business in, 11, 197–211; consequence of, 25–27; historical context of, 2–4; key concepts and argument, 23–27; and linguistic racial realism, 161; in the 1960s and 1970s, 10, 65–97; from the 1980s to the present, 99–129; problem of, 7–8; from slavery to the civil rights movement, 10, 29–63; in social sciences, 27, 29–63, 65–97, 99–129; systemic racism and, 177–179, 187; today, 4–6; the view beyond, 177–179. *See also* racial accommodation; words: importance of;

individual authors and book titles, specific topics, e.g., racism evasiveness
linguistic racial confrontation (LRC), x, xvi, xviii, 2, 9, 13–27, 35–36, 65, 68, 73, 80, 96, 100, 133, 142, 232n10; by conceptualizing racism as system of oppression, 10–11, 163–188; study for the advancement of, 193–195; unfinished business in, 11, 197–211
linguistic racial dominance, 30, 58, 69, 156
linguistic racial idealism, 23, 142–148, 161, 166–169, 194
linguistic racial realism, 23, 62, 141–148, 161, 166, 194
Little Rock, Arkansas, 52
Locke, Alain, 46
Los Angeles, California, 8, 77, 110, 121
Louima, Abner, 110
Louis, Joe, 38
Louisiana, xiii, 117, 118
LRA. *See* linguistic racial accommodation
LRC. *See* linguistic racial confrontation
Luckman, Thomas, 16
Lukes, Steven, 15
Lyman, Stanford M., 62
lynchings, 30, 36, 38, 53, 118

Maddern, Darlene Alvarez, xvi, 160
Malcolm X, 66
Mammy, 40
Mannheim, Karl, 16
manufacturing consent, 19
March on Washington for jobs and freedom, 59, 66, 93
Marcuse, Herbert, 76
Marshall, Thurgood, 51
Martin, Trayvon, 6, 119–120
Marx, Karl, 16, 49, 76, 88, 92, 125
Marxism/Marxist theory, 15, 46–47, 49, 53, 55–56, 58, 76–78, 81, 85, 144, 183. *See also* conceptual colonization
mass media, 173
McBride, Renisha, 120
McCarthy, Joseph, 53, 56, 220n63
McDuffie, Arthur, 100
McIntosh, Peggy, 170
McKay, Claude, 32
McKee, James B., 30–31, 53, 61–62, 219n40, 220n83

Memmi, Albert, 123
Memphis, Tennessee, 93
meta-racism, 21, 76–77
Meyers, Barton, 199, 231n2
Miami, Florida, 100–101, 110
Michigan, 42, 73, 120
micro-aggressions, 207–208
middle class, 40, 94
Middle East, 51, 116, 117, 203
Miles, Robert, 138
militancy, 50, 56, 75, 79, 88
Mills, C. Wright, 14, 183–184, 206
Mills, Charles, 17, 21–22, 216n12
mini-racism, 10, 154–156, 161–162
"minority group", xvii, 13–14, 176, 197–200, 202–203, 231n2
Mississippi, 71
Mississippi, University of, 66, 119
Missouri, 30, 120–121
Mitchell, Faith, 116–117
mobilization of bias, 15
Montgomery Bus Boycott, 51
morality, 41, 139, 201
"Moral Monday" movement, 144
Morrison, Toni, 170
Mouzelis, Nicos, 180
Moynihan, Daniel Patrick, 75–76, 94, 116, 222n26
Mullins, Nicholas, 180
Muslims, 69, 117; Black Muslims, 109; Muslim and Arab Americans, 117, 143
"My Brother's Keeper" initiative, 120
Myrdal, Gunnar, 42–50, 54, 57, 68–69, 109, 116, 218n27, 218n37, 222n43; See also *(An) American Dilemma: The Negro Problem and Modern Democracy*

NAACP (National Association for the Advancement of Colored People), 38, 51, 144
National Advisory Commission on Civil Disorders, 73
nationalism: black, 32–33, 71, 102, 172, 214n3, 222n46; white, 172, 230n15
National Welfare Rights Organization, 208
Native Americans, xvii, 108, 169, 205
The Nature of Prejudice (Allport), 54–56, 58

Nazi Germany, 52–53, 136–137, 154
"the Negro complex", 37
the "Negro problem", xvi, 19, 31–32, 36, 85, 91, 94–95, 109, 111, 132, 150, 166, 192, 194, 199; race relations scholarship and, 80–84, 161; See also *(An) American Dilemma: The Negro Problem and Modern Democracy*
Negro Subscale, 53
neoliberalism, 106
Netherlands, 202, 231n9
Neubeck, Kenneth, 127, 202, 209
New Abolitionists, 171
New Negro Movement, 32
New Orleans, Louisiana, xiii, 117
New York City, 30, 42, 110, 120
Nibert, David, 199
Nigeria, 69
1920s–2010s (specific decades). See under race relations: 1920s, 1930s, etc.
Nixon, Richard, 74
Nobel Peace Prize, 51
nonviolence, 66
no-race premise, 166–167
the North, 21, 31, 38, 42, 46, 51, 76; migration of African Americans to, 32, 38, 41, 51
North America, history of race concept in, 167–168
North Carolina, 66, 120, 144

Obama, Barack, 1, 4–6, 100, 117, 118–120, 171, 214n13–215n15
Odom, Howard, 31
Olympics, 38
Omi, Michael, and Howard Winant, 81, 108, 124, 127, 142, 157, 162, 178, 204; race concept of, 112, 140, 167–168; See also *Racial Formation in the United States*
oppression, 152; class, 77–78, 85, 93; economic, 144–145, 156; ethnicity-based, 33–34; power and, 152, 181; systems of/racism as system of, 2, 8–9, 20, 124, 160, 163–188, 203–205, 210. *See also* intersectionality; racial oppression; social oppression
otherization, racialized, 4
Owens, Jesse, 38

parables, 108
Park, Robert E., 32–38, 43–44, 52, 57, 67, 69, 78, 217n11–217n13, 219n40; Booker T. Washington and, 2, 33, 35, 85, 214n4, 217n11, 217n13; race relations cycle theory of, 33–38, 39, 42, 43–44, 54, 60–61, 85, 88, 91. *See also* Chicago school of race relations; *Introduction to the Science of Sociology*
Parker, Robert, 38
Parks, Rosa, 51
paternalism, 83, 146–147
Paul, Ron, 119
peer group pressure, 7
people of color, 8, 66, 79, 87–89, 100, 109, 123, 137, 160, 170–172, 190. *See also specific groups by name/description*
personality development, 39–40
personal racism. *See* individual racism
Pettigrew, Thomas, 30, 35, 88, 190
Philadelphia, Mississippi, 101
Philadelphia, Pennsylvania, xiv, 5, 117
The Philadelphia Negro (Du Bois), 32
Piven, Frances Fox, 209
Plato, 2
Plessy v. Ferguson, 1, 30, 51
pluralist theory, 13–14
police: brutality, 66, 89, 100, 110; and killings of unarmed African Americans, 110, 120–121, 194, 214n14; misconduct, 89, 110, 175. *See also* criminal justice system; "law and order"
policy: makers, x, 8, 10; racist, 168, 211. *See also* public policy
"political economy of race", 91
politics, 173, 183; of denial, 132; discourse, political, 15, 199; politicians, 14–15, 115; race concept and, 143; social theory work as political, 184. *See also* Democratic party; racial politics; Republican party
Portraits of White Racism (Wellman), 85–87, 105, 158
positivism, instrumental, 150
post racial America argument, 1, 4, 118
poverty, 95, 111, 173; African American, 79, 83–85, 91, 93–95, 192, 201, 222n46; culture of, 79, 85, 111, 120,

129, 191, 200, 222n46; race-neutral antipoverty policies, 222n43
power, 3, 26, 57, 217n13; differences, race-based, 139; language and, 18–19, 26, 164; oppression and, 152, 181; pluralist view of, 205; and powerlessness, 15–16; power theories, 13–16, 22; three dimensions of, 15; two faces of, 15
Power, Racism, and Privilege (Wilson), 80–84, 155
power elite theory, 14–15
Powers, Retha, 197, 231n1
power structures, x, 13, 14–15, 40, 46, 215n2. *See also* white power structure
prejudice, 51–59, 69, 88, 116
prison, 78, 89, 101
privilege, xviii, 141, 160. *See also* white racial privilege
profiling, racial, 5–6, 21, 110, 119, 143, 174
progressives, political, 136, 143, 145. *See also* Democratic party; liberals
propaganda, 48
protest, social. *See* social protest
public policy, 5, 8, 14, 34, 56, 69, 94–95, 110, 116, 132, 200, 222n43
Puerto Rico/Puerto Ricans, 111, 124, 174, 213n2

quantitative research methods, 148–151
quiescence, 15–16, 51, 102

race, 136; as agency concept, 10, 122, 136–141, 147–149, 161, 178, 192; class vs., 92, 94; ideology of, 123, 160, 184; "issue" of, ix–x, 2, 6, 13, 106, 133, 139, 147, 164; as most racially accommodative topic, 94, 187; "Myth of", 166; running race as a variable, 82, 96, 99, 136, 141, 147, 148–149, 151, 178; the term, ix, 2, 13–14, 122, 133, 139, 146–147, 164, 176. *See also* race concept, below
Race and Racism (Benedict), 48
Race and Racism (van den Berghe), 68–71. *See also* van den Berghe, Pierre L
race concept, 48, 58, 69–70, 104–105, 106–107, 112, 123, 125, 127, 132,

136–141, 149, 155–156, 158, 173, 206; American politics and, 143; as bogus concept, 165–166; history of, in North America, 167–168; linguistic racial realism and uncritical acceptance of, 146–148; science and, 170; and systems of race-justified oppression, 186
Race Matters (West), 110–111
"race project", 162
race relations, xviii, 2–4, 190–191, 206, 228n22; American sociology and, 10, 31–32, 59–62, 69–70, 161, 191, 206; as America's moral dilemma, 41–51; biological justification of white supremacy and, 30; as caste relations, 38–41; changing, 10; Chicago school of, 32–38, 217n11, 217n13; civil rights movement and, 63, 66–67; conception/perception and, 132, 134; conflict and, 68; cycle theory of (Park), 33–38, 39, 42, 43–44, 54, 60–61, 85, 88, 91; discursive rules of, challenging, 165; the Kerner Commission report and, 73–74; linguistic framing of, 21; and linguistic racial realism/idealism, 142; and LRA/LRC, 164; misconceptualization of, 132; in the 1800s, 30–32; in the 1920s, 32–38, 63; in the 1930s, 38–41, 63; in the 1940s, 41–51, 63; in the 1950s, 51–59, 63; in the 1960s, 66–74, 96; in the 1970s, 74–97; from the 1980s to the present, 99–129; paradigm, failure of, 10, 59–62; paradigms, dominant, 178, 218n20; perception/conception and, 132, 134; quantitative research methods, 148–151; and race, contemporary concept of, 141; racial oppression and, 106, 110, 142, 144, 161, 220n81; and racism, 72, 137, 161, 192; social epistemology theory and, 17; and social psychology/sociology of prejudice, 51–59; sociology, failure of race relations paradigm of, 10, 59–62; Southern, 39, 218n27; structural-functional theory and, 181–183; studying/trends in studies of, 129, 148–151; the term, 60; and terminology, 133, 137. *See also individual names,* e.g., Park, Robert E., van den Berghe, Pierre, Washington, Booker T.
Race Relations: Elements and Dynamics (Cox), 84–85, 91, 222n46
race relations research, 44–45, 48, 52–53, 59, 69–70, 74, 78, 96, 206
race relations scholarship, American, 10, 32, 43–44, 61, 78, 161; *The Declining Significance of Race* and, 95–96; and focus on the "Negro problem", 80–84, 161; linguistic racial realism and, 142; of the 1960s, 96; of the 1970s, 74–76, 96–97, 110; of the 1980s to the present, 110, 128–129; the white backlash and, 80–84
race relations theory, American, 43–44, 61, 63, 78, 84, 96, 109
"race war," Nazi doctrine of, 136, 154
racial accommodation/being racially accommodative, ix–xi, xiii, xvii, xix, 1–5, 23, 53, 142; African American scholars and, 35; African American "underclass" and, 113; career-driven, 79, 84; historical context of, 2–4, 33; meaning of, 23; and the misconceptualization of racism, 1–11; and personality development, 39–40; pressures toward, 6, 35; problem of, 2; race relations and, 4; racial formation theory and, 106; and racial oppression, 6; shift to social protest from, 51, 59, 71; the social sciences and, 29, 35; structural-functional theory and, 182; today, 4–6. *See also* linguistic racial accommodation (LRA)
racial accommodationism, 2, 33, 84–85, 217n13
racial animus. *See* animus, racial
racial attitudes, 23, 62, 109, 110, 115, 124, 128, 151
racial barriers, 103
racial behavior, 23, 109
racial bias, implicit, 209–210
racial conflict, 32, 67–68, 75–76, 80, 91–92, 96, 103, 152, 191
Racial Conflict in American Society (Himes), 80
racial contract theory, 17, 21–22

racial control mechanisms, 106
racial discourse. *See* discourse, racial
racial dominance, linguistic. *See* linguistic racial dominance
racial equality. *See* equality
racial formation, 81, 102–107, 112, 140, 142, 178, 223n8, 224n14, 228n12
Racial Formation in the United States (Omi and Winant), 102–107, 157, 223n8, 223n10, 224n14, 228n12, 229n34
racial formation theory, 102–103, 105–107, 140, 142, 224n14
racial frames, 20, 126–127
racial idealism, linguistic. *See* linguistic racial idealism
racial inequality. *See under* inequality: racial
racial internment, 184
racialized linguistic common sense, 19
racially accommodative language, ix–xi, xiii, 3–5, 19, 26, 135, 190; African Americans as challenging, 68; confronting, by conceptualizing racism as system of oppression, 10–11, 163–188; confronting, unfinished business in, 11, 197–211; continuity and change in, 65; problem of, 7–8. *See also* linguistic racial accommodation (LRA)
racially oppressed standpoint, 49–50
racial oppression/the racially oppressed, xi, 1, 4, 6, 16, 20, 23, 25, 42, 49, 77, 84, 95, 100, 111, 122, 125–127, 131, 133–135, 205, 207, 210; contemporary, 152; core of, 152; the Feagins' six themes of, 185; language of the racially oppressed, 188, 190, 192, 194; racial accommodation and, 4, 6, 9, 16, 23, 29, 35, 62, 70, 94, 190; systemic racism as core concern of, 135, 152; the term(s), 9, 14, 108, 140, 144–145, 200, 220n81. *See also* oppression; race relations; *specific topics*, e.g., conceptual misdirection, conflict theory
Racial Oppression in America (Blauner), 77–79, 158
racial politics, xix, 60, 91, 106, 117–128
racial prejudice. *See* prejudice

racial profiling. *See* profiling, racial
racial realism, linguistic. *See* linguistic racial realism
racial state, 21, 103, 105–106, 183
racial status quo. *See* status quo, racial
racial structure, 26, 112, 123, 125, 190
racism, 136–138, 203–205, 223n10; America as racist, 169, 175–176; "as atmosphere", 138; as beliefs or ideologies, 82, 154–156, 157–158; "big racism," rise and fall of, 137–138; class and, 70, 200; conceptually minimalist approach of, 122–126; conflict theory and, 181–183; cultural, 204; defining, 10, 131–162, 170–175; as discriminative behavior and practice, 157, 159; emotional component of, 209; everyday, 207–208; as global, 186, 211; as ideology, 82, 137, 154–156, 157–158; individual, 72–73, 159; linguistic racial realism and, 144–146; new and multiple forms of, 204; "permanence of", 108, 170; race relations and conceptualizations/definitions of, 137, 161, 192; racial accommodation and the misconceptualization of, 1–11; "as result", 137–138; "reverse", 137; systemic nature of/as systemic racism, 157–158, 160–161, 175–177; as system of domination, 79, 158; as system of oppression, 8–9, 20, 124, 160, 163–188, 203–205, 210; toward a more honest conceptualization of, 11, 189–195; unconscious, 55, 209–210; Western, 69–70; the word, 72, 96, 108, 140, 144–146. *See also* aversive racism; "black racism"; dominative racism; institutional racism; meta-racism; mini-racism; racist; systemic racism; white racism; *individual authors,* e.g., Bonilla-Silva, Eduardo; *specific topics,* e.g., conceptual inflation, stereotypes
Racism: From Slavery to Advanced Capitalism (Wilson), 20, 113–114, 205
racism blindness, 1, 23, 83. *See also* color-blind ideology
racism-centered perspectives, 88, 95, 193, 210

racism denial, 6–7, 74; language-centered, 9–10, 23–26, 33–34, 48, 55, 63, 91, 95, 97, 153, 188, 190–191, 198, 200, 202; language-centered, practices of, 24

racism evasion/racism-evasive language, ix, xi, xiii–xiv, 5–7, 10, 23, 26, 49–50, 53, 62–63, 72, 74, 95, 106, 114, 120, 123, 128, 178, 197, 203–205; double-whammy of racism-evasive politics, 132; LRA and, 25, 70; *See also under* language: racism-evasive

racism studies, x–xi, xv, xviii, 9, 11, 48, 53, 67, 72, 76, 87, 90, 95, 105, 107, 127, 129, 153, 170, 188, 190, 193–195, 206; emerging developments in, 207–211; historically grounded cross-national research, 210–211. *See also individual names,* e.g., Wilson, William J.

racism theory, x–xi, 19–22, 103, 113, 126, 128, 144, 157, 183, 188, 202; graphic representation of theories, 22; institutionalized, 90, 127, 157; racial contract theory and, 21; and radical antiracism theory, 184; sociology/social sciences and, 193; underdevelopment of, 95, 180–181. *See also* systemic racism theory

racist: actions, 127, 174; attitudes, 6, 175–176, 192, 210; behavior, 209; culture, 175; "racist relations", 220n81; the word, 163, 175; *See also under* ideology: racist; stereotypes: racist

Randolph, Asa Philip, 41

Rattansi, Ali, 152–153

Reagan, Ronald, 100–101; the Reagan backlash, 100–109

realism, conceptual. *See* conceptual realism

realism, linguistic racial. *See* linguistic racial realism

rebellion, 15–16, 66, 73, 76–77, 192, 199

Reconstruction, 29, 43, 75

"Red Scare". *See* McCarthy, Joseph

Regulating the Lives of Poor Women (Abramovitz), 209

Regulating the Lives of the Poor (Piven and Cloward), 209

Reid, Ira De A., 46

relations/relationships, 106, 139. *See also specific relationships,* e.g., hierarchies

religion, 4, 183

reproductive rights, 143, 194

Republican party, 101, 117, 118; "Southern strategy", 74, 101. *See also* Right, political

resistance, 20, 35, 57, 185

revolution, 20, 48, 70, 84, 191

revolutionary theory, 185

Right, political/right-wing ideology, 4, 115, 117, 143, 144, 156. *See also* Republican party

rights. *See* civil rights; human rights; voting rights

riots, 30, 53

Robeson, Paul, 41, 51

Roediger, David, 171

Romney, Mitt, 119

Roosevelt, Franklin D., 38, 41

Roosevelt, Theodore, 30

Rose, Arnold, 57, 58

Ross, Edward, 30

Rwanda, 69

Sanford, R. Nevitt, 53

San Quentin prison, 78

Santorum, Rick, 119

Schattschneider, E. E., 14–15

Schermerhorn, R. A., 57, 58

Scott, Walter L., 121

Scottsboro Nine, 38

segregation, racial, 1, 3, 30–31, 37, 39, 41, 51, 54, 59, 66, 74, 76, 101, 127, 157

Selma, Alabama, 66

separate but equal doctrine. *See* Brown decision, U.S. Supreme Court; Plessy v. Ferguson

September 11, 2001, 117

sexism, 87–89, 159

sexuality, 146–147

sexual orientation, 133, 199

sexual politics, 146

Sikes, Melvin P., 171

Simpson, O. J., 110, 119

Sinclair, Upton, 29

sit-ins, 66

slavery, 3, 21, 29–31, 40, 48, 68–70, 75–76, 104, 106, 125, 127, 136, 207,

209–210, 218n27; abolition of, 30, 75; American sociology and, 31; Emancipation, 29, 46; enslavement, 55; justifying, 168, 192
Smedley, Audrey, 105, 167–168, 224n17, 230n7
Smedley, Brian, 230n7
Smelzer, Neil, 116–117
Smith, Gerald K., 53
SNCC (Student Nonviolent Coordinating Committee), 71
social control, 19, 34
social epistemology theory, 17
"social fact", 169
social inequality. *See under* inequality: social
socialism, 4, 33
social justice, 160
social movements, 62, 102, 106, 157, 200, 208
social oppression, xviii, 8, 32, 62, 103, 133, 160, 199–200, 203, 205, 208–210. *See also* conceptual inflation; intersectionality
social protest, 6, 38, 41, 51, 56, 62, 63, 111, 117, 137, 194
social psychology, 51–59, 69, 88
social reformers, 219n40
social science/American social science, x–xiii, xv, xviii–xix, 192–194, 205–209; concepts and definitions in, 132–134; and facing racism, xix, 131–162, 192–194, 198, 201, 203; in highly racialized societies, 190; LRA in, 27, 29–63, 65–97, 99–129, 190, 192, 197; race, teachings on, 165; research, 116, 151, 176; value neutrality ideology of, 44–45, 52, 60. *See also* African American scholars; linguistic racial accommodation; sociology; theoretical perspective; *individual names,* e.g., Myrdal; *specific topics,* e.g., racism-evasive language
social structure, 26, 30, 33, 53–59, 63, 76, 79, 87, 104
social theory, 179–183
societies, highly racialized. *See* democracies; United States

socioeconomic status, 82, 91–95, 97, 102, 109, 113–114, 150, 156, 201. *See also* class; poverty
"sociological imagination", 184
The Sociological Imagination (Mills), 183–184
sociology/American sociology, 29; failure of race relations paradigm of, 10, 59–62, 191; in highly racialized societies, 190; LRA in, 29–59, 62–63, 190; and the nation's racial order, 190; professionalized, breaking free of, 205–206; and race relations research, 69–70; and racism theory, 193; white, 79–80. *See also* African American scholars; race relations; social science; *individual names, specific topics,* e.g., knowledge: sociology of
Sociology and the Race Problem: The Failure of a Perspective (McKee), 61–62, 219n40, 220n83
Sorokin, Pitirim, 204
the South, 3, 21, 34, 37–40, 42, 44–46, 50–51, 53, 60, 109, 118, 144; the civil rights movement in, 66; migration of African Americans from, 32, 38, 41, 51; race relations in, 39, 218n27. *See also* Civil War; Jim Crow system; segregation; slavery; "Southern strategy"; *specific events and locations*
South Africa, 60, 70, 89, 198, 202
South Carolina, 121–122
"Southern strategy", 74, 101
"The Spook Who Sat by the Door", xiv–xv
St. Louis, Missouri, 30, 120–121
standpoint theory, 49
stand your ground laws, 120, 194
Stanfield, John, xi, 52, 214n4, 217n11, 218n37
Staten Island, New York, 120
"states' rights", 101
status quo, racial, 13, 27, 67–68, 72, 86, 93, 109, 122, 132–134, 145, 228n31; American sociology's first century and, 29–32, 34–35, 38–39, 41–42, 44, 48–50, 62–63; language and, 134, 142, 152, 161, 164, 193, 211; power elite theory and, 14. *See also* conceptual realism

status quo theory, 185
Stefancic, Jean, 157
Steinberg, Stephen, xi, 37, 61, 71, 78, 91, 95, 144–145, 147, 220n81, 222n43
stereotypes, racist, 5, 40, 109, 126, 133, 149, 163–164, 174, 176, 181
Stinchcombe, Arthur, 133
Stone, Alfred Holt, 31–32, 61
storytelling, 108
structural determinism, 108
structural-functional theory, 181–183
structural racism perspective. *See* systemic racism
Student Nonviolent Coordinating Committee (SNCC), 71
Sullivan, Shannon, 17
Sumner, William Graham, 30–31, 31, 44
Supreme Court, U.S. *See* U.S. Supreme Court
symbolic interaction theory, 58, 81, 140, 181–183
systemic racism/systemic racism theory, 20–22, 102, 105–106, 108, 152, 165, 177–183, 203; advocates of systemic racism approach, 85–87; contemporary racial oppression and, 152; LRA and, 177–179, 187; racial formation theory and, 106–107, 142; racism as, 160–161, 175–177; theoretical perspective on, 176–187; as underdeveloped, 126–128, 129, 178, 185; *See also under* Feagin, Joe; racism; white racism: systemic; Wilson, William J.
systems awareness and systems blindness, 206–207
"systems literacy", 207

Taylor, Howard, 182
Tea Party, 4
Tennessee, 93
terministic screens, 18, 199
terroristic violence, 30, 51, 72, 101, 117
theoretical fragmentation, 99–129
theoretical perspective, 16, 67, 140, 176–187, 193, 222n46
theory/theories, 22, 177–181. *See also* knowledge theories; language theories; power theories; racism theories; *specific theories*

Thomas, Melvin, 201
Thomas, W. I., 31
three dimensions of power, 15
"thugs," the term, 120
Till, Emmett, 51
Timasheff, N. F., 134
tolerance, 166
transgender rights, 143, 194
Truth, Soujourner, 107
Tuana, Nancy, 17
Tuskegee Institute, 3, 46, 50, 218n37
two faces of power, 15

underclass, xv, 41, 81–82, 96, 113, 191, 222n46
United Nations (UN), 202–203, 211
United States, 60, 70; as highly racialized society, ix, xi, xvi, 1, 8, 19, 26, 65, 124, 132, 135–136, 147, 151, 161, 177, 187, 192, 194, 202; post racial America argument, 1, 4, 118; as racist, 169, 175–176; September 11, 2001, 117. *See also* race relations; *specific events and locations, specific topics,* e.g., white racism
Universal Negro Improvement Association, 32
Uprooting Racism (Kivel), 160
urban unrest, 66, 68, 73, 76, 100–101, 192
U.S. Commission on Civil Rights, 88, 159
U.S. Supreme Court, 1, 30, 38, 51, 54

value neutrality, ideology of, 44–45, 52, 60
values, 43
van den Berghe, Pierre L, 59, 68–71, 80–83, 91, 155, 168
Vera, Hernan, 150, 160, 171–172
victim-blaming, 35, 199
Vietnam War, 76
vigilante killings, 6, 100–101, 119–120, 194, 214n14
violence, 8, 30, 65, 101, 118–119, 121, 157, 194
Virginia, 119
voter suppression, 117, 143
voting rights, 30, 51, 194, 214n14
Voting Rights Act of 1965, 66

Wallace, George, 74

Index

Wallerson, Dena, 216n12
Ward, Lester Frank, 31
Warner, W. Lloyd, 39
War on Poverty, 66, 115, 225n35
Washington, Booker T., 2–4, 31, 33, 35, 46, 85, 218n37; Robert Park and, 2, 33, 35, 85, 214n4, 217n11, 217n13. *See also* Tuskegee Institute
Washington, 1963 March on. *See* March on Washington for jobs and freedom
Watts rebellion of 1965, 77
Weber, Max, 92, 223n62
welfare racism, xv, 127–128, 202
Welfare Racism: Playing the Race Card against America's Poor (Neubeck and Cazenave), 127, 202, 209
welfare terminology as racial code words, 101
Wellman, David, 85–87, 105, 158
West, Cornel, 110–111
West, Kanye, 117
White, Walter, 46
white antiracists, 171, 230n15
white backlash, 10, 63, 65–66, 74–75, 80–84, 91, 93, 96–97, 99–129, 137–138, 143, 145, 148, 156, 191–192, 206, 213n2
"white," defining/the term, 8, 122, 146, 170–175, 176, 213n2. *See also* European Americans
white nationalists, 172, 230n15
white power structure, xvi, 1–3, 15, 27, 42, 73, 93, 113, 131, 175, 184, 187, 191, 194, 213n2
white racial frame, 20, 126–127
white racial hegemony, 8–9, 21, 65, 145–146
white racial identity, 90, 127, 170–171, 175–176, 186, 230n15
white racial privilege, 6, 86, 90, 105, 127, 170, 175–176, 186, 201
white racism, x, xvi–xviii, 2, 5, 157–160; and black poverty, 94–95, 156; definition of, 175; institutionalized, 116; right-wing ideologies and, 156; systemic, xvi, 7, 15, 17, 22, 69, 75, 82–83, 109, 115, 165–177; the term, 19, 96, 108, 114, 140, 145, 164, 188; and the U.S. social system, 20, 73, 95, 116,

176, 194. *See also* racism; White Racism course; *specific book titles,* e.g., *Portraits of White Racism* (Wellman); *specific topics,* e.g., Kerner Commission report
White Racism (Feagin, Vera, and Batur), 160
White Racism: A Psychohistory (Kovel), 76–77, 96, 113, 157, 184
White Racism course, xvi–xviii, 140, 164–177, 181
white sociology, 79–80
white supremacy, 21, 30–32, 218n37
White Supremacy and Racism in the Post-Civil Rights Era (Bonilla-Silva), 122
Wilkinson, Doris, 200
Williams, Johnny, 201, 214n13, 231n8
Williams, Robin M., 109, 221n2
Wilson, Carter A., 20, 113–114, 205, 209
Wilson, Willliam J., 45, 88, 97, 103, 109, 112, 124, 162, 200–201; focus of, 178, 200–201; and systemic racism theory, 80–84, 113, 127, 200–201; and the white racial backlash, 156. *See also America Becoming*; *Power, Racism, and Privilege*; *(The) Declining Significance of Race*
Wilson, Woodrow, 30
Winant, Howard. *See* Omi, Michael, and Howard Winant; *Racial Formation in the United States*
Wirth, Louis, 198–199
women. *See specific topics,* e.g., feminist perspective, reproductive rights
words: importance of, ix, xvi, xviii, 8–9, 132–135, 142, 163, 189, 194–195; racial code words, 101. *See also* language; *specific words,* e.g., "racist"
Work, Monroe, 35, 61
working class, 76–77
World War I, 32
World War II, 30, 41, 52, 56
Wright, Reverend, 5

X, Malcolm, 66

Zimmerman, George, 119, 120

About the Author

Noel A. Cazenave is professor of sociology at the University of Connecticut. He is also on the faculty of the Urban and Community Studies program of UConn's Greater Hartford Campus and is a faculty affiliate with the Institute for African American Studies and with the American Studies Program. His interests include racism, poverty policy, political sociology, urban sociology, and criminal justice. In addition to many journal articles, book chapters, and other publications, he coauthored *Welfare Racism: Playing the Race Card against America's Poor,* which won five book awards, and has more recently published *Impossible Democracy: The Unlikely Success of the War on Poverty Community Action Programs* and *The Urban Racial State: Managing Race Relations in American Cities.* He is currently working on a book tentatively entitled *Killing African Americans: Police and Vigilante Violence as a Racial Control Mechanism.*